THE
SCIENCE
OF
GHOSTS

JOE NICKELL

THE SCIENCE OF GHOSTS

SEARCHING FOR
SPIRITS OF THE DEAD

Prometheus Books
59 John Glenn Drive
Amherst, New York 14228–2119

Cover image © 2012 Jill Battaglia/Archangel Images
Cover design by Nicole Sommer-Lecht

Inquiries should be addressed to
Prometheus Books
59 John Glenn Drive
Amherst, New York 14228–2119
VOICE: 716–691–0133
FAX: 716–691–0137
WWW.PROMETHEUSBOOKS.COM

16 15 14 13 12   6 5 4 3 2

Library of Congress Cataloging-in-Publication Data

Nickell, Joe.
    The science of ghosts : searching for spirits of the dead / by Joe Nickell.
        p. cm.
    Includes index.
    ISBN 978–1–61614–585–9 (pbk.)
    ISBN 978–1–61614–586–6 (ebook)
    1. Ghosts. I. Title.
BF1461.N53 2012
133.1—dc23

2012004780

Printed in the United States of America

CONTENTS

PART 1: THE HAUNTING IMPULSE

PART 2: SPIRITED TRAVELS

PART 3:
COMMUNICATION WITH THE DEAD

PART 4: GHOST HUNTING

ACKNOWLEDGMENTS

Numerous people deserve credit for helping to make this book possible. Paul Kurtz, chairman and founder of Prometheus Books, believed in this project, and the skilled staff at Prometheus Books were again a pleasure to work with, including Steven L. Mitchell, Cate Roberts-Abel, Jade Zora Ballard, Brian McMahon, and Nicole Sommer-Lecht.

At the Center for Inquiry I am grateful to Timothy Binga, director of the Center for Inquiry Libraries for research assistance, aided by librarian Lisa Nolan; Paul E. Loynes for typesetting; Thomas Flynn for photographic expertise and other advice; my assistant, Ed Beck, for scanning and organizing illustrations; and indeed the entire CFI staff for help at all levels—especially Ronald A. Lindsay, president and CEO; Barry Karr, executive director of CFI's Committee for Skeptical Inquiry; Kendrick Frazier, editor of *Skeptical Inquirer* (CFI's science magazine); and Patricia Beauchamp, Chris Fix, Julia Lavarnway, and many others. Special thanks to Ed Behr of the James Randi Educational Foundation.

I am also grateful to my wife, Diana Harris, for her assistance, and for the support of my daughter, Cherie Roycroft, and grandchildren, Chase, Tyner, and Alexis Jo, as well as my cousin John May.

In addition to those mentioned in the text, I am also indebted to the many scholars, scientists, popular writers, and other generous folk who assisted me at numerous sites around the world over the many years of this investigative effort. To all I am most appreciative.

INTRODUCTION: TOWARD A SCIENCE OF GHOSTS

W hat is a ghost? Numerous, often confusing, even contradictory definitions are advanced, but most commonly a ghost is held to be a type of *revenant*, an entity that returns from the dead. If in solid form—that is, one of the "walking dead"—the revenant is usually said to be either a *vampire* (a corpse that rises from its grave at night to drink the blood of the living), a *ghoul* (a revenant that inhabits graveyards and other isolated places and feeds on human flesh), or a *zombie* (a corpse reanimated by a voodoo sorcerer). However, if the revenant is in nonsolid form, it is typically viewed as a type of *spirit*. Spirits are alleged discarnate beings that range from angels and demons to elves, fairies, and some types of monsters, among other alleged entities.

Most people think of ghosts as spirits of the dead. Anciently, these were held to be disembodied souls. In Western religious belief, on death the soul departs for heaven or hell or, in Catholic dogma, perhaps an interim place called purgatory (from which the "poor souls" might return in phantasmic form to request prayers from the living). Protestants did not generally believe the dead could return, and so revenants were regarded as diabolical beings that masqueraded as the dead—a belief that continues, especially among Christian fundamentalists (Guiley 2000, 150–52, 158, 354–55, 356–57; Nickell 2011, 121–25, 151–55; Stravinskas 2002, 626–27).

Ghosts are, by definition then, allegedly paranormal—that is, supposedly beyond the range of nature and normal human experience. The term *paranormal* encompasses all of the alleged supernatural, as well as those things—like flying saucers and Bigfoot—that, if they actually exist, might be perfectly natural phenomena after all.

But are ghosts real? Do they actually exist in some otherworldly realm? Or are they merely figments of the human imagination? I have spent more than four decades investigating the widespread belief in ghosts, looking for solid evidence that can answer those questions. I have approached the subject with an open mind, convinced that paranormal claims should be carefully examined with the intent of explaining them.

To that end, I have applied my background as a professional stage magician and mentalist (including three years as resident magician at the Houdini Magical Hall of Fame in Niagara Falls, Ontario). Later, I studied and worked as a private investigator and undercover operative for a world-famous detective agency, hence my insistence on the investigative approach and the rules of evidence. Still later, I returned to university for advanced studies, receiving a doctorate in English literature with an emphasis on literary investigation and folklore.

I trust that the fruits of this relevant background will be evident in my work, which began in 1969 and continues to the present. For many years I worked closely with psychologist Robert A. Baker (1921–2005), and we were dubbed the "Original Ghostbusters." In the process, Bob designated me an honorary psychologist.

Since 1995 I have been senior research fellow of the Committee for Skeptical Inquiry in Amherst, New York, becoming apparently the world's only professional—that is, full-time, science-based—paranormal investigator. My findings have not only appeared in our own *Skeptical Inquirer* science magazine but also in some thirty books, including *Entities*, *Looking for a Miracle*, *Real-Life X-Files*, and *Tracking the Man-Beasts*. I have also been featured in documentaries on the Discovery, History, and National Geographic channels, among many others.

In these works and elsewhere I have tried to avoid the approach of "believers" and "debunkers" who too often start with an answer and work backward to the evidence, looking just for that which seems to support their prior convictions, thus exhibiting what is termed *confirmation bias*. I have sought instead to discover the best evidence and let it lead to the most likely solution, following the precept known as Occam's razor, which holds that the simplest tenable explanation—the one requiring the fewest assumptions —is most likely correct. And I have recognized that the burden of proof is always on the claimant—not on someone else to prove a negative.

I have naturally taken a hands-on approach. For the investigations in this book, I have visited sites around the world, spending days and nights in "haunted" places. I have also gone undercover (in disguise when necessary) to reveal deceptions, applied various forensic sciences to the evidence, conducted linguistic analyses and folkloristic studies, delved into psychological realms, and so on, believing that we serve humankind when we investigate—and hopefully solve—mysteries at the very fringes of science.

Here, then, is *The Science of Ghosts*. I have grouped the chapters into four parts as follows:

Part 1, "The Haunting Impulse," looks at the history, phenomena (such as auras, apparitions, and near-death experiences), and cultural and psychological forces that relate to belief in ghosts.

Part 2, "Spirited Travels," presents case studies that take us to numerous supposedly haunted places, from an Alaskan bordello to lonely lighthouses, European castles, Australian jails, and more.

Part 3, "Communication with the Dead," studies spiritualism and the claims of mediums who allegedly make contact with those from the other side.

And part 4, "Ghost Hunting," examines the evidence of those who visit allegedly haunted places in an effort to detect phenomena they believe are associated with ghosts.

In addition, an appendix, "The Haunted Mind," provides a glossary of mental phenomena associated with supposed otherworldly encounters.

So let us begin our journey into this life-and-death subject, entering whatever dark and mysterious realms we find, but in doing so always holding aloft the lamp of reason and seeing the progress of science as a series of solved mysteries.

PART 1:
THE HAUNTING
IMPULSE

Chapter 1

GHOSTS:
A BRIEF HISTORY

Among humankind's persistent beliefs is the conviction that ghosts, or spirits of the dead, actually may exist, may return to haunt a particular place, or can even be communicated with. Polls show that approximately a third of the American public holds such beliefs, although the number appears to be declining (Moore 2005).

In *Appearances of the Dead: A Cultural History of Ghosts*, R. C. Finucane (1984) observes that, over time, different cultures have had very different beliefs about spirits, and as those changed so did the spirits themselves.

For example, in the Old Testament, the dead could be called up—as "gods ascending out of the earth"—by someone with occult powers. The raised entities might express annoyance with having been thus "disquieted"—as did Samuel when King Saul had the Witch of Endor conjure him forth. He appeared as an "old man . . . covered with a mantle" (1 Samuel 28).

What may be "the first record of the classic chain-clanking ghost" (Guiley 2000, 25) has also been "regarded as the first investigated ghost story" (Finucane 2001, 17). It involved a house in Athens (about 1 CE) haunted by the phantom of an emaciated man in fetters. Rattling its chains at night, it supposedly brought disease and death to visitors, and it scared even skeptics who came to mock. Then a stoic philosopher named Athenodorus purchased the house. According to the story, he tried first to ignore the beckoning specter, but finally he followed it into the garden, where it disappeared. The next day he had local officials dig at the site, whereupon— the tale concludes—they discovered the skeleton in rusty chains. Following a proper burial, which appeased the ghost, the haunting ended (Cohen 1984, 39–41; Guiley 2000, 25; Finucane 2001, 17).

Now this hearsay story, related by Roman writer Pliny the Younger (ca.

100 CE) was already a century old when he told it. It had probably been retold many times, like so many folktales. It is what folklorists call a "legend"—that is, a narrative reflecting a folk belief, in this case belief in the reality of ghosts. Indeed it is a subtype called a "proof legend," one that supports a belief with alleged evidence. (In this case skeptics are supposedly discredited by the discovery of bones and chains that confirm the reality of the ghost.) The story is also an example of a "legend trip": a visit, to a site that has a legend about uncanny events there, made to test the legend (Brunvand 1996, 437–40).

In medieval Europe, ghosts were often portrayed—in accordance with Roman Catholic doctrine—as souls suffering in purgatory (a state or place wherein those who have died in God's grace atone for their sins). By 1527, at the latest, such ghosts were reportedly communicating with the living through physical rapping sounds, as happened when the spirit of an expelled French nun tapped out messages to a novice. These supposedly confirmed the reality of purgatory, thus discrediting the skepticism of heretical Protestants. It was also reported that she had seen the devil and had asked that she be absolved from her sins and that her bones be buried in the convent (Finucane 1984, 106–108, 223).

Allegedly paralleling such pious ghosts were evil spirits—devils or demons. The Catholic Church had methods for distinguishing ghosts from demons (and keeping the latter away), but Protestants generally believed that souls of the dead went immediately to heaven or hell and never returned. Therefore, apparitions—if they were not frauds or illusions (inspired, say, by fear or drink)—were likely to be either good angels or demons masquerading as ghosts, not actual spirits of the dead (Finucane 1984, 92–93).

One type of alleged spirit, usually more mischievous than malevolent, was the *poltergeist* (after the German term for "noisy spirit"). Invariably unseen, poltergeists have since ancient times thrown objects, made noises, engaged in vandalism, or otherwise wreaked havoc. However, the phenomena have typically centered around youngsters, who have sometimes been caught and confessed that they were simply playing pranks on superstitious adults (Nickell 2001, 219).

A skeptical view of evil spirits was offered by English writer Reginald Scot, who was concerned less with the ghost controversy than with a more dangerous consequence of emotional belief in the supernatural, the witch mania. In his *The Discoverie of Witchcraft* (1584), Scot devoted only a single chapter to ghosts, but therein he pilloried the beliefs of Catholics and his fellow Protestants alike. He held that only those apparitions and visions that came from God, Christ, or angels were to be considered; devils, he insisted, could not affect humans physically, since they were only spiritual beings.

King James (1566–1625) regarded Scot's views to be heretical and ordered the burning of his book, although copies survived and it became an important work in the next two centuries. Kings James's opinion—that there was a "fearful abounding" of witches and that all ghostly apparitions came from the devil—prevailed for a time (Scot 1584; Summers 1930; Finucane 1984, 93–95).

In Elizabethan culture—as reflected in the plays of William Shakespeare (1564–1616)—ghosts began to adapt to England's having made the transition from Catholicism to Protestantism (Finucane 1984, 111–14). The dead continued to have otherworldly, even old-fashioned trappings, yet they were purposeful and part of the psychological situation. For example, in *Hamlet* (where, states one scholar, "Shakespeare makes by far the fullest use of the belief in ghosts current in his own day" [Moorman 1905]), the ghost of Hamlet's father demands revenge for his foul murder (*Benet's* 1987, 421).

In the seventeenth century certain religious figures, like Anglican minister Joseph Glanvill (1636–1680), began to collect ghost accounts. This was with the intention of combating materialism (the philosophical doctrine that nothing exists but matter and the effects it produces), using supposed evidence of the supernatural.

One such story was published by Richard Baxter (1615–1691) in his *The Certainty of the Worlds of Spirits*. The story centered on an English servant who robbed and murdered his master, afterward fleeing into the military service in Ireland. However, at night a headless ghost would stand beside his bed and ask, "Wilt thou yet confess?" Eventually he became so depressed that he did confess to his commanding officer (Finucane 1984, 128). (Today a knowledgeable psychologist or neurologist would recognize the incident as a "waking dream," which occurs in the twilight between being fully asleep and awake. Such experiences typically include ghosts, aliens, angels, and the like. An encounter of this type can seem quite real, and the person experiencing it often insists that he or she was not dreaming [Baker and Nickell 1992, 226–27].)

Stories of this type continued to be reported, and to be collected by ghost chroniclers, in succeeding centuries. However, in the Enlightenment (the eighteenth-century European movement that emphasized rational and scientific knowledge), ghost tales increasingly began to be dismissed. They were regarded as representing what today would be termed "anecdotal evidence"—that is, as consisting of mere anecdotes (entertaining little tales) and nothing more. Serious thinkers generally relegated ghost stories to the domain of the ignorant and superstitious.

Most of the "real" Victorian-era ghosts that were the subject of such stories were quite dull, "silent grey ladies"—a marked contrast with some of history's more purposeful ghosts (Finucane 1984, 223). In one famous English haunting of the 1840s, the apparition of a woman (seen under conditions that suggest it was another waking dream) was described as "attired in grayish garments." Indeed, as related in the classic text of the period, *The Night-Side of Nature; or, Ghosts and Ghost-Seers* by Catherine Crowe (1848, 312, 318), the figure "generally appeared in a shroud"—it having been very common at times to depict ghosts as wearing grave clothes (see Haining 1982, 154, 167, 248; Cohen 1984, 253–254). (Today's Halloween ghosts, so often attired in sheets, may be an extension of this tradition.)

Belief in ghosts began to change in the mid-nineteenth century with the rise of modern spiritualism, a popular movement based on alleged communication with the other world. It began on March 31, 1848 (All Fools' Eve!), at a house in Hydesville, New York, when two schoolgirls, Maggie and Katie Fox, began to seemingly communicate with the ghost of a murdered peddler. Four decades later, the sisters confessed it had all been a trick. They publicly demonstrated how their "spirit rappings" (akin to those of 1527 mentioned earlier) had been produced surreptitiously in response to questions addressed to the invisible spirit. (For more on the Fox sisters and the origins of spiritualism, see chapter 23.) In the intervening years, however, spiritualism had spread like wildfire across the United States and beyond.

Self-styled "mediums" (those who supposedly contacted spirits of the dead for others) conducted dark-room séances wherein they produced a variety of phenomena that supposedly proved the reality of spirits. The Davenport Brothers, for example, were tied up and placed in a "spirit cabinet" with musical instruments that nevertheless were heard playing in the dark, after which the brothers were found still securely tied. They were occasionally caught cheating, however, and late in life one surviving brother confessed to the magician Houdini how they had secretly slipped from, and back into, their bonds to effect their spirit trickery (Nickell 1999).

Other mediums pretended to conjure up spirits who performed by writing on slates, speaking through levitating tin trumpets, causing tables to tilt mysteriously, and performing other wonders. Some mediums persuaded the spirits to "materialize" and appear to credulous sitters, but there were repeated exposés. For instance, in Boston in 1876 a reporter carefully searched the séance room after the alleged materialization of the medium's "spirit guide," whereupon he discovered the woman's accomplice hiding in a recess (Christopher 1970, 175–76).

Spiritualists claimed that a substance called "ectoplasm," which was tangible and produced by the medium's body, could be used by spirits to effect physical phenomena. Like a sort of magical modeling clay, ectoplasm allegedly enabled spirits to fashion an extra limb (or "pseudopod") on the medium, create an artificial larynx to make spirit speech possible, or simply become visible in a photograph. This was faked in a variety of ways, such as by using chiffon or gauze to produce "eerily convincing" effects according to confessed medium M. Lamar Keene in his *The Psychic Mafia* (1997, 100–101). Also used were chewed-up paper, concoctions of soap and gelatin, and so forth (Guiley 2000, 116–17).

Many people tried communicating with spirits through automatic writing (in which, supposedly, an entranced person's hand is guided by the spirits), or by use of a *planchette* (a moveable device fitted with a pencil that scrawled "spirit" messages), or by using a "talking board" (such as the later Ouija board, which had a planchette-style pointer that moved mysteriously to letters printed on the board in order to answer questions) (Guiley 2000, 291–92, 377). We now know that such activity is produced due to the sitter's "dissociation." In a dissociated state, the consciousness is split so that the individual is able simultaneously to perform one set of functions that he is aware of and another that he is not (Baker 1990, 106–107). Such unconscious muscular activity also explains dowsing, a technique that is sometimes used for attempted spirit communication (Christopher 1970, 132–41; Warren 2003, 169–71).

Spiritualistic "evidence" provoked much investigation. In her book *Ghost Hunters: William James and the Search for Scientific Proof of Life after Death*, Deborah Blum (2006) tells how a small band of scientists set out with the intention of proving the reality of the supernatural—ghosts included—

and thereby uniting religion and science. In 1882, in London, they founded the Society for Psychical Research (SPR). Unfortunately their credulity, even outright gullibility, did not serve them well.

The notorious medium Eusapia Palladino (1854–1918) was able to confound even some of Europe's most distinguished scientists with her spiritualistic effects. She produced a variety of phenomena, such as rapping noises, even though her hands were placed on the séance table and "controlled" by a sitter on each side of her. Skeptical scientists and investigators soon discovered that she used a number of tricks. Since the control of her hands was of her own devising, consisting of each of her hands simply touching the hand of the sitter on either side, by slowly moving her hands close together, she could eventually let one hand do double duty. This gave her a free hand with which to make raps, touch people at the table, move objects, and so on (Christopher 1970, 188–204).

In contrast to the SPR, genuinely skeptical scientists and investigators uncovered many deceptions and self-deceptions. For instance, noted physicist Michael Faraday (1791–1867) conducted table-tipping experiments that proved mediums and amateur spiritualists were actually putting pressure on tabletops, often unconsciously (Blum 2006, 30–21, 67). In 1876, British zoologist Ray Lankester caught the medium Henry Slade faking "spirit" writing on slates. And Houdini (1874–1926), who spent the last years of his life crusading against spiritualistic fraud, routed many phony mediums (Houdini 1924). Some of his work was on behalf of *Scientific American* magazine, which in the 1920s offered $2,500 to anyone who could produce an "objective psychic manifestation of physical character" (quoted in Brandon 1983, 175). (We will return to the phenomena of spiritualism again and again in this book.)

Beginning in the twentieth century, a major venue for hauntings has been the Hollywood movie, but it had less to do with the supposedly "real" realm of ghosts and more to do with horror, like Cecil B. Demille's *The Ghost Breaker* (1914), or with comedy/horror, like a 1940 movie of the same title starring Bob Hope and Paulette Goddard (*The Ghost Breakers* 2007), or *Ghost Catchers* (1944) (Internet Movie Database 2007).

Among other movies, *The Amityville Horror* (1979) featured one of the most notorious "haunted" places in the world. Made from the book *The Amityville Horror: A True Story*, it was anything but true. To various investigators, the tale told by George and Kathy Lutz—that their family had been driven from the house by occult forces—had seemed a questionable hodge-podge of phenomena, part traditional haunting, part poltergeist disturbance, and part demonic possession, including elements that seemed to have been lifted from the movie *The Exorcist* (1973). Eventually, William Weber, the attorney for the man who had murdered his family in the house, confessed how he and George Lutz had "created this horror story over many bottles of wine that George Lutz was drinking" (quoted in Nickell 1995, 128).

The popularity of the *Ghostbusters* movie of 1984—which featured three wacky parapsychology professors who set out to trap and remove super-natural entities—may have helped cause today's ghost-hunting clubs to pro-liferate. Many other movies have promoted interest in ghosts and spirits. *Poltergeist* (1982) took the idea of disruptive spirits to the extreme, with the science-fiction horrors of angry trees and homicidal dolls. *Ghost* (1990) was based on a murder victim (played by Patrick Swayze) whose earthbound spirit enlisted the services of a medium to help him protect his girlfriend. *The Sixth Sense* (1999) told the story of a troubled boy who could "see dead people" and the child psychologist who sought to help him. And *White Noise* (2005) featured a man who contacted his wife beyond the grave, using elec-tronic voice phenomena. Discussed later, this physical aspect is widely touted by today's ghost hunters.

Television has also long been in the ghost business, with such fare as *Topper* (1953–1955), *Great Ghost Tales* (1961), *The Ghost and Mrs. Muir* (1968–1969), *The Ghost Busters* (1975–1976), *Shadow Chasers* (1985), and *Pol-tergeist: The Legacy* (1996), as well as made-for-TV movies like *The Woman in White* (1978), *Amityville 4: The Evil Escapes* (1989), *The Ghost Writer* (1990), and many, many others. (For a "Filmography," with TV and movie listings from 1898–1999, see Edwards 2001.)

Chapter 2

NAKED GHOSTS!

Whether ghosts exist remains a controversy of our day—not within science but rather between science and what is called *parascience*. A subsidiary of parascience is termed *paraphysics*, defined as "the investigation of the nature, and modes of action, of forms of energy not described in traditional Western physics" (White and Krippner 1977, 24–25). Many parascientists (who are sometimes indistinguishable from mystics) postulate a "life force" or "life energy" that they believe can survive death and may explain such supposed "survival phenomena" as apparitions (White and Krippner 1977, 23).

This "energy" accounts for the "aura," an alleged radiance that is supposed to emanate from and surround all living things, which is perceived not by ordinary vision but by clairvoyance (psychic "clear seeing"). The human body does in fact give off certain radiations, including electromagnetic emanations (from the electrical activity of nerves), sonic waves (produced by physical actions with the body), chemical emissions (such as body odors), and so forth. However, while paranormalists sometimes equate these radiations with the aura (Permutt 1988, 57–58), they do not constitute a single, unified phenomenon; neither have they been shown to have the mystical properties attributed to auras (Nickell 2001a, 142–49).

Still, parascientists have touted techniques for supposedly recording the imagined life energy. These include Kirlian photography (a noncamera technique in which a high voltage, high-frequency electrical discharge is applied across a grounded object), but this technique merely records a corona discharge on the photographic plate. A similar claim is made for infrared imaging, but the recorded emanations are only those of body temperature. At a psychic fair I investigated alleged aura-imaging technology that yielded my own "full body aura photograph," but it was actually a simulation produced by a colored-light display (Nickell 2001a, 142–49). (See figures 2.1–2.3.)

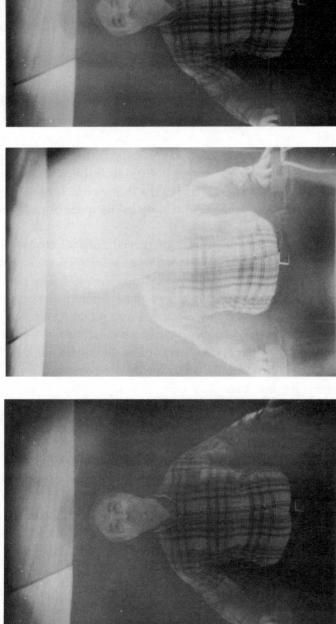

Figures 2.1–2.3. *Left:* Author poses for "aura" photo, placing hands on sensors. *Center:* Resulting "full-body aura photograph" shows dramatic burst of yellow-white radiance. *Right:* Second "aura" photo—made just minutes later—yields subdued tones of green and blue. (Author's photos.)

Again, proponents have invoked quantum mechanics in defense of ideas like "haunted" places having "residual emotions" and "spirits emitting emotions" (Belanger 2007, 166), but they have done so out of gross misunderstandings of the complexities of quantum theory, engaging in unwarranted extrapolations from particle physics to assumptions about the dubious realm of the paranormal. (For a serious discussion see Stenger 1990, 236–52.)

Indeed, science cannot substantiate the existence of a "life energy" that could survive death without dissipating or that could function (e.g., enable one to walk or gesture) without benefit of the physical organ known as the brain. As is well known from the science of neurology, when the brain dies, brain function ceases. The attempts of so-called ghost hunters to detect alleged postmortem "energy" with electronic gadgets, dowsing rods, and "psychics" continues to represent a fool's errand (as we shall see later).

If ghosts did, however, represent the survival of a soul or life force, how is it that—as confirmed by countless published sources as well as my own more than forty years' experience as a ghostbuster—the reputed entities are almost always seen wearing clothing (which is, of course, inanimate)?

GHOSTLY GARBS

The question is not new, having been posed by skeptics at least as early as the mid-nineteenth century (Roffe 1851) and addressed more recently to me by *Esquire* magazine (Answer Fella 2005). Psychical investigator Frank Podmore (1856–1910) wondered, since ghosts invariably appear dressed, "Have clothes also ethereal counterparts? Such was and is the belief of many early races of mankind, who leave clothes, food, and weapons in the graves of the dead, or burn them on the funeral pyre, that their friends may have all they require in the spirit world." However, he notes, "these ghosts commonly appear, not in the clothes which they were wearing at death—for most deaths take place in bed—but in some others" (Podmore 1909, 25–26).

Indeed, the ghosts of popular stories are garbed in many ways, according to cultural and dramatic expectations. For example, while medieval ghosts were typically wrapped in their burial shrouds, they could appear in full armor or other costume as the situation required, just as a woman of a more recent era saw her husband's ghost "dressed in a double-breasted suit long out of fashion" and "wearing equally unfashionable shoes" (Maxwell-Stuart 2006, 7, 62–63).

At the first "haunted" site I investigated (1971–1972), Toronto's Mackenzie House, there were purported sightings of a ghostly man in a frock coat—appropriate attire for its former historical resident, William Lyon Mackenzie (1795–1861), Canada's rebel-statesman (Nickell 1988, 17–27). Again, at Gettysburg, site of the historic Civil War battlefield, "ghosts" were properly outfitted in military dress—although some reportedly were only reenactment soldiers playing nighttime pranks (Nickell 1995, 56–59)!

Ghostly attire may even be modified according to some dramatic purpose. For example, the ghost of an eighteenth-century murder victim who sought revenge wore garments that were "all gory" (Finucane 1984, 60). Again, the wife of a corrupt moneylender who prayed at his grave beheld him after seven years wearing a black gown, but after another seven she saw him dressed in a white one and having a cheerful expression (Finucane 1984, 82).

Moreover, according to G. N. M. Tyrrell (1953, 66), one is "not only expected to believe in ghostly skirts and trousers, but also in ghostly hats, sticks, dogs, horses, carriages, doors, curtains—anything, in fact, with which a human being is commonly surrounded." He adds, citing many cases, "that there is no difference in existential status between one part of an apparition and another. In whatever sense the central figure is 'there,' the auxiliary objects, the additional figures, and the environment are 'there' too."

I even investigated one instance in which an item of clothing—an old wedding dress displayed in a museum—was itself claimed to be haunted. However, no one reported seeing a nude, ghostly bride donning the gown, whose ghostly movements in any event were attributable to people stepping on loose floorboards near the display case (Nickell 1995, 59–60).

IN THE BUFF

Despite their rarity, there *are* reports of naked ghosts. Yet even in these cases, the nudity is typically present because the alleged otherworldly situation requires it. For example, in London, from the mid-fifteenth to the mid-eighteenth century, came reports of five naked male ghosts. There, in 1447, a gang of ruffians were publicly hanged. Subsequently, their bodies were stripped and their clothing flung into the clamorous crowd, after which they were drawn and quartered. According to the legend, a notice of reprieve arrived belatedly and was read to the crowd, whereupon a misty ghost arose from each man's remains. The naked specters asked for their clothes to be returned and, when they were not, they ran away, only to be seen intermittently thereafter (Waters 1993, 114–16).

Again, the grounds of Scotland's Holyrood House Palace are supposedly haunted by the nude specter of Agnes Sampson, who was tried for witchcraft in 1592. She was stripped of her clothing, had all her body hair shaved off (in search of a "devil's mark"), was tortured into confessing, and then was executed by being strangled and burned (Cawthorne 2006, 118–20). Her ghost is reportedly seen as naked or, alternately, wearing a white shroud (Waters 1993, 55–56).

There are other instructive examples. One involved the naked and shivering ghost of a priest. This was explained by the bishop and his executors having milked the priest's estate to such an extent that he was left "spiritually naked" (Finucane 1984, 82). In some instances the overtones are decidedly sexual, as in the fourteenth-century case of an unclothed maiden's ghost running from a wood near Ravenna, pursued by a spectral knight on horseback (Maxwell-Stuart 2006, 8). Another story, "The Gypsy Girl and Her Lesbian Lover," tells of a tryst, followed by the disappearance and possible murder of the gypsy, whose subsequent apparition "was said to walk across the field behind the inn, and vanish through the wall into the hayloft where the two women had been found in a naked sexual embrace all those years ago" (Waters 1993, 117–20).

APPARITIONAL DRAMA

Proponents of ghosts do not have a ready answer for the question, why aren't ghosts naked? According to Hilary Evans, "We need clothes in this world, either to keep warm or to conform with notions of propriety, but surely in the next world the spirits will abandon the use of clothes with all their inconveniences?" He continues, "do we suppose that they change back into Earth-style clothes when they return as ghosts, so as not to offend us, and perhaps so as to be recognized?" (Evans and Huyghe 2000, 151).

Do ghosts clothe themselves either out of their modesty or to conform to ours? (In fact, there are even ghost encounters in which the spirits "are naked except for a small scrap of cloth concealing their private parts" [Maxwell-Stuart 2006, 62].) However, this rationale only further raises the question of how spirit entities obtain their spectral costumes. Are there really otherworldly shops that offer clothes, shoes, belts, hats, and other items—analogous to early theater or movie-studio prop departments?

The real answer, of course, is that Occam's razor applies—the principle that the simplest tenable explanation, the one relying on the fewest assumptions, is to be preferred. In this instance the simplest explanation is that apparitions and their accompaniments are just as they are in dreams, and in our memories and imaginings as well—mental images all. The items of clothing and other inanimate objects, as well as animals and additional elements of human surroundings, exist because they are necessary to what has been called the "apparitional drama" (Tyrell 1953, 83–115).[1]

Like "ghosts" themselves, the clothes and defacto dramatic props are part of the apparitional experience. Such experiences typically occur when the percipient is in an altered state of consciousness, such as in a "waking dream" (which occurs in the borderland between wakefulness and sleep) or in a daydream or similar state (Nickell 2001b, 216–17). No matter how much we wish otherwise, they are dramas—not of another world, but of this one.

Chapter 3

HEADLESS GHOSTS
I HAVE KNOWN

In the popular imagination, ghosts are a form of "energy" that survives death. Yet, as we have seen, ghosts are invariably portrayed as wearing clothing, uniforms, or costumes of their era, even though articles of dress are *inanimate* objects—an obvious contradiction.

Moreover, the science of physiology has established the simple fact that once the brain has been destroyed, brain function ceases, and so, too, surely the cessation of brain function ends the ability to think and move. Science therefore considers ghosts—alleged spirits of the dead who yet supposedly speak and walk about—to be figments of the imagination. Doubly unlikely, it would seem, are headless ghosts, whose existence utterly defies logic.

Nevertheless, storytellers have produced many colorful examples, notably Washington Irving's 1818 "The Legend of Sleepy Hollow," which tells how schoolmaster Ichabod Crane is frightened out of town by his rival, masquerading as a headless horseman. In contrast, many headless-ghost tales are told as true—or ostensibly so, for the teller's tongue may occasionally seem to stray into his cheek. I have investigated several of these.

SPECTER OF McCLANNAHAN HILL

In the mountains of eastern Kentucky, there are many such folk narratives, including an interesting one I learned while growing up in Morgan County. It concerns a Civil War skirmish that occurred on McClannahan Hill (approximately four miles northwest of the county seat of West Liberty, my hometown).

The story begins on October 6, 1863, when some Union soldiers (from Company B, Fifth Ohio Independent Cavalry Battalion) had passed through

West Liberty en route to Morehead. Rebel captain John T. Williams was able to cut across the river and reach McClannahan Hill ahead of them. He and his band waylaid the Federals, firing upon them from behind fallen trees.

Reportedly, one soldier was killed and a few others were wounded. (One of those was taken to the home of my great-great-grandfather, Milton B. Cox, himself then a second lieutenant serving in the Confederacy. There, the Cox family, in one of the common acts of the war, nursed the enemy soldier back to health [Nickell 1991].)

Over time, the superstitious Appalachian folk yielded up a tale about the ambush. "Some still say," wrote my old schoolteacher Arthur Johnson (1974, 330), "that a man with no head has been seen walking around on top of the hill there. It is believed that this is a ghost of the Union soldier who was killed there." (See figure 3.1.)

Figure 3.1. A headless soldier's ghost reputedly roams an eastern Kentucky site. (Ink sketch by Joe Nickell.)

Well, so "it is believed." But I recall once mentioning the tale to my father, the late J. Wendell Nickell, who had come to own the woodland property in question. A skeptic about such things, he retorted that in all his time on the site, he had never once seen the headless ghost of McClannahan Hill.

How the man supposedly lost his head is not explained. That he did is, in fact, doubtful, because—almost certainly—the ambushing rebels were without cannon; neither is there any other suggestion from the historical record of any beheading having taken place by that or any other means during the skirmish (Nickell 1991).

Therefore, I suspect we do not have the wandering ghost of a headless soldier, but rather the wandering motif (or story element) of a headless ghost that travels from region to region and tale to tale via the process known as folklore.

Such a narrative can take many forms, like the following example of what we might call "jokelore." It was related by the late Kentucky writer Joe Creason (1972, 217):

> Two boys in eastern Kentucky were discussing their town ghost. Just the night before, one vowed, he was walking past the haunted house when the ghost, head conveniently tucked under arm, floated out a window toward him.
>
> "What was that ol' ghost doin' the last time you saw him?" the other kid asked breathlessly.
>
> "Son," came the logical answer, "he was fallin' behind, fallin' behind!"

GHOST AT A RHINE CHAPEL

One of the defining characteristics of folklore is the existence of different versions of a tale—called "variants"—which are indicative of the oral tradition behind them. On an investigative tour of Germany in October 2002—accompanied by Martin Mahner, executive director of the Center for Inquiry/Europe—I saw evidence of such variants in several interesting cases (including that of "Satan's Footprint" [Nickell 2003, 27–28]).

An intriguing example turned up in an investigation that took us to two sites—Reichenstein Castle and a nearby chapel—located in the beautiful Rhine Valley. According to Dennis William Hauck's *The International Direc-*

tory of Haunted Places (2000, 113–14), the castle headquartered a gang of robber-knights. In 1282, they were captured, whereupon their leader, Dietrich von Hohenfels, entreated emperor Rudolf von Habsburg to spare his nine sons. The emperor stated that Dietrich was to be beheaded but, with his sons lined in a row, every one he could afterward run past would be spared. When the executioner's sword fell, "Dietrich's head rolled to the ground, but his bloodied torso stood erect and lunged forward, stumbling and swaying, until it passed every one of his sons. Finally, the headless body fell to its knees, a fountain of blood shooting high into the air where his head had been." The sons were spared, and afterward, on the execution site, the repentant family erected the St. Clement Chapel. According to Hauck, Dietrich's headless ghost is sometimes seen inside the chapel. Also, "Dietrich is buried on the property and his red sandstone marker depicts a knight in armor with no head."

Actually, the stone, described by Victor Hugo after visiting the castle, did not bear Dietrich's name, and Hugo said it was from the fourteenth century. In any event, it had been in a pile of rubble, and its whereabouts are now unknown. As to the chapel, an archaeology student at work there, Mirko Gutjahr, told us the chapel existed before the time of Dietrich's purported execution and that it was probably built in memory of sailors who drowned in the rough waters of the Rhine. Moreover, according to a history of the castle (*Tour Guide of Burg Reichenstein* n.d.): "Contrary to the legend, Dietrich of Hohenfels was not decapitated, but escaped. His 'companions' were hung on the trees in the valley by order of Rudolf von Habsburg."

Significantly, Martin Mahner recalled a variant of the beheading tale and tracked down a source ("Pirate Biographies: Klaus Störtebeker" 2002). The tale features a pirate, Klaus Störtebeker, who was captured in 1401. Kneeling before the executioner, he proposed a deal: "All those companions should be reprieved whom he could manage to walk by after being beheaded. This way he saved the lives of eleven pirates before the malicious executioner tripped him."

I suspect the robber-knights' tale is actually a late variant derived from the pirates' tale, but that both—describing a physiological impossibility (the postbeheading walk)—seem ultimately to derive from a fictional account.

PHANTOM OF THE WELL

At the mouth of the Niagara River—where the water from four Great Lakes flows into Lake Ontario—stands Old Fort Niagara. For over three centuries, garrisons maintained defenses at the site, beginning with the French (1678–1759), then, following a siege, the British (1759–1796), and, as a result of negotiations after the Revolutionary War, the Americans (1796–1963). It was subsequently restored as a historic site, open to the public, the only vestige of active military use being a Coast Guard station located there (Dunnigan 1985).

I have paid several visits to the fort and spent many pleasant hours there, much of the time investigating the reputed haunting of the well inside the "French Castle" (figures 3.2 and 3.3). The nucleus of the original fort, that structure is said to be "probably the oldest building in North America between the Appalachian Mountains and the Mississippi River" (Dunnigan 1985, 44).

Figure 3.2. Reenactment soldiers entertain visitors to Old Fort Niagara and its supposedly haunted French Castle. (Photo by Joe Nickell.)

Figure 3.3. The stone well inside Fort Niagara's French Castle is said to be home to a ghost soldier who's eternally searching for his head. (Photo by Joe Nickell.)

According to an elaborate folktale, the stone building was once the site of a gruesome tragedy. During the French occupation, the garrison was supposedly hosting a frontier ball, the dance being intended to relieve the long winter months. Unfortunately, an excess of wine sparked an argument over one of the Indian women. Two men drew their swords. After much dueling, one forced the other down the stairs to the ground-floor vestibule. The latter lost his step and fell, whereupon the other ran him through.

The victor panicked, fearing the consequences of his act, and determined to dismember and dispose of the body in turbulent Lake Ontario.

However, no sooner had he dispensed with the head than he heard others coming and quickly heaved the body down the well. Reportedly, "the evidence disappeared with a splash, and the fate of the missing officer was never determined. For years afterwards, however, on nights of a full moon, British and American occupants of the castle often saw and heard a headless apparition restlessly seeking its missing head!" (Dunnigan 1989)

The earliest published version of the ghost story is much skimpier. Appearing in Samuel De Vaux's *The Falls of Niagara* in 1839, it reads:

> There were many legendary stories about the fort . . . and it was a story with the soldiers and believed by the superstitious, that at midnight the headless trunk of a French general officer was often seen sitting on the curb of the old well, where he had been murdered and his body thrown in.

Over the years, raconteurs and authors of local guidebooks embroidered the tale, which became known across the Niagara region (Dunnigan 1989).

Despite ghostly shenanigans such as unexplained noises and other occurrences—potentially the result of misperceptions of mundane phenomena (a loose shutter on one occasion, for instance)—"the elusive ghost of the French Castle has yet to appear to modern eyes," according to castle historian Brian Dunnigan (1989, 104). Dunnigan himself once thought he saw the ghostly figure sitting hunched on the well, but when he got closer, he recognized the shape as a heap of Christmas greenery and other decorations to be disposed of (Diachun 2003). The apparition was a simulacrum (a random pattern that the brain interprets as something specific—the face of the Man in the Moon, for example [see Nickell 2004]).

Tour guide Elaine Kasprzyk (2002) confirmed that, to date, no one had reported seeing the ghost during overnight stays there. She added that the story was implausible in its details—for instance, there never would have been such a party with the Indians. Moreover, excavation of the well failed to uncover the expected bones of the murdered soldier. She said that typically (as did happen on our tour) a child would persist in believing the haunting tale. After she had explained that the story was untrue and the ghost nonexistent, a boy or girl would ask, "Have you ever seen the ghost?" or "Has he ever found his head?"

SPIRITS AT THE TOWER

Among the world's most famous headless ghosts is that of Anne Boleyn (1507–1536), King Henry VIII's second wife, who in 1536 was beheaded at the Tower of London. Hers is "one of the gruesome ghosts" alleged to haunt the medieval fortress and royal palace turned prison (Hauck 2000, 52). It is called "England's Most Haunted Building" (Jones 2004, 59). Anne was among many—including one of her accusers, Thomas Cromwell, and a later wife of Henry, Catherine Howard—who were beheaded at the tower.

As with the later Catherine, Anne Boleyn was charged with adultery. Actually, Henry had tired of her and had fallen in love with another (Jane Seymour, who would become her immediate successor), and the charges seemed largely or completely trumped up. All of her six alleged lovers denied the accusations, although the torture chamber elicited a confession from one (Hibbert et al. 1971, 52–55). The charge against another, her half brother, with whom she allegedly committed incest, was "invented by Thomas Cromwell" (*Webster's* 1997, 147). Perhaps the most celebrated of the accused was Sir Thomas Wyatt (ca. 1503–1542), the poet who introduced the Petrarchan sonnet to England. (Interestingly, my own ancestry traces back—through Rev. Haute Wyatt, a minister at Jamestown—to the famous bard.[1]) Wyatt was twice imprisoned in the tower but never lost his head.

Also reportedly seen at the tower is the apparition of Lady Jane Grey (1537–1554). A nominal queen of England during a power play, she reigned just nine days before she and her husband were imprisoned and beheaded. It is unclear whether her specter is headless, being that it is described as a "white shapeless ghost" (Hauck 2000, 52).

The same uncertainty attends the most dramatic of the tower's spirits, the reputed ghost of Margaret Pole, Countess of Salisbury. A target of Henry VIII's political vengeance (her son had vilified his claim to be head of the Church of England), she was ordered executed. The tough old lady supposedly refused to kneel for the executioner, who chased her screaming around the scaffold and "literally hacked her to death" (Jones 2004, 61). A less sensational account (Hibbert et al. 1971, 65) states:

> The proud woman had refused to put her gray head on the block as that was what traitors did. She had so shaken it from side to side—as though inviting

the executioner to get it off as best he could—that her neck and shoulders were hideously hacked about before the decapitation was accomplished.

Nevertheless, suiting the more dramatic version of the events, in some tales, her head has been restored so that "her screaming phantom continues to be chased throughout eternity by a ghostly executioner" (Jones 2004, 61). A quite serene ghost of Margaret Pole reportedly also haunts Dundridge Manor in St. Leonards, Buckinghamshire. It is "seen in broad daylight walking through the manor corridors, and sometimes the swishing of her skirts can also be heard" (Hauck 2000, 59).

Markedly different apparitions aside, we find that, as is typically the case at other reputed haunting sites, apparitions are really relatively scarce. Richard Jones, author of *Haunted London* (2004, 8), admits that

> hauntings can assume many different forms. It is, in fact, very rare for people to actually "see" a ghost. People sense them, smell them, and hear them, but a full-blown manifestation tends to be the exception rather than the rule.

This is consistent with the skeptics' view that it is not places, but people who are haunted. Seeming to sense a ghostly presence may be no more than the imagination at work. Apparitions can result from a "waking dream" (that occurs in the twilight between being fully awake and asleep) or other dissociative state (such as daydreaming), when imagery can well up from the subconscious and be superimposed briefly on the visual scene, something of a mental double exposure. Ghosts are thus invariably clothed as expected, a requisite of the apparitional story and setting (Nickell 2001).

When I visited the Tower of London many years ago[2]—walking among the regalia-clad Yeomen Warders known as Beefeaters, exploring the forbidding white tower, with its winding corridors, and perusing the dazzling crown jewels—I neither saw nor experienced any ghosts. Yet, like anyone else, I could feel the impress of history and, had I been so inclined, could easily have imagined myself in the midst of a ghostly drama, subjectively directing whether the ghosts would be headless or not.

Chapter 4

EXPERIENCING
THE OTHER SIDE

Belief that the human spirit survives bodily death is common to all religious traditions—except classical Buddhism, which does not accept the existence of a soul—as well as to the animistic beliefs of tribal societies in Asia, Africa, Australia, and the Americas. Various experiences have prompted belief in survival (Guiley 2000, 372–74). Here, out of my more than forty years of investigating paranormal phenomena, are cases of some main types of such experiences—waking dreams, near-death experiences (including out-of-body experiences), and past-life memories—that I have personally investigated.

WAKING DREAMS

My very first haunted-house investigation was at Toronto's historic Mackenzie House, the former home of Canadian rebel-statesman William Lyon Mackenzie (1795–1861) (figure 4.1). Mackenzie died in the house, and almost a century later it began to be known as a haunted house when new caretakers, Mr. and Mrs. Alex Dobban, related their experiences to the *Toronto Telegram*. Subsequently, previous caretakers—an army pensioner and his wife, Mr. and Mrs. Charles Edmunds—came forward to tell of their own spooky happenings (Nickell 1988, 17–27). During their tenure, from August 1956 until April 1960, Mrs. Edmunds often saw a woman, or sometimes a small man in a frock coat, presumably Mackenzie's ghost, standing in her room. For example, she told the *Telegram*:

Figure 4.1. The most haunted address in Canada is Toronto's Mackenzie House. (Sketch by Joe Nickell.)

One night I woke up at midnight to see a lady standing over my bed. She wasn't at the side, but at the head of the bed, leaning over me. There is no room for anyone to stand where she was. The bed was pushed against the wall. She was hanging down like a shadow but I could see her clearly. Something seemed to touch me on the shoulder to wake me up. She had long hair hanging down in front of her shoulders. . . . She had a long narrow face. Then she was gone. (quoted in Smith 1970, 44)

Now, Mrs. Edmunds's apparitions can be attributed to what are called "waking dreams." These are simple hallucinations that commonly occur when one is neither fully asleep nor awake. Formerly called "night terrors," they are technically termed *hypnagogic* or *hypnopompic* hallucinations (depending whether they occur, respectively, while going to sleep or while awakening). Because one is between states, one experiences features of both sleep and wakefulness: fantasy, dreamlike elements perceived as realistic occurrences. On some occasions one also experiences an inability to move, called "sleep paralysis," since the body is still in the sleep mode (the body's neural circuits keeping our muscles relaxed to help preserve our sleep). This can prompt the experiencer to "see" a demon (incubus or succubus) sitting on his or her chest, extraterrestrials strapping him or her down on an operating table, or the like.

NEAR-DEATH EXPERIENCES

Another type of experience also seems to provide a glimpse of the Other Side. Some years ago I came across an antique lithographed poster advertising a newspaper feature about people who "came back from the dead" (figure 4.2). With the assistance of CFI librarian Timothy Binga, I was able to track down a copy of the paper, the October 14, 1906, *Boston American* (Nickell 2007, 259–63).

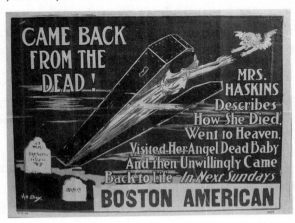

Figure 4.2. Poster from 1906 features a quaint depiction of what today would be called a near-death experience. (Photo by Joe Nickell from his collection.)

The main story concerned a Mrs. James A. Haskins, who had "apparently died during a recent attack of pleuro-pneumonia," during which time she had recovered after having appeared neither to breathe nor to have a heartbeat for some twenty-three minutes. (Of course, if this had actually occurred, she would have suffered irreversible brain damage.) Afterward, Mrs. Haskins would state that she heard a nurse say, "Well, she's gone," whereupon she felt the nurse close her eyes and heard her mother sobbing. "Then," she said, "my little dead baby, Doris, came to me. I held out my arms to her and held her close to my breast. Oh, I was so happy." She added: "Her coming back to me was not a shock. It seemed perfectly natural that she should come in that way. So I gathered her up in my arms and together we floated away in perfect happiness." However, in time, Mrs. Haskins became conscious of gasping for breath, feeling the pain of her illness, and finding herself in her own mother's arms. "Returning to life was the hard part," she insisted. "Dying was peace and happiness."

Her encounter has much in common with today's typical near-death experience (NDE)—a term coined by physician Raymond Moody in the 1970s to describe the mystical experiences some report after apparently returning from death's door. Although each person's experience is unique, *Harper's Encyclopedia of Mystical and Paranormal Experience* states:

> In an NDE people generally experience one or more of the following phenomena in this sequence: a sense of being dead, or an out-of-body experience in which they feel themselves floating above their bodies, looking down; cessation of pain and a feeling of bliss or peacefulness; traveling down a dark tunnel toward a light at the end; meeting nonphysical beings who glow, many of whom are dead friends and relatives; coming in contact with a guide or Supreme Being who takes them on a life review, during which their entire lives are put into perspective without rendering any negative judgments about past acts; and finally, a reluctant return to life. (Guiley 1991, 399)

Mrs. Haskins reported many of these experiences. Although she did not mention the dark tunnel, she did refer to "brightness."

From a scientific standpoint, out-of-body experiences are actually hallucinations such as can occur when one is nowhere near death: under anesthesia, when one is falling asleep or even merely relaxing or meditating, or during attacks of migraine or epilepsy. Also hallucinatory is the tunnel-travel experience, attributable to the particular structure of the visual cortex (the part of the brain that processes visual information (Blackmore 1991) or to pupil widening due to oxygen deprivation (Woerlee 2004). The life review results from the dying, oxygen-starved brain stimulating cells in the temporal lobe and thus arousing memories. And it is not surprising that people's longing for dead loved ones should manifest in dreamlike imagery.

As Mrs. Haskins's poignant story demonstrates, examples of people recovering from "death" and telling of their supposedly near-death experiences can be profound—even life transforming. Blackmore (1991) observes that the NDE has aspects "that are ineffable—they cannot be put into words." Such an event can seem so real, so powerful in its import, that—even though it is "essentially physiological"—it can profoundly change the lives of those who experience it.

PAST-LIFE MEMORIES

In her book, *Across Time and Death*, Jenny Cockell (1993), a British wife and mother who also works as a registered podiatrist, tells an unusual story. As a self-described "withdrawn and nervous child," she says she often woke sobbing with memories of her earlier death as an Irish woman named "Mary." She also recalled "constantly tidying and clearing out my room and toys," as well as "sweeping with a broom, and acting out other chores" (1, 5, 14). Jenny also frequently sketched maps of Mary's Irish village, although there were, admittedly, variations in the supposed landmarks.

In 1988, Cockell underwent hypnosis, whereupon she seemingly became Mary. Although while hypnotized she felt she existed partly in the past and partly in the present, she emphasized: "Yet I was Mary, and the past had become very real. I could smell the grass on the slopes outside a large farmhouse, and I breathed in the fresh spring air." Under hypnosis she also explored what she believed were her "psychic abilities." In addition, as "Mary," whose death she supposedly relived, she seemingly drifted outside herself on occasion to view the environs of her "now vacant body" (1993, 40, 55).

Jenny then engaged in research—making queries, acquiring maps, and so on—eventually turning up a village named Malahide and a woman named Mary Sutton who roughly fit her "memories." The story—also told on the television program *Unsolved Mysteries*—ended with Mrs. Cockell making contact with some of Mary's surviving children who—ironically and bizarrely—were old enough to be her parents. Nevertheless, she was satisfied with her "reunion" and began to look into her "next life" as a twenty-first-century Nepalese girl (1993, 117–53).

I carefully examined Mrs. Cockell's intriguing and no doubt sincere saga, but it did not withstand critical analysis. In addition to the overwhelming lack of factual information provided by her dreams and hypnosis (she had not even known Mary's surname or the name of her village), she made numerous errors (such as giving the husband's name as Bryan rather than John) and she rationalized her mistakes and omissions throughout her book. But if Jenny Cockell's story is untrue, where did it come from?

An analysis of her autobiographical statements (Nickell 2001, 137–41) reveals her to possess many of the traits that indicate a propensity to fantasize. For example, she is an excellent hypnotic subject; she spent much time fantasizing as a child and had imaginary playmates as well as a fantasy identity; she not only recalls but relives past experiences, has out-of-body experiences, and believes she has psychic powers; and so on. Taken together, these traits are strong evidence of what is termed a fantasy-prone personality (see Wilson and Barber 1983).

Being an excellent hypnotic subject is particularly relevant because, as the late psychologist Robert A. Baker observed (Baker and Nickell 1992, 152):

> For a long while it was believed that hypnosis provided the person hypnotized with abnormal or unusual abilities of recall. The ease with which hypnotized subjects would retrieve forgotten memories and relive early childhood experiences was astonishing. . . .
>
> However, when the veridicality of such memories was examined, it was found that many of the memories were not only false, but they were even outright fabrications. Confabulations, i.e., making up stories to fill in memory gaps, seemed to be the norm rather than the exception. It seems, literally, that using "hypnosis" to revive or awaken a person's past history somehow or other not only stimulates the person's desire to recall and his memory processes, but it also opens the flood gates of his or her imagination.

As Cockell herself acknowledges, she was forever dreaming: "Sometimes it was about the future, sometimes about the past, but hardly ever about the present." She adds, "My escape into the past grew as I grew, and it was like a little death in my own life, a death of part of me that replaced part of my life (1993, 16). As with other classic fantasizers, her need to retreat from an unpleasant reality led her to create a reality that took on—so to speak—a life of its own.

Experiences such as these—waking dreams, near-death experiences, and past-life memories—must extend far back in time. Indeed, one suspects they are as old as humankind. No doubt they have persuaded countless people to believe—profoundly, if wrongly—that they have actually had an other-worldly experience.

Chapter 5

ENTOMBED ALIVE!

It is a horrifying concept: being buried—or walled-up—alive. Fears of such possibilities were once rife.

In earlier times even physicians could not always determine infallibly whether an individual was dead or instead in a comatose or cataleptic state. Actual cases of people seemingly returning to life may have inspired ancient folktales about persons being raised from the dead.

Moreover, in Europe, untimely inhumation helped spread fears of vampires—those who returned from the dead to prey on the living (Bunson 1993, 211). Edgar Allan Poe (1809–1849) expressed, with his usual genius, the grotesque horror of living interment with his tale "The Premature Burial."

Then there were incidents—real or imagined—in which for some motive such as punishment or revenge a person was deliberately entombed alive, the theme of another Poe story, "The Cask of Amontillado."

One such alleged occurrence was in St. Augustine, Florida, at the Spanish-built fortress Castillo de San Marcos. Purportedly, an eighteenth-century colonel discovered his wife was having an affair and chained her and her lover to a wall in the dungeon; he "mortared a new wall of coquina stone in front of them" (Hauck 1996, 125). In fact, however, investigation shows that the event is historically unrecorded, and the tale is traceable only to the rumors and outright concoctions of tour guides in the early twentieth century (Nickell 2005, 26). (This case is explored more fully in chapter 17.)

In my travels, I have encountered other living-burial stories. Here are three that I have investigated, two being of the deliberate-entombment type, namely a walled-up nun in the Netherlands and a castle's mystery room in Switzerland, and the third belonging to the premature-burial genre, featuring a vault with a view in a Vermont graveyard.

WALLED-UP NUN

During a lecture and investigation trip to the Netherlands and Belgium in 2006 (Nickell 2007), I was escorted by Dutch skeptic Jan Willem Nienhuys to Singraven, an estate near the small town of Denekamp in northeastern Netherlands. Built on old foundations in the first quarter of the fifteenth century, the estate's manor house or "castle" is said to be haunted.

Its secluded location helped give it an air of mystery and, as is the case with many historic sites, the ambience helped spawn ghostlore. After one lord of the manor began a cemetery on the grounds, superstitious folk began to say he invited bad luck. When his beard caught fire from an oil lamp, burning him severely, and when his wife died in childbirth, people would say, "The ghost of Singraven has struck again" (Wynia et al. 2006).

A young Dutch "psychic," Robbert van den Broeke, visited Singraven and claimed to perceive numerous ghostly presences. Robbert—who busies himself giving dubious readings, producing questionable otherworldly photos, conveniently discovering crop circles near his and his parents' home, and so on (Broeke 2005)—did not, however, perform at his psychic best. He incorrectly identified an oil portrait as that of the noble with the burned beard (probably because he had seen a television show that made the same misidentification). He also placed the incident in the wrong room (Wynia et al. 2006).

In the mansion's drawing room, Robbert "saw" various ghosts sitting in chairs or moving about. However, tour guides at Singraven pointed out that there had never been reports of ghosts in that particular chamber, which, in fact, had been added relatively recently (Wynia et al. 2006). At Singraven and elsewhere, Robbert has produced "ghost" photos, but these seem on a par with his "alien" ones (see Nanninga 2005, 28), which are indistinguishable from ridiculous fakes.

The main target of Robbert's psychic and photographic efforts at Singraven is the colorful, spooky legend of a walled-up nun. A cloister occupied the estate from 1505 to 1515. According to a popular tale, one night a young nun slipped away for a clandestine liaison with her lover. Returning late, she attempted to sneak up the stairs, but they creaked and awakened the mother superior, who decided to make an example of her. The unfortunate nun was sealed up in the wall near the foot of the stairway. As she slowly starved to death, her shouts of despair served as a warning to the other sisters (Wynia et al. 2006).

Now, this tale is implausible on the face of it—not only because it has an ostensibly devout prioress capriciously violating one of the Ten Commandments, but also because the cloister at Singraven was not for nuns at all. Rather, it housed Beguines (lay sisters). It is, in fact, a proliferating and often-debunked folktale. It has found its way into literature, for example in the epic poem *Marmion* by Sir Walter Scott (1808). Catholic scholar Herbert Thurston said of the legend:

> To anyone who honestly looks into the matter, it will be clear that no statutes of any religious order have yet been brought forward which prescribe such punishment; that no contemporary records speak of its infliction; that no attempt is made to give details of persons or time; that the few traditions that speak of discovery of walled-up remains crumble away the moment they are examined; that the growth of the tradition itself can be abundantly accounted for; that the few historians or antiquaries of repute, whether Catholic or Protestant, either avowedly disbelieve the calumny, or studiously refrain from repeating it. (quoted in Catholic 2006)

Thurston's skepticism is fully justified by the facts of our investigation at Singraven. The wall in which the nun was allegedly sealed—now graced with a mirror (see figure 5.1)—was actually opened up in the early 1990s. This was done by workmen who were replacing the manor's electric wiring. The workers discovered no bones inside the wall, thus discrediting the local legend and with it the ghost sightings of the nun at the alleged site of her horrible death (Wynia et al. 2006).

Such legends of nuns being walled-up for punishment may be derived from the fact that ascetics were sometimes voluntarily enclosed, hermitlike, for solitary meditation. We learned of a church in Utrecht with just such a history. Visiting there the day following our investigation at Singraven, Jan Willem Nienhuys and I found an incised stone tablet in the walkway at the side of the edifice. It reads (in translation): "Sister Bertken Lived Here as Hermit Walled in a Niche in the Wall in the Choir of the Buurkerk 1457–1514."

Called "anchoresses," the walled-up penitents were not nuns (they did not take vows, for example), and while they led very austere lives, their "cells" could be quite roomy and often had a door that led into the church.

Figure 5.1. In a "haunted" manor house, Dutch paranormal investigator Jan Willem Nienhuys investigates the wall (behind the mirror) inside which an errant nun was reputedly sealed alive in the early sixteenth century. (Photo by Joe Nickell.)

Such hermits even kept in touch with both common folk and nobles, dispensing spiritual counsel and practical advice. When, after the Council of Trent (1545–1563) the Roman Catholic Church became increasingly male-dominated, the urban anchoresses disappeared (see Mulder-Bakker 2005).

MYSTERIOUS CASTLE ROOM

Another entombed-alive legend is attributed to a curious little structure high atop a medieval castle in Switzerland. Overlooking the village of Oensingen, near Solothurn, Bechburg Castle could have been built as early as the mid-thirteenth century, although the earliest document relating to it dates from 1313 (Schloss 2007).

The enigmatic structure is at the highest part of the castle, except for an adjacent tower that continues upward (see figure 5.2). Roofed but doorless and windowless, the structure is the subject of a legend of uncertain vintage.

Figure 5.2. At the eastern end of Switzerland's Bechburg Castle is a roofed little room (upper left) in which an evil knight allegedly was sealed after contracting leprosy. (Photo by Joe Nickell.)

Reportedly entombed there was a certain Kuoni, a despicable robber-knight who terrorized the populace and shed much innocent blood. Finally, though, he received a kind of justice when he became afflicted with leprosy or some other contagious disease. According to the tale, he was walled inside the chamber, and servants fed him food and water through a small opening. When he died, this was closed with a stone. Supposedly, however, the chamber could not contain the restless soul of the evil man, which still haunts the castle on certain nights (Roth and Maurer 2006).

The fanciful tale of a leprous knight being walled-in sounds less like historical fact (especially since the spot seems an unlikely place for such confinement) than folkloric fiction inspired by accounts of walled-up ascetics. Nevertheless, the name Kuoni—a diminutive of Konrad—has been common among the barons of the Bechburg, and there is an old document that could seem to support the legend. Dated 1408 and penned by Count Egon von Kyburg, it reports repair work occurred on the "alcove" (or "little chamber") in which "Kuoni reposes" (Roth and Maurer 2006). Ghost proponents assume that this refers to the mysterious structure and so confirms that someone named Kuoni is entombed there. But might it not also refer to another place on the premises where, say, a child—little Konrad—slept?

In any case, there is no apparent evidence that the small roofed structure ever had a door or windows. Moreover, when I visited the castle with German skeptic Martin Mahner on May 25, 2007, we discovered something that none of our sources mentioned: its shape is peculiar. While one side meets the front at right angles, the other curves smoothly into it (again, see figure 5.2). This suggests that, architecturally, its purpose may have been partially or even totally stylistic.

As we learned from files at the city hall in Oensingen (Schloss 2007), a further possibility was suggested by a provincial historical-building supervisor. He had a worker use a jackhammer to drill into the mysterious structure from the top. While this was in progress, a severe lightning and hail storm arose and ended the exploration, but not before a depth of one meter had been reached. This led the supervisor to conclude that the little prominence has incredibly thick walls, indeed that it is probably not hollow at all but instead just a defensive bulwark.

Of course, even if the entire Kuoni folktale is untrue, that does not disprove the claims that the place is haunted. But what is the evidence that it is? Well, a tour guide who "usually" leaves the tower door open sometimes returns to find it closed again. Since it is latched from the inside, this cannot happen accidentally, and he dismisses suggestions that it could be a prank by visitors. He continually feels that he is not alone, and he sometimes hears voices along an empty hallway, but he is unsure whether they belong to ghosts or whether it is simply the wind carrying the voices of people who are walking nearby. Once, years ago, a volunteer worker during spring cleaning heard footsteps behind him as he descended the tower stairs. When he looked there was no one behind him, yet as he continued on so did the sounds. He insisted they were not the echoes of his own footsteps (Roth and Maurer 2006, 105–108).

Such anecdotal evidence, however spine-tingling it may be to some, has no weight in the scientific investigation of paranormal claims. If spooky happenings at Bechburg Castle are not due to the suggested causes already given—a prankster latching a door, the wind carrying voices, or the echo of one's own footsteps—clearly there are other possible explanations (see Nickell 1995, 39–77; 2001). We must ask: how, without a brain, can a disembodied spirit think, walk, or say *boo*? Science has never attributed a single occurrence to the alleged supernatural realm.

VAULT WITH A VIEW

A large, grassy mound seems strangely out of place near the front of Evergreen Cemetery in New Haven, Vermont. At the top of the mound is a small glass window encased in a square of cement that invites passersby to peer into the grave below (figure 5.3). The window was placed there at the behest of its tenant, and therein lies a spooky tale.

The deceased was Dr. Timothy Clark Smith (1821–1893). Between stints as a schoolteacher, merchant, and Treasury Department clerk, he studied medicine at New Haven (1834–1844) and the University of New York (1853–1855), obtaining his medical degree in 1855. He subsequently became a staff surgeon in the Russian army (1855–1856). Afterward, he served as US consul, first at Odessa, Russia (1861–1875), and then at Galatz (1878–1883) (Robinson 1950, 117). One source states that Smith's travels earned him the sobriquet "Odessa" Smith (Marquard 1982).

Figure 5.3. Atop this Vermont cemetery mound is a concrete-encased window to the grave below. The man interred reportedly feared "premature burial." The stone in the foreground seals the stairway to the arched vault. (Photo by Joe Nickell.)

Smith died on February 25, 1893, at Middlebury, Vermont. I found his obituary in a later (March 3) *Middlebury Register*. It reported that he "died suddenly on Saturday morning at the Logan House [hotel] where he had been living. After breakfast, he walked out into the office and stood by the stove when stricken." A local news article in the same issue noted that he was "formerly a resident of this town," adding that "many will remember the old red store where Timothy Smith, Sr., traded, and afterwards his son." The article also noted that "the deceased leaves a wife and several children."

A modern newspaper feature story on the grave (Marquard 1982) says of Smith's era:

> It was the late 1800s—in times before embalming—and folks didn't have to travel far to hear tales of people who had been presumed dead, only to be buried alive.
>
> One legend has it that Smith particularly feared contracting sleeping sickness, and waking up on the cold side of a coffin cover.

Smith therefore devised a plan that involved postponing his burial until he was assuredly dead and having his arched burial vault provided with stairs and a viewing window at the top of a glassed shaft.

One of Smith's children, Harrison T. C. Smith of Gilman, Iowa, reportedly traveled to New Haven "to supervise construction of the unusual crypt" (Marquard 1982). The vault has two rooms, cemetery sexton Betty Bell told me (2003), the second being for Smith's wife, Catherine (Prout) Smith.

According to the feature article, there are other legends about the tomb. One is that Smith had it outfitted with "tools for his escape." Although condensation and plant growth inside the shaft now block one's view, residents in years past claimed to see the tools along with Smith's bones. Said one, "You can see the face of the skeleton down there with a hammer and chisel crossed on the ground next to it" (Marquard 1982). Another source claims that when Smith was interred, "in the corpse's hand they placed a bell that he could ring should he wake up and find himself the victim of a premature burial" (Citro and Foulds, 2003, 292).

Curiously perhaps, ghost tales about the grave seem scarce. The authors of *Curious New England* (Citro and Foulds 2003, 292) attempt to provoke the credulous. Mentioning the bell allegedly placed in Smith's hand, they say, "So if you decide to visit the cemetery, keep very quiet . . . and listen." I did but, not surprisingly, heard nothing.

Area resident John Palmer (2003) told me that for fun he used to send impressionable children to the site to scare them. He still felt guilty about one such event. He had his two older boys take a couple of six-year-olds to the grave, telling them a person was alive down there. Then suddenly they exclaimed, "The ground is moving!" whereupon Palmer—who had hidden in the trees—jumped out screaming. The two youngsters were so scared that they ran into each other's arms and fell down.

Actually, Palmer told me, although as a child he had himself played there with other children, he never saw any ghosts or even heard any ghost tales. I guess Timothy Clark Smith is dead after all.

Chapter 6

GHOSTLY
LORE AND LURE

In the search for spirits of the dead, one often encounters legends—proliferating tales that can prove as elusive as the ghosts they tell of. Here are three examples of "haunted" places that illustrate how things may not be quite what they are reputed to be.

WINCHESTER MYSTERY HOUSE

A stacked and sprawling architectural wonder, the Winchester Mystery House in San Jose, California, once comprised an estimated 500 rooms, although it was significantly reduced by the 1906 San Francisco earthquake. However, when Sarah Winchester died in 1922, the house she obsessively built onto still contained 160 rooms with 2,000 doors (including some that opened onto blank walls), 10,000 windows, 47 stairways, and as many fireplaces, secret passageways, and more, including, controversially, a blue séance room where she reportedly rendezvoused secretly with spirits. (See figure 6.1.)

Sources claim that Sarah Winchester, grief stricken at the death of her husband, William, heir to the Winchester Rifle fortune, sought out a medium to contact his spirit. The medium allegedly directed her to make amends for the deaths caused by the rifles, to appease the victims' ghosts by building a house for them. As a consequence, the Winchester Mystery House is claimed to be America's most haunted mansion, tenanted by perhaps thousands of ghostly guests (Nickell 2004, 128–30; Guiley 2000, 405–407; *Winchester Mystery House* 1997; Hauck 1996, 75–76; Winer and Osborne 1979, 33–49).

Figure 6.1. The Winchester Mystery House is far more immense than this view conveys. (Photo by Joe Nickell.)

The house attracts legends, certainly, but are they true? I investigated the site on October 24, 2001, as part of a California lecture and investigations tour, accompanied by colleague Vaughn Rees.

In fact, there is no proof that Mrs. Winchester ever contacted a medium, and her companion for many years, Miss Henrietta Severs, denied the widow was ever a spiritualist. The séance room was really a bedroom, and the tower's bell that supposedly summoned spirits at midnight was instead used to call workmen, as well as to serve as an alarm in case of fire. Reports of "ghostly music" were due to the fact that, when she was unable to sleep, Sarah Winchester typically played the pump organ in the Grand Ballroom.

Of course it would be unusual if such a rambling old house did not have the characteristics that often lead to reports of ghostly activity, including drafts, odd noises (caused by temperature changes and settlings of an old structure), and the legends and ambiance that create a climate of expectation. On one occasion, for instance, a shadowy figure turned out to be a Winchester staffer. As with other "haunted" places, there is no scientific evidence that the great mansion hosts a single ghost—"only," as the late psychologist Robert A. Baker loved to say, "haunted people" (Nickell 2004, 128–39).

GHOST OF CLEMENT HALL

On a visit to the University of Tennessee at Martin to give a well-attended lecture on March 24, 2010, I learned of UTM's Ghost of Clement Hall, termed "one of the most popular ghost stories of West Tennessee" ("Ghost of Clement Hall" 2006). I determined to look into the case, ably assisted in my investigation by members of the group that sponsored my talk, Campus Freethinkers Society (president Angelia Stinnett, who helped throughout; Stetson Ford, who did online research; Trey Hamilton, who video-recorded my on-site interviews with staff; and advisor Lionel Crews, who also assisted in various ways).

Reportedly, the apparition of a young woman in white confirms the legend of a student who committed suicide on the fourth floor of the campus's oldest dormitory (figure 6.2). The story was also the subject of a 2008 movie, *A Rose for Caitlin*, made by Virtual Light Films (UTM students). Caitlin or Caitlyn is simply the nickname students have given to the "spirit of the unknown girl" ("Haunted Tour" 2010).

In addition to apparitions, other allegedly ghostly phenomena include flickering lights and strange noises—in other words, nothing of a convincing evidential nature. Consider one reported sighting made by David Belote (2006), assistant vice chancellor for student affairs. He remains unsure just what he saw in the building's attic in the early 1980s. Something moved quickly between some stacked boxes, but, he says, the movement could be attributed to a bird or something else. "It could have been my imagination," he concedes, admitting he has embellished the story over the years when relating it to students. Stephanie Mueller (2010), an advisor to special-needs students—having worked in the building for years, both day and night—attributes the flickering shadow she once saw on the floor to a failing light bulb. She added that the building's radiator heat, which expands and contracts pipes, could be responsible for many noises.

Figure 6.2. Clement Hall, oldest dormitory at the University of Tennessee at Martin, is supposedly haunted by the "spirit of an unknown girl." (Photo by Joe Nickell.)

UTM's director of housing, Earl Wright (2006), believes the ghost story originated in an incident in the early 1970s. Wright's sister and her roommate, who were working on an art project, had left some life-sized Halloween-themed figures standing in a shower stall to dry. These frightened a fellow student who came upon them and, Wright thinks, sparked the ghost story. (Again see "Ghost of Clement Hall" 2006.) However, the hypothesis fails to explain many factors, including how the cutouts, promptly revealed as such, were transformed into a persistently haunting spirit.

In any case, housing director Wright (2006) insists that the allegation of a student having committed suicide on the top floor of Clement Hall is untrue. And Stephanie Mueller told me pointedly that there were "different versions" of the tale. These are what folklorists call *variants*, and they are evidence of the folklore process at work. The differences include the supposed reason for the "suicide" (the young woman was simply jilted, or she walked in on her cheating boyfriend *in flagrante delicto*) as well as the place and manner of death (she hanged herself in a men's shower stall where there is a bent curtain rod, or perhaps she died in another way, as evidenced by "blood" splatters on a hallway door). Another women's dorm, McCord Hall, likewise has a story of a suicide by hanging—possibly indicating that the *legend* (i.e., a supposedly true folktale) is *migratory* (to use other folklorist terms).

Indeed, the UTM tale's cluster of *motifs* (or narrative elements) provided a basis for an Internet search (generously conducted for me by CFI Libraries director Timothy Binga). This showed that similar stories of a suicidal dorm resident who returns to haunt the place of tragedy are found not only on other Tennessee campuses but also across the country, from Charlotte to Tulsa and beyond. The evidence thus suggests that it is a migratory legend— part of the narrative lore of college folk, transmitted widely. It seems that no matter how much the imaginary ghost wanders, she can always find a place to stay: among those who can most empathize with her.

TRAGICALLY "HAUNTED"

Formerly called the Winecoff Hotel, it was the site of the most tragic hotel fire, not only in Atlanta, but in all US history. Thus, it surely should be haunted—if, that is, ghosts are something more than figments of the romantic imagination. During the popular Dragon*Con festival in September 2009 and 2010, I investigated ghost claims at the refurbished hotel, collecting published tales, taking photographs, interviewing the manager, and more.

A historical marker on the property relates the horrific story. Before dawn on December 7, 1946, the hotel was filled with 280 guests. At that time, the brick structure was believed to be fireproof but—lacking sprinklers, fire escapes, and even fire doors—it was actually a death trap, which claimed 119 lives. Although firemen from Atlanta and surrounding towns fought valiantly for some two and half hours, "their ladders reached only to the eighth floor, and their nets were not strong enough to withstand jumps of more than 70 feet." Consequently the bodies of those who perished by jumping were scattered on the sidewalks and piled in the alley at the rear of the building. Within days, however, reports of the horror prompted enactment of fire-safety ordinances across the country, and today the shell of the building has been transformed into the modern, safety-conscious Ellis Hotel.

Authors of ghost books—typically a superstitious, mystery-mongering lot—are at pains to give the hotel sufficient ghostly tales to befit its tragic history. Reese Christian—whose book *Ghosts of Atlanta* (2008) bills her as an "elite psychic medium" and member of Ghost Hounds Paranormal Research Society—warms to the task. Although lacking specific sources, she touts such phenomena as workmen's unaccountably moved tools, the sounds of noisy but empty hallways, and the repeated smell of smoke when there was no fire (Christian 2008, 51–57).

Such reports may be unexplained, but they are hardly unexplainable. Workmen may mislay tools, or fellow workers may play pranks on them; guests can hear noises from other floors; and smoke may be imagined or simply come from someone's cigarette. Some ghostly experiences in hotels—including vivid apparitions—may stem from a guest's "waking dream," a state that occurs in the interface between wakefulness and sleep (see appendix).

At the Ellis, as at many other allegedly haunted buildings, people outside sometimes imagine they can see ghostly faces in the windows (Bender 2008, 131–34). When these are not actual faces—of guests or housekeepers—they may be nothing more than simulacra: these are the result of one's ability to perceive images in random patterns (such as the play of light and shadow upon a window), like seeing pictures in clouds. I did some experimenting with my camera at the hotel and produced the "faces" shown in one window here (figure 6.3).

The manager of the Ellis, Peter Minervini (2010), very kindly took a few minutes to sit and talk with CFI Libraries director Timothy Binga and me when we lunched at the hotel on September 4, 2010. He said he had worked there about a year and had no ghost experiences. The only thing he mentioned was an odd odor, occasionally perceived in one room, that he did not attribute to anything otherworldly. He said he was himself a skeptic regarding ghosts. The year before, I was startled when a young woman with a tour company told me there were so few credible ghost accounts in Atlanta that they were changing the name of their "Ghosts and Legends Tour." Will wonders never cease!

Figure 6.3. "Faces," seen in the play of light and shadow of windows, are often attributed to ghosts—as shown here at Atlanta's Ellis Hotel. (Photo by Joe Nickell.)

Chapter 7

THE DOCTOR'S GHOSTLY VISITOR: TRACKING "THE GIRL IN THE SNOW"

Although skeptics insist ghosts are unreal, there are many ghostly encounters that seem to present startling evidence to the contrary. One such incident is presented in the book *The Telltale Lilac Bush and Other West Virginia Ghost Tales* by Ruth Ann Musick (1965, 28–30). The story is indeed spine tingling, but is it true as well? I first began to investigate the case for my book *Entities: Angels, Spirits, Demons, and Other Alien Beings* (1995).

"HELP"

Musick's narrative, titled "Help," relates how "Doctor Anderson" was awakened by a knock at the door "just past midnight." He found on his doorstep a girl of twelve or thirteen who was dressed in a blue coat and carrying a white muff. She implored him to hurry to "the old Hostler place," where her mother was desperately ill, and then she darted down the road. Anderson picked up his doctor's bag, quickly saddled his horse, and hurried on his way until "he saw the glow of a lamp in the old Hostler house."

Finding a bedridden woman inside, the physician put wood on the dying fire and set to work to treat her fever. When she had rallied, he told her how fortunate she was that her daughter had fetched him. "But I have no daughter," the woman whispered. "My daughter has been dead for three years." Anderson described to her how the girl had been dressed; the woman

67

admitted that her daughter had had such clothing and indicated where the items were hanging.

Thereupon, relates the narrative's final paragraph, "Doctor Anderson strode over to the closet, opened the door, and took out a blue coat and white muff. His hands trembled when he felt the coat and muff and found them still warm and damp from perspiration."

How do we explain such an event? Well, first we remember to apply an old skeptic's dictum: before attempting to explain something, make sure it really happened.

ANOTHER VERSION

As it turns out, a book by Billy Graham contains a remarkably similar story (1975, 2–3), wherein the implication is that the little girl in the tale is not a ghost but rather an angel:

> Dr. S. W. Mitchell, a celebrated Philadelphia neurologist, had gone to bed after an exceptionally tiring day. Suddenly he was awakened by someone knocking on his door. Opening it he found a little girl, poorly dressed and deeply upset. She told him her mother was very sick and asked him if he would please come with her. It was a bitterly cold, snowy night, but though he was bone tired, Dr. Mitchell dressed and followed the girl. . . .
>
> As *Reader's Digest* reports the story, he found the mother desperately ill with pneumonia. After arranging for medical care, he complimented the sick woman on the intelligence and persistence of her little daughter. The woman looked at him strangely and said, "My daughter died a month ago." She added, "Her shoes and coat are in the clothes closet there." Dr. Mitchell, amazed and perplexed, went to the closet and opened the door. There hung the very coat worn by the little girl who had brought him to tend her mother. It was warm and dry and could not possibly have been out in the wintry night. . . .
>
> Could the doctor have been called in the hour of desperate need by an angel who appeared as this woman's young daughter? Was this the work of God's angels on behalf of the sick woman?

Graham provides no documentation beyond the vague reference to *Reader's Digest*, which in any event is hardly a scholarly source. In fact, I soon discovered that the tale is an old one, circulated in various forms with conflicting details. For example, as "The Girl in the Snow," it appears in Margaret Ronan's anthology of *Strange Unsolved Mysteries*. While Graham's version is of implied recent vintage, that by Ronan is set on a "December day in 1880." Whereas Graham states that the doctor was "awakened by someone knocking on his door," Ronan tells us "the doorbell downstairs was ringing violently." Absent from the Graham version is the suggestion that the little girl was a ghost, not an angel; for example, Ronan says the child looked "almost wraithlike in the whirling snow," and that "at times she seemed to vanish into the storm." In Graham's account, the doctor is credited with simply "arranging for medical care," while Ronan insists Mitchell "set about at once to do what he could for her" and "by morning he felt that at last she was out of danger." Although both versions preserve the essential element that the woman's little girl had died a month before, Graham's version quotes the mother as saying, "Her shoes and coat are in the clothes closet there," while Ronan's has her stating, "All I have left to remember her by are those clothes hanging on that peg over there." Indeed the latter account does not describe a coat and shoes but states: "Hanging from the peg was the thin dress he had seen the child wearing, and the ragged shawl" (Ronan 1974, 99–101).

VARIANT TALES

There are many other versions—or *variants* as folklorists say—of the proliferating tale. Of the five others I discovered, all feature the physician S. Weir Mitchell, but only two suggest the time period. Unlike the Graham (1975) and Ronan (1974) versions, which have the garments in a "clothes closet" and hanging from a peg, respectively, four of the other five variant tales say the clothes are in a "cupboard"; one has them in a "shabby chiffonier" (Edwards 1961, 52). There are differences in the clothes: Colby (1959) lists a "little dress" and "tattered shawl"; Edwards (1961) a "heavy dress," "hightop shoes," and "gray shawl" with a "blue glass pin"; Hurwood (1967) "all the clothes the child had worn when he saw her earlier"; Tyler (1970) that exact same wording; and *Strange Stories* (1976) "her shoes and [folded] shawl."

No doubt there are still other versions of the story. Variants are a "defining characteristic of folklore," according to distinguished folklorist Jan H. Brunvand (1978, 7), since oral transmission naturally produces differing versions of the same story. In this case, however, Brunvand notes that many of the variants are explained by writers copying others (Tyler from Hurwood, for instance) but adding details and making other changes for literary purposes (Brunvand 2000, 132). In any case, Brunvand (1981, 21) observes that when there is no certain original, the multiple versions of a tale provide "good evidence against credibility." But was there an identifiable original of the Mitchell story?

Brunvand (2000, 123–36) followed up on the tale (with some assistance from me). Eventually he turned up a couple of versions that supposedly came from Mitchell himself. One was published in 1950 by R. W. G. Vail, then director of the New York Historical Society:

> One day in February, 1949, Dr. Philip Cook of Worcester, Mass., while on a visit to New York City, told me this story which he had heard the famous doctor and writer S. Weir Mitchell tell at a medical meeting years ago. (Dr. Mitchell died in 1914).
>
> "I was sitting in my office late one night when I heard a knock and, going to the door, found a little girl crying, who asked me to go at once to her home to visit a very sick patient. I told her that I was practically retired and never made evening calls, but she seemed to be in such great distress that I agreed to make the call and so wrote down the name and address she gave me. So I got my bag, hat, and coat and returned to the door, but the little girl was gone. However, I had the address and so went on and made the call. When I got there, a woman came to the door in tears. I asked if there was a patient needing attention. She said that there had been—her little daughter—but that she had just died. She then invited me in. I saw the patient lying dead in her bed, and it was the little girl who had called at my office."

Brunvand (2000, 123–36) also turned up an interesting letter from the Mitchell papers. Dated November 2, 1909, it had been written to Mitchell by physician Noel Smith of Dover, New Hampshire. It read:

> S. Weir Mitchell, M.D.
>
> My dear Doctor:—
>
> Please pardon my intrusion upon your valuable time, but—as I should like the truthfulness, or otherwise, of what follows established, I have taken the liberty of addressing you.
>
> A travelling man, a stranger, accosted me a few days since at one of our principal hotels, knowing that I was a physician, asking me if I believe in

the supernatural, communications with the spirits of departed friends, etc.—I assured him that I had never experienced any personal observations or manifestations that would lead me to any such belief. He then related to me the following story, vouching for its authenticity.—He was a member of some organization, I think, in N.Y., and they had lectures now and then upon various topics. One evening it was announced that prominent men were present who would in turn relate their most wonderful experiences. You was [*sic*] the first called upon, and you stated that you could tell your most wonderful personal experience in a few words. You went on to say that you were engaged in writing late one evening in your library when somebody knocked three times upon the library door. This was thought to be very strange, as electric bells were in use. Upon opening the door, a little girl, about 12 years of age stood there, having a red cloak for an outer garment. She asked if you were Dr. Mitchell, and wished you to go at once to visit her mother professionally, as she was very ill. You informed her that you had given up general practice, but that Dr. Bennett lived diagonally across the street, and that you would direct her to his door, which you did. In a few moments the raps upon your door were repeated, and you found the girl there a second time. She could not obtain Dr. Bennett's services, and urged you to accompany her home; and you did so. She conducted you to a poor section of the city and up a rickety flight of stairs into a tenement house. She ushered you into a room where her mother lay ill upon a bed. You prescribed for the sick lady, giving her some general directions for future guide, and assured her that it was only at the very urgent and persistent efforts of her daughter that you were prevailed upon to come to her. The woman said that that was strange: that she had no daughter—that her only daughter had just died and her body reposed in a casket in the adjoining room. You then looked into this room & viewed the remains of a girl about 12 years of age, while hanging upon the wall was a red cloak.

I am curious to know, doctor, whether you ever had any such experience, or any approach thereto. Hence these words. Let me say right here that Mrs. Smith & myself enjoyed very much the reading together the "Red City" when running in the Century Magazine.

Thanking you in advance for your reply to this inquiry. I am

Yours Sincerely
  Noel Smith

THE REVELATION

Mitchell wrote the following at the top of Smith's letter in his own hand-writing: "One of many about an early [illegible] ghosttale of [mine?]"—a seemingly tacit admission that the ghost narrative was pure fiction.

Indeed, Mitchell must surely be alluding to this very matter when, in his novel *Characteristics* ([1891] 1909, 208–209), the protagonist, North, observes:

> It is dangerous to tell a ghost-story nowadays. . . . A friend of mine once told one in print out of his wicked head, just for the fun of it. It was about a little dead child who rang up a doctor one night, and took him to see her dying mother. Since then he has been the prey of collectors of such marvels. Psychical societies write to him; anxious believers and disbelievers in the supernatural assail him with letters. He has written some fifty to lay this ghost. How could he predict a day when he would be taken seriously?

So there we have it: Mitchell's oblique confession that he had simply conjured up a ghost tale, filled it with literary verisimilitude (semblance of truth), and sent it forth. Later, as Brunvand (2000, 129) notes, Mitchell was "chagrined to find the public believing that he was presenting the story as the literal truth." Mitchell—like the Fox sisters, whose phony spirit communications spawned the modern spiritualist movement (Nickell 2007, 39)—discovered that the genie could not be put back into the bottle.

Chapter 8

ELVIS LIVES! INVESTIGATING THE LEGENDS AND PHENOMENA

Legendary American singer Elvis Presley is heralded not only as the major innovator, "The King," of rock 'n' roll but also as a godlike figure inviting comparison with Jesus—complete with alleged healings and resurrectionlike appearances. Looking at this mythology in the making can provide insights into the mythology that developed around the central figure of Christianity two millennia before. Here, we analyze Elvis's developing myth, study a recorded séance, visit two sites—one where Elvis's apparitions have been reported (figure 8.1) and another where the apparitions sometimes eat (figure 8.2)—and consider other sidelights.

ELVIS

Elvis Aron Presley was born January 8, 1935, in East Tupelo, Mississippi. Influenced by the music around him (including that of the Pentecostal church he attended with his parents), he went on to blend largely white country-and-western music with predominantly black rhythm-and-blues to help create a new American pop-music genre, rock 'n' roll. With songs like "Heartbreak Hotel," "All Shook Up," and "Jailhouse Rock," plus more than thirty movies (beginning with *Love Me Tender* in 1956), he became a superstar.

However, by the late 1970s, Elvis's performances were deteriorating, and his overweight appearance had begun to draw jokes. In 1977, allegations of drug abuse and odd behavior surfaced in a book by three of his former employees titled *Elvis: What Happened?* Before the star could respond to the charges, he was discovered dead on August 16 at his Memphis, Tennessee, mansion—Graceland. An autopsy revealed that drugs were a contributing factor (*Collier's Encyclopedia*, s.v. "Elvis Aron Presley").

Along with countless others, I can still recall where I was when the news of Elvis's death came. I was in my apartment in West Los Angeles (where I was working as an armed guard while attending Paul Stader's Hollywood Stunt School). As I noted in my personal journal for that Tuesday: "While [I was] writing, there was a knock at my door. I found a young man—about 19, drunk, beer can still in hand, tears streaming down his face—who told me Elvis had just died. That incident is evidence of the impact he had."

DEVELOPING MYTHOLOGY

Others, however, reacted with much deeper emotion. Many of Elvis's followers began to exhibit a "deitific regard" toward the dead star (Banks 1996, 222), prompted in part by Elvis himself. Before his death, the biography *Elvis: What Happened?* reported:

> While the rest of the world recognizes that Elvis Aron Presley is something more than an ordinary human being, the one person who believes that most passionately is Presley himself. He is addicted to the study of the Bible, mystical religion, numerology, psychic phenomena, and the belief in life after death. He firmly believes he has the powers of psychic healing by the laying on of hands. He believes he will be reincarnated. He believes he has the strength of will to move clouds in the air, and he is also convinced that there are beings on other planets. He firmly believes he is a prophet who was destined to lead, designated by God for a special role in life. (West, West, and Hebler 1977, 157)

Now, following Elvis's death, grandiose claims began to proliferate. Someone noticed that "Elvis" is an anagram of "lives." Parallels have been drawn between Elvis and Jesus:

- For example, Elvis was said not to be buried in his grave but to be hiding elsewhere (Southwell and Twist 2004, 20). (In Matthew [28:1–15], when

Jesus' tomb was found empty, the chief priests told the soldiers to say, "His disciples came by night and stole him away while we were asleep.")

- After his death Elvis was reportedly witnessed boarding an airplane (Southwell and Twist 2004, 20), and there were subsequently "numerous accounts of 'Elvis sightings' in malls, burger restaurants, and airports throughout the United States" (Banks 1996). An Elvis Is Alive Museum was even created by a Baptist minister with displays of photographs, FBI files, and other memorabilia that supposedly provide evidence that the singer never died ("Elvis Is Alive" 2008). (In the Gospels, after his resurrection, Jesus made appearances to his disciples and many others [e.g., John 20:19–29; 1 Corinthians 15:4–8].)

- In time, Elvis's mythological status began to include "tales that recount his healings of illness, blindness, and sorrow through dreams and his music" (Banks 1996, 222). (As related, for example, in Luke [4:40–41; 18:43], Jesus went about healing the sick, the blind, and the possessed.)

- On the wall around Graceland, Elvis's followers have written inscriptions: "Elvis, we believe always and forever"; "Elvis, you are my God and my King"; and "Elvis, every mountain I have had to climb, you carried me over on your back" (Banks 1996, 222). (The New Testament contains passages such as these: "The grace of our Lord overflowed for me with the faith and love that are in Christ Jesus" [1 Timothy 1:14] and "I rejoice in the Lord. . . . I can do all things in him who strengthens me" [Philippians 4:10–13].)

- Great numbers of the faithful—some 10 percent of the American public—have visited Graceland "as a place of pilgrimage" ("Elvis Presley Phenomenon" 2008). (Christians make pilgrimages to Jerusalem and other sites associated with Jesus in order to venerate him.)

- There have even been "weeping" effigies of the star, like a plaster bust owned by a Dutch Elvis impersonator ("Is 'Weeping' Elvis Statue a Hose Job" 1997). (The phenomenon of weeping icons—rife with misperceptions and pious hoaxes—is frequently associated with Jesus, Mary, or a Christian saint [Nickell 2004, 324–30].)

ENCOUNTERS

The "Elvis sightings" are especially persistent. They stem from the notions of conspiracy theorists who believe the star faked his death. The "evidence" is generally laughable. For example, on his gravestone, Elvis's middle name appears not as Aron but "Aaron," as if it were "a method of saying, 'It's not me'" (Brewer-Giorgio 1988, 55). In fact, although it is clear he himself used "Aron" (probably for its similarity to the name of his stillborn twin, Jesse Garon Presley), the more common spelling often appears and may even have been the original form (Brewer-Giorgio 1988, 50–61; "Elvis Presley Phenomenon" 2008).

Nevertheless, a still-alive Elvis has reportedly been seen by thousands of eyewitnesses. Critics, on the other hand, have suggested that the sightings can be explained by glimpses of Elvis impersonators ("Elvis Presley Phenomenon" 2008) or even simple lookalikes. Some modern sightings—which emphasize Elvis pigging out on fast food—are obviously satirical (Elvis Sighting Bulletin Board 2008) and examples of jokelore.

Other close encounters of the Elvis kind involve his ghost or spirit allegedly communicating with others through such means as automatic writing (in which Elvis guides the sensitive's hand), séances (spirit-communication sessions often held by a "medium"), and astral encounters (achieved through out-of-body experiences). All of these have been utilized by one Dorothy Sherry, "a simple housewife" who has been billed as a "psychic go-between" for Elvis. "Ghost hunter" Hans Holzer tells her story in *Star Ghosts*. He insists: "Dorothy Sherry has never met Elvis Presley. She has not been to any concerts of his, does not collect his records or consider herself a fan of his" (1979, 61–62). Yet he says her contacts with Elvis are among the most "evidential" of his career.

Why, Sherry can even be possessed by Elvis, or at least Holzer claims (though shows us no photos) that he watched "the usually placid face of Dorothy Sherry change to a near-likeness of Elvis" as the star supposedly "controlled her." Elvis then provided statements "in rapid succession which left no doubt," Holzer insisted, "about his identity and actual presence in our midst" (1979, 63). Through Sherry, Elvis not only provided information supposedly unknown to her, but he also revealed to her that, in her words, "he had known me in a previous life, and that I had been his wife" (67). "Dorothy," Hans Holzer tells us, "went astral traveling with Elvis practically night after night" (68).

We thus receive the distinct impression that far from being uninterested in Elvis, Sherry is obsessed with him. Moreover, she has several traits that are associated with a fantasy-prone personality (such as professing psychic powers, having out-of-body experiences, receiving messages from higher entities, seeing apparitions, and so on) (Nickell 2001, 215; Wilson and Barber 1983).

Holzer does concede: "Although I haven't the slightest doubt that Dorothy never read any books about Presley, nor any newspaper stories concerning him, the fact that these sources exist must be taken into account when evaluating the evidence obtained through her entranced lips" (1979, 62). Indeed, Holzer must know that the very sources used to authenticate spirit communication may be used by a medium (consciously or not) to glean the information in the first place. Alleged psychics and mediums have long made a practice of conducting secret research using the results as evidence, convincing the credulous of their paranormal ability. (For example, according to his former secretary, notorious medium Arthur Ford [1897–1971] traveled with a suitcase crammed with notes and clippings about whomever was to attend one of his séances [Christopher 1975, 143–44].)

In fact, some of the very information Dorothy Sherry offered as coming from Elvis's spirit (for example an incident about a friend's leg injury [Holzer 1979, 64]) was readily available in the book *Elvis: What Happened?* (West, West, and Hebler 1977, 165). Moreover, some of the alleged information is doubtful. Sherry has Elvis telling her his mother had a weakness for drink, "a fact which has never been publicized for obvious reasons," says Holzer (1979, 65). Actually, the allegation had indeed been made by "some Presley detractors," but it was emphatically denied by Elvis's close companions (West, West, and Hebler 1977, 139). In any event, why would Elvis—otherworldly or not—choose to reveal derogatory information about the woman he regarded as a saint?

Holzer's use of "psychics" in ghost hunting was once examined in the *Journal for the Society for Psychical Research*. The reviewer found that Holzer's verification methodology was so unsatisfactory as to "cast considerable doubt on the objectivity and reliability of his work as a whole" (quoted in Berger and Berger 1991, 183). I myself have reviewed Holzer's work and have reached a similar conclusion (Nickell 1995, 61–63).

ELVIS'S GHOST

Among the places Dorothy Sherry claims to have astrally traveled with Elvis is the Las Vegas Hilton. His spirit reportedly haunts "numerous locations" in the building ("Haunted Places" 2008), and the site is listed in Dennis William Hauck's *Haunted Places: The National Directory* (1996, 262). (Again, see figure 8.1.)

Figure 8.1. Statue of Elvis in the Las Vegas Hilton, where the late rock 'n' roll legend's ghost is said to appear. (Photo by Joe Nickell.)

In hopes of catching a glimpse of the specter, I visited the Hilton during a stay in Las Vegas. (Although I was there to receive an award, I decided to make the trip a working one as well.) I was accompanied to the famous hotel and casino by colleague Vaughn Rees (then with our CFI/West office in Los Angeles).

We prowled the spacious resort's byways but were unable to see the King's ghost. A security guard discounted the idea that Elvis haunted the site. So did an information agent, who responded, "Absolutely not!" She told us she had worked there for thirty-five years, extending back to the time when Presley actually performed at the hotel. (She added that her father had once received a Cadillac as a gift from him.) Yet she stated that she had neither experienced nor even heard of Elvis's ghost haunting the premises.[1] Here, as elsewhere, it seems ghosts are only likely to appear to those with vivid imaginations.

Figure 8.2. The author at an Elvis-Eats-Here site (a restaurant at Underground Atlanta), part of American jokelore. (Author's photo.)

However, on one occasion I was challenged to explain a "spirit" photo of Elvis and his twin Jesse that supposedly depicted their visages and hands. In the photo, they appeared in mist behind an erstwhile Elvis impersonator who purports "to host the soul" of Jesse ("Best Epiphany" 1994). The singer made highly emotional claims about the picture (a rejected shot from an entertainment magazine's photo session). He called it "miraculous" and "supernatural." However, I explained otherwise when he and I appeared together on the radio show *The Night Side with Richard Syrett* (CFRB Toronto, February 25, 2001).

I had in the meantime investigated the case with photo expert Rob McElroy. We learned from those on the photo shoot that the "mist" was cigarette smoke blown in blue light for effect. The photo effects were "an accident," according to the art director. It was she who actually snapped that photo while a writer at the shoot darted in and out of the scene to adjust the singer's collar. "I always knew it was me," the writer admitted. The glitch was affected by the combined burst of light from the electronic flash and the slower (quarter-second) exposure from the camera's shutter. The result was that the singer's right hand and face were both sharp and blurred and that the intruding writer's underexposed hand and face appeared as extra images (McElroy 2001). Not surprisingly, perhaps, the singer did not accept this explanation.

The impulse that prompts Elvis encounters is the emotional unwillingness of fans to accept his death. This is the same impulse that has helped fuel the Elvis-impersonator industry,[2] just as it made possible the impostors of an earlier time who claimed to be the "real" death-surviving cult personalities of John Wilkes Booth, Jesse James, or Billy the Kid (Nickell 1993). However, no credible evidence that Elvis survived has surfaced since his reported death at age forty-two. And as the pathologist who performed the autopsy on him is quoted as saying, "If he wasn't dead before I did the autopsy, he sure was afterwards!" ("Elvis Presley Phenomenon" 2008).

Although his rocky life shows he was in many ways ill-suited for stardom—let alone mythology or, heaven forbid, deification—Elvis Presley does remain a larger-than-life figure for his influence on pop culture and, especially, for music that will no doubt last for generations.

Chapter 9

ENCOUNTERING PHANTOM SOLDIERS

Tales of spectral soldiers, who haunt battlefields or other sites, abound, and they are told in numerous books such as *Ghosts of 1812* (Winfield 2009), *The Field Guide to Ghosts and Other Apparitions* (Evans and Huyghe 2000), and *Haunted Places: The National Directory* (Hauck 1996). But are such stories true?

TRUTH BE TOLD

No doubt many stories are sincere accounts of a ghostly encounter, yet that does not mean the perceived phantoms were real. Even ghost hunter Jeff Belanger (2006) admits, "Battle sites are hallowed grounds, and one doesn't have to be a psychic or sensitive to stand in the middle of a battlefield such as Gettysburg, Pennsylvania, and imagine what it must have been like." Indeed, some people's imaginations are so intense they can easily "see" soldiers and actions that exist only in their minds.

This is certainly true at Gettysburg, where the clash of armies claimed thousands of Union and Confederate lives in three days. In his *Ghosts of Gettysburg* and *More Ghosts of Gettysburg* (see a pattern?), Mark Nesbitt reveals himself as a credulous raconteur. While faulting skeptics and attempting to invoke science, he offers little more than dubious ghost tales—many of which sound like yarns spun around a campfire. Others appear to have been collected in that fashion. For instance, "Now, on particularly sultry moonlit summer nights on the battlefield, when the mists hang low in what is appropriately known as the Valley of Death between Little Round Top and Devil's Den, there can be seen, slowly picking his way down the rocky western slope of the much-fought-over hill, a lone horseman, replete in the finery of a Civil War officer" (Nesbitt 1991, 60). Or so unnamed informants allegedly claim. (For more, see Nickell 1995, 56–57.)

STRANGER THAN . . .

And then there are the suspicious stories. For example, during the filming of *Gettysburg*, some Civil War reenactors went to the famous battlefield's Little Round Top site to view a beautiful sunset. They were surprised by a haggard old man, in the garb of a Union private, who appeared, smelling of sulfur from gunpowder. He walked up to the trio and handed them some musket rounds, saying, "Rough one today, eh boys?" then turned and—as the men examined the rounds—"vanished into thin air."

If the story sounds too good to be true—an ethereal spirit looking completely solid and carrying real, nonethereal ammo—it apparently is. According to a posting on a reenactors forum ("Ghosts" 2006), the tale "was entirely made up." Indeed, "the originator of the story (who went so far as to tell it on *Unsolved Mysteries*) admitted it as being false." Noting that, another tale actually resulted from "a student's creative writing project," the source adds, "the battlefield used to be a quiet, peaceful, reflective place at night, but that has changed. Now, it is impossible to sit atop Little Round Top without seeing a flurry of flashbulbs of people in Devil's Den, and hearing gaggles of teenage girls shrieking at the top of their lungs whenever a squirrel causes a branch to move."

A classic of the made-up ghost-soldiers genre is a First World War tale called "one of the most curious in the annals of the supernatural" (Haining 1993, 19). It grew out of the horrific Battle of Mons on August 23, 1914, when British soldiers—outnumbered ten to one—stood off fifty German divisions and greatly assisted in the withdrawal of the French. Soon a story was told of a British infantryman who uttered a prayer in Latin and in response saw phantom bowmen firing silvery arrows into advancing German troops. The enemy fell by the hundreds and, when their bodies were examined later, they bore no wounds! A published account, "The Bowmen," inspired countless readers, and, eventually troops returning from France told how they had *witnessed* the ghosts—by then called angels—raining destruction on the enemy from the sky.

As it happened, however, "The Bowmen" was entirely a work of fiction—a short story penned by Arthur Machen (1863–1947). Hearing the. testimonials, Machen quickly came forward to insist that he had made up the tale. However, probably in part due to his being a journalist, having attributed the alleged occurrence to a real and impressive battle, and publishing it in the London *Evening News*, many people did not listen to his protests (Haining 1993, 19–22).

MISTAKEN IDENTITY

Reenactors are even frequently mistaken for ghosts. For instance, at Kennesaw Mountain Battlefield in Georgia, I was investigating with CFI librarian Timothy Binga and videographer Adam Isaac at the site of Kennesaw's fiercest fighting. We saw coming toward us on a trail what appeared to be a lone Confederate soldier (figure 9.1). When he came close, I asked him if he had ever been mistaken for a ghost. This brought a smile and a story. He had once been off by himself, sitting quietly and meditating on the history of the place. From behind, a tourist approached him cautiously and gently touched him on the shoulder, wanting to know if he was real and alive (Hawkins 2011)!

He told us he had even shown up once, inadvertently, in a "ghost" photo. This happened at Gettysburg, where a tourist snapped his picture from a distance, then took the supposedly paranormal photograph to the visitor's center to show it off. Although himself a believer in ghosts, he admitted that at least half of the "apparitions" he had experienced were surely nothing more than his vivid imagination responding to his intense desire to commune with the past. I suspect all of the apparitions were so caused, especially when he stated that the more intense ones invariably occurred where his own Civil War ancestors had fought.

Another story is related by a teacher in Smithfield, North Carolina:

I was on a scavenger hunt for my Johnston County history class, and I was in full uniform, because I had just taught a 4th Grade class about the life of a soldier during the War Between the States. One of the places on the list was River Side Cemetery, the oldest Cemetery in Johnston County, and I was walking through there going from tree to tree looking for the oldest tombstone. Next thing I know I hear a car slam on brakes and people are looking at me with their mouths wide open in amazement. They looked like they saw a ghost. ("Mistaken for a Ghost?" 2011)

Figure 9.1. This reenactment soldier, at Kennesaw Mountain Civil War battlefield, has been mistaken for a ghost! (Photo by Joe Nickell.)

MISCHIEVOUS "GHOSTS"

And then there are outright pranks. At Gettysburg's historic bullet-pockmarked Farnsworth House, I interviewed the manager (O'Day 1993). She told me that some of the battlefield sightings of "ghosts"—especially those at night—are believed to result from the mischief of reenactment soldiers.

Such pranks are common. For instance, one Gettysburg reenactor writes:

One night, at around 11:30–midnight, I decided for no particular reason to just put on my uniform and go for a stroll down some of our very pretty country roads. So I'm walking along in the moonlight, and these cars are slowing waaaaaay down as they pass me and staring as they go by. I'm not overly concerned with them, so I just ignore them like they aren't even there. Eventually, this one car with a guy and a girl who are somewhere in their late teens actually follow alongside of me for about 30–40 yards. Then they pull ahead, and I see them start to turn around in a drive way. Well, I couldn't resist: I jumped off the road and hid behind a tree and laughed while they freaked out trying to figure where I had gone. ("Mistaken for a Ghost?" 2011)

(Such pranks are distinctively reminiscent of certain "Bigfoot" hoaxes perpetrated by persons dressing in fur suits [Nickell 2011, 68–73, 77–83].)

ON BALANCE

Many reenactors are like one I talked with at Kennesaw Mountain who was giving demonstrations of cannon firing. The soldier stated that he had been a reenactor for many years and had never encountered a ghost—even though he had often camped out at Kennesaw and other sites, which should have provided many such opportunities.

Yet ghost hunters and ghost-tour operators are doing a thriving business. According to a source quoted earlier:

The ghost stories have done more damage than anything else. People are no longer using the National Military Park for its intended purpose—to honor and study the people and deeds of the past. They're using it as a cheap-thrill amusement park. I summarily reject the notion that "oh, it gets the kids interested in history." When I was growing up, there were no *Ghosts of Gettysburg* books, tours, videos, t-shirts, or glow sticks, and yet by some miracle, I found myself enamored with the battlefield, the Civil War, and history.

The inscriptions on the battlefield monuments tell us something. "Entrusted to the care of a nation we were proud to serve." "In memory of our fallen comrades." "Erected by the survivors." These men wanted to be remembered for who they were. REAL PEOPLE. To instead focus on questionable stories serves only to cheapen their memory and trivialize what actually happened here. Particularly those stories which are blatantly made up, and sold to tourists who seem to have no better use for their money. When you consider that the Civil War was as real to those who experienced it as WWII was to our veterans alive today . . . why are there no ghost tours at Normandy or Iwo Jima? Why aren't people charged $5 a head to walk by a VA Medical Center to have someone carrying a lantern tell the tale of PFC Jones who went crazy after he came back from the war and there are those who say he still walks these halls today, ooooOOOO ooooOOOooohhh? Because it's tasteless and disrespectful. ("Ghosts" 2006)

Chapter 10

CONJURING GHOSTS: THE HAUNTING OF VAN HORN MANSION

The historic Van Horn Mansion in the Village of Burt, New York (Newfane township), was built in 1823 by James Van Horn Sr., an early settler whose gristmill was burned by the British during the War of 1812 (Townsend 2005, 8). Now, allegedly, the mansion hosts both the living and the dead (figure 10.1). I have spent quality time on the grounds over the years, even attending some séances there undercover, and I have learned much about how such a place can become "haunted."

Figure 10.1. Historic Van Horn Mansion provides lessons in how a previously unhaunted place acquires "ghosts." (Photo by Joe Nickell.)

THE PERAMBULATING TOMBSTONE

The mansion's resident ghost is supposed to be "Malinda"—actually Malinda (Niles) Van Horn, wife of James Van Horn Jr. She died in 1837, at the age of twenty-one. The rumormongers have had a field day with her. One source, reporting her marriage in 1836, adds:

> But within a year, Malinda died under strange and unknown circumstances. Some say she was killed by James Van Horn Sr. Others say she was thrown down the stairs by her husband because she could not bear children. Whatever the case, the Van Horns hid the scandal carefully, burying her on the grounds of the mansion on January 13, 1837, ten days after her 21st birthday. (Townsend 2005, 8)

On the other hand, some sources state she was killed by a falling tree limb (Winfield 1997, 64), while others insist Malinda simply died in childbirth (Wiseman 2000; Lee 2008, 64).

Another legend gives the site of Malinda's burial as the flower garden near the mansion. However, my investigation (which included visiting the relevant sites and archives) revealed that hers, like all the Van Horn graves, was originally in the family cemetery at some distance from the house. From there the various remains were relocated in the 1930s to the Glenwood Cemetery in Lockport (Smitten 2004, 195) where they were given newer granite stones. The old gravestones, including Malinda's, were afterward stored in the carriage shed. That is where Malinda's reposed when the Newfane Historical Society acquired the mansion ("Van Horn Mansion" 2011). However, the stone did once reportedly lie at the present flower garden site "for many years," although, significantly, it had not been there earlier, during the tenure of grounds workers from 1909 to 1933. It may have gotten there about the time the Van Horn graves were relocated to the Glenwood Cemetery, at which time, according to a rumor, one of the stones fell off the wagon transporting them to the carriage shed. (See the report of the Newfane historian, Heck n.d.) This could account for the marble tombstone having once been broken, but the township historian stated that the stone "had been broken by vandals at the Van Horn family plot" (Heck 1989).

Subsequently repaired, the tombstone was placed in the flower garden (figure 10.2) because two dowsers—Bill Tolhurst and Dorothy Ludemann (who has also had various ghostly encounters)—"located" Malinda's supposed gravesite using "dowsing rods" and other doubtful approaches ("Van Horn Mansion" 2011).[1] The dowsers' error in believing Malinda Van Horn was buried in the flower garden may have been compounded by the stone's earlier existence there, as well as its inscription (which could seem to refer to the flower garden, but no doubt does not):

> Sleep Malinda Sleep;
> Sleep [softl]y here
> Where flowers blo[om &] zephyrs sigh
> [Wher]e I may come to shed the tear
> That streams unbid from sorowing [*sic*] eye.

Now, several sources (copying from others) ignore the fact of a word in the first line being illegible and give it as "calmly" (e.g., Lee 2008, 64)—I suspect because of the current notion of Malinda's troubled spirit. Having actually examined the stone, I believe the initial letter was *s*, and I and reconstruct the word as "softly," which fits the space better.[2] "Softly" also comports better with tombstone versification of Malinda's time. The township historian (Heck n.d.) inquired about the actual location of Malinda's grave and concluded: "Malinda was not buried in the garden; but her stone became located there through an accident."

Malinda's actual remains were almost certainly never removed from the original family burial site; otherwise, there should have been a stone for her at the Glenwood Cemetery. Some reports insist that, indeed, "her grave is several hundred feet east of the marker's present location" (Nelson 1970). While the old tombstone, beautifully carved and inscribed with profound sentiment, bespeaks a loving burial, Malinda's grave does appear to have suffered neglect by the time the graves were relocated nearly a century later. I suspect this was in part a consequence of her husband's later remarriage—a familiar story in such circumstances.

THE SIGHTINGS

Of course, that her remains lie elsewhere does not preclude her imagined ghost from seeming to haunt the garden and house, but it does detract from the pretty story used to promote the "ghost."

Figure 10.2. Tombstone of Malinda Van Horn is the stuff of legend. (Photo by Joe Nickell.)

Moreover, famed Western New York ghost raconteur (and author's friend) Mason Winfield (1997, 64–65) observes that Malinda is not alone among reported ghosts at Van Horn. Indeed, the list is long and is summarized by Lee (2008, 61):

Groundskeepers swore they saw a young woman, in a long white dress, walking on the lawn. Volunteers in the interior of the mansion heard crying and footsteps in unoccupied rooms. Workmen ran from their jobs, spooked. Motorists jammed on their brakes to avoid a mysterious child in the road who then disappeared. Internal lights were seen in the dark, empty mansion. A certain coolness is felt in a certain bedroom. A rocking chair is seen moving of its own volition in the nursery.

But all such incidents have ready explanations: the effects of suggestion and expectation, misperceptions, simple physical causes, pranking, and so on. The devil—or ghost in this case—is in the details.

The stories have been told and retold in such a way that it is difficult to determine precisely what happened originally in each case. Moreover, incidents became altered, or even multiplied, or were otherwise exaggerated. For instance, a motorist who reportedly skidded to avoid a girl darting from the mansion and then vanishing (Winfield 1997, 64) might only have had a common apparitional experience in which a mental image springs from the subconscious (see appendix). Or it might even have been a real girl who was lost sight of by the seriously distracted motorist. On the other hand, a version of the tale says the girl was Malinda and that she was "standing in the middle of the street" (Hauck 1996, 296). In time the happening supposedly became repeated: "Motorists [plural] jammed on their brakes to avoid a mysterious child in the road who then disappeared" (Lee 2008, 61). So sketchy are the reports that they should not be described as unexplained mysteries but rather as worthless evidence.

Where more facts are known, however, inferences may be made. For instance, a senior guide at Van Horn told me that several people had seen a spectral woman looking out a front upstairs bedroom window. However, the solution was an easy one, she noted, pointing to a manikin fitted with a white wedding dress that had previously stood in the window! She had herself had two sightings of, she believed, Malinda. However, one occurred while she was "cleaning," when, at such times of doing routine work, one's mind may be near a daydreaming state, conducive to having an apparitional experience. Her other encounter occurred while she was giving a tour and was brief and vague. Another guide, who has worked at the mansion for many years, told me she had never experienced a ghost and, in fact, believed that ghosts were contrary to Christian teaching.

And then there is the mansion's reputedly haunted dollhouse (figure 10.3), which "is said to have miniature furnishings that get rearranged seemingly on their own" (Crocitto 2011). However, my guide explained what she thought was actually happening. As an experiment, she told me, she had deliberately removed the clear plastic cover and specially positioned items, such as a chair, then monitored the site to see if anything actually moved. It never did (Nickell 2011). She concluded people were probably just misremembering the prior arrangement.

Figure 10.3. Dollhouse at the Van Horn Mansion is reputedly a haunted house within a haunted house. (Photo by Joe Nickell.)

EVOLVING PHENOMENON

We have better luck tracking the Van Horn Mansion's transformation into a "haunted" place. From the time the mansion was completed in 1823 until 1967 (including use as a restaurant from 1949 to 1959), there is no published contemporary record or authentic oral tradition of the house ever being haunted. Indeed, Newfane historian Judson Heck contacted several former residents of the house and they universally "denied any mysterious episodes" (Sherwood 1986).

It was during the period between 1967 and 1970, when the place became abandoned, that it acquired a reputation for being haunted (Lee 2008, 60). A volunteer at Van Horn stated that the mansion "was all boarded up and neglected, the porch was falling off, the grass was untended and it did look spooky." She stated, "I don't think there are any ghosts in the house and I don't think there ever were." She concluded that the spooky aspect prompted people to invent ghosts (Smitten 2004, 193). Derelict buildings do seem to invite notions of ghosts and hauntings—as happened, for example, to the Belhurst Castle (an inn at Geneva, New York) and the historic Octagon House (at Genesee County Village, Mumford, New York) (see Nickell 2001, 294–95; 2004, 321). When such houses are restored and opened as businesses, the "haunting" lore is frequently seized upon as a convenient promotional gimmick.

In 1970 the budding ghostlore gained a boost when a newspaper story—published on Halloween—told of a recent series of séances held in the deserted mansion. "Was it just our imagination, or could we hear a woman softly crying?" asked the mystery-mongering reporter (Nelson 1970). Scratching sounds, footsteps, a "cold spot" greeted an unlikely group of "researchers." In the dark, distinct raps were heard in response to questions posed. "The taps told us it was Malinda; she was not alone; that she was unhappy, frightened and more." Because similar rapping communications had marked the beginning of modern spiritualism in 1848 but later proved to have been a hoax (see chapter 23), I also suspect deception in this instance of too-good-to-be-true, copycat spirit communication.

Once the Malinda fakelore was established and publicized, it would not abate; rather, it increased as a bandwagon effect over subsequent years. In 1989 a "psychic" named "Lady Salem," who was "dressed in a floor-length black shroud," led a small group through the house while engaging in other occult antics, including holding a séance in which a candle flame answered questions by being unresponsive for *no* and animated for *yes*. (I suspect someone may have been surreptitiously blowing.) Also, "Lady Salem" placed one member, Kathleen Ganz, in a "trance" by having her stare into a flame, whereupon, says Ganz (1989), "a soldier named Jeremy started talking through me."

I myself sat in on some séances there in 2003 (Nickell 2011), including one, conducted by a medium using the table-tipping phenomenon. (Sitters place their hands on the top of, usually, a pedestal table, and it tips once for *yes*, twice for *no*. See appendix for "ideomotor effect.") I got loving messages from an aunt and uncle—whom, alas, I had just invented! I never saw anything I regarded as authentic spirit communication, but I was impressed by the credulity of superstitious folk.

Meanwhile, Van Horn Mansion gained an entry in *Haunted Places: The National Directory* (Hauck 1996, 296) and then in other compendia like *Ghost Stories of New York State* (Smitten 2004, 192–95). The Van Horn Ghost bandwagon was merrily rolling on.

Indeed, it seems to be running out of control. After Malinda's grave was supposedly located in the flower garden and her tombstone placed there, a sign was installed that read: "Since this work was started there have been no sightings of Malinda." Yet on my visits there in September 2011, that statement had been covered over, proof that once a ghost tale gains traction it may be very difficult to rein in.

Chapter 11

ANIMAL SPIRITS

Animal ghosts are, well, a strange breed. In the popular imagination animals may, like their human counterparts, continue their existence after death.

A PHANTOM HORSE

Such was the case of a phantom horse, "Gloa," I investigated in Germany in 2002. Colleague Martin Mahner and I found ourselves in the village of Wehrheim, sitting on bales of hay in a horse shed and listening to an interesting story.

The horse, Gloa, was the beautiful and beloved pet of its owner, Rosemarie Schäuble (2002), who was still grieving over the Icelandic mare's death some two years earlier. Ms. Schäuble was convinced that Gloa had since manifested herself in two dramatic ways. First, the vegetation had withered at the very spot where she had died, leaving a bare area in the shape of Gloa's silhouette. Second, one day while visiting the field where Gloa had grazed, Ms. Schäuble suddenly saw the mare approach, only to then vanish just as suddenly.

Although these reported phenomena seem striking, an on-site investigation readily revealed plausible explanations. Regarding the bare spot, there were similar barren patches here and there in the surrounding area. It seems likely that whatever soil conditions caused these also caused the supposedly paranormal patch. Its appearance after the horse's death may have been coincidental, or the bare spot may simply not have been noticed previously.

The silhouette of the horse formed by the bare patch is in the eye of the beholder. People whom I showed photos of the spot did not recognize a horse's shape until it was pointed out to them. The human brain, wishing to make sense of things, has the ability to perceive random shapes as specific images. That is how we see pictures in clouds, inkblots, and so forth, a popular example being the Man in the Moon. Such images are known as *simulacra* (see appendix).

As to Ms. Schäuble's fleeting glimpse of Gloa's ghostly figure, such apparitional experiences tend to occur when people are performing routine chores or are otherwise close to a daydream state, and they "may be related to the dreamer's current concerns" (Baker 1990, 179–82). I suspect that when Ms. Schäuble visited the pasture to feed the horses, a memory of Gloa was triggered subconsciously and was momentarily superimposed on the visual scene. As Ms. Schäuble told me, Gloa often used to come up to the fence to greet her, just as the apparition of her did.

While explanations for the reported phenomena in this case seem mundane, they nevertheless serve to remind us that appearances can be deceiving—especially when they involve our most cherished wishes and beliefs. Understandably, when a loved person or pet dies we may have trouble "letting go," and wishful thinking may prevail.

SPIRITUALIST CONTACT

As the belief in spirit contact arose in the mid-nineteenth century, certain self-styled "mediums" (those who claim to intercede between ordinary folk and spirits of the dead), occasionally mentioned a pet—often a dog—in a reading. Now, some pet psychics like Christa Carl conduct "séance readings" for animals that have "passed over."

Thus, the owner of a dog named Brandy, Carl said, who had broken away from her kennel and was killed, wanted to communicate with her spirit. "I learned from her," the pet medium claims, "that she didn't know why she had been put in the kennel. She had felt abandoned, unloved, uncared for." Carl explained things to Brandy, she said, "and now she's at peace" (Cooper and Noble 1996, 102). Of course there is not a shred of proof that the spirit was contacted or even existed—except in the imaginations of Christa Carl and the dog's grieving, guilt-ridden, and credulous owner.

SPECTRAL HOUNDS

In addition to hopes, fears may prompt belief in ghostly entities. Sir Arthur Conan Doyle's Sherlock Holmes novel, *The Hound of the Baskervilles*, is based on a gigantic hound that appears on the moor to foreshadow the death of one of the Baskerville clan. Although fictional, the story was based on a widespread ancient English tradition of a spectral hound (Cohen 1989, 144). Such folklore is common to areas steeped in the supernatural, such as Devon, Essex, Suffolk, and Norfolk. Often called Black Shuck, the creature is said to be entirely black and as big as a calf, sporting glowing eyes—even when he is described as headless! (Guiley 2000, 48–49). Also in Scotland, Vaughn family members were supposed to see a black dog before one of them died.

Another spectral English canine was a white dog. It was said to appear prior to executions at the infamous Newgate Prison. It would be spotted outside the gates (Cohen 1989, 144).

GHOSTLY MONGOOSE

Mischief may be at the root of other encounters. Take the bizarre case of Gef, the supposed ghost (or poltergeist) of a talking mongoose! He appeared in 1931 on the Irving farm on the Isle of Man (in the Irish Sea). He was never reliably seen but instead tossed stones at unwelcome visitors, "urinated" through cracks in the walls, and performed other mischief. However, doubters—of which there were many—noted that the events centered around the family's twelve-year-old daughter, Viorrey; indeed Gef allegedly lived in the girl's room. The skeptics were convinced Viorrey was simply playing pranks, using ventriloquism and other tricks, the effects then being hyped by reporters and credulous paranormalists. Indeed a reporter for the *Isle of Man Examiner* caught the girl making a squeaking sound, although her father insisted the noise came from elsewhere in the room (*Psychic Pets* 1996, 72–83). (Poltergeist phenomena will be taken up more fully in later chapters.)

PART 2:
SPIRITED TRAVELS

Chapter 12

GHOST OF AN ALASKA MURDERER?

Spirits of the dead are among the supernatural beings historically encountered by Native Americans. Alaskan Eskimos, according to a Smithsonian ethnography report (Murdoch 1885), often used weapons to fend off ghosts, even carrying a drawn knife for protection when traveling at night.

Today, not even weapons, apparently, can rid Juneau's Alaskan Hotel of its ghosts, one of whom was allegedly even created by an angry man's vengeful axe.

❚ALASKAN BORDELLO❚

Built in 1913 as a hotel and bordello (prostitution was legal in Alaska until 1956), the Alaskan (figure 12.1) experienced a colorful history before declining (under the name Northlander Hotel, beginning in 1961) and finally being condemned in 1977. It was subsequently restored and, in 1981, placed on the National Register of Historic Places.

On May 31, 2006, when a cruise ship I was on made a stopover in Juneau (and I gave a scheduled talk and radio interview), I was able to tour the area courtesy of Michael S. Stekoll, professor of chemistry and biochemistry at the University of Alaska Southeast. We stopped to investigate the historic "haunted" hotel, where we were given a tour by owner Bettye Adams and her son Joshua (see figure 12.2).

Figure 12.1. The very "haunted" Alaskan Hotel in Juneau is a historic landmark. (Photo by Joe Nickell.)

Figure 12.2. Joe Nickell looks for ghosts at the Alaskan Hotel. (Author's photo.)

The Adamses and their excitable staff reported various ghostly goings-on in several rooms of the Alaskan. In number 311, a manager having died there the previous February, staff members believed they could sense a ghostly presence, a subjective impression I was unable to share. Room 313 had yielded a photo by a former resident that showed several "orbs," bright spheres believed by many to be a form of "spirit energy"; actually, however, when they are not mere reflections from shiny surfaces, orbs commonly result from the camera's flash rebounding from dust particles or water droplets close to the lens (Nickell 2006, 25).

MURDEROUS ATTACK?

It is room 315, however, that is most discussed, although the phantom habitué is supposedly the same as "the specter in room 321" and elsewhere in the hotel, according to the author of *Haunted Alaska*, Ron Wendt (2002, 71). He elaborates:

> The ghost of the Alaskan Hotel carries a tragic story. In life, she was once the bride of a gold prospector. The man told her he was going to the Haines area to search for gold. He put her up at the Alaskan Hotel and said he would return in three weeks.
>
> When her husband failed to return, the woman became desperate. She was out of money and had nowhere to run. An acquaintance told her there was a way she could support herself, and so she turned to prostitution.
>
> About three months later, the miner returned. When he found out that his wife had been working as a prostitute, he killed her at the hotel. (73)

Although the names of these *dramatis personae* are unrecorded, someone has somehow learned that the woman's name was Alice and that her husband killed her with "a hatchet" dislodged "from beneath his waistcoat" (Adams 2006, 5–6). But wait: maybe it was really a revolver with which he "shot her dead in that very room"—room 315 (Adams n.d., 56). Sources are also unsure whether the man was really the woman's husband or merely her suitor; they are equally uncertain as to whether he was indeed a miner or instead "captain of his own fishing boat" who "went out to fish and possibly to whale"[1] (Adams n.d., 55).

According to the latter version, inexplicably, while at sea, this captain heard rumors of his girlfriend's infidelity and attempted to return to Juneau in a storm. According to a version of the story that does not involve murder (Adams n.d., 55–56):

> Death came quickly to all beneath the turbulent waves, but the man continued, unhindered by flesh. He knocked, bodiless at the door, but none answered. So they say that the man simply stays there, waiting for his love to answer him, right around the time of month that he died.

Or so "they say."

That there are proliferating versions of this story is at once evidence of folklore in the making and reason to be skeptical of its historicity. Its basic folk motifs (or story elements)—involving unfaithfulness, revenge, tragedy, and haunting[2]—persist, even when the factual details are questionable.

ENCOUNTERS

Some form of the ghost tale apparently traces back at least to the time the building was called the Northlander Hotel and Marguerite Franklin was owner. She gave a discounted rate on the "haunted" room to a young, poor employee who worked the "graveyard" shift (midnight to eight a.m.). That woman soon reportedly sensed the presence of a "smelly fisherman," even hearing his creaking footsteps and heavy breathing as well as smelling him. She seems to have been an impressionable, possibly even "fantasy-prone," young lady who may have had "waking dreams," which occur in the twilight between being fully asleep and awake (Nickell 1995, 40–42). Or, since she slept during the daytime, one wonders if she might merely have perceived the occasional hotel guest in the hallway. Supposedly the incidents occurred from the twenty-fourth to the thirtieth of each month, but there is no convincing record of such consistency (Adams n.d., 55–56).

As to reported apparitions, those are said to be of the legendary woman turned prostitute. States Wendt (2002, 71), "Witnesses have observed her walking down the hall, then simply vanishing from sight." My own investigations, as well as research data, demonstrate that such experiences often derive from altered states of consciousness, such as when a person is tired or in a relaxed state or performing routine chores. In imaginative individuals, a mental image might be superimposed upon the visual scene as a sort of mental double exposure (Nickell 2000, 18).

Certainly, the Alaskan Hotel's ghosts seem to have much in common with those alleged at other "haunted" sites, as well as with other mysterious entities—monsters and aliens—of the Pacific Northwest and elsewhere. "Where do entities come from?" asked noted psychologist Robert A. Baker (in an afterword to Nickell 1995, 275). He answered, "from within the human head, where they are produced by the ever-active, image-creating human mind."

Chapter 13

LIGHTHOUSE SPECTERS

Remote sentinels on rocky shores, lighthouses have been called "America's castles" (Hermanson n.d.). Certainly, they are places of scenic beauty, romance, and legend. From the late eighteenth century until the last lighthouse tower was automated in the 1960s, lighthouse keepers and their families worked around the clock at the lonely job of maintaining light stations—keeping the beacons lit and, when necessary, the fog signals sounding. If many popular writers are to be believed, the spirits of some keepers, shipwreck victims, and others still maintain their lonely vigils (Elizabeth and Roberts 1999, vii; Thompson 1998, 7).

INVESTIGATING ON-SITE

Over the years I have visited and investigated many of these "haunted" sites. I climbed the 219 steps of the 165-foot lighthouse at St. Augustine, Florida. As "assistant keepers," my wife, Diana Harris, and I stayed a few days in the remote Big Bay Point Lighthouse on Michigan's upper peninsula, perched on a cliff overlooking Lake Superior. We did the same at Thirty Mile Point Light on Lake Ontario (so named because it is thirty miles east of the mouth of the Niagara River) (figure 13.1). A bonus of the latter was access to a few years' worth of entries recorded in its guest books—or maybe I should say *ghost* books, given the various mentions, pro and con, of spooky phenomena.

In addition, I have visited other reputedly haunted sites, such as Lake Michigan's Seul Choix Point Lighthouse (figure 13.2) (escorted up to the lantern room by Coast Guard maintenance men); the "French Castle" (officers quarters) at Old Fort Niagara, which had a navigational light placed atop it in 1780 (Grant and Jones 2002, 112–13); and the old and new lighthouses at Presque Isle, Michigan, on Lake Huron; as well as other lighthouses and proximate coastal areas.

Figure 13.1. The author was once "assistant keeper" at the Thirty Mile Point Light on Lake Ontario. (Pencil sketch by Joe Nickell.)

Figure 13.2. The author and his wife (Diana Harris) picnic at "haunted" Seul Choix Point Lighthouse on Lake Michigan. (Watercolor sketch by Joe Nickell.)

At some of the sites—such as Peggy's Cove, Nova Scotia, and Cape Hattaras and Ocracoke, North Carolina—ghosts are not reported in the lighthouses per se but rather are experienced as apparitions seen along the nearby seashore.

APPARITIONS

Among apparitional experiences—which involve the supposed sensing of a dead person (by sound, scent, or even touch)—a minority are visual sightings (Guiley 2000, 16). For example, as with supposedly haunted inns, some historic lighthouses and keepers' cottages have overnight guests who may awaken to see a spectral figure. Such was the case with intrepid lighthouse photographers Bob and Sandra Shanklin, who were able to spend a night at Plymouth Bay, Massachusetts. According to Bob: "I saw a woman's face hovering about fifteen or sixteen inches above Sandra's face. She had a blue-green, iridescent appearance, and she was wearing an old-timey garment that buttoned tight around her long neck." When he looked away for a moment, she vanished. "I hate that I didn't wake up Sandra, so she could see her, too," he added (Shanklin 1999).

Given the woman's quaint dress, the Shanklins thought she might have been the ghost of Hannah Thomas. Hannah had carried on the duties of her husband John while he served in the Revolutionary War and for a period following, when he failed to return and was presumed dead. In 1790, officials made her the first designated female lighthouse keeper in America (Elizabeth and Roberts 1999, 15–21).

The report of another spectral sighting comes from Big Bay Point Lighthouse. Several years ago, a lady saw "a man in a beard and hat" standing at the foot of her bed. The credulous believe he was the "restless spirit" of former lighthouse keeper William Prior who—despondent over the death of his son—hanged himself in the woods in 1901 (Stonehouse 1997, 32).

Actually, however, neurologists and psychologists attribute such "ghost" sightings to a type of dream that occurs in the twilight between sleep and wakefulness (as we discussed in several earlier cases). Called "waking dreams" (known in earlier times as "night terrors"), they are quite common and are very realistic to those who experience them (Nickell 1995, 41, 117).

But what about apparitions that are seen during normal waking activity? My own investigative experience, as well as other research data, demonstrates that apparitions are most likely to be perceived during daydreams or other altered states of consciousness. Many occur, for example, while the experiencer is in a relaxed state or concentrating on some activity like reading or performing routine work. Under such conditions, particularly in the case of imaginative persons, a mental image might emerge from the sub-conscious and be briefly superimposed on the visual scene, yielding a "sighting" (Nickell 2001, 291–92). Researcher G. N. M. Tyrrell (1973) noted that apparitions of people appear fully clothed and are often accom-panied by objects, just as they are in dreams, because the clothes and objects are required by the apparitional drama.

Such mental images may be the basis for sightings of figures like the "Lady in Blue," who has allegedly been seen over the years near the light-house at Peggy's Cove, Nova Scotia ("Peggy's Cove" 2008b); the "girl wearing a red dress" in the keepers' dwelling at St. Augustine Lighthouse (Elizabeth and Roberts 1999, 41–45); the apparition of a shipwrecked "old salt" at Ram Island Light in Boothbay Harbor, Maine (Thompson 1998, 71); or the figure of Aaron Burr's daughter, Theodosia, on the beach near Cape Hattaras Lighthouse (or is it the lighthouse on Ocracoke Island?) (Elizabeth and Roberts 1999, 65–73; Elizabeth and Roberts 2004, 9, 11; Zepke 1999, 78–81). In any event, all of these sightings are accompanied by multiple con-flicting stories—what folklorists call *variants*, evidence of the transmission process that produces folklore (Brunvand 1978, 7). Dissemination of the tales prompts more sightings from imaginative individuals, giving the sup-posed ghosts something of a life of their own.

OTHER PHENOMENA

In addition to visual apparitions, other touted phenomena at lighthouses (and their environs) are similar to those reported at other alleged spirit-dwelling sites. They include the following:

Ghostly footsteps. The sounds of footfalls are frequently reported in haunted lighthouses or keepers' homes. This is despite the irony of ghosts being such ethereal entities that they pass through walls yet allegedly depress floorboards as they walk.

My wife Diana and I failed to hear the footsteps that have been reported in the lightkeeper's dwelling at Seul Choix (pronounced Sis-shwa) on Lake Michigan (again, see figure 13.2). Supposedly, they were heard once by a carpenter while he was nailing subflooring at the base of the staircase. Because the footsteps stopped whenever he ceased nailing, he concluded that the sounds were merely echoes of his hammering—that is, until he finally put down his hammer and still heard "heavy footsteps" upstairs. Reportedly he "packed up his tools and left, 'vowing never to return by himself'" (Elizabeth and Roberts 1999, 85–86).

The precise truth of this tale is anybody's guess, but there are a number of likely causes for audible footsteplike noises in a "haunted" place. Among them are simple creaking sounds caused by an old building's settling, from woodwork that yields knocking and popping sounds as the result of temperature changes, or from myriad other causes (Nickell 1995, 47–48; Christopher 1970, 169, 171). At Thirty Mile Point Light on Lake Ontario, one overnight guest commented in the log book, "People write of ghosts. We haven't heard any yet, just a lot of noises from the pipes when the heat turns on!" ("Thirty Mile Point Light: 2001–2007").

Still another force seems a likely culprit for the "footsteps" heard in the tower of Battery Point Lighthouse near Crescent City, California. They invariably occurred "during stormy weather," indicating that the sounds were probably caused by the wind. Although previous keepers had experienced many such "ghostly" happenings at Battery Point, a subsequent couple did not. The wife attributed her lack of haunting incidents to the fact that she absolutely did not believe in ghosts (Elizabeth and Roberts 1999, 50–63).

Moans and shrieks. Eerie sounds attributed to mournful or distraught spirits are commonly reported—as if vocalizations are possible without a larynx. In one instance, such sounds were found to come from the wind blowing through an open sewer pipe. Comments William O. Thompson in his *Lighthouse Legends and Hauntings* (1998, 33), "Perhaps this is how some of our ghost stories get started. Every lighthouse is exposed to strange sounds and an active imagination can be very creative."

Consider New Presque Isle Light Station on Lake Huron (north of Alpena, Michigan). According to ghost mongers, the site is haunted by the unrequited spirit of a former keeper's wife. She went insane (according to one version of the tale) due to the stark isolation and numbing boredom of lighthouse life or (says another version) due to being locked in the tower whenever her husband visited his mistress in town. In any event, the woman supposedly died at the site, and "people have reported hearing her screaming" near the tower. In a rare moment of skepticism, however, the writers concede that "perhaps it's just the fierce Lake Huron wind screaming around the tower" (Elizabeth and Roberts 1999, 12).

Thompson (1998, 73) observes that lighthouses are "natural places" for people to have "ghostly experiences," and he mentions the effects of wind whistling through cracks in the structures as among the causes of unaccountable noises. As well, analogous to what happens to woodwork, he notes, old steel "creeps and moans" due to expansion by sunlight and contraction by cold, night air.

Again, at Thirty Mile Point Light, guestbook entries report various ghostly sounds, while others give skeptical interpretations, like this one: "Ghosts? Well we heard all kinds of strange noises but it was very windy." Another person wrote, "The very windy nights added to the 'ghostly sounds' of the building" ("Thirty Mile Point Light: 2001–2007").

Phantom smells. Among other "ghostly" phenomena at lighthouses are strange smells. For example, from Old Presque Isle Lighthouse, now a museum, comes a touching story by Lorraine Parris, a worker in the gift shop. Previously, she and her husband George were caretakers at the site for fourteen years, until he died of a heart attack at the beginning of 1992. According to *Lighthouse Ghosts* (Elizabeth and Roberts 1999, 8), "Sometimes she feels George in the dwelling with her." Moreover, "she recalls waking up some mornings smelling eggs and sausage cooking—a familiar aroma since that's what George used to cook for her for breakfast every morning." But surely, rather than a ghostly visitation the experience is instead the poignant effect of a memory arising lovingly from the subconscious.

At other sites, such as St. Augustine Lighthouse, the motif of lingering cigar smoke appears in circulating ghost tales (Elizabeth and Roberts 1999, 40–49). Again, combined with the previously mentioned footsteps in the keeper's house at Seul Choix Point Lighthouse, the "strong smell of cigars" convinces some "that a lighthouse keeper is still at work" there ("Seul Choix Point Lighthouse" 2005), although others attribute the phenomena to a ship's captain named James Townshend, who died in the dwelling in 1910 (Elizabeth and Roberts 1999, 82–89; Smith 2003, 124).

However, not only is the identity of the phantom questioned, but so is the nature of the smoke itself. In her *Ghost Stories of the Sea*, Barbara Smith (2003, 124) attributes the phenomenon to Captain Townshend but refers to it as "the smell of the man's ever-present *cigarettes*," again stating that "the smoky smell from the man's *cigarettes* can still occasionally be detected" (emphasis added). Here, I think, is an important clue to what is really happening. The smell of actual smoke—whether from area chimneys or cigarettes or whatever other source—is interpreted as cigar smoke because that is what has been suggested and is therefore expected.

Proof of this is evident from an incident at Seul Choix reported in *Haunted Lakes II* (Stonehouse 2000, 4). Two visitors, smelling what they thought was burning wiring, ran to tell the tour guide they thought the house was on fire. If "cigar smoke" can be mistaken for burning wiring, some other burning material could in turn be mistaken for it.

Pranks. Mischief attributed to ghosts at various sites may have a far simpler explanation: the pranksters may not be dead after all!

Consider, for instance, the shenanigans attributed to the aforementioned spectral cigar smoker at Seul Choix. Supposedly the ghost of Captain Townshend liked to "play pranks." A docent claims that

> he sometimes turns over the silverware on the table (Captain Townshend used to hold his fork upside down when he ate). Once in a while the old captain shuts the Bible that's on display in the dwelling, and he seems to take great pleasure in turning the hat around on the mannequin that's dressed in an official keeper's uniform. Occasionally, Captain Townshend even puts a cigar or two in the pocket of the keeper's coat! (Elizabeth and Roberts 1999, 87)

No, the cigars were not materialized from the Great Beyond. They had been set out "in strategic places in the house," once by a group doing a magazine story and again by a couple of Boy Scouts and their Scoutmaster (Stonehouse 2000, 10). The temptation each time for someone to play ghost must have been irresistible. Over the years I have encountered many such pranksters (Nickell 2001), even catching a few red-handed myself (Nickell 2008).

PHANTOM LIGHT

The Old Presque Isle Light, first lit in 1840, was extinguished when the "new" lighthouse was built about a mile away in 1870. Yet according to some, the spirit of an old keeper still maintains a "phantom light" in the tower, which has been witnessed on numerous occasions.

Nevertheless, there are reasons to believe that whatever the source of the mystery light, it has nothing to do with spirits. It is crucial to note that it is never seen by anyone who is actually inside the lantern room. And it is described as lacking the intensity and whiteness of a true lighthouse beam. Indeed, it is not a beam at all (see the photo in Grant and Jones 2002, 139), and it is certainly not a rotating beam; rather, it tends to be only a "yellow glow" (Elizabeth and Roberts 1999, 6).

Indeed, I think we can take a clue from similar reports; the motif of a ghost light is common in spooklore. The late magician and psychic investigator Milbourne Christopher (1970, 172–73) told of a deserted house wherein persons at a distance from the structure could see a lantern, supposedly carried by a specter, moving from room to room. It always went from right to left. However, an investigator discovered that the light was not an interior one at all but rather the reflection of headlights on the window's glass each time a car approached the house. Other spirit lights in windows often turn out to be reflections from the moon or other light sources, an effect I have witnessed on more than one occasion (Nickell 1995, 50–51).

Now, we are told that attempts have been made to stop Presque Isle's phantom light from shining. "We've had the glass covered inside and the lens covered, but the light was still there," says Lorraine Parris. "It seems to shine right through. There's just no way to stop it" (quoted in Grant and Jones 2002, 139). Reportedly, coastguardsmen remained baffled, as the light persisted even when nearby lights were extinguished for a while one night (Elizabeth and Roberts 1999, 6).

But all such actions are obviously predicated on the assumption that reflection is the logical culprit. Indeed, the fact that the light still shone after the glass was covered on the *inside* is telling: it seems a safe bet that it would not continue if the glass were covered on the *outside*. Moreover, the reflection hypothesis is given weight by the light's dependence on viewing conditions. It is reportedly best seen from a certain spot on the pier. Also, if the viewer is traveling along the road near the marina or in a boat on the lake, the "spirit light" will "blink on and off," thus "making it appear to be the beam from a rotating beacon"—while it is, of course, no such thing. That effect may well be due to a light reflecting first from one flat pane of glass then another as the viewer's line of sight changes. And so it appears that here, as with other lighthouses, ghosts are really only illusions of our sometimes-haunted minds.

Chapter 14

THE STORIED LIGHTHOUSE GHOST

At Yaquina Bay on Oregon's central coast stands a historic lighthouse with a unique story—the spine-tingling tale of a young girl murdered to keep a ghost company!

YAQUINA BAY LIGHT

The lighthouse, or "light" in sailors' parlance, was built in 1871, just after the establishment of Newport, a fishing and fur-trade outpost on the bay's north shore. The light's prominence was shortened in 1873 by the building of another, the Yaquina Head lighthouse, just three miles to the north. Its more powerful lamp reached some twenty-two miles, almost twice that of the "old" bay light, which was decommissioned in 1874.

The Yaquina Bay structure is the only one in Oregon with the lighthouse keeper's living quarters combined with the light tower in the same building—looking rather like a two-story house with a great lantern atop. When the keeper and his family moved out, the premises remained empty for fourteen years. Then in 1888, the US Army Corps of Engineers began to use it for housing while building jetties at the mouth of the bay. The premises were acquired for a state park in 1934, but after a dozen years the derelict lighthouse was set to be razed. Citizens formed the Lincoln County Historical Society to save the structure, which was fully restored during the 1970s. Today, as the only wood lighthouse in Oregon, it is listed on the National Register of Historic Places ("Yaquina Bay Lighthouse History" 2011).

GHOST STORY

The Yaquina Bay Lighthouse's singular ghost tale is often told. As related in *A Haunted Tour Guide to the Pacific Northwest*:

> A ship landed at Newport and a man calling himself Trevenard came ashore. He left his daughter Zina (or Muriel) at a small hotel until he returned. In 1874 she joined a group of teenagers investigating the lighthouse. They discovered a metal door in the lighthouse third floor closet. They were preparing to leave when Zina said she had left her handkerchief in the lighthouse. She reentered, and in a few minutes they heard screams for help coming from inside. A trail of blood drops led upstairs, where they found her bloody handkerchief in the room where they had found the hidden door.
>
> Many visitors have reported eerie sensations when walking through the building. Some have reported a light emanating from a second floor room late at night. . . . Other people have spoken with volunteers who confirmed a ghostly presence haunts the lighthouse. (Davis 2001, 15–16)

Elsewhere, the same author concedes that "there are several stories about the Yaquina Bay Lighthouse, which conflict in some details, like the name of the missing girl," and he has therefore "summarized the most popular stories" (Davis 1999, 158). Another source (Castle et al. 1979, 22) reports:

> There is an old story that the lighthouse is haunted. A century ago a young woman was believed murdered there, although her body was never found. Later, those venturing nearby were supposed to have heard moaning and cries for help. Ships at sea were said to have been guided by a strange light.

Sources often pair the girl's specter with the wandering ghost of a murdered sea captain. According to Dennis William Hauck in his *Haunted Places: The National Directory*, the latter ghost, with "the face of a skeleton," told a housewife he was searching for "a place to stay and someone to join him in death" (1996, 346). Apparently the abandoned Yaquina Bay Lighthouse filled the bill, and you know the rest of the story. The apparition of the captain, says Hauck, "and that of a young woman in a white dress, would be encountered by scores of witnesses over the next 120 years."

As we have discussed before, those differing versions of the story—what folklorists term *variants*—are evidence of folklore at work. They result from stories being passed by word of mouth or, in more recent times, by writers copying other writers—a process clearly accelerated by the Internet.

VERISIMILITUDE

We must ask, however, do ghostly sightings and reports of spectral activity confirm the reality of the original story? Emphatically, the answer is no, because the narrative of the young lady who entered the recently abandoned lighthouse never to be seen again is, in fact, *fictional*. It derives from a short story about the seeming murder of a young girl, Muriel Trevenard, by a ghost. Titled "The Haunted Light," it was penned by Lischen M. Miller and published in the *Pacific Monthly* in 1899.[1]

Lischen M. Miller was actually a founder of the *Pacific Monthly* (which ran from October 1898 to April 1900). A sister-in-law of western writer and adventurer Joaquin Miller (pen name of Cincinnatus Hiner Miller, 1837–1913), she was a writer of stories, meditations, and poems. One of the latter, complementing her haunted-lighthouse tale, is "Sea-Drift":

> Once in a twelvemonth given,
> At midnight of the year,
> To rise from their graves as vapor
> That shadows the face of fear,
> And up through the green of surges,
> A sweep to the headlands base,
> Like a white mist blown to landward,
>
> They come to this lofty place—
> Pale as the heart of sorrow
> Dim as a dream might be—
> The souls of ship wrecked sailors,
> And them that drowned at sea.
> In swift and silent procession
> Circle the lonely sweep,
> Where the wild wind faints before them,
> And hushed is the roar of the deep.

Miller's "The Haunted Light" is clearly a work of prose fiction, though naïve readers may have mistaken its verisimilitude for truth. Among those taken in were the coauthors of *Historic Haunted America* (Norman and Scott 1995, 288–91), who cite Lischen M. Miller but refer to her short story as "an account compiled by" Miller! Yet these ghost mongers seem not even to have consulted the original story: for example, they omit it from their bibliography. They also have errors in what folklorists call *motifs* (or story elements), notably having Muriel seek to retrieve her "scarf" rather than the "handkerchief" of the original story (Norman and Scott, 1995, 290, 436). (Other sources refer to "gloves" [Hauck 1996, 346] or merely to "something she left behind" [Castle et al. 1979, 22].)

The story was reprinted as a pamphlet in 1973 by the historical society (which operates the lighthouse as a museum), and the ghost story was included in a short video that used to be shown to visitors. Area resident Sue Garner—whose daughter Kenna Warsinske interned at CFI in 2011 and first alerted me to the fiction-to-folklore story—recalls that when Kenna and her sister were little the video played about every thirty minutes in the lighthouse basement.

LIGHT OF TRUTH

Now, however, reports Sue Garner (who generously revisited the lighthouse on my behalf and provided much of the research material for this chapter), the historical society is working diligently to downplay the ghost tale, so the video is no longer shown.

Among those getting the true facts out is cameraman/producer Scott Gibson. His 2007 DVD *Oregon Lights*, a documentary on the state's historic—and often "haunted"—lighthouses, debunks the ghost tale and concludes with his poignant comment: "I don't know if any of the other ghost stories have any credibility, but lighthouses are truly remarkable structures. It's sad to think another one will never be built."

It will be interesting to see if the ghost-girl genie can ever be put back in its bottle and the bottle effectively stoppered, although the effort is commendable. Meanwhile, we can continue to monitor the "haunting" of the old Yaquina Bay Lighthouse—a fictional one that, truth be told, may be as authentic as they get.

Chapter 15

PIRATES' GHOSTS: AAR-R-GH!

They embody legend: romantic, swashbuckling, heroic figures—
enchanting rogues whose ghosts eternally guard their buried treasures, search for their lost heads, or simply beckon to the credulous from
their supposed coastal haunts. I have sought their specters from New
Orleans to Savannah, from North Carolina's Ocracoke Island to Oak Island
in Nova Scotia's Mahone Bay. Here is a look at some of what I found; as
usual, not everything was as it seemed.

JEAN LAFITTE

I began to think about pirates' ghosts on an investigative trip to Louisiana in
2000, when a nighttime tour of New Orleans "haunted" spots took me to
two sites associated with an unlikely American hero, Jean Lafitte.

Lafitte (ca. 1780–1825) became known as "the Terror of the Gulf" for
his exploits as a smuggler, privateer (one licensed by a government to seize
its enemy's ships), and later pirate. Lafitte was transformed into a hero
during the war of 1812. Suspected of complicity with British forces, he
proved his loyalty to American general Andrew Jackson in 1815, spurning a
British bribe of £30,000 and fighting heroically in defense of his adopted
homeland during the Battle of New Orleans (Groom 2006).

Dead since approximately 1825, Jean Lafitte still reportedly gets around,
haunting, some say, a New Orleans bar, Lafitte's Blacksmith Shop, at 941
Bourbon Street. One ghost guide claims the structure was built "around
1722" (Belanger 2005, 91), but other sources place it at least half a century
later—no earlier than 1772 (Dickinson 1997, 54). (See also Herczog 2000,
255; Cook 1999, 52; Bultman 1998, 95.) Of *briqueté entre poleaux* construc-

tion (i.e., bricked between posts), it was stuccoed over at a later period and now is in "alarmingly tumbledown" condition (Cook 1999, 52). (See figure 15.1.) Some sources (e.g., Nott 1928, 37, 39) are skeptical of tales that Lafitte actually ran a blacksmith shop as a cover for smuggling, but, says one, "it makes a good story" (Downs and Edge 2000, 197).

Figure 15.1. Jean Lafitte's ramshackle blacksmith shop in New Orleans is allegedly home to his ghost. (Watercolor sketch by Joe Nickell.)

Certainly, as I can attest, the place is darkly atmospheric, and both the ambiance and imbibed spirits, together with the power of suggestion, no doubt contribute to reported sightings of the pirate. However, even one ghost promoter concedes, "Such sightings may not withstand a sobriety test, but this does little to dampen the pervasive appeal of Lafitte's Blacksmith Shop and Bar" (Sillery 2001, 110). In other instances—as when a bartender reported that "a short, stout man walked out of the fireplace" (Belanger 2005, 91)—the circumstances are suggestive. The bartender may well have been tired (it was "late one rainy night") and in a daydreaming state (he was "alone" with the soothing patter of rain), just the conditions known to prompt apparitional sightings in which images from the subconscious can momentarily be superimposed on the individual's surroundings (Nickell 2001, 290–93).

This is most likely to happen with imaginative individuals, especially those having fantasy-prone personalities. Psychics and mediums typically have characteristics associated with fantasizers (such as encountering apparitions, communicating with paranormal entities, and so on [Wilson and Barber 1983]). Consider a New Orleans ghost guide who calls herself "Bloody Mary"—a self-described "mystic," "psychic," and "medium" who believes she has had previous lives (quoted in Belanger 2005, 88–90). She writes:

> The first time in this lifetime that I entered Lafitte's I was compelled to stare into the dual smithy (now turned fireplace). Staring at me from the center was a pair of eyes—free floating, with no face to be seen. My eyes and his were locked in a trance for some time until the eyes simply *poofed* into two bursts of flame and disappeared. That, of course, broke my trance, and when I bent down again to recheck the scene, nothing was to be seen. I checked for mirrors, candles, and such mundane things that might explain what I saw, but I found none. Shrugging my shoulders, I simply decided it was a sign of welcome. (quoted in Belanger 2005, 91)

Elsewhere she has felt rooms "calling" to her, has sensed a "time portal," and has been lured to a room by "astral travel," saying, "I truly believe I had stayed there before." She has spirits who travel with her, sees a spectral resident in her hallways, and will "occasionally invite inside and outside spirits to parties" (quoted in Belanger 2005, 88–91). Over the years I have observed a correlation between fantasy proneness and intensity of ghostly experiences (Nickell 2001, 299). "Bloody Mary" provides further evidence of the link.

"Ghost" photos taken by patrons at the Lafitte Blacksmith Shop and Bar have been described by Victor C. Klein (1999, 54) as exhibiting "strange luminous, somewhat amorphous, translucent cloudlike images." Although he does not reproduce the photos, the descriptions are consistent with the camera's flash rebounding from smoke or mist. Note Barbara Sillery's comment that "the pirate has been frequently sighted in the *smoky haze* of the dimly lit rooms" (2001, 110, emphasis added) that are illuminated entirely by candles (Herczog 2000, 255). Not a single ghost has ever been authenticated by mainstream science, which attributes them to myriad nonsupernatural causes (see Nickell 1994, 146–59; 2008).

Not far from Lafitte's Blacksmith Shop is a slate-paved pedestrian walkway known as Pirate's Alley. It is supposedly haunted by the famous pirate, but—as one source acknowledges—"every historic site in New Orleans claims the ghost of Jean Lafitte" ("Pirate's Alley Café Reviews"

2009). The claim for Pirate's Alley is that Lafitte met Andrew Jackson there in 1815 to plan the Battle of New Orleans; however, the alley was not actually constructed until the 1830s (Cook 1999, 25). (See figure 15.2.)

Figure 15.2. Pirate's Alley is another supposedly haunted site in New Orleans's French Quarter. (Photo by Joe Nickell.)

Lafitte's ghost is also reputed to make appearances at La Porte, Texas (east of Houston). Legendarily, Lafitte buried a treasure there, consisting of gold and jewels and allegedly protected by his ghost. However, the treasure-guarding ghost is a common folklore motif (or story element) (Thompson 1955, 2:429), and reports of some residents having been "awakened in the middle of the night by Lafitte's ghost, dressed in a red coat, standing at the foot of their beds" are easily explained as waking dreams. These occur in a state between wakefulness and sleep, and they are responsible for countless ghostly visitations (Nickell 1995, 41, 46, 55).

CAPTAIN FLINT

Some sources associate Lafitte (if not his ghost) with another place, Pirates' House Restaurant in Savannah, Georgia, where I investigated and had a pleasant lunch on March 24, 2004. A more cautious source states only that "famous pirates such as Jean Lafitte came to port in Savannah," so it is "reasonable to suppose that many of them came to the Pirates [*sic*] House to enjoy a bit of grog, a sea chanty, and a coarse joke or two." This source adds:

> There are some who believe that the spirits of pirates still inhabit the Pirates [*sic*] House. Mysterious lights have been seen in the old seamen's quarters, and noises heard, apparitions that cannot be pegged to any human activity. There are those who have sensed presences and scenes of ancient violence. Yet others have passed years without noticing anything unusual in the building suggesting that the only piratical activity still in the house is the imbibing of generous quantities of ale by the witnesses to these events. ("Legend of the Pirates' House" 2009)

A popular ghost guide—*Haunted Places: The National Directory*—alleges that the restaurant was once Lafitte's home, adding, however, that "it is the ghost of another notorious pirate known as Captain Flint, who haunts the place" (Hauck 1996, 141).

A history provided by the restaurant's website states:

> 'Tis said that old Captain Flint, who originally buried the fabulous treasure on Treasure Island, died here in an upstairs room. In the story, his faithful mate, Billy Bones, was at his side when he breathed his last, muttering "Darby bring aft the rum." Even now, many swear that the ghost of Captain Flint still haunts the Pirates' House on moonless nights. ("History" 2009)

It helps here to realize that "Captain Flint" was a fictitious character in Robert Louis Stevenson's tale of greedy pirates and revenge, *Treasure Island* (1883). Although it is claimed that "Captain Flint" was modeled on a historical character, that remains unproved, and there is only a supposed connection to Pirates' House ("Legend of the Pirates' House" 2009; "Captain Flint" 2009). This case is instructive in showing that an apparently fictional character can haunt a place just as convincingly as a real one!

CAPTAIN KIDD

Treasure Island appears to be a source for other tales involving pirates' ghosts and the buried treasures they allegedly guard—none more famous than that of "Captain" William Kidd. A seventeenth-century privateer for the British against the French off the coast of North America, Kidd later became an outright pirate. British authorities declared him such, arrested him at Boston, and transported him to England. There he was tried, convicted, and hanged in 1701. His remains were displayed publicly, in a dangling iron cage, as a warning to others (Cawthorne 2005, 169–91; Klein 2006, 51–64).

"After his death," according to a scholarly source, "Kidd became a legendary figure in both England and the U.S. He became the hero of many ballads, his ghost was seen on several occasions, and numerous attempts were made to discover a fabulous treasure that he supposedly buried in various points ranging from Oak Island, Nova Scotia, to Gardiner's Island, New York" (*Benet's* 1987, 529). In addition to *Treasure Island*, the Kidd legend also strongly influenced Edgar Allan Poe's short story "The Gold Bug" (1843). Treasure was recovered from Kidd, but even before his hanging rumors spread that there was much, much more (Klein 2006, 58). (See also Shute 2002; Beck 1973, 337–38.)

Although proof or even credible evidence is lacking, Oak Island in Mahone Bay, Nova Scotia, is believed by many to contain a fabulous treasure—possibly Kidd's imagined trove. The island is steeped in legends about ghosts who guard the fabled "money pit." The focus of "the world's longest and most expensive treasure hunt" (O'Connor 1988, 4), this is a shaft, dug and redug for some two centuries, representing an inverted monument to greed, folly, and even death (Crooker 1993, 92–93; Nickell 2001, 219–34).

I visited Oak Island in mid-1999 after giving a presentation at a forensic conference in nearby New Brunswick. Although at the time the area was guarded by a no-trespassing sign rather than pirates' ghosts, I was able to access the island by a causeway and spend quality time with Dan Blankenship, dubbed "Oak Island's most obsessive searcher" (O'Connor 1988, 145). The next day I viewed the remainder of the island by boat, piloted by local private eye Jim Harvey. After considerable subsequent research (Nickell 2001, 219, 234), I concluded that the "money pit" and accompanying "pirate tunnels" were natural cavern features, that the treasure was fictitious, and that many of the cryptic elements in the Oak Island saga were attributable to "Secret

Vault" rituals of the Freemasons. Indeed, the long "search" for Oak Island's legendary treasure was carried out largely by prominent Nova Scotia Masons.

Over the years, the legendary pirate-guarded treasure has also been the target of dowsers, psychics, dream interpreters, and other mystics—not one of them successful. If the site was indeed guarded by a ghost—of Kidd or an anonymous pirate—he seems not to have known he was wasting his effort on a nonexistent treasure trove.

BLACKBEARD

Of history's most notorious pirates, Edward Teach surely tops the list. Born possibly in Bristol, England, circa 1680, Teach, like others of his ilk, turned from privateering to piracy, his trademark jet beard earning him his sobriquet "Blackbeard." His "terrifying appearance, daring raids and murderous exploits" made him an enduring legend (Klein 2006, 76). He plundered the Atlantic coast, but when he planned to establish a fort at Ocracoke, an island off North Carolina's Outer Banks, the governor of neighboring Virginia responded. The governor persuaded the Virginia Assembly to post a £100 reward for Blackbeard, dead or alive, and lesser rewards for his men.

On November 22, 1718, two sloops under the command of Lt. Robert Maynard confronted Blackbeard's *Adventure* at Ocracoke. After unleashing a broadside against the *Jane*, Teach and his men boarded her, only to be overwhelmed by armed men hidden in the cargo hold. In the ensuing fight Maynard attacked Teach with pistol and sword, finally decapitating him. When its companion sloop pulled up, decks of the *Jane* were awash in blood. Maynard suspended Teach's head as a trophy from his sloop's bowsprit (Klein 2006, 76–87; Cawthorne 2005, 199–207).

Today, Ocracoke is as lush with legends as it is with scenery. My wife and I visited Ocracoke on our honeymoon in 2006. The name itself has a Blackbeard legend attached: supposedly, during the night before his encounter with Maynard, Blackbeard was impatient for dawn, crying out, "O crow cock! O crow cock!"—hence the name of the inlet and the island. Actually, long before Blackbeard, old maps show the area below Cape Hatteras with the name Wokokon. Sometimes spelled Woccocock, this apparently Native American name evolved (its W dropped) to Occocock (various spellings) and then to the present Ocracoke (Rondthaler n.d.).

Other Blackbeard legends fare no better. One holds that after he was decapitated, his corpse was tossed overboard, where it swam "three times" around the sloop before finally sinking (Cawthorne 2005, 205). Of course, since this is scientifically impossible, it little matters that another source says it was "several times" (Klein 2006, 86). Still another best describes it with appropriate sarcasm as "seven times, or was it eleven times, or perhaps by this time it is seven times eleven" (Rondthaler n.d.). There are variations of the tale (to folklorists, *variants* are evidence of the folkloric process). One version states "that Teach's headless body ran wildly around the deck before throwing itself into the sea" (Pickering 2006, 74). Another variant combines two legends, having Blackbeard's severed head circling the ship and simultaneously crying out "O crow Cock! O crow, Cock!" supposedly because Blackbeard wanted morning light to help him find his body (Walser 1980, 12–14).

Sightings of Blackbeard's ghost commonly involve familiar folklore motifs. Endlessly, we are told, Blackbeard wanders Ocracoke searching for his lost head (Elizabeth and Roberts 2004, 13). So ubiquitous is this motif that I have encountered it in various countries (see, for example, chapter 3, "Headless Ghosts I Have Known," and Nickell 2006). It is one that neither raconteurs nor the credulous can resist, though for others it is so hackneyed as to seem a caricature of the ghost-tale genre.

So is the legend of Blackbeard's ghost searching for his treasure—not at Ocracoke but at the Isles of Shoals in Maine and New Hampshire, as well as on Smith and Langier Islands in Chesapeake Bay (D'Agostino 2008, 110–11). But these have a suspiciously literary quality and seem of relatively late vintage, probably deriving from the Kidd legends.

Blackbeard is just one of four ghosts alleged to haunt Ocracoke—or only three if the "old man with a big, bushy beard" that appears in a museum's upstairs window (Elizabeth and Roberts 2004, 10) is the pirate himself. But that is not claimed, and the ghost of the historic David Williams House (now the Ocracoke Preservation Society Museum) not only has his head on his shoulders, but the house dates from 1900, long after Blackbeard's time. The ghost tale is even more recent. Julia Howard (2006), the museum's director since 1972, told me she believes the story was fabricated by a docent (since deceased) whom she described as "a character." Howard also related how a volunteer once accommodated a mother whose boys had wanted to see the ghost. While they were outside looking up, the volunteer surreptitiously jiggled the curtains, creating a "ghost"—as real as any, pirate or not.

Chapter 16

AN AUSTRIAN CASTLE HAUNTED BY PARACELSUS?

Among the significant European figures of the sixteenth century, Paracelsus (1493–1541) was a transitional figure in the contest between magical and scientific thinking. On the one hand, he was part charlatan: his work was riddled with mystical nonsense about alchemy and the search for immortality. On the other, he rejected much ancient nonsense, advocated experimentation, developed the idea that chemical substances might have medical value (Cridlan 1997, 881; Chavallier 1996, 21–22), and famously observed that whether or not a poison is lethal depends on its dose (Chevallier 1996, 22).

Although he adopted the name Paracelsus—apparently to suggest superiority to Celsus, the Roman medical writer—he was born Theophrastus Bombastus von Hohenheim in 1493. He was known not only for his revolutionary ideas but also for his argumentative manner; some claim—wrongly—that the word *bombastic* was derived from his name (Hauck 2000, 99).[1] An inveterate traveler, he settled into the role of town physician and university lecturer at Basel from 1526 to 1529, when he lost a lawsuit over a professional fee. He continued wandering throughout Europe, Asia Minor, and Africa until he was invited to Salzburg, Austria, by the prince-archbishop in 1541. However, Paracelsus died there on September 24, 1541, at the age of forty-eight (*Collier's Encyclopedia* 1993; "Paracelsus" 2008).

There are those who say that Paracelsus continues to be a transitional figure of another kind: a spirit interacting with the living and even being sought for miraculous cures. On a trip to Europe in 2007, I visited two sites in Salzburg where these activities are reputed to continue, Salzburg Castle and the tomb of Paracelsus.

SALZBURG CASTLE

Located on the river Salzach, Austria's beautiful city of Salzburg is capital of the state of the same name, both of which take their appellation from the salt—the so-called white gold—mined from mount Dürnberg. Salzburg was the birthplace of Mozart, and today it offers many sights, including a baroque cathedral, a palace (Schloss Mirabell), and gardens, and (as part of the latter) a poignant little dwarf park bearing statues of the wee people who once graced the royal court ("Salzburg Sightseeing Tours" n.d.; "Mirabell Palace and Gardens" 2007).

The castle, the Hohensalzburg Fortress, overlooks—actually towers over—Salzburg from atop the Mönchsberg, one of five mountain peaks in Salzburg. Built in 1077, the structure is accessible by a steep footpath or by the funicular (a cable-operated railway), and it offers impressive interior scenes together with commanding views of the historic city. The fortress was so imposing that for a thousand years it was never attacked, although "when Napoleon stopped by, the city wisely surrendered" (Steves 2007).

According to paranormalist Dennis William Hauck (2000, 99) in his book *The International Directory of Haunted Places*:

> Psychics say [Paracelsus's] ghost roams the castle grounds searching for his many manuscripts that were taken from his room after his death and hidden away by the Prince Bishop. American tourist Deb Dupre was one of many to feel the presence of Paracelsus in the castle. Her encounter during a visit in 1986 changed her life, causing her to become more unconventional and creative and open to the deeper symbolism of alchemy. She even started painting dramatic and colorful depictions of alchemical forces in her own life. Dupre also picked up paranormal energy in several photographs of the castle, including the spiraling mist that followed her around.

A copy of one such "ghost" photo is reproduced in Hauck (2000, 99). Unfortunately, science has not found such "spiraling mist" to be due to "paranormal energy." Instead, much evidence shows it is simply the result of the camera's flash rebounding from the wrist strap!

I did a pioneering study of this effect (Nickell 1996, 13–14) and have replicated it many times under controlled conditions. Depending on the nature of the strap (round, flat, braided, smooth, etc.), the orientation and closeness of the strap to the camera, as well as other factors including lighting conditions, a considerable variety of effects can be produced. Even so, other instances of camera-strap "ghosts" in Hauck (2000, 110, 120, 157) are recognizable. (The interested reader should compare an example in Hauck [2000, 110] with one of mine [Nickell 1996, 13] to see how similar the effects can be.)

Visiting Salzburg Castle with my colleague Martin Mahner, I sought out the site in question and snapped some experimental photographs, one of which is shown in figure 16.1. (At the bottom of the white curve, the more mistlike blurring is due to the corresponding portion of the strap's greater distance from the lens, an effect that occurs along the entire length of the analogous curved line in the tourist photo, showing that that section of the strap was the farthest from the lens when the flash went off.)

Figure 16.1. A ghostly shape appears in this experimental photograph taken at Austria's Salzburg Castle at a spot where a similar photo effect was attributed to the ghost of Paracelsus. (Photo by Joe Nickell.)

Except for the photo and that reference to what "psychics say," Hauck offers no further proof that Paracelsus's ghost, or any other, haunts the fortress grounds. Indeed we queried one castle shopkeeper who insisted that there was no ghostly lore—no specific story or generalized topic—that she was aware of; neither were there any reported ghostly experiences that had come to her attention. Virtually no one, she told us, asks about ghosts. Subsequently, at the castle's museum shop, a young lady attendant echoed the first shopkeeper's sentiments.

Of course, no one can prove there is not a ghost at the fortress, but fortunately no one has to. Rather, the burden of proof falls on claimants, and thus far they have utterly failed to meet the challenge.

PARACELSUS'S TOMB

After searching for the ghost of Paracelsus at the castle, Martin and I visited the adept's tomb at St. Sebastian's church cemetery. We were there because of a statement by Hauck (2000, 99) regarding Paracelsus: "To this day, many ill and crippled people visit his gravesite hoping for a miraculous cure from the spirit of the greatest doctor of all time." (Hauck's specific source is unclear, since he supplies only a generalized bibliography.)

Located on a line of sight that runs due north from the castle, the cemetery is entered from the street Lizer Gasse and is at once a place that is quintessentially baroque and Italian—as well as one of quiet repose. Its centerpiece is the grave of Prince-Archbishop Wolf Dietrich (1587–1612). The cemetery also contains the Mozart family tomb (with the graves of the composer's wife and father, Mozart himself being buried in Vienna), as well as the graves of other Salzburg notables.

Paracelsus's grave niche in the church's exterior, shown in figure 16.2, bears a bas-relief profile of him. It also includes a Latin inscription stating, "Here are the effigy and the bones of Philippus Theophrastus Paracelsus, who has won such fame in all the world through his Alchemy, until they are again clad in flesh. When this church was repaired in 1752 they were lifted from their mouldering grave and interred at this spot."

Alas, while we were at the tomb, taking photographs and making notes, we watched in vain for the pathetic pilgrims who were expected to visit, hoping for magical healings. Only a curious tourist couple stopped briefly. Finally, I spied a young priest hurrying by, and I called out, "Excuse me, Father, do you speak English?"

"Some," he answered.

Figure 16.2. The grave niche of Paracelsus is alleged to draw pilgrims seeking magical healings. (Photo by Joe Nickell.)

I told him a book claimed that people came to Paracelsus's tomb to be cured of their ailments, and I asked if this were indeed so.

"I've never heard such a claim," he told me. He did say that there was a group that made annual visits to the tomb, but he was unaware of any healing tradition at the site.

Even Hauck makes no mention of any actual healings being claimed at the site. If there are, their numbers would no doubt still pale in comparison to the French healing shrine, Lourdes. More than five million people visit Lourdes annually, yet only sixty-seven alleged "miracle cures" have been officially recognized since 1858 (D'Emilio 2008). Not only is that an abysmal record, but the claims at such healing shrines are invariably only examples of the logical fallacy called arguing from ignorance (that is, drawing a conclusion from a lack of knowledge): "One does not know why the condition abated, so it must have been a miracle." In fact, some "cures" are attributable to poor investigation, while others may simply represent misdiagnosis, psychosomatic conditions, prior medical treatment, the body's own healing power, and other factors (Nickell 2007, 202–205).

Despite our disappointing search, Paracelsus does continue to be among us—not as a spirit plaguing our photos or providing miraculous healings, but as a transitional figure in man's gradual emergence from the shadowy underworld of ignorance and superstition into the bright realm of science and reason.

Chapter 17

INCARCERATED GHOSTS: HAUNTED DUNGEONS, PRISONS, AND JAILS

"Stone walls do not a prison make," wrote the English poet Richard Lovelace (1618–1658). That would seem especially—and literally—true for ghosts, yet, if much evidence is to be believed, many spirits of the dead seem unable, or at least unwilling, to leave the places of their incarceration. Here is a look at some "haunted" jails, prisons, dungeons, and the like I have personally investigated.

CONVICTS, BARRACKS

On a sojourn in Australia in November 2000, I investigated several myths and mysteries, beginning with the Hyde Park Barracks—reputedly "the most haunted building in Central Sydney" (Davis 1998, 2). Constructed as secure housing for government-assisted male convicts in 1817, it opened in mid-1819 with its central building holding an average of six hundred men. (It became an immigration depot for single females in 1848, a government office complex in 1887, and today it is a museum featuring its original history.)

No ghosts were reported at the barracks until the 1950s, when a clerk saw an apparition, "a figure in convict garb hobbling down a corridor" (Davis 1998, 2). Now that the facility is open to steady streams of visitors, various strange phenomena are reported, especially by those who spend the night. These include security guards and schoolchildren on sleepovers that give them a bit of the "convict experience." The barracks maintains a ghost file, which records experiences just after they occur, and curator Michael Bogle generously allowed me to study this file in his office.

It is clear from these personal accounts that the spend-the-night experiences were designed to stimulate the imagination, and it is therefore not surprising that they provoked dreams or even triggered apparitions of historical figures. Indeed, some persons described apparent "waking dreams" that occur in the twilight of being partially awake. For instance, one girl described "a man standing beside my hammock looking at me"—dressed of course in period clothes. She admits she had "tried to imagine what it must have been like for the convicts who stayed there," thus helping set the stage for such an experience.

Also not surprising, on occasion the narratives contain hints of possible pranking. For example, one of a group of forty-seven schoolchildren reported having felt a "long hand" reach in under her sleeping bag to touch her on the hip. Or was that instead only the effect of a runaway imagination, prompted by talk of ghosts? Or was it, perhaps, yet another waking dream? On one occasion, ghostly tappings proved to have been only the sounds of a mechanized display. Suggestions and expectation can be powerful, especially in such a setting (Nickell 2001, 15–16).

THE MELBOURNE GAOL

Likewise, the Old Melbourne Gaol (British spelling of *jail*), which I visited with skeptics from that Australian city, is "the repository of many troubled spirits, the ghosts of criminals who suffered and died there"—or so "some say" (Davis 1998, 174).

Certainly the old gaol is a stark showing of Australian penal life in the nineteenth century, exhibiting many grim implements of restraint and punishment as well as *mementi mori* ("reminders of death"). For example, there is the pistol, homemade armor, and death mask of the notorious "bushranger" (i.e., highwayman) Ned Kelley, as well as the scaffold on which he was finally hanged for his crimes.

Despite the spooky ambiance (figure 17.1), reported ghostly phenomena at the site are somewhat scant, even though an advertising brochure promises: "Experience the haunting and eerie atmosphere of the gaol, and by listening carefully, you can almost hear the clank of the prisoners' chains."

Figure 17.1. If the Old Melbourne Gaol, Australia, is not haunted, its spooky ambiance says it should be! (Photo by Joe Nickell.)

Nevertheless, when I broached the topic of hauntings to a gift-shop employee, she brought out, rather halfheartedly, a questionable "ghost" snapshot. She conceded that some people reported their "feelings" at the site, but added that, while she had been employed at the gaol for ten years, she had had no paranormal experiences of her own. However, noting that she worked just one day a week, she joked that maybe "the ghosts take Tuesdays off" (Nickell 2001, 16).

FORTRESS "DUNGEON"

The Castillo de San Marcos in St. Augustine, Florida (figure 17.2), is the oldest masonry fort in the continental United States. Built by the Spanish in response to a 1668 raid by English pirates, the castillo today is allegedly home to various ghosts. These include the spirits of Señora Dolores Marti, wife of Colonel Garcia Marti, who was assigned to the fort in 1784, and her lover, Captain Manuel Abela. When the colonel learned of the affair, he "chained them to a wall in the dungeon and mortared a new wall of coquina stone in front of them," according to *Haunted Places: The National Directory*

(Hauck 1996, 125). (The story motif of being entombed alive is common to folklore and fiction. See Nickell 2008, 17–20.)

Figure 17.2. Reenactment soldier at Castillo de San Marcos— like a ghostly sentry—evokes the past. (Photo by Joe Nickell.)

On visiting the fortress, however, and being shown about by staffer John Cipriani, I learned there never was a "dungeon," despite the castillo's having been used as a prison on various occasions—for example, for Americans during the Revolutionary War (Brownstone and Franck 1989, 8). The raconteurs' "dungeon" is in fact a small room that was part of the powder magazine. When found to be too humid for storing gunpowder, the room was sealed off.

It was rediscovered, storytellers say—in 1833, 1838, or 1938—by an engineer who noted that when a section of the wall was tapped it sounded hollow. "He chipped away at the mortar, and the lantern he held illuminated two skeletons" (Moore 1998, 147). In fact, however, the room was rediscovered in 1832 when a cannon accidentally fell through from the fortress' gun deck. Although "bones" were reportedly found among the debris inside, it is uncertain whether they were human. Besides, those who portray skeletons chained to a wall need to recall that bones are not wired together like the articulated skeletons studied in science class. Thus, as the imagined bodies decomposed, they would have fallen apart, the bones landing in a heap on the floor.

Besides, the story of the colonel sealing his wife and her lover in the chamber is only a fable. As one source admits, correctly, "history does not record the event" (Lapham 1997, 146). Another agrees but nevertheless offers the hope that "perhaps some visitors may still experience an eerie feeling when visiting the small room in the northeast corner" (Cain 1997, 22). However, as John Cipriani assured me, "There aren't any ghosts." Noting that he had slept in Castillo de San Marcos all night on occasion and had experienced nothing paranormal, he pointed out that places with genuine history did not need to resort to using ghosts for tourist promotion (Cipriani 2004).

JAIL TURNED INN

According to *Haunted Inns of America*, "sometimes late at night, strange moaning, groaning, and blood-curdling screams can be heard" emanating from the cell of a man who died painfully in the old Nelson County, Kentucky, jail—now a popular bed and breakfast (Smith and Jean 2003, 84). (The jail began as a single cell in 1797, then was expanded into a larger structure in 1819; this in turn became the jailer's residence when a new jail wing was added on in 1874 [Greco 1994, 131–35].)

Interestingly, while the story of the haunted cell was first published in 1909 ("Haunted Jail" 1909), it appears to have sunk into relative obscurity long before I "did time" there, spending a restful night in 1993.

Not only was my sleep not broken by ghostly cries, but the innkeeper at the time, Ann Hurst, told me she had never seen or heard a ghost, even though, as she said, "I stay here a lot at night and I always felt very secure." She added, "I never had any reason to believe in anything other than what I can touch." Two others I interviewed—owner Fran McCoy and tour guide Cathy Lawrence—described themselves as "believers" in ghosts, yet even they had had no ghostly experiences in the historic jail—especially no moans, groans, or screams.

Nevertheless, today's mystery-selling ghost buffs chronicle spectral encounters at the Jailer's Inn. These tend to follow familiar patterns. For example, one sleeping guest "was awakened at 1:00 a.m. and witnessed a man standing on the other side of the room. He stood there for a long time and then faded away" (Smith and Jean 2003, 84). This was obviously another "waking dream" like those discussed earlier. At least the specter did not scream.

AUSTERE PENITENTIARY

The gothic, castellated Eastern State Penitentiary in Philadelphia was once a marvel of prison architecture. Its floor plan was designed so that a single guard—stationed in its rotunda—could peer down each of its seven long cellblocks, the corridors arrayed like spokes of a wheel. The prison opened on October 23, 1829. "It was the world's first true penitentiary," claims a brochure, "a prison designed to inspire penitence—or true regret—in the hearts of criminals." In 1842, Charles Dickens visited the prison and wrote in his travel journal:

> In its intention, I am well convinced that it is kind, humane, and meant for reformation; but I am persuaded that those who devised this system of Prison Discipline, and those benevolent gentlemen who carry it into exe-cution, do not know what it is that they are doing. I believe that very few men are capable of estimating the immense amount of torture and agony which this dreadful punishment, prolonged for years, inflicts upon the suf-ferers; and in guessing at it myself, and in reasoning from what I have seen written upon their faces, and what to my certain knowledge they feel within, I am only the more convinced that there is a depth of terrible endurance in it which none but the sufferers themselves can fathom, and which no man has a right to inflict upon his fellow-creature.

It remains today an extremely foreboding place, attracting with its "super-natural atmosphere" so-called paranormal investigators, including of course

Jason Hawes, Grant Wilson, and their team that comprises Sci Fi Channel's (now Syfy Universal's) *Ghost Hunters*. They visited the prison in September 2004 and, in their typical fashion, chased after anomalies. Something darted by their thermal camera but turned out to be "only a cat"; another thermal image, a bright spot, at first seemed interesting but proved to be a reflection; and a "black shape" that passed before two people after one had taken a picture was explained by Jason: "The flash must have screwed up their eyes for a second." Their best effort was a moving image on a video that, although "a little vague," resembled someone in a dark robe, although the duo conceded it could have been a hoax (Hawes and Wilson 2007, 99–113).

Other such teams "investigating" at Eastern State have employed "the usual ghost hunting equipment," in addition to plying dowsing rods to supposedly effect spirit communication and photographing "orbs"—seeming balls of "spirit energy" that are actually caused by the camera's flash rebounding from dust particles. Ghost hunters have also relied on alleged psychic powers—on members' alleged "clairvoyant," "clairsentient," and "intuitive" ability, including their "feelings" of various kinds (Sarro 2008, 11–54). In short, they have engaged in the usual pseudoscientific and superstitious silliness that characterizes most of today's ghost hunting.

Accompanied by Philadelphia skeptic Bob Glickman, I visited Eastern State on May 15, 2010. We explored the crumbling facility, including the comfortably furnished cell of "Scarface" Al Capone, talked with staff, and even ducked into one dark cell to conduct an experiment in making orbs. We took some trial snapshots, then shook dust in the air and—in a flash—captured images that many ghost hunters mistakenly believe provide scientific evidence of spirit survival. Alas, we otherwise came up empty.

As these examples and others show (I have saved Alcatraz for separate treatment), old places of imprisonment stir strong emotions. The idea that ghosts are, well, free spirits still haunting such literally confining spaces is a romantic as well as ironic one. Add to the romance the eerie feelings such ominous sites inspire and indeed "ghosts" of the imagination may well appear to the impressionable.

Chapter 18

CONVICT SPECTERS
AT ALCATRAZ

Alcatraz! Its very name is synonymous with incarceration. An island fortress that became a military prison turned federal penitentiary, Alcatraz was a place from which escape was deemed impossible (figure 18.1). Yet a man whom I saw as a boy on my hometown's sidewalks would dramatically challenge that notion. His amazing act, together with persistent stories that ghostly prisoners still unaccountably inhabited the forbidding place, lured me to "The Rock," accompanied by fellow investigator Vaughn Rees, in May 2010. Here is some of what I found.

Figure 18.1. Alcatraz is an island fortress where—some insist—ghostly prisoners are still confined. (Photo by Joe Nickell.)

BACKGROUND

Located in San Francisco Bay, the small, stark island was discovered in 1769 by Spanish explorers who named it *Isla de los Alcatraces* ("Island of the Pelicans"). It became a possession of the United States in 1851 and was soon fortified; a lighthouse followed (1854), along with prison buildings (1868). Over the years it housed troublesome soldiers, Native Americans, and—during World War II—foreign enemies. Transferred to the Department of Justice in 1933, it began to serve as a maximum-security prison for dangerous inmates. Usually enveloped in fog, surrounded by icy, treacherous currents, and buffeted by wind, the facility was an isolated, foreboding place until it closed in 1963 (*Collier's Encyclopedia* 1993; Vercillo 2008, 7–39).

Thought to be escape-proof, it received such most-wanted criminals as Al Capone and murderer Robert Stroud. (Stroud, the "Birdman of Alacatraz," who was played by Burt Lancaster in the 1962 movie of that title, was transferred to the island from Leavenworth, where he had become an amateur ornithologist of some celebrity, and hence a nuisance to officialdom. Hollywood notwithstanding, Stroud never kept birds at Alcatraz [Heaney 1987, 97]).

Notwithstanding the formidable security, men with little to lose and much time on their hands dreamed of escape, and several tried. In 1962, for example, three desperados—Frank Lee Morris and the Anglin brothers, John and Clarence—made a daring escape from the Rock and were never seen again. Some believe they got away for good, but most likely they perished in the icy currents. Six months later came a more successful escape, although—well, I am getting ahead of a good story.

John Paul Scott—"Mr. Scott" to me as a boy of eleven[1]—had come to my hometown of West Liberty, Kentucky, to work as a lab technician at the hospital. I remember him as not too tall, slender, making a neat appearance in his white lab coat, and having a pleasant personality. I had no idea that he was a twice-convicted bank robber or that he would soon be involved in a sensational aborted break-in at a bank in the next county. The attempt—in the early-morning hours of Sunday, January 6, 1957, made with his brother Don and another man—ended with Scott shot in the mouth and arm by the bank's night watchman and Sheriff Little wounded in both knees by a spray of a submachine-gun fire from the trio. I remember the big headlines about the subsequent state police manhunt and capture of the gang.

All three drew lengthy prison terms, and Scott—sentenced to thirty

years and sent to prison in Atlanta—attempted escape and soon found himself at Alcatraz (Nickell 1991; Esslinger 2003; 397–412).

On December 16, 1962, however, six months after the previous Alcatraz
escape, Scott and another prisoner, Darl Lee Parker, while working on kitchen
detail, removed precut bars and went out a window, climbed up pipes to the
roof, and used a knotted extension cord to lower themselves to the ground at
the rear of the library. They tumbled down a steep hill and slid down a sewer
pipe to the water's edge. Using "water-wings" improvised from parts of a
prison shirt, the sleeves stuffed with inflated rubber gloves (stolen from the
hospital), the pair swam toward shore. Parker, having apparently broken his
foot in a fall, struggled against the currents, then took refuge on the nearby
rock formation known as Little Alcatraz, where he waited to be rescued. Scott,
however, successfully swam to shore, the mile-and-a-quarter distance length-
ened by strong currents pulling him off course. Some boys discovered him
unconscious and near death on rocks beneath the Golden Gate Bridge, and
they alerted police (Blackwell 1962; Esslinger 2003, 402–403). Scott was soon
returned to Alcatraz, but he had entered history as the only man ever to escape
the Rock and unquestionably reach the mainland alive.[2]

STILL INCARCERATED?

Although Scott died in 1987 in a federal prison at Tallahassee, Florida, his
ghost could, one supposes, still be among those who allegedly haunt Alca-
traz today. Yet few of the former inmates—neither Capone, nor "Birdman"
Stroud, for instance—actually died at Alcatraz (an exception being Joe
Bowers, who was shot to death after crossing a fence in an attempt to escape)
(Vercillo 2008, 79–115).

Yet if the urge to be free is so powerful, and not only among attempted
escapees, then why do ghosts remain—as they purportedly do—at so many
"haunted" places of confinement? Do they choose to stay for some inexpli-
cable reason, or is it that the dungeons and jails themselves somehow retain
"vibrations" of those who have lived there? Among believers in haunted
places, there is no generally agreed-upon explanation (Guiley 2000, 180–
81), and none that makes any scientific sense. Could it be that at Alcatraz, as
elsewhere, the evidence for ghosts is untrustworthy, as I have indeed found
in over forty years of active investigation?

With these thoughts in mind, on May 10, 2011, Vaughn Rees and I took an excursion boat to the Rock, where we toured the island and cellblocks—Vaughn with a still camera, I with a camcorder[3]—and talked with staff. Word spread among park rangers and interpreters of my connection with Scott, and I related what I knew. A young National Parks Conservancy member was soon guiding us about, asking if we would like to see some areas where tourists are not allowed. Of course we said yes, and after he fetched a bunch of keys, we were shown the hospital, the "psycho cell" (where I was shut in for the experience), a site associated with Robert Stroud, and other areas. As it happened, no ghosts put in an appearance.

PHENOMENA OF GHOSTS?

Claims of ghostly happenings at Alcatraz are largely products of folklore. *Ghosts of Alcatraz* (Vercillo 2008), like so many other mystery-mongering books, is rife with such unattributable constructions as "were said to" (58), "is said to" (67), "it is said that" (71, 73, 87, 97), "are said to" (74, 75, 99), "some say that" (89), "it is believed that" (93, 96), and so on—prefatory statements that demonstrate how worthless the anecdotes are as evidence.

Some claims are assigned to Alcatraz employees. Like our conservancy guide, most Alcatraz professionals do not claim ghost experiences, although "occasionally, one of them will admit that weird things happen here that they cannot explain" (Vercillo 2008, 123). Actually, the notion that an unexplained occurrence is proof of the supernatural is simply a logical fallacy called an argument from ignorance. Nevertheless, what about the movement of objects reported in the old prison administration office, which is visible to visitors through glass windows? According to Vercillo (2008, 71), "It is said that the chair . . . winds up in different locations of the room. And occasionally, the typewriter is shifted to a different spot on the desk." But she admits there is a nonsupernatural possibility: "Most people believe that the security guards who keep an eye on the tourists of Alcatraz are just moving things around as a prank to pass the time and frighten their co-workers." Now, I have uncovered many such pranks in my ghostbusting career (Nickell 2008), but there are also other possible explanations: maybe the objects are simply moved during cleaning, for example.

Other claims of ghosts at Alcatraz supposedly come from self-styled psychics. According to one source, "Numerous psychics have reported cold spots, harsh and sudden emotional outbursts, apparitions claiming abuse, vibrations and a myriad of other ghostly traces" ("Alcatraz Hauntings" 2007). However, admits Vercillo (2008, 118), "not too many psychics have reported on their findings at Alcatraz," and "the records of these reports are mostly lost to time." These alleged "findings" are therefore worse than worthless, and no psychic phenomenon has ever been validated by mainstream science.

Sylvia Browne, "the most well-known psychic to have visited the island" (Vercillo 2008, 118), is also one of the most notorious, once even failing to foresee her own criminal conviction. (See chapter 32.) Browne was also taken to task by the TV show *Inside Edition*, which exposed her claim to have solved a police case that, in fact, continued to remain unsolved (Nickell 2001, 124–25). Thus, we may be suspicious of the claim that she was "called in" by the National Park Service to investigate spooky phenomena at Alcatraz—especially since the Park Service does not promote ghosts there and, as Vercillo (2008, 106) concedes, "Reports of who precisely called Browne in to investigate the ghostly activity are varied." And second- and thirdhand accounts of her "psychic" feelings—utilizing such phrases as "some say" and "are reported to" (Vercillo 2008, 106–107)—do not represent evidence that science should, or even can, study. Psychics like Browne typically offer unsubstantiated claims, even unverifiable ones, or information that is obtainable from research or other sources (Nickell 2001, 297–98).

Still other ghost claims at Alcatraz stem from would-be ghost hunters. For example, Vercillo (2008, 143–47) cites the use of such silly devices as dowsing rods and Geiger counters, without, unfortunately, giving many specifics, other than reporting on photographs of ghostly "orbs" (88, 120). These are supposed to be due to spirit energy but actually result from the camera's flash rebounding from particulate matter floating in the air. Vaughn and I demonstrated the making of orbs at Alcatraz by shaking a dust cloth in front of the camera: click, flash, voila! Orbs on demand! Ghost Science 101.

In his *Ghost Stalker's Guide to Haunted California*, Richard Senate (1998, i) refers to "haunted places" where people report "things that by all science, should not be there." So maybe they really are not there, or maybe they are misperceived. Senate went to Alcatraz for a radio station, hoping to record some ghostly sounds for broadcast. Alas (apart from feelings he and a "psychic" had), "there was only the sound of terns and the awful silence of the prison," he admits, so "the radio people were unhappy with the ghost hunt" (1998, 124–25). Although Vercillo (2008, 50, 70) tells us "voices are reportedly still heard" in the prison, elsewhere she admits, "Sound carries easily here and there are always plenty of people to keep the place occupied."

And then there are supposed tape-recorded spirit voices, so-called EVP or electronic voice phenomena. But EVP might be better explained as the experience of verbal pareidolia. *Pareidolia* (see appendix) is the tendency to see pictures in clouds or to hear apparent words in random sounds—either from the tape recorder's own electronic and mechanical noise or from external, nonghostly sources (e.g., background noise). Alcatraz EVPs were analyzed by audio expert Paul Ginsberg (2009). He concluded that the recordings were "not the speech of a human being," explaining, "These sounds are well above the range of the human-voice spectrum, so I would say without any question that these sounds were not made—could not be made—by any human" adding whimsically, "at least not a live one." More seriously he concluded, "I would love to have some *hard* evidence that this, in fact, is a connection to the Beyond and that there are other worlds out there, but right now I'm still skeptical."

Moreover, certain other sounds—if they indeed actually occurred—might have similar nonghostly explanations. For instance, alleged "unearthly screams" may be nothing more than the cries of seagulls, which "sound almost like human screaming" (Vercillo 2008, 50, 122). And the claim that visitors to Alcatraz sometimes hear Robert "Birdman" Stroud's "distinctive whistle attempting to reach his beloved birds from beyond the grave" (Smith 2004, 174–76), might be explained as only the whistling notes of other birds. Of course, the imagination is yet another ready source for perceived sounds.

Indeed, the imagination plays a crucial role in all ghostly encounters. If ghosts are not the stuff of science—no matter how much they are pseudo-scientifically mischaracterized by the word *energy*—then they are figments of our romantic attitudes. And so convict ghosts remain forever trapped—not behind bars and walls that could never hold them, but in our minds. There they offer perpetual penance, having at least escaped, we can imagine, the greatest confinement of all: death.

Chapter 19

GHOSTS IN THE MIRROR

Given the illusory nature of mirrors, with their reflective and ever-changing surfaces, they have long been used for *scrying*. In this activity (of which crystal gazing is a form) shiny surfaces are stared upon at length until clairvoyant visions are perceived in the mind's eye—that is, the mind of a "psychic" (or fantasy-prone person). Some believe mirrors are portals into the spirit world, so it is not surprising that the ghost-in-the-mirror phenomenon is common. Indeed, it represents a distinct genre of ghostly encounters, indicated by a book, *Ghost in the Mirror*, by Leslie Rule (2008), as well as by my own investigations. Among my ghost-mirror cases (in addition to one at the "haunted" Myrtles Plantation in Louisiana [Nickell 2007, 1–10] and the story of another mirror, now lost, in which Abraham Lincoln witnessed a strange double image of himself [Nickell 2001, 109–13]) are more recent investigations.

MYSTERY AT THE LOWE HOTEL

According to a number of sources, Point Pleasant, West Virginia, offers haunting experiences—literally: ghosts have supposedly checked in at the Lowe Hotel and never left!

Three times I have visited this Ohio River town to investigate its mythical Mothman monster, a fanciful statue of which now stands across the street from the historic inn. (Once, I conducted an experiment in perception for the History Channel's popular TV series *Monster Quest*, and I include a chapter on Mothman in my *Tracking the Man-Beasts: Sasquatch, Vampires, Zombies, and More*, 2011.) In so doing, I have twice stayed at the Lowe, each time daring to bed down in its especially haunted room 314.

The Lowe is one of those grand hotels of yesteryear. Built in 1901 on the bank of the Ohio River, it is very near the site of the 1774 Battle of Point Pleasant (which Congress later decreed the first battle of the American Revolutionary War). Originally named the Spencer Hotel (in honor of a local judge), it was operated by the Lowe family from 1929 to 1990, when it was acquired by its present owners, Ruth and Rush Finley.

When I asked Rush Finley (2011) if he had had any ghost experiences, he replied that he was "not of that mind-set." Guests did occasionally have an experience, however. Ruth told a reporter, "We used to keep all those stories quiet, because we thought it would be bad for business. But in the last several years, these kinds of experiences have come into vogue, and we've encouraged guests to share their experiences" (see "Ghostly Encounters," *Charleston Gazette-Mail*, Feb. 18, 2007).

On my first stay (April 12, 2002), I interviewed Ruth Finley as she graciously gave me a tour of the old inn, a place filled with ambiance. She said that the wife of a railroad employee had stayed in room 314 for a week and had once awakened to see a man standing there. The woman also reported seeing the man in a large framed mirror when she did her hair. But are such experiences evidence of ghosts, or does science have another explanation?

MYSTERY SOLVED

To explain the Lowe Hotel's ghost-revealing mirror, we must look at how the phenomenon originated. Recall that a guest staying in room 314 for a week had first awakened to see a man standing in the room. This is a rather obvious description of a hypnopompic experience or "waking dream." As we previously discussed, this is a type of common hallucination that occurs in the interface between sleep and wakefulness. In this state, people often "see" ghosts, angels, extraterrestrials, or other entities. The woman also reported that the man appeared in the mirror when she did her hair—another, similar type of apparitional experience that typically occurs when one is in an altered state of consciousness, like daydreaming or performing some routine chore, as in this instance. (See appendix for "apparitional experiences.") It would not be at all unusual for a person having the one experience to have the other. Probably, the provocative nature of mirrors, together with the prior experience, played a part in triggering the subsequent sightings.

Paranormal writer Rosemary Ellen Guiley has more to say about the man in the mirror. In cataloging other ghostly activity at the Lowe in an article, she writes: "The third floor is the most active. In room 314, a tall, thin man in a 1930s suit, with a long beard, has appeared in a mirror. The solemn-looking fellow has not been identified, but he bears a strong resemblance to Sid Hatfield of the famous McCoy-Hatfield feuding families fame" (Guiley 2007).

Now, Guiley does not say it *was* Sid Hatfield (1893–1921) who, incidentally, was not a member of the feuding family, although he bragged that he was. A photo of him in his prime (apparently not long before he was killed while serving as police chief of Matewan, West Virginia) shows him clean-shaven. And he died a decade before he would have been dressed in 1930s attire. He also lived several counties away from Point Pleasant and had no known connection with the Lowe (although Rush Finley thinks it possible he *could* have stayed there). Nevertheless, various Internet postings and published articles suggest the ghost was indeed Sid, often using similar wording. (Indeed, one ghost-hunter's site uses—without attribution—four sentences verbatim from another site that acknowledges Guiley as its source.)

Still another source ("Lowe Hotel" 2010) has somehow learned that Sid's mirrored reflection did not appear to just one person but "has been seen by many." But if there were indeed "many" sightings of Sid, we would think *someone* would see his sheriff's badge or even his most prominent feature—"the gold caps on every one of his teeth"—that earned him his nickname "Smilin' Sid" ("Sid Hatfield" 2011).

I did not see Sid—or any other ghost—on the nights I stayed in room 314. I did photograph some "ghost orbs" (bright balls of "spirit energy" that seem to hover in haunted places). The orbs even appeared in the magical mirror on the wall! However, it probably helped that I pointed the camera at the mirror and then shook a dust cloth in the air in front of it. Real investigators know that orbs are merely the result of the camera's flash rebounding from particles of dust or debris—or, alternately, droplets of moisture—close to the lens.

My last night at the Lowe, I had to move down the hall, giving up my room to a party of ghost hunters from Kentucky who had prebooked it. I chatted with them until midnight, and one agreed with me on the fundamentally unscientific nature of ghost hunters endlessly seeking "anomalies" in "haunted" places, using equipment for which there is no scientific proof that it detects ghosts.

MARILYN AT THE HOLLYWOOD ROOSEVELT?

Reminiscent of the Lowe Hotel's "haunting" is an earlier case I investigated at the Hollywood Roosevelt Hotel in June 2000. (I have also stayed at the hotel on other occasions—once when I was in Southern California to make a giant Nasca-geoglyph re-creation on an area ranch for National Geographic Television.) Over the years, I kept meaning to write up this case; obviously, an appropriate time has now presented itself.

Among many ghostly phenomena claimed in *former* promotional material from the hotel is the story of "Marilyn Monroe's Ghost in Mirror" ("Marilyn" 2000). It is one of a collection of brief ghost stories related under the heading "Tall Tales," which perhaps gives an idea of the seriousness with which we should approach the report.

In any case, the initial sighting was in mid-December 1985, shortly before the hotel reopened following a two-year restoration. "With the opening so close," the account reads, "all office workers, managers and secretaries spent the day cleaning, sweeping and dusting." Indeed, several of the "tall tales" have their origin around this time, suggesting a bout of psychological contagion, whereby one report sets up expectations in others, prompting them to have questionable perceptions and experiences. (This is also the cause of many UFO and monster "flaps.") Ghost stories might also have been hyped for publicity purposes.

As it happened, while a staff member named Suzanne Leonard was cleaning the tall, framed mirror (then located in the general manager's office) she saw "the reflection of a blonde girl right where her hand was dusting." She looked around to find no one there, "yet when she looked back at the mirror, the reflection was still there." She did not say the girl resembled Marilyn Monroe, but the manager later told her the mirror had come from the star's former suite near the pool, and the identification has stuck. (The mirror was later relocated to the area outside the lower-level elevator. See accompanying illustration [figure 19.1], which I created for fun, bringing to the site a Marilyn cutout folded in my suitcase.)

How do we explain the ghost in the mirror? As at the Lowe Hotel, the Hollywood Roosevelt employee was performing a routine chore and, in the resulting reverie, may have had an apparitional experience (in which an image from the subconscious becomes superimposed on the visual scene). I do not know if apparitions are more likely to happen when a mirror is involved—that is, if there is a scrying effect. However, in such an experience, when the person shifts his or her gaze (as happened with the "Marilyn" sighting), the "spell" is usually broken and the illusory image dissolves. That it did not in this instance could suggest that another factor was involved.

Figure 19.1. "Haunted" mirror at Hollywood Roosevelt Hotel is shown here with a cutout of Marilyn Monroe, since her ghost would not put in an appearance! (Photo by Joe Nickell.)

I suspect that in the constantly changing surface swirls and streaks caused by her cleaning, the percipient briefly saw a *simulacrum*—that is, an image resulting from the brain's tendency (called *pareidolia*) to perceive recognizable images in random patterns—such as seeing pictures in clouds, inkblots, or the like. That the image appeared "right where her hand was dusting" seems to support this hypothesis. If the simulacrum effect was involved, it probably combined with the apparitional experience to trigger the appearance of the "blonde girl" who was not reflected in the mirror but who appeared *on* it—before, of course, being dusted away!

As an example of the utterly shoddy "research" that is often done on such cases by ghost-mongering types, consider the account by Richard Senate (1998, 13–14). Giving no sources for his alleged facts, Senate erroneously attributes the mirror sighting to a "maid"; wrongly places its occurrence "near the elevators" (where the mirror was relocated); incorrectly reports that, when the percipient turned back to the mirror, "the image of the beautiful blond [*sic*] was gone"; adds imaginative details to the original vague and apparently monochromatic image ("that silky golden hair, those crystal blue eyes, those lustrous lashes, the pouting red lips"); has somehow learned that the domestic was not "dusting" but "polishing" the mirror; and so on. Other sources imply additional sightings of Marilyn in the mirror, as well as sightings of other deceased guests in other mirrors in the Roosevelt's hallways, as what began as single incident obviously becomes mythologized (see Hauck, 1996, 47).

EXPERIENCING THE PSYCHOMANTEUM

These cases bring us to the psychomanteum. That is a chamber with a mirror into which one gazes in hopes of seeing spirits of the dead. The chamber is dark, save for a dim lightbulb or a candle.

On June 26–27, 2010, my wife Diana Harris and I were visiting the charming spiritualist village on Cassadaga Lake in Western New York, the subject of the book *Lily Dale: The True Story of the Town That Talks to the Dead* by Christine Wicker (2003). There, in the basement of a three-story Victorian dwelling known as Angel House (figure 19.2), is a psychomanteum. Screened off with fabric panels, and containing a mirror that is slightly tipped up so sitters do not see themselves, the chamber is the topic of chapter 18 of Wicker's book.

Through a spiritualist friend (with whom we also sat during the evening's healing ceremony performed by visiting Tibetan monks), we were invited with another couple to visit the Angel House's psychomanteum. There we five sat for several minutes and looked in vain for the ghostly figures. Christine Wicker had looked longer on two separate occasions with Lily Dale mediums and had similar results, although one medium's friend reportedly had better luck.

Figure 19.2. Angel House at Lily Dale spiritualist village in Western New York contains an alleged spirit-conjuring chamber called a *psychomanteum*. (Photo by Joe Nickell.)

The psychomanteum was popularized by Dr. Raymond Moody—the professor of psychology best known for coining the term *near-death experience* (NDE)—whose 1993 book *Reunions* is based on the mirror chamber. He has used his own psychomanteum as a research tool, encouraging persons to contact the dead as a means of resolving grief. Moody's setup is contained in his rural Alabama facility, the John Dee Memorial Theater of the Mind. Dee (1527–1608) was court magician to Elizabeth I; he touted scrying (using an obsidian mirror) as a technique for predicting the future.

The technique of scrying involves relaxing and placing the mind in an unfocused state, whereupon the shiny surface may seem to cloud over as a prelude to the appearance of mental imagery.

Thus, the psychomanteum invites use of the imagination. As Francis X. King (1991, 151) cautions in *Mind & Magic*, with scrying, you may not be seeing clairvoyantly but "just getting better acquainted with the contents of your own unconscious mind."

Chapter 20

HAUNTED DUTCH MINES

While the country's official name is the Netherlands, most people elsewhere call it Holland (even though that term really applies to only two of its thirteen provinces). Just about a tenth the size of California, the Netherlands is still one of Europe's most densely populated countries (after Monaco and Malta). It has historically been a treasure trove of geniuses—from the Dutch masters, like Rembrandt and Vermeer, to such scientific pioneers as Antoni van Leeuwenhoek (1632–1723), who first identified bacteria, and Christiaan Huygens (1629–1695), who proposed the wave theory of light. Indeed, seated in the front row during my talk at a skeptics congress in Utrecht on October 28, 2006, was Gerard 't Hooft, cowinner (with Martin Veltman) of the 2000 Nobel Prize in Physics.

Of course, like people everywhere, the Dutch can also be superstitious—hence the conference theme, "the paranormal." I spoke on the relationship between Dutch and American psychics and for several days before the event toured the country with noted Dutch skeptic Jan Willem Nienhuys, investigating a number of mysteries and legends. These included an Amsterdam woman's visions, haunted coal mines, the well-known boy-with-his-finger-in-the-dike tale, and more. (Our investigation of a mansion haunted by the ghost of a walled-up nun appears in chapter 5.)

The Netherlands's Limburg Province (the country's southernmost) rests on coal deposits that are some 270 million years old. Coal, once an important Dutch commodity, was mined in the region, which contains many labyrinthine mines as well as cave systems (Harmans 2005, 365).

Nienhuys had learned of a "haunted" mine, the Emma, but it is unfortunately now closed. Nevertheless, we were able to visit, about twenty kilometers to the south, a historical mine, Steenkolenmijn, which is open to the public as a sort of mining museum. (As Nienhuys learned, however, one must be constantly skeptical: this "coal" mine is actually an old marl pit, centuries old, that was converted to a "model mine" in 1917.)

In addition to touring a mine to get a sense of the setting of mine ghost tales, we also visited the Meertens Institute in Amsterdam, which conducts research on language and culture, including ethnology and folklore. There we met with senior researcher Theo Meder, who helped us sort out versions of the Emma mine's ghost tale.

The story is elaborated as a children's adventure, *Kaspar*, by Pierre Heijboer, who was himself from the village of Hoensbroek, where the Emma mine is located. In the story, Little Jo had just turned fifteen and had gone to work in the mine, even though his grandmother thought this work too dangerous for him. His job was to regulate the weather-doors, leather flaps that regulated airflow.

One day there were no coal cars, but as he sat there he was visited by an old man dressed in a miner's clothes, wearing a beard, and using a walking stick. He told Jo his name was Kaspar and that he could determine who could see him and who could not. He took Jo through a hole into an old section of the mine that Kaspar said was his domain. Everywhere old supports had fallen, and at one place Jo saw, sticking out, the bony hand of a miner who had been killed in a collapse. He also saw fossil trees of the type coal was made from, as well as bright crystals and other sights. Although hours passed, he was not tired, thirsty, or hungry.

Meanwhile, because he had not returned, Jo's grandmother was worried, especially when she learned that his name-token—kept on a hook during working hours as a safety precaution—was missing. After two days, everyone had given up hope of ever finding him alive again, although his grandmother kept praying for his safe return.

Then, on the third day, Jo reappeared. When asked to explain what had happened, he began by saying that no one would believe him. In fact, as his family rejoiced, mine officials had a doctor examine him, and a mine policeman accused him of deserting his post. The miners' chaplain was also skeptical of his story, but his grandmother knew not to worry about him in the future because he was protected by "Kaspar, the mine ghost" (Meder 2005; 2006).

Obviously, this narrative has a fairy-tale quality, not the least of which is its motif of passing through a hole into a mystical realm. (In Lewis Carroll's

1865 *Alice's Adventures in Wonderland*, for example, little Alice falls down a rabbit hole and into a strange land where everything occurs with fantastic illogicality.) Then there is the supernatural figure of Kaspar. Common to Dutch mine legends and myths, Kaspar is a sort of god of the underworld. He is generally malevolent, angry at humans who pillage his rich hoard of coal (Dieteren 1984, p. 33). So when miners arrived at work and found cracked supports, they would suggest, "Kaspar has been here," or when a coffee can or sandwiches went missing they would suggest, "Well, Kaspar may have taken them" (Lemmens 1936, 62).

If the Emma mine story is based on an actual event, it had to have occurred between 1913, when that mine first opened, and 1936, when a version of the tale appeared in a book of mine legends (Lemmens 1936, 77). Meder (2006) suggests that the boy may simply have wandered off, become lost, and fallen asleep, dreaming about the old man or inventing him to provide an alibi for himself.

Asked about haunted mines, our guide at Steenkolenmijn was very dismissive, saying that ghost stories were simply used to scare beginning workers. Even so, Nienhuys did turn up some illuminating tales of mine "ghosts." One specter proved to be a living miner who was covered in chalk, while another was a goat that had been surreptitiously released underground!

Still another tale, "the ghost in the mine wagon," tells about a miner who was attempting to fraudulently change the tags on coal cars to give himself credit for greater production. Suddenly, his hand was grabbed—in one version by a ghost, in another by the supervisor who had hidden in one of the cars (Nienhuys 2006).

As all these folk narratives about mine ghosts indicate, they have less insight to provide about the reality of ghosts than about the storytellers' desire to entertain or instruct within their own cultural environment.

Chapter 21

STAGE FRIGHT: THEATRICAL HAUNTINGS

W hich is more likely to be "haunted," a university engineering building or an old theater? That it is the latter seems obvious—for reasons we shall soon consider. When Tom Ogden (2009, x) began to collect tales for his book *Haunted Theaters*, he discovered that "the hard part wasn't finding theaters that are haunted. If anything, it was finding theaters that *aren't* haunted. For some reason, it seems that more spirits have taken up residence in playhouses than just about any other type of venue." My own assessment is similar, except that I suspect theaters are believed to be haunted because people *expect* them to be.

First of all, theaters are places where magic and mystery are presented on stage—along with "ghosts" themselves. For example, Shakespeare brought several specters on stage, including Banquo's ghost in *Macbeth* and the shade of the prince of Denmark's father in *Hamlet*. That the bard really believed in ghosts is by no means certain, for he also wrote this exchange in *Henry IV, Part I* (act 3, scene 1): When Glendower boasts, "I can call spirits from the vasty deep," Hotspur replies, "Why, so can I, or so can any man; but will they come when you do call for them?" Nevertheless, dramatists found many ways of producing ghostly figures on stage (such as magician de Philipstahl's "phantasmagoria," utilizing a magic lantern, which debuted in London in 1802 [Nickell 2005, 126]).

Not only could "ghosts" appear on stage, but they could be seen offstage as well—especially by imaginative (even fantasy-prone) people, as theatrical folk are often likely to be. Also, when one is tired (say at the end of a performance), or daydreaming, or otherwise in a period of reverie (as when performing routine chores, for instance) one is more likely to have an apparitional experience, in which a dreamlike image from the subconscious is briefly superimposed on the visual scene (Nickell 2001, 216–17). As people relate their supposed encounters, they set the stage, so to speak, for others to do likewise. In such a climate, exaggerations—even pranks—are almost sure to follow. And as Ogden (2009, 11) says with more justification than he seems to be aware of, "once they've manifested, phantoms tend to stick around."

More than most places, theaters offer a variety of ghost-inspiring factors: dramatized stories, scenes of make-believe, historical figures in period costumes, romantic ambiance, plays of light and shadow, opportunities to be virtually alone in a spooky building late at night, the effects of faulty wiring and noisy steam pipes, and so on. Here are some "haunted" theaters I have investigated.

BIRD CAGE THEATRE

Tombstone, Arizona, has been called "one of the most haunted places in North America" (Smith 2002, 26). Among the sites I visited there on Halloween 2003 (with fellow investigator Vaughn Rees), was the notorious Bird Cage Theatre [*sic*]. It opened under that name on December 23, 1881, when Tombstone had swelled from a silver-mining camp to a boomtown. It is an original entertainment hall—a combination saloon, gambling hall, opera house, and brothel—where Wild Bill Hickok and Diamond Jim Brady once played poker. Suspended from the ceiling are fourteen "cribs," seven on each side, where prostitutes were displayed, and reportedly, with the red velvet curtains drawn, where they entertained clients. According to a persistent legend, the hall originally opened under another name but changed it after a popular song's refrain, "She's only a bird in a gilded cage." The song was penned by British lyricist Arthur J. Lamb, after (says the legend) he stood at the theater's bar and, in an inspired moment, saw the girls in their "cribs" as caged birds:

> She's only a bird in a gilded cage,
> A beautiful sight to see.
> You may think she's happy and free from care,
> She's not, though she seems to be.
> 'Tis sad when you think of her wasted life
> For youth cannot mate with age;

And her beauty was sold for an old man's gold,
She's a bird in a gilded cage.

(Cottrill 2005, 170–71; Ogden 2009, 66–75;
Smith 2002, 26–30)

Actually the story falls apart when we realize that Lamb (born August 12, 1870, died August 10, 1928) would have been only eleven years old when the Bird Cage was named. And the song was not published until 1900 ("Harry Von Tilzer" 2011; "Arthur J. Lamb" 2011).

Be that as it may, the Bird Cage is reportedly a hive of ghostly activity, having been featured in various television ghost hunts, books, and Internet sites. It is "allegedly home to 31 different ghosts" ("Bird Cage" 2011a), one of which is the most often reported. A version of the story was collected by Hauck (1996, 23) and related in a single sentence: "The apparition of a man wearing a celluloid visor and carrying a clipboard has been seen walking across the stage."

Now, for some time I have been working with CFI Libraries director Timothy Binga to track story elements—folklorists call them *motifs*—in narratives that offer paranormal claims. For example (as discussed in chapter 6), Tim tracked for me on the Internet motifs from a University of Tennessee legend about a dorm resident's suicide (which had actually never occurred there). This turned up many similar tales across the country, recognizable as variants (to use another folklorist term) of "a migratory legend—part of the narrative lore of college folk, transmitted widely" (Nickell 2010).

We used a similar approach for the onstage man with the visor and clipboard, turning up a number of hits. While these were consistently linked to the Bird Cage, they nevertheless showed many variants—evidence of the folkloric process at work. For example, in various Internet sites the specter is described as "a stagehand," "a man in black," and "a stage manager." He sometimes wears a visor but carries no clipboard, or he had both and is dressed in "period clothing."[1] Two books on haunted theaters provide other variants. One is based on an interview with the theater's owner, Bill Hunley (Smith 2002, 28). He recalled several purported sightings of the ghostly figure, who, he explains, "walks from stage right to stage left." Hunley mentions no visor but states: "He's wearing pinstriped pants and carrying a clipboard. He's intently looking at the clipboard. You see him for about a second, maybe a second and a half, then he's gone."

In contrast to Hunley's description of a simple action played over and over, Tom Ogden presents in his book (2009, 72–73) what is termed a "residual haunting" (Kachuba 2007, 26)—a more elaborate version, attributed to one "Charlotte." In this, the "man dressed in black," with visor and clipboard, is not briefly walking across the stage but is actually at work "onstage setting up"; indeed he "busied himself near the back curtain." This version even has a punchline: when "Charlotte" tells a tour guide of seeing the man—whom, importantly, she did not perceive as spectral—she is told, "'The man you saw' the guide started cautiously, 'well, he was one of our ghosts.'" Some sources take the ghost even further beyond the single action, one saying of the man with the clipboard: "He is not fond of being shoved in the chest. The ghost was also known to smoke cigars" ("Bird Cage" 2011b). However, this is clearly an example of motifs from "other" ghost tales of the Bird Cage becoming grafted onto the narrative of the clipboard-carrying man (see, e.g., Smith 2002, 740).

Such evidence by itself does not conclusively disprove the existence of the ghost with the clipboard, but of course the burden of proof falls on whoever would make such a claim, not on someone else to disprove it. The principle of Occam's razor—that the explanation with the fewest assumptions is to be preferred—favors the nonghost hypothesis: that however the spectral figure originated—as a mistake, a prank, or a trick of the mind—it has persisted and multiplied due to processes best understood by psychologists and folklorists.

LANCASTER OPERA HOUSE

Lodged in an Italianate building whose first floor houses the Lancaster, New York, Town Hall, the Lancaster Opera House is a charming two-story theater that opened in 1897. (It later became a distribution center for the needy during the Great Depression, a parachute factory during World War II, and a civil defense headquarters after the war. It was restored beginning in 1976, and it was revived as a theater in 1981 ["Area Landmarks: Lancaster Opera House" 1998].)

The most-talked-about phantoms of the opera house are twofold. One is "William," a gaslight-era prankster "who moves objects about, opens and closes doors and plays with the elevator" ("Area Landmarks" 1998). Such "poltergeist" phenomena, however, may be simply due to some mundane cause of which the percipient is unaware; for example, certain openings of locked doors were attributable to the janitor (Nelson 1992). As well, a given door might not have been pulled completely shut so that the latch clicked in place; thus it could pop open unexpectedly later, perhaps with changes in temperature. As to the "haunted" elevator, it was known to occasionally malfunction (Kazmierczak 1998). Also, as I have found in many other cases, the urge in some people to play ghost pranks on others is practically irresistible (Nickell 2008).

The other opera house entity is known as "the Lady in Lavender," so called because she reportedly wears a lavender gown. Her name is said to be "Priscilla." She is only glimpsed, however—invariably in the theater's balcony (figure 21.1)—and these sightings are as rare as they are brief (Nelson 1992; Winfield 2006, 78–79). She has never appeared to me on my visits, even when my wife Diana Harris and I sat in that very area during a February 28, 2009, performance of *Hound of the Baskervilles* (based on the Sherlock Holmes novel). Significantly, both "William" and the lavender-gowned "Priscilla" were first identified—perhaps we should say conjured up, if not invented—by local psychics (Nelson 1992).

Figure 21.1. Balcony of Lancaster Opera House, where the "Lady in Lavender" is said to appear on occasion. (Photo by Joe Nickell.)

Given the opinion of many psychologists that it is people—not places— that are haunted, I used a questionnaire to collect and study the experiences of five people associated with the Lancaster Opera House. The question- naire is designed to record and quantify one's alleged ghost encounters as well as measure the individual's propensity to fantasize. The results showed a clear correlation: the more experiences a person reported, the higher his or her fantasy-proneness (FP) score proved to be. (That is, one person with no ghost experiences had a very low FP score; three persons who each claimed a few experiences had a moderate FP score; and one person who reported numerous experiences had a high score, indicative of a fantasy- prone personality.)

The highest-scoring person—both in ghost experiences and in traits associated with fantasy proneness—was a self-described spiritualist medium. Among such traits (identified in a classic study by Wilson and Barber 1983), she reported a claimed "psychic" ability, a "healing touch," past-life experi- ences, vivid dreams, ease of being hypnotized, ability to speak with spirits of the dead, and so on. As a child she had also had "make-believe friends," another trait commonly associated with a fantasy-prone personality. As this and other evidence I collected shows, the ghosts of the Lancaster Opera House appear to be figments of the imagination, pure and simple.

RIVIERA THEATRE

Located in North Tonawanda, New York, the Riviera Theatre [sic] was built in 1926 in Italian Renaissance style from plans drawn by well-known theater architects Leon H. Lempert and Son. Installed in the new theater, a Wurl- itzer theater organ, called "an orchestra in a box," provided accompaniment for the latest movies, vaudeville acts, and music events. Over the years, the theater became part of the Shea's and Dipson chains, was sold and resold several other times, then was finally acquired in 1989 by the Niagara Fron- tier Theatre Organ Society, which began extensive renovation.

According to the Riviera's artistic director David Bondrow (2008), the "main story" relating to the theater's alleged haunting tells of the accidental death of a child performer named "Mary." Supposedly, scenery was being changed at the wrong time and the girl was struck by a *batten* (a long strip of lumber used, for example, to strengthen or fasten canvas). "Whistling cues" were reportedly being used to signal the scenery changes, and someone was whistling a tune at the time, thus causing confusion that led to the tragic accident.

Unfortunately, this rather implausible tale is completely unsubstantiated, there being no evidence that such a girl was a historical person. Nevertheless, a "psychic entertainer" in recent years kept sensing "Mary," so the name became attached to the legendary girl. In time, "Mary" was credited with any odd occurrence at the Riviera. Indeed, late one night she reportedly put in an appearance. Technicians were designing a show and "went to a blackout" (i.e., all lights on stage being turned off in anticipation of the next lighting cue), whereupon a ghostly figure was seen (whether by one or more persons is unclear) floating down stage. It was reported to be "Mary."

Now, the fact that the ghost appeared just after the lights were turned out suggests the alleged apparition may have been a type of optical illusion— the negative afterimage (a well-understood retinal phenomenon) of, say, someone on stage who had been bathed in bright light. The resulting spectral figure—retained by the eye in the dark—would thus move, while appearing to float in midair, as the viewer's head turned, and then it would dissolve. Even one person having had such a striking experience could have spread it to others by suggestion (a process called *folie à deux*—see appendix).

But could a completely fictitious entity come alive—so to speak—as a ghost? Just such a possibility was demonstrated by a famous long-running experiment, conducted by a group of eight psychical researchers under the direction of Toronto parapsychologists Iris M. Owen and her husband, A. R. G. Owen, during the 1970s. The group invented an imaginary ghost named "Philip Aylesford." According to his make-believe biography, he was born in 1624, served as a knight and a spy for Charles II, and had an extramarital affair with a gypsy girl who was burned at the stake after his wife accused her of witchcraft, whereupon he committed suicide in 1654 at age thirty. One of the researchers even painted a portrait of "Philip."

Then the group, none of whom were psychics, began trying to communicate with the nonexistent entity. At first all they felt was "a presence," but after several months they opted for the improved ambiance of a Victorian séance. Soon "Philip" was communicating with rappings (once for *yes*, twice for *no*), followed by table tipping and other occurrences, even with some sitters (inspired by electronic-voice phenomena) perceiving whispered responses to questions from Iris M. Owen. The researchers believed they were producing psychokinetic effects with their minds (Guiley 2000, 286; Winfield 2006, 134–38). Instead, of course, they were demonstrating how belief, leading to expectation, could produce ghostly effects best attributable to misperception, imagination, unconscious muscular activity, and so on (see appendix).

GHOSTLIGHT THEATER

Converted in 2001 from an old German Methodist Church (built in 1889), a theater in North Tonawanda, New York, soon became the Ghostlight Theatre, and therein lies a tale.

Despite reports of paranormal activity at the theater, *ghost light* is a theatrical term. Found in every theater, the ghost light is simply a lamp or, typically a naked light bulb set atop a light standard. Rolled onstage before the manager locks up at closing time, it is used as a sort of night light, for safety, so that anyone who enters later will not trip over stage props or fall into the orchestra pit. It probably gets its name from the idea that the only ones left in the building when the light is lit are "ghosts." Hence, the superstitious say that the light is to keep ghosts at bay or, contradictorily, to keep the spirits company during long nights ("What's a Ghost Light?" 2008; "Ghost Light" 1995).

Certainly, Ghostlight Theater welcomes the association with ghosts. I attended a 2009 pre-Halloween performance there based on Washington Irving's ghost tale "The Legend of Sleepy Hollow," and the program noted that previous productions have included such paranormal fare as *Night of the Living Dead*, and *Nosferatu: The Legend of Dracula*. One actress's program bio mentions that she "loves to ghost hunt" and "tries to go to every haunted house, real or otherwise during the autumn season." The program also contains an ad: "Buffalo Erie Paranormal Society/For when things go bump in the night. . . . If you are experiencing paranormal activity give us a call" (*Legend of Sleepy Hollow* [program booklet] 2009).

Such alleged activity at the Ghostlight is the subject of a chapter in *Haunted Buffalo* (Claud and O'Connor 2009), as well as a segment of a documentary DVD, *Ghostlights: Folklore, Skepticism & Belief*, on which I appear, filmed at various Western New York theaters, including the Ghostlight. (I attended the film's premier in 2008 at the Riviera Theatre [LaChiusa, LaChiusa, and Kupezyk 2008].) One highlight has local actor Paul

McGinnis observing—not surprisingly—that ghostly phenomena seem more plentiful whenever the Ghostlight is putting on a play with "supernatural aspects," such as the ghost in Dickens's *A Christmas Carol*.

Indeed, one ghost seems to have stepped off the stage of that show's performance. A young theater worker was busy painting bricks for a set—and so was engaged in the kind of routine activity that can lead to a reverie and hence to a ghost sighting. (See appendix for "apparitional experience.") She began to feel as if someone were watching her, and this set the stage, so to speak, for her subconscious to conjure up a ghost—the figure of a lady sitting in the front row of the otherwise empty Ghostlight seats. Of course the lady was dressed in quaint attire, which the stagehand described as being of the era of *A Christmas Carol* (LaChiusa, LaChiusa, and Kupezyk 2008).

The young lady's father, the Ghostlight's technical director, Jesse Swartz, compared her description to the one given by an actress who had also seen a ghost lady on another occasion, and he declared a match. But not so fast: the actress reported the dress of the lady she saw as being consistent with the 1895–1900 period, whereas attire comparable to that of *A Christmas Carol* (published in 1843) dates from more than half a century earlier—so there would seem not to have been such a good match after all.

Nevertheless, folk at the Ghostlight have already dubbed their female ghost "the Lady in Red" (LaChiusa, LaChiusa, and Kupezyk 2008)—seemingly their version of the Lancaster Opera House's "Lady in Lavender" —and now they even say she has company from yet another costumed lady, a "woman in black" (Claud and O'Connor 2009, 109–12). Offering a dubious photo, sightings, noises "that can't be explained," ghost hunters' "orbs," and alleged psychic impressions (LaChiusa, LaChiusa, and Kupezyk 2008; Claud and O'Connor 2009, 109–12), the Ghostlight's reputation of "being deeply haunted" (Dabkowski 2006) can be expected to attract an even larger cast of theatrical ghosts.

PALACE GRAND THEATRE

A red-haired beauty, Kathleen "Klondike Kate" Rockwell (1876–1957), was a true dance-hall queen (not a lady of the evening like those of Tombstone's Bird Cage Theatre). As a talented dancer, she spun many yards of bright red chiffon about her to create a "flame dance" that impressed audiences in frontier Dawson City, Yukon. This was the boomtown of the great Klondike Gold Rush at the turn of the last century. Kate was called the "Darling of Dawson" and "Belle of the Klondike," especially when, her glory days long past, she was selling picture postcards of herself (figure 21.2) and telling gold-rush-era tales wherever she could fine a venue. She had spent only two years in Dawson, having arrived in 1900 and left when the gold rush was dying out. Yet today she has allegedly returned to grace Dawson's Palace Grand Theatre once more—this time as a backstage ghost.

Figure 21.2. "Klondike Kate" Rockwell, with whom the author has had many posthumous connections—though never as a ghost. (Author's collection.)

I came to feel very close to Kate—to her memory, at least, not her sup-posedly earthbound spirit—when I, likewise, spent much of two years in Dawson, in 1975 and 1976. I worked as a blackjack dealer and crown-and-anchor croupier (with waxed mustache, sleeve garters, and all) in Diamond Tooth Gertie's Gambling Hall (named in memory of another dance-hall queen, Gertie Lovejoy). I attended the Place Grand's shows and got to know many of the theatrical folk. (Actor and mime Brian Jones, for example, who, like most seasonal outsiders in Dawson, worked two jobs, often fixed my breakfast as short-order cook at the Flora-Dora Café overlooking the Yukon River.) During my second summer I also worked as a manager of a riverboat tour company, whose owner, Captain Dick Stevenson, also had a fishing camp on a little island, and we once hosted the entire Palace Grand crew there for one of our famous salmon barbeques. On that day I ferried the the-atrical folk (actors, stagehands, etc.) to the island using "my" boat: a small paddle wheeler named—tah dah!—"Klondike Kate."

I had another connection with Kate. I had stayed in Dawson through the winter to serve as exhibit designer for a grant-supported renovation and redesigning of displays for the Dawson City Museum. The museum had acquired from an estate sale a few of Kate's belongings: a dress, a beaded purse, and another item or two, including, if I recall correctly, a lady's fan. I set aside a small room, which we finished with period wallpaper and out-fitted with an antique brass bed and small dressing table. Putting the small items on the latter and installing a glass-paneled wall case for the dress, I created "Klondike Kate's Bedroom" (Rubinsky 1976). Even so, Kate's ghost never came by.

Before, however, one attributes the alleged ghost's absence to the fact that the bedroom was a reproduction, we must realize that is just what today's Palace Grand Theatre is: a replica. The original 1899 building had largely succumbed to time (notably from having been built on ground that alternately froze and thawed). By the 1950s it was in tumbledown shape, and it was replaced in 1962 with a replica. (Now in modern, far-north restora-tions, steel supports are set deep so they rest directly on the permafrost for stability.)

This replica, too, almost perished on the night of Tuesday, May 18, 1976, when fire engulfed the historic Bonanza Hotel. Only a vacant lot intervened between it and the Palace Grand, and firemen fought valiantly to save the latter. As I wrote at the time in my journal:

One brave fireman [I believe it was Peter Jenkins] sat against a smoldering [electric] pole . . . and played his stream of water along the blackening side of the Palace Grand. He didn't move even after the burning building slowly leaned over toward him and finally fell over, fortunately collapsing from underneath to land in its own blazing territory.

Such a rush of flame billowed up that the crowd was forced back further but eventually the fire—and the threat—died down.

Had the theater also succumbed, the entire downtown district would have gone too, in a chain reaction of each burning building kindling the next. People were crying in the streets, and the scene remains one of the most vivid of my lifetime.

During my time in Dawson, I never heard a word about Kate's ghost inhabiting the Dawson landmark. Although devoting a ten-page chapter titled "The Queen of Klondike" to her in his *Haunted Theaters*, Tom Ogden (2009, 185) offers merely a single sentence of utter hearsay in that regard: "She's said to have returned to haunt the dressing rooms of the Palace Grand, the theater where she had her first triumphs in her youth." He does add one sentence: "If you . . . decide to tour the old Palace Grand Theatre, look closely: If you see someone with blazing red hair backstage surrounded by red chiffon, you just might have stumbled across the ghost of the 'Darling of Dawson' herself, Klondike Kate" (186).

Then again, of course, you may see nothing at all. That is the familiar story of all theatrical ghosts: there is no evidence they actually exist, but often they play roles in little dramas that take place in our imagination.

Chapter 22

WORLDWIDE HAUNTINGS

Hauntings—of one kind or another—are reported worldwide. Here are selected examples—from Europe, Canada, Argentina, Australia, Russia, China, and Morocco—both specific cases and generalized claims that I have investigated during years of travels. I think these brief reports convey some of the flavor of the different cultures involved, while demonstrating the persistence of belief that is a common thread throughout.

THE WHITE LADY (EUROPE)

A phantom figure, the White Lady of the Hohenzollerns, has been called "one of the world's most mobile ghosts," having "appeared in castles all over Europe" (Hauck 2000, 113). I have crossed her spirited path on occasion, including once in Franconia (the northern region of the German state of Bavaria) with my friend Martin Mahner in 2002. It is said that every town in the region has a legend of die Weisse Frau ("the White Lady"), who walks about at night terrifying the populace. Her saga is most firmly attached to the Plassenburg, a Renaissance fortress overlooking the Franconian town of Kulmbach.

Tradition says the White Lady was Kunigunde von Orlamünde, whose husband's ancestors erected the castle. After she was widowed, she sought to marry a certain Albrecht von Hohenzollern, who was agreeable except for what he characterized as the "four eyes between us." Although he apparently meant his parents, Kunigunde assumed he referred to her two children, so she secretly murdered them. So it would appear they died a natural death, she used a needle—a "golden needle" according to one of the many variant folktales—to pierce the children's skulls. However, a guilty conscience drove her to Rome, where the Pope promised forgiveness in return for her commitment to a life of monastic devotion. Supposedly, she went on her knees from the Plassenburg to the valley of Bernick to establish a monastery.

Some versions of the legend say she died in the attempt, while others have her succeeding, then dying in her early thirties. They agree that, ever since, she haunts the numerous castles of the Hohenzollern dynasty—appearing in some simultaneously!

The saga was first mentioned in the latter part of the fifteenth century. At the old castle of Bayreuth, says the revealing account, whenever the Cavaliers wished to be rid of the visiting ruler and his entourage, the White Lady would be conjured up to frighten them away. That is, one of the court ladies would secretly dress in a white gown and roam the dark chambers and corridors of the Plassenburg. The castle residents especially enjoyed fooling a gullible Count Friedrich. Once, however, a man who donned a white garment to play ghost and chase away the Hohenzollerns reportedly came to a tragic end. In one version of the tale, he fell drunkenly down the stairs; in another, he was pushed by the man he attempted to frighten. In any case, he reportedly broke his neck (Wachler 1931; Nickell 2007, 276–74).

Whether the early accounts of ghostly hoaxing are true—and they deserve at least as much credit as the later ghost legends—the story of die Weisse Frau herself is cast into doubt by the historical record. Although the Countess Kunigunde did enter a monastery, she died not in her thirties but in her seventies. More important, her marriage had been childless (Wachler 1931). According to my guide at the historic castle, the true story about Albrecht's refusal to marry her was that she was impoverished. Another castle worker—who had herself never seen the specter and noted that there were no recent sightings—stated her belief that the White Lady of the Hohenzollerns was "only a legend" (Nickell 2007, 274).

SPECTRAL SHIP (CANADA)

Ghosts and ships seem made for each other, combining the spine-tingling attraction of hauntings with the enduring romance of the sea. Among the beguiling stories are those of vessels that are themselves phantoms—linked to shipwrecks and other disasters. Such is the mystery of the *Teazer* light, an example of "ghost lights" or "luminous phenomena" (see Corliss 1995)—in this instance, interpreted as the spectral appearance of a fiery sailing ship.

The story begins on June 26, 1813, when a privateer's vessel, the *Young Teazer*, was hemmed in by British warships in Nova Scotia's Mahone Bay. The pirates' commander, seeing that they were doomed to be captured and hanged, ordered the ship set ablaze, whereupon, according to legend at least, all men perished (Blackman 1998). However, soon afterward came reports of eyewitnesses that the vessel had returned in the form of a fiery ghost ship! Almost always, it was observed on foggy nights, especially those occurring "within three days of a full moon" (Colombo 1988, 32; Nickell 2001, 188–89).

In 1999, at Malone Bay to investigate the mystery of Oak Island's legendary treasure (Nickell 2001, 219–33), I determined to also maintain a vigil for the *Teazer* light, since I was there about three days after a full moon. Alas, the phantom ship was a no-show, but that was hardly surprising, since one of the last sightings was reported in 1935 (Colombo 1988, 32). (I wondered whether the diminishing of apparition reports could be due to encroaching light pollution, from homes, marinas, and so on, obscuring the spectral phenomenon.)

Nevertheless, my research into the case led to a revealing account by one local man who, with some friends, had actually witnessed the phenomenon of the fiery ship from Borgal's Point. Shaking their heads in wonderment, they went indoors for about a quarter of an hour. When they then returned to have another look, "there, in exactly the same place, the moon was coming up. It was at the full, and they knew its location by its relation to Tancook Island." The young man understood what had happened.

> It struck him that there must have been a bank of fog in front of the moon as it first came over the horizon that caused it to appear like a ship on fire, and he now thinks this is what the Malone Bay people have been seeing all these years. If the fog had not cleared away that night he would always have thought, like all the other people, that he had seen the *Teazer*. (Creighton 1957)

HAUNTED CEMETERY (ARGENTINA)

It is a memorable sight, "a city within a city," as one writer describes it (Winter 2001). It is really a city of the dead, located in Buenos Aires (which I visited for the 2005 Primera Conferencia Ibroamericana Sobre Pensamiento Critico, i.e., the First Latin American Conference on Critical Thinking). A necropolis consisting of narrow alleys lined with ornate crypts and mausoleums, Cementerio de la Recoleta offers a prestigious final address to the once rich and powerful, including Eva Peron (the late actress turned controversial first lady). Recoleta is considered "one of the world's grandest graveyards" (Bernhardson 2004, 72). See figure 22.1.

Figure 22.1. Recoleta Cemetery in Buenos Aires is a veritable city of the dead. (Photo by Joe Nickell.)

Some say the cemetery is haunted, while an Internet search turned up a cautionary remark: "Everybody will tell you the stories about this interesting place, but don't believe all of them; ghosts don't walk there at night" (Fodors.com 2004). Sure enough, two days after my visit, a local guide told me just such a tale about the cemetery.

As the story goes, one night a man met a woman in the neighborhood and the pair went to the cemetery for a tryst. She borrowed a jacket from him but then suddenly ran away. He followed, searching for her. Eventually, he found his jacket at a crypt bearing a picture of a young woman who was entombed there. It was the same young lady!

The guide who related the tale, Paola Luski (2005), told me she was dubious of it. She said one reason to question the story was the general absence of pictures of the deceased at the tombs of Recoleta.

More important, the tale seems especially doubtful because of its obvious similarity to the widespread "Vanishing Hitchhiker" urban legend (albeit without that story's automobile). Shared narrative elements (or *motifs* as folklorists say) include the meeting of the pair, their linking up, the young lady's disappearance, and the cemetery as the final destination and scene of revelation. The jacket (like the coat, sweater, etc., present in some versions of the proliferating hitchhiker tale) is clearly intended to provide verisimilitude (a sense of truthfulness) to the story, and it represents an unmistakable link with the famous roadside-phantom narrative.

Thus, the Recoleta tale is simply another variant of the ubiquitous legend that has antecedents as far back as 1876. Again, as American folklorist Jan Harold Brunvand (1981, 21) points out, multiple versions of a tale provide "good evidence against credibility."

A GESTURING GHOST (AUSTRALIA)

Called "Australia's most famous ghost" (Davis 1998, 16), the alleged specter of Frederick Fisher has attracted such notables as Charles Dickens (who published a version of the story in his *Household Words*) and magician John Pepper (who featured it as the subject of his "Pepper's ghost" stage illusion in a circa 1879 Sydney performance). The tale has been presented in poems, songs, plays, operas, books, and countless newspaper articles, as well as being the inspiration for a movie and the focus of an annual festival in Campbelltown. In 2000, I investigated the case on-site, assisted by magic historian Peter Rodgers (with whom I shared other investigations and adventures [Nickell 2004, 289–95, 331–34]).

Briefly, the story began with Fisher's disappearance on June 17, 1826. He was a paroled convict who had built a shack in Campbelltown, where he caroused with other parolees and ne'er-do-wells, including his neighbor George Worrell. To protect his assets while he was in prison, he had signed over his property to Worrell, only to discover on his release that his supposed best friend had been claiming it as his own. When Fischer conveniently disappeared, Worrell told inquirers that the ex-con had returned to England. However, suspicions were raised when Worrell began wearing Fisher's clothes and "proved" his ownership of one of Fisher's horses with a crudely forged sale receipt.

The Colonial Secretary's Office on September 23 offered a reward for "the discovery of the body of the missing man," or a lesser amount for proof that he had indeed "quitted the Colony." At this point, a townsman named James Farley reportedly encountered Fisher's ghost! Walking near Fisher's property one evening, he spied Fisher's apparition, sitting on a fence, emitting an eerie glow, and bleeding from a gashed head (figure 22.2). Moaning, the specter "pointed a bony finger in the direction of the creek that flowed behind Fisher's farm." The sighting prompted a police search of the area, and soon Fisher's corpse was unearthed. Subsequently, Worrell was arrested, convicted, and executed—reportedly confessing just before he was hanged (Fowler 1991, 13).

Figure 22.2. Artist's depiction of Fisher's ghost appearing to a fellow Australian. (From a nineteenth-century wood engraving.)

So Fisher's ghost acted like many another purposeful phantom of yore that sometimes "advised where their bodies might be discovered" (Finucane 1984, 194). Or did it? An examination of the records in the proceedings of the Supreme Criminal Court of February 2, 1827, shows that nowhere is there any mention whatsoever of the ghost. In fact, the proceedings demonstrate that Fisher's missing body was located in a purely rational—not supernatural—manner. Constable George Looland testified that blood on fence rails at Fisher's paddock led him to search the area, assisted by two Aboriginal trackers. They came to a marshy spot where there was apparently a surface disturbance and probed with an iron rod before procuring a spade to excavate farther. Soon they had revealed "the left hand of a man lying on his side," but left further exploration for the coroner. When the corpse was subsequently examined, "several fractures were found in the head" (Supreme Criminal Court 1827).

The fanciful story of the gesturing ghost may have been launched by an anonymous poem, a *fictionalized* narrative published in 1832. And over time the tale shows evidence of folkloric evolution. For instance, the earliest account of the tale has Fisher sitting on the rail of a fence, but that motif was eventually transformed into the rail of a bridge, and, when the bridge over Fisher's Ghost Creek was rebuilt at a different site, the supposed apparition followed. One such sighting in 1955 proved to be only a white cow in the distant darkness! (Nickell 2004, 304–10)

↓GHOSTLY PORTENTS (RUSSIA) ↑

According to *The International Directory of Haunted Places* (Hauck 2000, 129–31), Russia has haunting phenomena similar to those now reported around the world. However, a published photograph showing a "Moscow ghost" looks like nothing more than a wandering fingertip bouncing back the flash!

Of more interest are the reported apparitions. At the Kremlin the specter of Ivan the Terrible has reportedly been seen on several occasions. Most appearances occurred during 1894, prior to the wedding of Nicholas II to Alexandra, when Nicholas was to accede to the throne after his father's death. Purportedly, the phantom of Ivan brandished his scepter while flames danced around his face (Nickell 2004, 311–12).

The ghost of Lenin (1870–1924), the Russian revolutionary, also allegedly haunts the Kremlin. His spirit purportedly contacted a medium in 1961 to tell her he resented sharing his mausoleum with the late dictator Joseph Stalin (1879–1953). The medium—herself a communist heroine who is devoted to Lenin and who was imprisoned by Stalin—disclosed Lenin's alleged feelings in an address she gave to the Party Congress; the following night the dictator's body was disinterred and relocated elsewhere.

These examples of apparitions—typical of those reported elsewhere and no doubt similarly explained (see appendix for "apparitional experiences")—demonstrate a tendency for Russian apparitions to serve as omens. People tend to perceive ghosts in terms of their own cultural attitudes, notes R. C. Finucane (1984) in his *Appearances of the Dead: A Cultural History of Ghosts*. As purposeful as are, say, the ghosts of Shakespeare's plays (recall how the specters of Hamlet's father and Banquo were motivated by revenge), those of Russian historical figures similarly function as portents in anxious times.

When I toured the Kremlin in 2001 and stood before Lenin's mausoleum in Red Square, I too (although not seeing ghosts) could feel the impress of history. Considering the frequently troubled past of the country, and magnified by history and legend, such personages as Lenin and Ivan the Terrible loomed large—haunting, so to speak, my thoughts.

ANCESTRAL SPIRITS (CHINA)

In Chinese culture, ghosts take many forms, from malevolent entities to revered ancestral spirits. Notable among the latter are certain practices dedicated to the memory and respect of one's deceased loved ones. One feature—comparable to Mexico's Day of the Dead (Nickell 2007, 127–29)—is a special day in early April on which occurs Qing Ming, or the "Tombsweeping Festival." At this time, families ritually cleanse ancestral gravesites and provide offerings to their spirits in the form of wine, food, and flowers, as well as something called "ghost money" (Mooney 2008, 60).

Ghost money is paper currency that is burned as an offering, intended for use by one's deceased loved ones. It is burned at graves, in passageways between buildings, and on roadsides—especially during Qing Ming and another popular festival (held in the seventh month of the lunar calendar) called the Ghost Festival. I learned of this practice during my three weeks in Beijing in October 2010 as CFI's visiting scholar (on an exchange program with the China Research Institute for Science Popularization).

During my stay, *China Daily* published a large feature article on the practice, which began as early as the Qin Dynasty (221–206 BCE), when Chinese people burned not only paper money but other paper items at funerals. In the Wei Dynasty (220–265 CE) and continuing to the present (although deteriorating during the "cultural revolution" of 1966–1976), people began to make small effigies of everyday items, crafted of paper and intended to be burned to assist the deceased in the afterlife. In time, luxury items—watches, cars, and digital cameras, even brand-name handbags—would be copied in paper and sold in the *ming zhi pu*, or "ghost money shops" (Cheng 2010).

Although fewer paper effigies are used today, the tradition continues, despite some environmental concerns that have resulted in prohibitions on burning by property-management companies and others. The skilled craft work, sometimes passed down from father to son, is demanding, given the unusualness of some requests. One master craftsman, Au Yeung, says clients may order items like special food dishes (such as sour and spicy pork, rice noodles, and black pepper chicken wings) from famous eateries. The paper re-creations must look like the real thing. As Au Yeung says, "I not only need to please the customer but also the person who is receiving the gift in the afterlife" (Cheng 2010).

MALEVOLENT SPIRITS (MOROCCO)

In mysterious Morocco for several days in 1971—traveling from Ceuta to Tangiers, Rabat, Casa Blanca, and Marrakesh ("the most African" of Moroccan cities [Barosio 2001, 13])—I experienced the country's often-superstitious subculture—where female fortune-tellers prognosticate by laying out bright, cheap playing cards; snake charmers perform (teasing cobras with a tangle of lesser serpents); "doctors" use dubious diagnostic methods (such as totaling the lengths of a patient's fingers and checking that against the length of his forearm) before administering colored powders; and so on. Islam is the reigning religion, and mosques are ever present, like Marrakesh's Koutoubia Mosque, an "architectural marvel of harmonious design" graced with a 226-foot-high minaret (Barosio 2001, 110) (figure 22.3).

Ghosts are not generally accepted in Islamic theology, which holds that the soul goes upon death to a first judgment, following which it stays grave-bound until the final resurrection (Eliade 1995, 548).

In Morocco, however, there has been a popular belief "that dead saints might appear to the living and the dead might come to see their friends but remain invisible." Moreover,

The Moroccans believed that the dead would be angry if they were offended by anyone and would punish him, and if children did not visit the graves of their parents they would be cursed by them. The voices of some of the dead were thought to be audible in cemeteries, though only good people, children, and animals could hear them. If a person had been killed, the spot would be regarded as haunted, and passersby might hear him groan. (Eliade 1995, 548)

Figure 22.3. Koutoubia Mosque graces Marrakesh, Morocco. (Travel sketch by Joe Nickell.)

More commonly believed in in Morocco are the *jnun*—referred to as *jinn* in other Islamic countries—which are various devils or demonic spirits with supernatural power. They are thought to have been pre-Islamic nature demons, later adopted by Islam, and mentioned in the Qur'an (51:52) as being created by Allah. A possible dualism is admitted, with some being good, others evil (Leach 1984, 552–53); there are even reported cases of possession (Morocco 2011). While at times the jnun may be believed to haunt Moroccan graveyards and other places, it must be remembered that those entities are supposedly created spirits and "not dead people" (Eliade 1995, 548).

As these several examples show, belief in ghosts or other "haunting" spirits is ubiquitous—common to differing cultures and times. These examples also show considerable diversity, together with a surprising commonality—not unlike the varied cultures of humanity themselves.

PART 3:
COMMUNICATION
WITH THE DEAD

Chapter 23

A SKELETON'S TALE: THE ORIGINS OF MODERN SPIRITUALISM

More than half a century after modern spiritualism began with pur-ported communications from the ghost of a murdered peddler, the reality of the messages was allegedly confirmed. A skeleton was report-edly uncovered in the cellar of the original farmhouse where the séances had taken place, along with the peddler's tin trunk. Now, a century after that, the claims are again being touted by spiritualists who have enshrined the exca-vated foundation (figure 23.1)—sort of a spiritualists' equivalent of the Mor-mons' Hill Cumorah (where Joseph Smith claimed he received a book written on gold plates from the angel Moroni [Nickell 2004]). Assisted by research librarian Timothy Binga, director of the Center for Inquiry Libraries, I sought to uncover the true facts in the case.

BACKGROUND

Modern spiritualism began in Hydesville, New York, in 1848. At the home of a blacksmith named John Fox, strange rapping noises began to occur in the bedroom of Fox's young daughters, Margaret ("Maggie") and Katharine ("Katie"). The girls claimed the noises were communications from the departed spirit of a murdered peddler. After a time, on the night of March 31 (All Fool's Eve!), the girls' mother witnessed a remarkable demonstration that she later described in a signed report.

Figure 23.1. CFI librarian Timothy Binga stands at the enshrined site of the birthplace of spiritualism. (Photo by Joe Nickell.)

Loudly, Katie addressed "Mr. Splitfoot," saying "do as I do," and clapping her hands. At once, there came the same number of mysterious raps. Next Maggie exclaimed, "Now do just as I do; count one, two, three, four," clapping her hands accordingly. Four raps came in response (Mulholland 1938, 30–33).

Next, the peddler's spirit began to answer questions by rapping, once for *no*, twice for *yes*. He claimed he had been murdered and his body buried in the cellar, but digging there produced only a few bones attributed to animals (Weisberg 2004, 57).

Before long, people discovered that the girls could conjure up not only the ghostly peddler but other obliging spirits as well. The demonstrations received such attention that the girls' older sister, Leah Fish, originated a "spiritualistic" society. "Spiritualism" began to take on the trappings of religion, with hymns being sung at the opening and close of a session (which they called a "séance"). Following a successful visit to New York, Leah took the girls on tour to towns and cities across the nation. Everywhere people were anxious to communicate with the souls of their departed loved ones.

However, scientists and other rational-minded investigators came forth to challenge Maggie and Katie's claims. Early on, University of Buffalo faculty members studied the girls' raps. The examiners excluded "spiritual causation" and asserted, curiously enough, that the raps were "produced by the action of the will, through voluntary action on the joints." In a much later investigation, the "spirits" gave out erroneous information, and investigators caused the rapping sounds to cease abruptly by controlling Margaret's feet (Mulholland 1938, 34–38).

Then, four decades after spiritualism began, sisters Margaret Fox Kane and Katherine Fox Jencken confessed it had all been a trick. On Sunday, October 21, 1888, the sisters appeared at the Academy of Music in New York City. With Katherine sitting in a box and repeatedly nodding in agreement while a number of spiritualists expressed their disapproval with groans and hisses, Margaret revealed all from the music hall stage. She explained how she had produced the rapping noises by slipping her foot from her shoe and snapping her toes. Placing her stockinged foot on a thin plank, she demonstrated the effect for the audience. As the *Evening Post* reported the following day, "Mrs. Kane now locates the origin of Modern Spiritualism in her great toe" (quoted in Christopher 1970, 181). Margaret went on to state:

> I think that it is about time that the truth of this miserable subject "Spiritualism" should be brought out. It is now widespread all over the world, and unless it is put down it will do great evil. I was the first in the field and I have the right to expose it.
>
> My sister Katie and myself were very young children when this horrible deception began. I was eight and just a year and a half older than she. We were very mischievous children and we wanted to terrify our dear mother, who was a very good woman and very easily frightened. At night when we were in bed, we used to tie an apple to a string and move it up and down, causing the apple to bump on the floor, or we would drop the apple

on the floor, making a strange noise every time it would rebound. Mother listened to this for a time. She could not understand it and did not suspect us of being capable of a trick because we were so young.

At last she could stand it no longer and she called the neighbors in and told them about it. It was this that set us to discover the means of making the raps.

Margaret explained:

My sister Katie was the first one to discover that by swishing her fingers she could produce a certain noise with the knuckles and joints, and that the same effect could be made with the toes. Finding we could make raps with our feet—first with one foot and then with both—we practiced until we could do this easily when the room was dark. (quoted in Mulholland 1938, 41–42)

Margaret also stated that Leah knew the spirit rappings were fake and that when she traveled with the girls (on their first nationwide tour) it was she who signaled the answers to various questions. (She probably chatted with sitters before the séance to obtain information; when that did not produce the requisite facts, the "spirits" no doubt spoke in vague generalizations that are the mainstay of spiritualistic charlatans.)

Margaret repeated her exposé in other cities close to New York. However, explains John Mulholland (1938, 43), "It was expected that this would give her sufficient income to live but she shortly discovered that while many people will pay to be humbugged few will pay to be educated."

Perhaps not surprisingly, then, Margaret returned to mediumship when she needed money again. After her death on March 8, 1895, thousands of spiritualist mourners attended her funeral.

Today, spiritualists characterize Margaret's exposé as bogus, attributing it to her need for money or the desire for revenge against her rivals or both. However, not only were her admissions fully corroborated by her sister, but she also demonstrated to the audience that she could produce the mysterious raps just as she said (Christopher 1970, 181).

THE DISCOVERY

The Fox sisters had seemingly fooled the world, but, after the turn of the century, new evidence for their supposed genuineness was allegedly discovered. As reported by the *Boston Journal* of November 23, 1904:

> The skeleton of the man who first caused the rappings heard by the Fox Sisters in 1848 has been found between the walls of the house occupied by the sisters, and clears them from the only shadow of doubt held concerning their sincerity in the discovery of spirit communication.
>
> The Fox sisters declared that they learned to communicate with the spirit of a man, and that he told them he had been murdered and buried in the cellar. Evacuation failed to locate the body and thus give proof positive of their story.

The *Journal* continued:

> The discovery was made by school children playing in the cellar of the building in Hydesville known as "The Spook House," where the Fox sisters first heard the wonderful rappings. A reputable citizen of Clyde, who owns the house, made an investigation, and found an almost entire human skeleton between the crumbling walls, undoubtedly that of the wandering peddler who it was claimed was murdered in the east room and buried in the basement.
>
> Examination revealed that a false and unobserved inner wall had been built. Between this false inner wall and the original outer wall and near the center of the basement, the skeleton was found. It is interesting to know that the false wall is composed of stones like those used fifty years ago to build stone fences. This recalls a statement made over fifty years ago by Miss Lucretia Pulver, that Mr. Bell [the earlier house owner and presumed murderer] worked each night under cover of darkness, carrying stones from the fence into the cellar. The finding of the bones corroborates the sworn statement made by Margaret Fox [the girls' mother], April 11, 1848. (quoted in Muldoon 1942, 20–24)

Additional stories appeared in other newspapers ("Bones" 1904; "Fox House Figures" 1904; "Headless Skeleton" 1904; "Topics of the Times" 1904).

This reputed discovery was trumpeted by spiritualists over the following decades, along with a "tin peddler's pack"—actually a tin trunk (figure

23.2)—that was allegedly discovered at the same site (Keeler 1922, 60). The trunk was later kept in the cottage that had been moved to Lily Dale spiritualist village in 1916 and used as a museum. The cottage remained there until it was destroyed by fire in the 1950s. While the trunk was saved, skeptics have long questioned its authenticity (Weisberg 2004, 266–67).

Figure 23.2. Joe Nickell examines the alleged "peddler's trunk" at Lily Dale Museum. (Author's photograph by Diana Harris.)

INVESTIGATION

To review the alleged discoveries at the Fox cottage's cellar, I twice visited the site, taking photographs and making a diagrammatic sketch of the stone structure; interviewed knowledgeable persons; examined Fox-related artifacts, including the reputed peddler's trunk at the Lily Dale spiritualist museum; with Tim Binga, conducted research at the public library at Newark, New York (where I joked that my work was so important I had "brought my own librarian"); and studied a valuable collection of old papers, clippings, and photographs that was generously sent over to the library for our use by the Newark-Arcadia Historical Society. We also sought out rare books and journals and did much other work, all of it demanding but ultimately paying dividends.

Unfortunately, as it happens, there is reason for skepticism of nearly every aspect of the case. To begin with, the earliest published testimonies never gave the peddler's name, only the initials "C. B.," with the *B* specifically applying to the surname (Lewis 1848, 10). Only later was the name said to be "Charles B. Rosna" or some variant; Sir Arthur Conan Doyle (1926, 1:64, 76) insisted it was actually "Charles B. Rosma." Another source gives "Charles Rosa" (Guiley 2000, 141).

In fact, no one has been able to find a single record or other proof of the existence of a peddler named Charles B. Rosna/Rosma/Rosa. One source was forced to conclude, lamely, that the name "might have been misspelled" (Pressing n.d., 63), but no peddler with any similar name has ever been identified. We, too, looked—in vain.

At the old cottage site we studied the restored foundation and its double wall, the "false" interior one having ostensibly been placed secretly to hide the peddler's corpse (Muldoon 1942, 20–21; Keeler 1922). However, it is apparent that the wall in question is actually just one of four inner walls that likely represent an original, boxlike foundation (figure 23.3). That foundation was apparently later enlarged into a rectangular shape by the addition of new walls around the old ones (creating unequal spaces between the walls at either end and thickening the front and rear walls at the same time). Perhaps the extra foundation resulted from the house having been expanded from a cabin into a cottage. We later discovered that the "two separate stone foundations" were confirmed in 1904 ("Headless Skeleton" 1904).

As to the bones themselves, their authenticity was questioned at the time of their alleged discovery. The *New York Times* reported that the bones had created a stir "amusingly disproportioned to any necessary significance of the discovery" ("Topics of the Times" 1904). That was because there was no proof either that the bones belonged to the "legendary peddler" or that the Fox sisters had done anything more than capitalize on a then-current rumor that a peddler was murdered at the site. The *Times* said of spiritualists' claims about the bones, "As usual, they are taking all possible pains to render a real investigation of the affair impossible, and are assuming as true a lot of things much in need of other proof than their own assertions."

Figure 23.3. A reputedly false inner wall (left) of Fox cottage is actually only part of a smaller, four-walled, inner foundation. (Photo by Joe Nickell.)

The *Acadian Weekly* ("Fox House Figures" 1904) opined that while the bones might have been hidden in the wall for half a century, they might equally have been "disinterred from some cemetery and placed there for effect." The paper referred to the original 1848 story of spirit communication at the cottage as "the old hoax."

Eventually, the true source of the bones was reported in an editorial in the *Journal of the American Society for Psychical Research* in 1909. A physician had been asked by another publication (the *Occult Review*) to investigate the alleged discovery:

He reports to us that he found a number of bones there, but that there were only a few ribs with odds and ends of bones and among them a superabundance of some and a deficiency of others. Among them also were some chicken bones. There was nothing about the premises to indicate that they had been buried there, but might have been put there by boys in sport. He also reports that within a few days past he has learned that a certain person near the place had put the bones there as a practical joke and is now too much ashamed of it to confess it. Whether there is any better foundation for these incidents than for the original story it is not possible to decide, but it is certain that the probabilities that there is anything more than a casual coincidence or than a trick played on the credulity of the defenders of the Fox sisters are very much shaded. ("Editorial" 1909)

But then what about the peddler's trunk, allegedly found at the same site and time as the bones? As a matter of fact, the trunk was never reported in any of the contemporary sources we uncovered. The earliest mention of it I have found is an account penned years later by one P. L. O. A. Keeler (1922), a Lily Dale medium who had a reputation for faking spirit writing and other phenomena (Nickell 2007). I examined the trunk at the Lily Dale Museum, whose curator, Ron Nagy (2006), conceded there was no real provenance for it or any proof of its discovery in 1904. And the trunk's condition appears far too good for its supposed half-century burial (again, see figure 23.2).

CONCLUSIONS

The modern unearthing of the Fox cottage's foundations did nothing to support the claim that in 1848 schoolgirls had communicated with the spirit of a murdered peddler. Instead, the excavation made it possible for everyone to see that no "false wall" had been built to hide the legendary peddler's remains but that it was merely part of an earlier, smaller foundation. The best evidence indicates that the 1904 "discovery" of the peddler's bones was a hoax; ditto the later appearance of the tin trunk. Therefore, the Fox sisters' confessions stand, corroborated by independent evidence that the spirit rappings they produced were accomplished by trickery.

Chapter 24

SPIRIT SEARCH: WILLIAM JAMES AND THE SPR

Rivaling the new burst of rationalism among philosophers and scientists that was spawned by Charles Darwin's theory of evolution in the late nineteenth century, a countermovement of "spiritualism" and "unexplained" phenomena spread among the credulous. The craze had been sparked in 1848 at Hydesville, New York, when two schoolgirls, Maggie and Katie Fox, supposedly channeled the ghost of a murdered peddler. Although four decades later they confessed that their "spirit rappings" had been produced by trickery (see previous chapter), in the meantime, "mediums" and "psychics" flourished.

In her book *Ghost Hunters: William James and the Search for Scientific Proof of Life after Death* (2006) (figure 24.1), journalism professor and Pulitzer Prize–winner Deborah Blum chronicles the response of the scientific community. She focuses on a small band of scientists who set out with the intention of proving the reality of the supernatural and thus uniting religion and science. In 1882 in London they founded the Society for Psychical Research (SPR).

In an apparent attempt at evenhandedness, however, Blum risks giving readers the impression (so criticizes the *New York Times*) that the SPR "was on to something" (Gottlieb 2006). She opens the book with a spine-tingling tale investigated by William James himself, the noted Harvard philosopher and psychologist. Blum tells how sixteen-year-old Bertha Huse of Enfield, New Hampshire, set out one October morning in 1898 for the mill where she worked. She left a trail of footprints in the frost but they soon disappeared, along with Bertha herself. One hundred and fifty people searched nearby woods and fields—even the waters of Mascoma Lake, traversed by an old

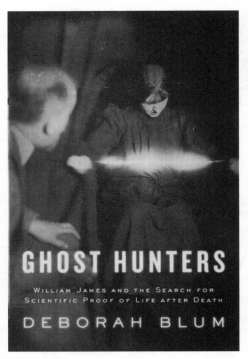

Figure 24.1. *Ghost Hunters: William James and the Search for Scientific Proof of Life after Death*, by Deborah Blum.

Shaker bridge. A Boston diver was called in, but he too failed to locate the girl. "It was as if," writes Blum, "Bertha had vanished into the dawn itself."

Then came "the nightmare that caused a woman in a nearby town to start screaming in her sleep" (Blum 2006, 2). Soon the woman, Nellie Titus, was very precisely directing the diver to a spot where, she said, the girl was wedged head down in the bridge's wooden structure, as indeed Bertha was soon found. James had his wife's cousin interview those involved, and he concluded, "My own view of the Titus case consequently is that it is a decidedly solid document in favor of the admission of a supernatural faculty of seership" (5).

Blum is prepared to leave readers with the distinct impression that only Mrs. Titus's clairvoyant powers could explain such a remarkable case. She writes: "When I started this book, I saw myself as the perfect author to explore the supernatural, and a career science writer anchored in place with the sturdy shoes of common sense." But her research changed the way she thought: "I still don't aspire to a sixth sense, I like being a science writer, still grounded in reality. I'm just less smug than I was when I started, less positive of my rightness" (Blum 2006, 323). She may also be less critical in her judgments.

CRISIS APPARITIONS

Blum does acknowledge the frequent revelations of genuinely skeptical scientists and investigators, like British zoologist Ray Lankester, who caught medium Henry Slade faking "spirit" writing on blank slates (Blum 2006, 67), and physicist Michael Faraday, whose table-tipping experiments demonstrated that mediums and amateur spiritualists were guilty of putting pressure on table tops, often unconsciously (20–21).

Yet she presents, for instance, case after unexplained case of what SPR researcher Edmund Gurney called "crisis apparitions." Typically someone encountered a loved one in a dream or apparition, only to discover later that—at that precise moment—the person had died. Blum seems to accept Gurney's evidence (in *Phantasms of the Living* [1886]) that the tales were well authenticated, rather than follow a journalist's instinct that they seem too good to be true.

Indeed, one early case reported by Gurney and his colleague Frederic Myers (1884)—supposedly providing irrefutable evidence for apparitional phenomena—is instructive. A Shanghai jurist, Sir Edmund Hornby, had been awakened one evening by a newspaperman who had arrived belatedly to get the customary written judgment for the next day's edition. The man, appearing "deadly pale," only left after the judge provided a verbal summary, which the reporter recorded in his notebook. The following day Judge Hornby learned that the newspaperman had died during the night; although his family attested that he had never left the house, *with his body was discovered a notebook containing a summary of Hornby's judgment*! The judge added that his wife would verify what he had told her on the night in question and that other details were confirmed by an inquest.

Alas, investigation soon revealed that the newspaperman had not died at one in the morning as reported, but between eight and nine a.m. "after a good night's rest"; that the judge could not have told his wife about the events at the time, because he was then between marriages; and finally, that although the story depends on a certain judgment that was to be delivered the next day, no such judgment was recorded. Confronted, Judge Hornby conceded, "My vision must have followed the death (some three months) instead of synchronizing with it." Bewildered, he added that had he not felt he could rely on his memory, he would not "have ever told it as a personal experience" (quoted in Hansel 1966, 188–89). This case clearly shows why investigators must be suspicious of such anecdotal evidence.

ON CREDULITY

Much of Blum's attention is appropriately given to William James and to "the medium that James knew best" (Blum 2006, 224), Leonora Piper, a medium who—in contrast to the likes of the infamous Eusapia Palladino[1]—was never exposed. But Blum could have profited from reading Martin Gardner's two-part treatise on how Mrs. Piper bamboozled James and others.

James (1992, 1:20), reports Gardner, "was too gullible and ignorant of methods of deception to appreciate the ease with which intelligent persons can be deceived by crafty charlatans." He adds: "As all magicians know, men of science who know nothing about magic are the easiest of all people to fool. As I like to say, electrons and microbes don't cheat, but psychics do." Gardner shows how Mrs. Piper "did an enormous amount of what was then called 'fishing' and today is called 'cold reading'" (1:23). She also appeared to use information learned in earlier sessions and to benefit from what was said and done while she was in a "trance." Notes Gardner (2:38), "Because believers in Mrs. Piper were convinced she could recall nothing of what was said during a séance, it never occurred to them that Mrs. Piper might be lying."

TOWARD A SOLUTION

But what about William James's report on the disappearance and clairvoyant discovery of the body of young Bertha Huse, mentioned earlier? Surely that cannot be explained away. Well, as it happens, I looked into that very cold case, and here is what I found.

The tragedy occurred on Monday, October 31—Halloween—1898. SPR's journal observed, regarding the supposed "supernormal character" of the case, that "the main question would seem to be how much information existed in the neighborhood about the girl's doings which might have furnished the material for Mrs. Titus's trance-impressions" ("Proceedings" 1907, 124).

As it happened, the missing girl had been seen not only on the street that led to the bridge but, by one witness, actually on the bridge itself. Moreover, according to contemporary reports, a light frost on the morning the girl vanished recorded her footprints "on to the bridge and up to a distance unrecorded upon it," a fact "known to all the town" ("Proceedings" 1907,

125). Of course, it may not have been known to everyone at the time of the initial search, and the diver may not have been apprised of it. He had searched the length of the long bridge on both sides in water so dark that he could not see at all. He would no doubt have benefited from having his search redirected to an area just beyond where the footprints had ended, where, indeed, he "found the body entirely by feeling" (125). In other words, Mrs. Titus's vision might have had a natural, rather than supernatural, explanation.

I suspect that an in-depth skeptical investigation at the time would have rendered the case even less astonishing than it now appears—in contrast to Deborah Blum's rather mystifying version of events. Although Blum has written a good book, a more skeptical and investigative approach would, I am convinced, have produced a better one.

Chapter 25

GHOSTWRITTEN TEXTS?

Did famed orator Robert Green Ingersoll communicate posthumously through a spiritualist medium to recant his atheism? Published texts claim just such a visitation and recantation, but were they authentically written by him?

DO SPIRITS WRITE?

Spiritualist mediums—those who purport to communicate with the dead—use many approaches to convince the credulous of their ability. Many have been caught cheating when spirits purportedly produce physical phenomena such as slate writing, paintings, vocalizations, and "materializations," as well as photography and other effects.

The great magician Harry Houdini (1874–1926) spent his last years exposing spiritualist fraud. After his death, several mediums claimed to have contacted his repentant spirit. One, Arthur Ford, was later shown to be a clever fraud artist (Nickell 1991, 57–58). In 1969, I sat with a medium in a séance I had arranged for a Canadian Broadcasting Corporation radio program. In the dimly lit Toronto studio, the medium went speedily into a "trance," then vocalized an implicitly apologetic speech, supposedly from Houdini in the spirit realm but actually a most unconvincing bit of fakery (Nickell 2004, 6).

One case I investigated supposedly involved an otherworldly Abraham Lincoln communicating by one of the two types of alleged spirit writing, slate writing—a "direct" form in which the entity itself wields the chalk. This occurred at a late-nineteenth-century séance conducted by fraudulent medium P. L. O. A. Keeler. In the brief text, "Lincoln" endorsed spiritualism and Keeler himself. However, in chapter 37 of this book, "Ghost Forensics," the writing is shown to be spurious.

Another allegedly reformed disbeliever, according to one Keeler séance, was famed orator Robert G. Ingersoll (1833–1899) (figure 25.1). His "signature" was among a group of facsimile signatures—supposedly from spirits (of mostly now-obscure spiritualists)—but actually attributable to the artistic hand of Keeler (Nickell 2004, 7). (Keeler was subsequently caught cheating—appropriately enough—by one of Houdini's undercover agents [Kalush and Sloman 2006, 465–66].)

Figure 25.1. Famed agnostic orator Robert Green Ingersoll (1833–1899) is an unlikely spirit author. (Photo courtesy of Robert G. Ingersoll Memorial Committee.)

Ingersoll also allegedly made after-death contact by means of the other type of reputed spirit writing: "automatic writing." Ingersoll was a tempting target for spiritualists. Although a confirmed atheist, he had cordial relations with many American spiritualists (Smith 1990, 344–45; Nickell 1999). His acknowledgment of the "other side" would have been greatly valued—if believed.

A version of the "Ingersoll" message first appeared in the June 1903 issue of the *Sermon* (a fact called to my attention by CFI Libraries director Timothy Binga. See figure 25.2), a spiritualist magazine published in Toronto by B. F. Austin, an excommunicated Methodist preacher and spiritualist convert. The message's recipient later said it was received in a somewhat "crude manner" and soon produced a more polished communication. This was published as a twenty-three-page pamphlet titled *A Message from Robert G. Ingersoll Transmitted by Automatic Writing through a Philadelphia Psychic* (1904).

Figure 25.2. CFI Libraries director Timothy Binga examines a scanned copy of a rare pamphlet containing a purported spirit message from Robert G. Ingersoll, the orator and atheist. (Photo by Joe Nickell.)

Asked by the psychic medium to explain how he communicated, "Ingersoll" replied in part:

> The pencil you are now holding is guided by my thoughts, but it is your physical strength which I use to move the pencil. The writing is inspired by me and I know that the work is as nearly automatic as many inventions worked by mortals.
>
> You hold the pencil and call a guide; the guide simply places their [*sic*] hand over yours to start the forces you possess into motion. The thought force we possess keeps the pencil moving until we have finished the work or your own mind becomes active. (*Message from Robert G. Ingersoll* 1904, 3–4)

AUTOMATIC WRITING

As this case indicates, many attribute automatic writing to spirits or other entities. In one famous instance, Pearl Lenore Curran of St. Louis discovered in 1913 that she was apparently taking dictation from a spirit. As her Ouija board's pointer spelled out: "Many moons ago I lived. Again I come—Patience Worth, my name." Curran soon found that "Patience" could communicate by speaking through Curran's own voice or by controlling her fingers as she typed. Alas, however, there was no evidence to confirm Patience's claim that she was born in England in 1649 or that, at age forty-five, she was killed in America by Indians. Investigator Milbourne Christopher (1970, 129) concluded that Curran had "discovered not a spirit but a way to express herself."

As another example, Swiss medium Hélène Smith (real name Catherine Elise Muller, 1861–1929) conducted séances in which she became entranced, spoke in tongues, wrote in Sanskrit, and channeled a spirit guide named Leopold as well as the spirit of the Italian sorcerer Cagliostro (for which she spoke in a deep voice). She made "astral visits" to Mars and produced automatic writing in an alleged Martian language (Guiley 1991, 553). However, that language proved to be structurally related to French, and an investigator who studied her for many years—Theodore Flournoy (1963, 44)—concluded:

> No one dares tell her that her great invisible protector is only an illusory apparition, another part of herself, a product of her subconscious imagination; nor that the strange peculiarities of her mediumistic communications

—the Sanskrit, the recognizable signatures of deceased persons, the thousand correct revelations of facts unknown to her—are but old forgotten memories of things which she saw or heard in her childhood.

I once received a letter from a man who claimed to be in Ouija-board communication with ancient entities. The man requested I investigate his claim, and I did agree to test him at his own expense. I proposed to use a Ouija-style board on which the letters were scrambled, which would be hidden from his view during the test, predicting that he would thereby only spell gibberish. I never heard from him again.

Automatic writing is produced while one is in a dissociative state. (See appendix.) It is a form of *motor automatism*, or unconscious muscular activity, the cause not only of Ouija-board planchette movement but also of such phenomena as table tipping, "trance" painting or music composition, dowsing, and so on. It is also responsible for some impulsive acts. (A second category, *sensory automatism*, includes apparitions, dreams, hallucinations, certain inspirations, etc. See Guiley 1991, 45–48; Gardner 1957, 109.)

INGERSOLL VS. "INGERSOLL"

But is the "Ingersoll" automatic writing merely the product of another imaginative person's fantasy? To assess its authenticity, I spent many hours comparing it with genuine Ingersoll selections, settling on one that was as seemingly comparable to the questioned text as I could find (Ingersoll 1887). The results were interesting.

Here is an authentic passage from Ingersoll (from his "A Tribute to Henry Ward Beecher" [1887, 421–22]):

All there is of leaf and bud, of flower and fruit, of painted insect life, and all the winged and happy children of the air that Summer holds beneath her dome of blue, were known and loved by him. He loved the yellow Autumn fields, the golden stacks, the happy homes of men, the orchard's bending boughs, the sumach's flags of flame, the maples with transfigured leaves, the tender yellow of the beech, the wondrous harmonies of brown and gold— the vines where hang the clustered spheres of wit and mirth. He loved the winter days, the whirl and drift of snow—all forms of frost—the rage and fury of the storm, when the forest, desolate and stripped, the brave old pine towers green and grand—a prophecy of Spring. He heard the rhythmic sounds of Nature's busy strife, the hum of bees, the songs of birds, the eagle's cry, the murmur of the streams, the sighs and lamentations of the winds, and all the voices of the sea. He loved the shores, the vales, the crags and cliffs, the city's busy streets, the introspective, silent plain, the solemn splendors of the night, the silver sea of dawn, and evening's clouds of molten gold. The love of nature freed this loving man.

Note the sophisticated poetic quality, complete with alliteration ("flower and fruit," "bending boughs," "silver sea") and the striking imagery ("evening's clouds of molten gold").

For comparison, here is a paragraph from "Ingersoll" (*Message from Robert G. Ingersoll* 1904, 20), allegedly written automatically:

You may believe I am drawing a fancy picture, my dear friends, but for the love of yourself, if not your fellow man, judge not what you do not believe, nor condemn not what is not absolutely wicked in the light of human kindness. Then remember that if man is capable of kindness and love the Creator of the universe is incapable of less love and kindness, and you are only a weak and ignorant vessel, touched with a spark for greater light, and when you wilfully destroy a human body you have done the utmost in your power, but you can so blacken your own soul by the desire to send others to your imaginary hell, that when you throw aside your mortal clothing you will see your soul marked with your evil intentions and hellish work, and ages may find you reaping, as you have sown, the seeds of hate and malice, and your victims reaping in your errors all the joys of eternal love in the mansions far above.

Note the biblical echoes—"reaping, as you have sown" (cf. Galatians 6:7) and "the mansions far above" (cf. John 14:2)—which seem unlikely to have come from the atheist orator.

Although the questioned text has a somewhat literary and even oratorical quality, it is ultimately unconvincing as the voice of Robert G. Ingersoll. Its long sentences are actually too long, and the percentage of polysyllabic words is too high (more than three times as much as in a comparative sample). That is to say, the style is superficially overblown. There are distinctively "wordy" passages, yet none reach the eloquence of Ingersoll. Another difference in the writings is shown by a method of literary analysis called *stylometry* (Nickell 1987, 95–97). Such an analysis includes common features like the frequency of the words *the*, *of*, and *and*—the most-used words in the English language—as a percentage of the text. In the sample, Ingersoll's use of *the*, for example, was almost four times that of the "automatically" generated "Ingersoll."[1]

While interesting, such statistical differences can fluctuate from passage to passage and may not ultimately prove dependable. Therefore, I looked at other, more revealing features.

Notably, the "Ingersoll" automatic writing has a number of grammatical errors that are missing from the authentic Robert G. Ingersoll composition. They include noun-pronoun agreement errors ("the guide . . . their," "one . . . they," "my remains . . . it," and "no mortal . . . their" [pp. 3, 7, 8, and 13]); faulty verb-subject agreement ("information and . . . inventions . . . is" and "There seems to be elements" [pp. 17 and 21]); run-on sentences (pp. 6, 9, 10); numerous instances of faulty punctuation, and at least one misspelling ("lead" for *led* [p. 12]). There is faulty parallelism ("Heaven is not ruled by forms and creeds, but [by] true love and God Almighty's laws" [p. 18]), and other writing faults as well.

TRUE AUTHORSHIP

The stylistic evidence does not support the claim that Robert G. Ingersoll posthumously wrote the spirit text attributed to him. Instead, it appears to be no more than an imitation produced by the automatic writer—however unconsciously or consciously.

The "message" pamphlet gave only the person's initials ("M. E. M."), and she was unidentifiable by standard bibliographic sources. Librarian Binga, however, finally discovered her name. It had been recorded on the Library of Congress's old catalog card as Mary E. Matter. We know little about her except that she described herself as a "Philadelphia Psychic," but we can infer something more.

Matter obviously exhibited several characteristics of what is termed *fantasy proneness*. Persons exhibiting a fantasy-prone personality are essentially sane and normal individuals who nevertheless exhibit such traits as being easily hypnotized (including falling into self-induced "trances"), claiming psychic abilities, allegedly being in touch with magical entities (e.g., spirits, alien beings, guardian angels, or the like), exhibiting automatic writing, and other traits. This personality type was characterized in a pioneering study that suggested that "individuals manifesting the fantasy-prone syndrome may have been over-represented among famous mediums, psychics, and religious visionaries of the past" (Wilson and Barber 1983, 371).

It seems curious that if Robert G. Ingersoll did indeed communicate through an automatic writer, he did not choose either to continue to do so or to find a way to provide better evidence of the reality of the "other side." His silence is revealing.

Chapter 26

THE SÉANCES OF "HELLISH NELL": SOLVING THE UNEXPLAINED

As the Allied Forces prepared for D-day toward the climax of World War II, Britain's highest criminal court was trying celebrity spiritualist Helen Duncan as a mediumistic fraud under the 1735 Witchcraft Act. Some thought she really was channeling spirits from the Beyond. But was the trial even about her questioned powers, or was it an attempt to silence her visionary revelations of top-secret naval events?

The case is treated in depth elsewhere (e.g., Shandler 2006), yet these treatments maintain an essential mystery of the affair: the precise nature of Duncan's séance materializations are left unexplained. Do clues remain that may help solve this very cold case?

"HELLISH NELL"

Today it is easy to see Helen "Nell" Duncan (1897–1956) as a successor to both the biblical Witch of Endor (1 Samuel 28:7–20) and a pair of nineteenth-century schoolgirls, Maggie and Katie Fox, who launched modern spiritualism in 1848. However, forty years later the sisters confessed that their otherworldly communications had no more substance than the alleged spirits themselves (Nickell 2001, 194). In the 1940s, spiritualists still produced "materializations" (appearances of spirits in the near-dark of séances), although these were repeatedly exposed as fraudulent.

Born Victoria Helen MacFarlane, the controversial medium had been a schoolgirl with "psychic" tendencies, earning her the sobriquet "Hellish Nell." She progressed from adolescent mill worker to unwed mother to wife of Henry Duncan, who would father seven more children with her while allowing her to support their family with her séances.

Today, Helen Duncan would be recognized as having a fantasy-prone personality (given her imaginary ghost friends, claimed magical powers such as clairvoyance, "trance" communications with higher entities, and so on [see Wilson and Barber 1983]). However, being fantasy prone does not preclude also being fraudulent if one wishes to convince others that one really does have special powers—which brings us to ectoplasm.

MATERIALIZATIONS

Ectoplasm is an imagined substance supposedly emanating from a medium in a trance state. Repeated exposés have revealed that ectoplasm is typically simulated with chiffon or cheesecloth. Easily compressible, these light fabrics are ideal for hiding and could—by inviting imagination in the near dark—simulate the spirit of a baby in a dress or, unfolded farther, a person in a transparent shroud.

Originally, spirit conjurers, such as the Davenport Brothers, would be tied up in a special "spirit cabinet" in which were placed musical instruments. After "spirits" were glimpsed outside the cabinet and music was heard playing, theater lights would eventually come on, and the brothers would be found still securely tied, "proving" no trickery was involved (Nickell 2001, 18–27).

Helen Duncan's cabinet consisted of a pair of black velvet curtains that hung from the ceiling and framed an armchair. The scene was dimly lit with a red light that produced an "unearthly glow" (Keene and Spraggett 1997, 101). The medium was first strip-searched by women in an anteroom, then confined in a large cloth sack that was closed at the neck with a drawstring, and finally bound to the chair with the knots sealed with wax.

Soon, Duncan was in an apparent trance, seemingly evidenced by her loud snoring. In time, "ectoplasm" might be seen creeping from the cabinet. Then Duncan's "spirit guide," one "Albert Stewart," would take over, engaging in banter with the sitters. An ectoplasmic blob might appear and be regarded as a baby's head; a shrouded figure, then another, might appear.

At times, a sitter would be permitted to touch the ectoplasm. It would often be described as feeling like soft cloth. One witness complained that the spirits were "fat and clammy, undoubtedly human," perhaps like Duncan draped in muslin.

At the end of the séance, Duncan might wander out from behind the curtain, "Albert" having been kind enough to free her from the tied sack. Yet the sack would be undamaged and the knots intact and still sealed. It was as if Duncan had been dematerialized to pass through the sack (Shandler 2006, 91–92).

SECRETS

Duncan was arrested on the evening of January 19, 1944. Well into the séance, bright lights came on. Although spiritualists claimed light could be fatal to a medium in the entranced state, Duncan was only dazed. She, her assistant, and the couple who ran the spiritualist church in Portsmouth were charged under the Witchcraft Act, which stated: "If any person shall pretend to exercise or use any kind of witchcraft, sorcery, enchantment, or configuration, or undertake to tell fortunes, every person so offending shall suffer imprisonment by the space of one whole year without bail" (quoted in Shandler 2006, 102).

The charges against Duncan really resulted from belated assertions that she was giving away wartime secrets: twice, it was said, she revealed the sinking of a warship—on May 24, 1941, the great battleship HMS *Hood* and on November 25 of that year, HMS *Barham*. (A rumor claimed she materialized the spirit of a sailor whose cap bore the latter ship's name [Shandler 2006, 40].) Some officials were concerned by these violations of Prime Minister Winston Churchill's order to keep all naval losses secret. Were Duncan's revelations merely the lucky result of after-the-fact matching of pronouncements and events? Or was she a true medium? Or perhaps a spy? (Surely, if the last were true, she was an especially foolhardy one!)

Whatever the case, officials seemed to be unwilling to take chances with D-day approaching. Duncan was jailed, tried, and convicted; she lost her appeal and served out her sentence at Holloway Prison. She failed to foresee a rocket strike on the prison in the summer of 1944, but she did escape injury (Shandler 2006, 206, 270).

Duncan's trial provoked a curt note from Churchill (1944) to the home secretary, wishing to know "why the Witchcraft Act of 1735 was used in a modern Court of Justice" and why officials "kept busy with all this obsolete tomfoolery." It has been claimed that Duncan's was the last witchcraft trial in Britain, but there was one more conviction under the act before Parliament replaced it in 1951 with modern legislation in the form of the Fraudulent Mediums Act (Shandler 2006, 217).

MORE SECRETS

Not everything was made clear by Helen Duncan's trial. True, there was evidence enough of her trickery, including the results of a disastrous séance in 1933. Duncan was observed creating a "Little Miss Peggy" who peeped from a nearby sideboard and lisped a nursery rhyme. Duncan created the fake spirit child and could be observed kneeling behind a cupboard, manipulating what proved to be "a woman's stockinet undervest" as if it were a sock puppet. As Shandler (2006, 172) describes it, "A dutiful sitter aimed a beam from a handheld lamp at Duncan. Flooded with light, the medium doubled over, [and] stuffed Peggy up her skirts, presumably the shortest route back to the Other Side."

Still, at the séance that led to Duncan's arrest in 1944, no trace of white cloth had been discovered. Unfortunately, while the séance room was thoroughly combed, the detective in charge chose not to have the attendees searched—Duncan, her husband, her attendant, the couple who ran the affair, and the sitters. Other detectives tried to catch Duncan *in flagrante delicto* by capturing her ectoplasmic cloth. Psychical investigator Harry Price had a doctor probe her orifices, but when he planned to take X-rays, the medium ran away. Price (1931) wrote a book suggesting that Duncan swallowed and regurgitated the cloth. Later, however, watching a famous regurgitator, Kanichchka, the Human Ostrich, who gagged loudly and brought up only small materials, Price may have harbored doubts about the hypothesis (Shandler 2006, 165–66).

And what about Duncan's escape from the bag she was confined in or, on occasion, from a specially designed séance suit? Recall that "Albert" freed her from the tied sack whose knots were still sealed. Once, in the early 1930s, psychical investigators placed her into a special suit that was stitched up the back; at the close of the séance, "Albert" pulled it off and flung it into the group of spectators, who found it intact while the medium shivered naked behind the curtains (Shandler 2006, 67–69).

REVELATIONS

Materializations are largely a thing of the past, although in recent times I have sat in dark-room séances including a "direct voice" scenario in which various voices—all sounding like versions of the medium's—speak through a supposedly levitating tin trumpet (Nickell 2004a, 42–43). As a magician and mentalist, I have studied séance magic for years, performing some feats myself and experimenting with many others (Nickell 2001, 267–75). Once, undercover, I was able to gain access to an out-of-the-way historic séance room at the spiritualist camp at Cassadaga, Florida, where séances like Duncan's had been held under the familiar red light (Nickell 2004b).

I have researched the cold case of Helen Duncan's materializations and have turned up some clues. Since Duncan was actually caught and convicted of cheating, my hypothesis is that she was always cheating and that, like both honest and dishonest tricksters, she employed a variety of techniques. My friend William V. Rauscher (2006, 537), an Episcopal priest and magician who has exposed many spiritualistic deceptions, says that among materialization cabinet mediums Helen Duncan "stands out in the history of psychical research as ultra devious, and even disgusting."

It cannot be doubted that Duncan's ectoplasm (or teleplasm when used to effect mind-over-matter feats) was cheesecloth. As pointed out by V. J. Wooley in the *Journal of the Society for Psychical Research* (1932), Harry Price's permitted flash photographs reveal that "the same holes and crease-marks [in the cloth] appeared in the pictures evening after evening." A materialized hand was obviously "a housemaid's rubber glove." Moreover, "the only non-photographic material secured was a portion of alleged teleplasm removed from the medium's mouth [where she was obviously disposing of the evidence] at the last sitting. This proved on analysis to consist of several layers of cheap paper stuck together with white of egg." Price (1933, 205) discovered from one photo that the spirit "Peggy" was "merely a picture of a girl's head cut from a magazine cover and stuck on the cheese-cloth."

If the fake medium did not introduce the cheesecloth by regurgitation—

and Woolley (1932) reminded readers that "Mrs. Duncan was never seen to swallow or regurgitate anything, nor was any foreign substance found in her pharynx"—then she hid it somewhere, not necessarily inside her body.

A very important clue, I believe, comes from the work she did to support her family before becoming a professional medium: she was a seamstress. Duncan went door-to-door by day—taking in sheets to be repaired, socks to be darned, collars and cuffs to be reversed—then worked into the night completing the tasks (Shandler 2006, 143). She could well have put her considerable sewing skills to clever use in perpetrating her spook-show deceptions.

Consider, for instance, a séance Price attended. He reports, "The medium wore her own garments (a pair of black sateen knickers, a man's coat made of the same material, and a pair of black stockings)." Although Price says casually, "We examined them carefully," he does not convince us the examiners turned the coat inside out, unstitched the lining, and looked for cheesecloth—although during the séance she was covered head to foot with seeming "yards" of it (Price 1933, 203).

On other occasions, Duncan might have used the search of her person as a diversion, allowing a confederate (such as her assistant) to pass the cloth to her after she was searched. Confessed fraudulent medium M. Lamar Keene (1997, 100–104) notes that mediums often used this method, along with other techniques. A small kit of materials could even be hidden in the folds of the séance curtain beforehand or placed there by a confederate while the medium was being searched. (Houdini, who effected handcuff escapes from a curtained cabinet, hid his lockpicks and other tools in this manner [Gibson 1930, 26–27].)

As to the sewn-up séance suit and the cloth sack in which she was tied up, Duncan might again have used her sewing skills. She could have opened a seam (say, at the bottom of the sack) to free herself. The coils of rope wound about the sack would have presented little difficulty. As Houdini knew (and I learned as a boy imitating him), a single rope wound willy-nilly leaves lots of slack; so does tying it over a coat or sack (Gibson and Young 1953, 40). Subsequently, while as "Albert" she was delivering a soliloquy, the freed medium could have used the time to quickly restitch the opened seam. (Interestingly, Houdini described various sack escapes—including "the Spirit Sack"—as early as 1921.)

Duncan's feat would actually have been far more mysterious had she still been sealed in the bag, since it would have been nearly impossible for her to return to the tied position and re-sew the bag from inside. In brief, instead of being gratuitously released by "Albert" at the end of the séance, she probably accomplished her own escape at the beginning of the performance. She then simulated the appearance of spirits and finally tried to disguise what really happened by pretending she had been supernaturally released. Her case is a study in audacity. A current movement to have her posthumously pardoned (Official Helen Duncan Website 2009) demonstrates her ability to continue fooling the gullible from the grave.

Chapter 27

SÉANCE UNDERCOVER

I have made several undercover visits to paranormal sites, such as the "haunted" Van Horn Mansion in Burt, New York (chapter 10), where, for a time in 2000, a private spiritualist circle held séances. I had infiltrated the group with the help of a friend, Ginger Burg. I sat at one table-tipping session (wherein the table tipped once for *yes*, and twice for *no*, as well as tipping to indicate letters of the alphabet, which the medium ran through out loud). I received loving messages from an aunt and uncle who, however, were nonexistent, since I had made them up on the spur of the moment. Here are a few other instances of my going undercover among the spirits.

AT CAMP CHESTERFIELD

Camp Chesterfield, the notorious spiritualist enclave dubbed "the Coney Island of spiritualism," is located in Chesterfield, Indiana. Among the many exposés it has suffered is a book-length revelation of séance trickery there by M. Lamar Keene (1976). Keene was a former Chesterfield medium who was persuaded by my friend, the Rev. William V. Rauscher, magician and psychical researcher, to confess his tricks to ghostwriter Allen Spraggett. The result was *The Psychic Mafia* (1976), a stunning chronicle of "materializations," disembodied voices speaking through floating spirit trumpets, and other séance deceptions.

I had long wished to visit Camp Chesterfield, especially after reading Keene's memoir, and in the summer of 2001 I was able to do so. Because mediums at Chesterfield were alert to anyone who might expose their frauds, and because I had recently appeared on *Dateline NBC* to help reveal the deceptions of "psychic medium" John Edward (see chapter 30), I determined to go undercover. I shaved my mustache and otherwise changed my

217

appearance, entering the spiritualist village in the person of "Jim Collins," after the name of Houdini's assistant. "Jim" limped with a cane as he strolled the grounds, sharing, with anyone who would listen, his grief over the recent death of his mother.

Among several bogus practices I would subsequently expose in the pages of *Skeptical Inquirer*—spirit card writing, dark-room spirit trumpet "vocalizations," productions of "apports" (supposedly materialized objects), and so on—there were sessions of "billet reading." In one of these, held in a chapel, I was given a slip of paper on which to list the names of loved ones who had supposedly crossed over, together with a question and my name. I was instructed to fold the paper in half, warned that to fold it otherwise would result in the medium not reading it. This would make it easy for the medium to surreptitiously flip it open with the thumb of one hand under cover of the lectern, while he held someone else's slip to his forehead. The trick would only work if all the slips looked identical by being folded the same. I penned the names, wrote the question ("Mother, will you be with me always?"), and dropped the folded slip into the basket that was passed around.

Soon the medium was drawing out the folded billets, one by one, divining their contents, and giving replies to questions supposedly from the sitters' deceased family members or friends. Some who received messages were crying in response, when the medium announced that he was "getting the Collins family." After I identified myself sitting in the back row, the medium divined each name I had listed and then said, "Your mother wants you to know she'll always be there for you." I was moved almost to tears, but then I remembered that my mother was still living and was not, in fact, named Mrs. Collins! And I felt much better—having caught another spiritualist trickster (Nickell 2004, 31–45).

CLUELESS MEDIUM

Spiritualist Phil Jordan was, he says, "raised on dreams." He claims to have experienced clairvoyant visions since he was about six years old, and he has worked as a so-called police psychic (he claims to have located a missing boy utilizing his psychic powers, although the facts in the case tell a much more mundane story [Nickell 2007, 231–35]). His fame as a psychic seemingly in decline, in 2001 he purchased the old Gould Hotel in Seneca Falls, New

York. There he offered a show, "The Spirit Connection," which his promotional literature characterized as "a show similar to *The John Edwards* [*sic*] *Show* on TV" ("Phil Jordan" 2003). (Apparently Jordan did not foresee the ultimate failure of his business venture.)

To investigate Jordan's alleged spiritualistic ability, I signed up for a show. On August 9, 2003, I disguised myself as a homely old yokel sporting slicked-back hair and nerdy horn rims. As "Johnny Adams" I took my seat at a small table bearing a nameplate lettered with a red marker, "Adams 1." Jordan soon began to give readings, attempting to provide one for each of the four dozen sitters. He employed a standard "cold-reading" technique, artfully fishing for information and making vague statements that he hoped the credulous sitter would accept, interpret, and validate. Even so, Jordan provoked a blank look from several audience members.

He did not fare so well with me. He saw a woman, he said, possibly my mother, who had swollen legs before she passed over. I scored that a miss. He also envisioned a man who had "raised hogs," which could describe my grandfather Nickell—a farmer and once member of the Kentucky state legislature—except that he was nothing like the plainspoken matter-of-fact type Jordan characterized. Other offerings were no better. And he utterly failed to have mentioned such powerful issues as my mother's Alzheimer's or the life-transforming news that came shortly thereafter: the revelation that I had a daughter, along with two grandsons, I had not known about!

And couldn't the alleged medium's spirit guides have given him my true identity? Couldn't he have gotten intimations of an impostor, or at least have sensed the overwhelmingly negative vibrations emanating from the person of "Johnny Adams?" Instead, Jordan obligingly inscribed a copy of his self-published book to "Johnny" and posed happily for a photo. I afterward dubbed him the "psychic sleuth without a clue" (Nickell 2007, 231–35).

MY SPIRIT GUIDE?

At Lily Dale, the spiritualist camp in western New York, a medium named Patricia Bartlett used to offer amateurish pastel drawings of sitters' "spirit guides," those supposed entities—typically Native Americans—who provide assistance from "the Other Side." Bartlett seemed a sweet little old lady, as I showed up at her cottage one off-season day in 2000, not many years before her death.

As she was setting out her crayons and getting her drawing board ready, I casually remarked, "You know ma'am, I think I saw my spirit guide once." She perked up, and I went on to tell her how, during a troubled time in my life, I had awakened one night to see an American Indian, who wore "three yellow feathers," standing at the foot of my bed. He said, "Everything will be all right my son," and then I must have gone back to sleep, I told her.

"That's your spirit guide!" Bartlett agreed. "We are permitted to give him a name," she went on to say, and she suggested "Yellow Bird," for the three yellow feathers he wore. "Would you like me to see if I can picture Yellow Bird?" she asked, and of course I nodded enthusiastically.

"I'm getting a big strong man," she suggested, eyeing me. "And his hair isn't . . .," she said hesitantly, indicating with her fingers hair falling straight on either side of the face, and I responded by shaking my head. "I see it as pulled back," she said, again gesturing, and as I agreed that that was Yellow Bird, she began drawing (figure 27.1). The process was a bit disconcerting, as, unlike a Coney Island sketch artist, she looked not at me but rather *past* me, as if seeing someone over my shoulder. At length, she showed me the picture. She stated that she also saw an aura around Yellow Bird and asked if I would like her to add that. I answered yes, and soon she exchanged the portrait (figure 27.2) for my fifty dollars.

Figure 27.1. The late spirit artist Patricia Bartlett produces a portrait of the author's supposed "spirit guide." (Photo by Joe Nickell.)

Figure 27.2. "Yellow Bird" was drawn by spiritualist artist Patricia Bartlett. (Photo by Joe Nickell.)

It was worth every penny for me to have a chance to investigate a spirit artist and experience the whole process myself. However, I never decided: Did she say to herself cynically that if I wanted a picture of an Indian guide she would merely give me what I wanted? Or was she sincere after all, simply imagining Yellow Bird from my word portrait and then drawing what her mind created? That is, was she a fake or a fantasizer? It was one or the other, because I had made up my story during the drive to the scenic little village.

Chapter 28

"MESSAGES" FROM THE 9/11 DEAD

On the morning of September 11, 2001, concerted terrorist attacks on New York's World Trade Center and the Pentagon building in Arlington, Virginia, claimed nearly three thousand victims. They also resulted in America's largest criminal investigation, a war in Afghanistan, and endless controversy sparked by conspiracy theorists.

Many of the family members and friends of the victims also began to convince themselves that there was a mystical aspect to the tragedy. Some claimed there had been intuitive foreshadowings of the event; others claimed that they had received certain signals from, or even experienced actual encounters with, their deceased loved ones. Now Bonnie McEneaney, whose husband, Eamon, was a 9/11 victim, has collected numerous such anecdotal accounts. Her book *Messages: Signs, Visits, and Premonitions from Loved Ones Lost on 9/11* (McEneaney 2010), bears a jacket blurb from spiritualist medium James Van Praagh (whom I once debated on a radio program). The evidence is revealing—if not in the way McEneaney intended.

BACKGROUND

At a quarter of a mile high, only eighty-six feet shorter than the Sears Tower in Chicago, the twin towers of Manhattan's World Trade Center were the second- and third-tallest buildings in the United States. One steel tower was crowned with a restaurant, the other with an observatory. Far below, beneath the multibuilding complex at the towers' bases, was a giant basement containing a five-level garage capable of parking two thousand vehicles. The World Trade Center was a huge target for terrorists. Indeed, more than eight and a half years before the towers were brought down, the garage was the site of a massive bombing that rocked the towers, led to an intense investigation by the FBI and the Bureau of Alcohol, Tobacco, Firearms, and Explosives (ATF), and culminated in the arrest and conviction of four terrorists, each of whom was sentenced to 240 years in the US penitentiary (Nickell and Fischer 1999, 237–45).

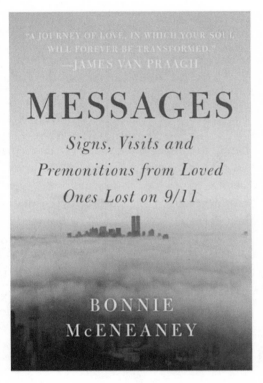

Figure 28.1. *Messages: Signs, Visits and Premonitions from Loved Ones Lost on 9/11*, by Bonnie McEneaney.

The horrific events now known as "9/11" occurred on September 11, 2001. Nineteen terrorists commandeered four commercial airplanes, crashing one into each of the World Trade Center's twin towers and another into the Pentagon near Washington, DC; only the heroic actions of passengers and crew aboard a fourth hijacked plane prevented it from reaching another target—probably the US Capitol—and instead caused it to crash in a rural Pennsylvania field.

The attacks prompted an immediate investigation by the FBI, which linked the strikes to the terrorist organization al Qaeda and its leader, Osama bin Laden (who initially denied involvement). On July 22, 2002, the National Commission on Terrorist Attacks upon the United States issued its report, which gave an account of the circumstances that surrounded the suicide attacks—including issues of preparedness and response.

The United States Department of Commerce's National Institute of Standards and Technology (NIST) conducted a technical investigation of the twin towers' collapse, culminating in a ten-thousand-page report explaining that the crashed planes caused severe initial damage and that the subsequent fires weakened the floors' support trusses, causing floors to sag and pull on the exterior steel columns, which then buckled and became unable to support the structures (Dunbar and Reagan 2006). As it happens, I was invited to lecture on critical thinking at NIST on June 28, 2007, and I was able to view some of the steel girders from the collapsed twin towers that had been analyzed by NIST experts (see figure 28.2). (In 2002, I had visited the "Ground Zero" site where the towers had stood.)

Figure 28.2. Steel girders from the collapsed World Trade Center twin towers that have been analyzed by NIST experts. (Photo by Joe Nickell.)

In time, however, conspiracy theorists began to make outlandish claims—some based on "scientific" evidence—that the towers' collapse was due not to airplane-crash damage and fire but to explosives previously installed in the buildings! Supposedly the US government intended to frame terrorists and so gain an excuse to launch the Iraq War (Griffin 2007, 2).

Meanwhile, the United States has responded to the 9/11 attacks by launching the War on Terror, beginning with the invasion of Afghanistan (whose Taliban rulers had harbored Osama bin Laden and his al-Qaeda followers) and enacting the USA PATRIOT (Uniting and Strengthening America by Providing Appropriate Tools Required to Intercept and Obstruct Terrorism) Act, which expanded both antiterrorism legislation and law-enforcement powers. Osama bin Laden has been caught and killed; an architect of the terrorist attacks, Khalid Sheikh Mohammad, and other coconspirators have been apprehended; repair of the Pentagon has been completed; rebuilding has begun at the World Trade Center site; and various memorials to the dead have been created.

SIGNS

It is not surprising that controversies and irreparable damages remain, among them the effects of the loss of so many victims. Although surviving family members and friends have tried to get on with their lives, much grief and longing remains—and the lure of superstition is not far away. Hence the quest for "messages" from the dead and the likelihood of a book such as Bonnie McEneaney's *Messages* appearing.

McEneaney gives a personal example of one of the myriad "signs" that supposedly indicates contact with victims. Seeking some such indicator regarding her husband, Eamon, she writes, "Everything around me was still—not a ripple in the air. Then all of [a] sudden, somewhere above me, I heard the beginning rush of a gust of new wind building up in intensity" (McEneaney 2010, 10). As she looked up, "I could see the wind! It created such a pattern through the leaves and the trees that it was easy to follow. It had the outline of a river." She concludes, "I didn't know how to explain the river of wind I had just seen and felt. . . . Yet I knew absolutely it was connected to Eamon and that the sad message it brought was true and real."

This seems a classic case of wishful thinking and the power of expectation. McEneaney (2010, 11) reveals that her father had twice promised, before his own death in 1993, "You know, Bonnie, when I die, I'll speak to you through the wind." Thus, she was predisposed to accept wind as a form of spirit communication, and when she witnessed a particular breeze after her husband's death, she interpreted it accordingly. Those looking for a sign are likely to find something they can interpret as such. Some pored over the things their loved ones left behind and selectively mined them for signs, engaging in a process of after-the-fact matching known as *retrofitting*.

Many of the supposed signs catalogued by McEneaney seem truly mundane: finding a coin (2010, 25–32, 195), having an experience with a bird or a butterfly (25, 28, 158), seeing a rainbow over the place where the World Trade Center once stood (134), and so on. A color photo that graces the back cover of *Messages* was taken by a woman whose husband died in the South Tower on 9/11. It shows their daughter with a streak that she interprets as a "beam of light" (4) but is probably only an effect caused by the intrusion of her camera strap. (As is typical of photographic glitches, nothing was seen until the photo was processed.) Over and over, McEneaney and those whose stories she features emphasize that an occurrence is "something that we can't explain" (e.g., 117), as if therefore it is proof of the paranormal. This is a type of logical fallacy called arguing from ignorance. ("We don't know what actually happened, so it must've been paranormal." In other words, "we don't know; therefore we do know!")

VISITS

Supposed visitations by the deceased 9/11 victims are among the most profound experiences described in *Messages* and are also among the most easily explained. Consider the seeming visit of victim Welles Crowther to a former roommate who stated: "I don't remember if it was one or two days after 9/11. I don't know if I fell asleep or not. But what I remember clearly is Welles standing in the doorway to my bedroom, saying, 'Hey, man, everything's going to be all right.' He was there just a second and then he said, 'I've got to go now'" (McEneaney 2010, 97). Another seeming visitation was reported by Deborah Calandrillo, whose husband, Joe, had worked as an accountant in the North Tower. "He appeared suddenly in the bedroom they had shared," writes McEneaney (51). "She was lying in bed. His arm was draped around her pillow. There was a solemn expression on his face. Deborah told me that she is positive she was awake when this happened."

That insistence on having been awake helps identify the experience as a common "waking dream," which occurs in the interface between being awake and asleep. This is the explanation for many paranormal encounters through the ages: visits from demons, ghosts, aliens. Along with ordinary dreams, events that are surely waking dreams are reported frequently in *Messages* (McEneaney 2010, 56–59, 101).

A rather typical waking dream was described by another friend of Welles Crowther, who—while lying on the sofa watching television (and having possibly drifted toward sleep)—heard footsteps and saw his late friend, who said, "Chuck, it's okay. I'm okay." Like most people who experience a waking dream, he thought he was not dreaming:

> First of all I don't dream very much. When I do, my dreams aren't realistic. If this was in fact a dream, it was completely realistic. I was wearing exactly what I was wearing; the television was playing exactly what it was playing. Everything was exactly as it is, and there was no break between sleeping and waking . . . between what happened and what was going on around me. It was of a piece.

He also said: "I don't remember what happened next. I don't remember if I blinked or if he just went away" (McEneaney 2010, 101). This case illustrates many of the characteristics of a waking dream, wherein, as the late psychologist Robert A. Baker noted, the experiencer "is unalterably convinced of the 'reality' of the entire experience." Baker also called attention to the fact that after the supposed encounter, the percipient typically just goes back to sleep (Baker and Nickell 1992, 130–31, 226–27).

Some percipients, like Lisa O'Brien, whose husband, Timmy, was a 9/11 casualty, appear to have had both dreams and waking dreams. "Lisa feels that Timmy is frequently in her bedroom," states McEneaney, "communicating with her in the night, sometimes when she is asleep and dreaming and sometimes just as she drifts off" (2010, 67).[1] Not surprisingly, Lisa's experiences have occurred only at night; "she has never actually seen Timmy when she is wide awake and moving about" (68). (When people claim to encounter spirits during waking activity, it is usually when they are tired, performing routine work, concentrating on some activity such as reading, or in an altered state of consciousness such as daydreaming [Nickell 2001].)

Children also often have ghostly experiences just like adults. Lisa's little daughter Jacie once told her: "Daddy is here too. He comes in the middle of the night and sits at the bottom of the bed. Sometimes he pats your hair and kisses you" (McEneaney 2010, 69). Such experiences typically express the percipient's own hopes and fears: the desire for a comforting message from a deceased loved one or the fear of an encounter with an extraterrestrial.

Jacie, at age four, was also seen at times to laugh and appear "to have conversations with invisible companions" (McEneaney 2010, 69). She said they were her daddy and his friends from work. Having invisible companions is common to those with a propensity to fantasize (Wilson and Barber 1983) and is not, of course, proof of spirit communication—no matter how often the former is equated with the latter.

PREMONITIONS

McEneaney begins her discussion of premonitions by relating a premonitory dream experienced by Abraham Lincoln, who "told several people about his dream, and he also wrote it down in his journal" (2010, 119). Lincoln described seeing a corpse upon a catafalque, around which were military guardsmen and many mourners: "'Who is dead in the White House?' I demanded of one of the soldiers. 'The President,' was his answer. 'He was killed by an assassin.' Then came a loud burst of grief from the crowd which awoke me from my dream. I slept no more that night and although it was only a dream, I have been strangely annoyed by it ever since."

Now, putting aside the fact that McEneaney's text is corrupted (differing from the original in some of its punctuation and containing—horrors!—a grammatical error), and given that Lincoln did not keep (as she reports) a journal, he probably did relate such a dream. However, he thought at the time that it was someone else who was killed, as he told Ward Hill Lamon, a friend who had accompanied him to Washington for his protection (Nickell 1999, 17). It was Lamon who, from memory, reconstructed Lincoln's words some three decades after the fact (Lamon 1895, 115–17).

The important point to make is that there is nothing remarkable about Lincoln having dreamed of death—even his own assassination. In the Civil War strife, death was all around him. Moreover, not only had an assassination plot been thwarted prior to his first inauguration in 1861, he had subsequently received numerous death threats and once had a hole shot through his top hat by an intended assassin. Lamon and others around him constantly remonstrated with him about his safety.

Likewise, it is really not surprising that World Trade Center workers and their family members had forebodings of disaster. The towers had already been the target of a most serious attack in 1993. Osama bin Laden had issued *fatwas* in 1996 and 1998 calling for *jihad* (holy war) against the United States. And the World Trade Center workers had not only the same unease that everyone has about their unforeseen future (even in the most peaceful times), they were also working in what had previously proven to be a prime terrorist target. As Martin Gardner wrote (concerning supposedly precognitive dreams of the sinking of the *Titanic*), "With respect to dreams about major disasters that make the headlines, we have no inkling of the millions and millions of times that people dream of such a disaster and nothing happens" (1986, 9). Not only will some people be motivated for various reasons to exaggerate or even fabricate such a dream (for personal aggrandizement, for example, or to promote supernatural beliefs), but even a completely honest person may unconsciously exaggerate. Gardner explains:

> After telling about a precognitive dream for the umpteenth time, one no longer recalls the dream's actual details, especially if it occurred many years ago. Dreams are hard enough to remember accurately ten minutes after waking! One is soon recalling not the dream itself but pictures that formed in the mind during previous tellings. The only way a precognitive disaster dream can have evidential value is when its details are written down before a disaster and dated in a way that can be verified, such as being described in a letter or published before the event or stated on a radio or television talk-show.

(In at least one instance—a prediction of the assassination attempt on President Reagan—even that was faked by a later, backdated taping [Frazier and Randi 1981]!)

So the after-the-fact stories McEneaney relates are simply not impressive. Take that of a woman who formerly worked in the South Tower who dreamed she was looking at "the southern tip of Manhattan" (i.e., in the direction of the World Trade Center) when she beheld "a huge explosion" and "saw something that looked almost like a mushroom cloud over the city." In the dream, she said to her husband, "Bin Laden just blew up New

York. Grab the dogs and get them away from the windows in case they shatter" (quoted in McEneaney 2010, 132). Another woman, known as "Julia C.," says she had a dream just two days before 9/11 concerning a previous country home: suddenly a big truck raced up the driveway and disappeared into the house, whereupon she saw "this huge gaping black hole with jagged edges" then "a flicker of a fire and black smoke"—images of a truck bombing she later equated with the destruction of the twin towers by crashing planes (135).

As still another example, one victim's dream journal contained a reference to an "atom bomb" that was "in the shape of a paper plane," but if that seemed significant in light of 9/11 (it was the last entry, made a month before the tragedy), it appears less so when we note that the 9/11 disaster did not involve an "atom bomb" and that, in any case, the journal's dream bomb "did not go off." Actually, the woman's dream occurred the day after she was hired to work at the World Trade Center (McEneaney 2010, 143) and may simply have been prompted by the previous bombing there. It is simply retrofitting to so selectively equate dream images with the 9/11 events. This is what yet another person (with only a late connection to the World Trade Center site) obviously did. She had had a dream of "two predatory birds"; however, McEneaney (2010, 139) states: "It wasn't until later" that she "came to see the birds as lethal aircraft."

MEDIUMISTIC OFFERINGS

Following the World Trade Center disaster, before the month was out, some family members had begun to visit so-called psychics and mediums (those who supposedly intercede on our behalf to relay messages from the spirit realm). Unlike the "physical mediumship" of the past—when spirits seemed to actually materialize or produce distinctive effects in dark-room séances, practices that repeatedly proved fraudulent—today's "mental mediumship" carries fewer risks of exposure. At the same time, the dead often seem uncertain, or perhaps they mumble, as when McEneaney herself received mention of a man whose "name was John or began with the initial *J*" (2010, 201). Not surprisingly, her husband indeed had a friend of that name. If not, a Jim or Jason or Jesse or another would have filled the bill.

McEneaney was really impressed with the psychic offering, "Your husband's name starts with *E*. Is it Emile?" (2010, 200). The fact is, his name was Eamon—yet McEneaney is willing to credit the reader with a hit. She wonders how a psychic could have gotten so close by identifying the first letter. Perhaps it was a lucky guess; perhaps McEneaney remembers exactly what was said and when. Or perhaps a friend of hers, who had apparently been to the psychic and recommended her to McEneaney, had mentioned her (and her husband's name) to the psychic—something the friend might not even remember having done.

McEneaney appears woefully unaware of psychics' techniques. Consider cold reading (so called because the psychic works "cold," without advance knowledge about the sitter). It is a method of artfully fishing for information while giving the impression that it comes from spirits of the dead. Often the reader uses what I call "the question trick": he or she asks a question that, if answered in the affirmative, is considered a hit, whereas otherwise the psychic will treat it as only part of the lead-up to a statement or to additional questions. Using body language, the sitter's own responses, and other cues and clues, the shrewd medium operates like a skilled magician but employs instead of legerdemain what might be called "sleight of tongue."

Such readings work better with the credulous, who often count only hits, while misses are either interpreted as necessary (retrofitting again) or forgotten. McEneaney does concede "that not everyone who received a message from a medium or psychic was happy with the experience" (2010, 202). One psychic told a woman that "in another life," her husband and son (both of whom had perished at the World Trade Center) "liked to go out in a bang and they were together when Mount Vesuvius blew up." The woman found such offerings neither helpful nor comforting (202).

The same woman, however, was more impressed with the clever, fast-talking "psychic medium" John Edward (real name John Edward McGee Jr.). Yet he had mentioned not a husband and son but a husband and father-in-law (apparently the latter was also deceased). Edward fared much better when he told her that she was "wearing a piece of clothing that had belonged to her husband," which she was (McEneaney 2010, 203). That seems quite accurate, but suppose he had actually asked if she had with her something of her husband's (which would perhaps be more likely than not) and the woman retrofitted the more specific "clothing" to the "something." It is difficult to judge the accuracy of such claims without complete and precise facts.

Edward uses a number of techniques, including a shotgun approach: a statement to an area of the audience rather than a single person, whereby he has multiple opportunities for someone to validate one of his offerings. He has also been known to use the technique of hot reading, passing off information *gleaned earlier* as having just come from the Other Side. He was caught cheating in this way on a *Dateline NBC* episode (for which I was both an advisor behind the scenes and an interviewee on camera [Nickell 2010]). If Edward or any other medium could actually communicate with the dead under scientifically controlled conditions, he or she could accept James Randi's Million Dollar Challenge, retire, and enjoy the accolades of science.

CONCLUSIONS

Given the overwhelming tragedy of 9/11, made very personal to those whose loved ones perished, we can well understand the emotions involved: the grief, the longing for a connection with the deceased, the wish for a final good-bye. Perceived signs, apparent visits, premonitions, or even pretended messages supposedly relayed by psychics and mediums may seem comforting—but at what expense? Such illusions come at least at the cost of sinking into superstition, at worst of falling vulnerable to fantasizers or charlatans. Sadly, this is the legacy of McEneaney's *Messages*.

Chapter 29

SYNCHRONICITIES: A PATHOLOGIST AMONG THE SPIRITS

J anis Amatuzio, MD, is a forensic pathologist—one who routinely conducts death investigations and performs autopsies to determine the cause, manner, and mode of death (as, for example, cardiac arrest resulting from arteriosclerosis due to natural causes).[1] She claims her work has also given her evidence of life after death.

In two books—*Forever Ours* (2002) and *Beyond Knowing* (2006) (figure 29.1)—she has gathered much evidence toward that end. However, it is of extremely poor quality. Consisting of "the dreams, visions, and extraordinary experiences that so many people report following the death of a loved one," the tales represent the very anecdotal evidence that science has found good reason to distrust, as we saw in the previous chapter.

For example, a woman named Laura, whose husband had succumbed to disease, was heartened by an experience that to her was profoundly mystical. While driving, she heard on the radio what she and her husband had regarded as "our song," containing phrases about "being well in heaven" and "watching over you." She told Amatuzio (2006, xv), "In that moment I changed; I mean, I knew without a doubt he was reaching out to assure me that all was well."

Now, what is Laura really saying? Of course, the experience was understandably poignant, and it no doubt seemed, as she said, "an astonishing coincidence." But to suggest that her husband was "reaching out" via a song implies that somehow his spirit controlled the record-playing mechanism at the radio station, or telepathically influenced the disc jockey to make that selection, or—the mind boggles.

Figure 29.1. *Beyond Knowing: Mysteries and Messages of Death and Life from a Forensic Pathologist*, by Janis Amatuzio, MD.

DREAM SYNCHRONICITIES

Amatuzio and many of the people reporting their experiences to her are impressed by coincidences—especially those she terms "extraordinary synchronicities" (2006, 6). (Psychologist Carl Jung [1960] used the term *synchronicity* to describe "meaningful coincidences" that appear to occur in an acausal manner.) One problem in this regard is that people tend to overestimate the rarity of such synchronous events. (For a discussion, see Falk 1981.)

Some of Amatuzio's synchronistic anecdotes involve dreams. For instance, after one of her lectures on mystical experiences, a woman named

Theresa told her of a dream she had had. In it, her friend Marge had taken her on a shopping trip and had tried on a maroon dress and gold locket. Theresa stated, "I remember I woke briefly after my extraordinary dream and saw it was midnight." The next day she learned from another friend that Marge had died during the night. When Theresa asked what time that had happened, she received the spine-tingling answer, "About midnight." The following afternoon, when she visited the mortuary, there lay Marge's body clad in a maroon dress and wearing a gold locket (Amatuzio 2006, 141–44).

Such tales are almost formulaic: someone appears in another's dream, the dreamer wakes conveniently to note the time, and he or she later discovers that the death transpired at exactly the time noted. (That the time in the foregoing story was "midnight" bespeaks of its fairy-tale quality.)

Psychologist C. E. M. Hansel (1966, 195–96) notes the elusiveness of dreams as evidence:

> Remembering some event from one's waking life of a few years back is a relatively clear-cut process compared with recalling a dream of last night. Many people recount dreams with the greatest confidence, but since a dream is a private experience there is no way of checking its factual content. It is not surprising that a large number of so-called psychic experiences involve them. The great danger in recalling the content of a dream is not only the ease with which it may be changed or embellished, but that the dating of a dream presents extreme difficulty. If a person after hearing about some event, remembers having dreamed some days before that it would happen, no one can check this fact. He may be remembering something that really happened, or the dream may have been produced and placed at a suitable position in his past at the time he hears the story.

He continues:

> Most memories of past events can be located at some point in time by virtue of the fact that they arise in a context; there are events before and after them. If this context is lacking, it will be difficult to place the memory in time, and it will lack reality. A dream largely lacks this context, and when it is recalled, there is little to guarantee that it happened last night, some other night, or that it was not primarily generated at the time of recall. Just as perception is affected by memory, recall is affected by contemporary conditions, and when the memory is vague, as when a dream is recalled, the amount of material added to it may be large.

Dream synchronicities and other anecdotally reported mystical experiences have been collected by the thousands, but, notes Hansel (189), "none of the stories investigated has withstood critical examination."

Amatuzio's anecdotes are no exception. As she presents them, they are not even admissible as evidence, lacking sufficient documentation, failing to meet the burdens of evidence and proof, violating the rule of best evidence, and consisting of mere hearsay—among other deficiencies (cf. Hill, Rossen, and Sogg 1978, 48–53, 131–35, 208–209).

EVIDENCE?

It is surprising that a forensic expert would be so inattentive to good evidence. Indeed, she actually admits, "I knew that as a scientist and a physician, I could not 'prove' these experiences to be real," placing the word *prove* in quotation marks as if proof were little more than a semblance of reality. Instead, in the most fuzzy, New Age fashion, she speaks airily about "the wisdom and truths arising from these mysteriously beautiful experiences" (Amatuzio 2006, x).

Like everyone, she recognizes that we humans are cerebral and emotional creatures. We both think and feel. For example, we can scientifically prove the fact of death and investigate its cause on the one hand, and, on the other, we can respond to death with appropriate sadness for the deceased and compassion for that person's loved ones, among other emotional responses.

The problem lies in trying to think with our emotions. Not only does Amatuzio (2006, 181, 199–201) advocate trusting "intuition" as a means of "knowing" (as if intuition never fails!), but she attempts to make it seem intellectually respectable through pseudoscientific speculations about quantum physics and cell biology (137–40). Thus, she concludes that when we begin to "awaken"—to use intuition—"we see the truth about life and gain a deep knowing, a glimpse through the mysterious veil separating the living and dead. I believe in my heart, I know, that life goes on . . . forever" (200).

But does she not know what neurological science has established, that once the brain has been destroyed, brain function ceases? With that cessation ends the ability to think and move, no matter how much we want to believe otherwise. Ghosts—even headless ones (Nickell 2006)—may haunt people's imaginations, but there is no scientific proof that they otherwise exist.

FANTASY PRONENESS

Nevertheless, like a number of other New Age doctors—such as Judith Orloff (2000), who claims psychic ability and advocates "intuitive healing"—Amatuzio "knows" the "truth" of her beliefs. Although she is intelligent and scientifically trained, she has many of the traits associated with a fantasy-prone personality—one common to many "mediums," "psychics," and "visionaries." (So does Orloff: see Nickell 2004, 215.) That personality type was characterized in a pioneering study by Sheryl C. Wilson and Theodore X. Barber (1983) that identified some thirteen shared traits. (Anyone may have a few of these—I do—and only rarely would someone have all of them. As in previous studies [Nickell 2004, 296–303], I consider six or more traits in an individual indicative of fantasy proneness. Called "fantasizers," such people are sane and normal, representing an estimated 4 percent of the population.)

Among the fantasy traits that Amatuzio exhibits are (1) *having imaginary companions in childhood* (she had "not one but two imaginary friends," named "Rara" and "Gerry" [4]); (2) *fantasizing frequently as a child* (with her "friends," for hours on end she "made up new games, fairy castles, and magic places" [4]); (3) *experiencing imagined sensations as real* (her imaginary friends and two stuffed animals "seem as real to me today as they did then" [6]); (4) *experiencing hypnagogic or hypnopompic hallucinations* (she describes a bedside visitation by "a large, light-filled being" [9]); (5) *receiving special messages from spirits, higher intelligences, or the like* (her "being" told her he was her "guardian and guide" [9]); (6) *having out-of-body experiences* (in one incident she has the sense of being "outside myself looking into the cadaver laboratory" [13]); and others.

I do not know if Amatuzio can see the obvious, that her spirit guide is merely a grown-up version of one of her childhood imaginary friends. That the notion comforts her—just as her storytellers say their dreams and synchronicities give them peace—does not establish the existence of a spirit realm. Neither does it recommend that we believe in such, lured by doubtful—even often disproved—evidence. To do so is to sacrifice reason on the altar of superstition, to be bewitched into coping with our real, natural world by embracing the fantasies of an unreal, supernatural one.

Chapter 30

JOHN EDWARD: SPIRIT HUCKSTER

Psychic medium John Edward is reemerging from relative obscurity after his popular television show, *Crossing Over with John Edward*, ended in 2004. He appears on another cable show, gives tours, has a website (http://www.infinitequest.com), and generally makes his living claiming to communicate with those who have "crossed over."

I was invited by Central New York Skeptics to join them in Syracuse, New York, for an evening with Edward. (It was held at Mulroy Civic Center on Sunday, October 11, 2009. I was accompanied by CNY Skeptics president Lisa Goodlin, David Harding, and Brian Madigan, all of whom afterward shared insightful observations on what we had witnessed.) The glib Edward—real name John Edward McGee Jr.—held forth for more than two hours. He began with a joke to the effect that although he is psychic, he nevertheless needed a GPS to get to the site. The highly credulous, adoring crowd found every gag hilarious, every platitude profound, and every lucky guess or shrewd deduction proof of communication with the dead.

OLD "SPIRITS" IN NEW BOTTLES

Edward is part of the new breed of spiritualists (like Sylvia Browne and James Van Praagh) who avoid the risky *physical* mediumship of yore. During the heyday of spiritualism, magicians such as Houdini and Maskelyne used to catch mediums at their dark-room séance deceptions, such as slate writing, floating spirit trumpets, and full-bodied "materializations." The investigators gave public demonstrations of the trickery. "Do Spirits Return?" a Houdini poster asked. "Houdini says No—and Proves It" (Gibson 1977, 157).

The new "psychic mediums" opt instead for the simpler, safer *mental* mediumship, the supposed production of messages from the Great Beyond. This itself is nothing new, but now instead of the flowery language supposedly channeled from talkative Victorians, we get fragmented bits of data from spirits seeming to have diminished memories and limited speech: "I feel like there's a *J*- or *G*-sounding name attached to this" is a typical Edward offering (Nickell 2001).

Styles change even in supposedly talking with the dead. Today's mediums employ the old fortune-teller's technique of "cold reading"—so named because the sensitive has no advance information about the sitter. He or she artfully fishes for information from the person, often asking a question which, if the answer is yes, will be treated as a "hit" but otherwise will become only part of the lead-up to a statement.

Not surprisingly, Edward has a background in fortune-telling. His mother, he acknowledges, was a "psychic junkie" who threw fortune-telling "house parties." Advised by one visiting clairvoyant that he had "wonderful psychic abilities," Edward began doing card readings for family and friends as a teenager. He progressed to giving readings at so-called psychic fairs. There he soon learned that names and other "validating information" could sometimes be better fitted to the dead than the living. Edward eventually changed his billing from "psychic" to "psychic medium" (Edward 1999), setting him on the road to financial success.

THE GROUP APPROACH

Edward's audiences typically find him accurate and convincing. However, a study I made of one television transcript revealed he was actually wrong about as often as not (Nickell 1998).[1] In Syracuse, for example, no one seemed to relate to a cat named Smokey. Nevertheless, in such cases Edward can still toss out something he "sees" or "feels," and he may get lucky. Besides, the onus is on his listeners to somehow match his offerings to their lives, and if one person can't oblige, someone else will give it a try. Thus, when no one seemed to be "going to Thailand," Edward doubled his options, suggesting the trip was for adoption. Finally, one woman shouted out that she had adopted a child from Korea. When no one had experienced an Edward-visualized tattoo removal, a young lady helpfully supplied her adventure of an excised mole. Edward then looked for validation of an imagined spirit named Lily: she soon morphed into a cat of that name, still living!

Edward sometimes joked his way out of a dilemma. For instance, when one woman's late husband had not had the envisioned "foot surgery," Edward quipped, "Do you have any other husbands?"

Joking aside, this group approach has been a boon to modern mediums. On occasion, when multiple sitters acknowledge a particular offering, the medium can simply narrow the choice to a single person and then build on that success—a technique definitely employed by John Edward (Ballard 2001).

GETTING BURNED WITH "HOT" READING

According to respected journalists, episodes of *Crossing Over* were edited to make Edward appear more accurate than he was (Ballard 2001), even to the point of apparently splicing in clips of one sitter nodding yes "after statements with which he remembers disagreeing" (Jaroff 2001).

Rarely, when the opportunity presents itself, Edward may turn from "cold reading" to the much more accurate "hot reading." Although I have no evidence of him using that technique in Syracuse, he was caught cheating with it on a *Dateline NBC* episode for which I was both a behind-the-scenes advisor and an on-camera interviewee. Edward was exposed passing off knowledge he had gained from a *Dateline* cameraman during a shoot hours earlier as otherworldly revelation during a reading session. He feigned surprise that his alleged spirit gleanings applied to the cameraman. As *Dateline*'s John Hockenberry subsequently told an evasive Edward, "So that's not some energy coming through, that's something you knew going in" (Nickell 2001).

In his book, *Crossing Over*, Edward disparaged Hockenberry, who, he said, "came down on the side of the professional skeptic they used as my foil . . . Joe Nickell" (2001, 243). Edward also referred to Hockenberry's "big Gotcha! moment." That's right, John, we gotcha! You were caught cheating. And your claimed psychic powers didn't even let you see it coming.

FAST TALKER

In his stand-up act, Edward keeps things going at such a pace that there is little time to critically analyze what is occurring. The average person is not much better equipped to avoid being fooled by John Edward's sleight-of-tongue tricks than he or she is to avoid being fooled by the artful illusions of a stage magician. Careful analysis of a recorded session by one knowledgeable of the techniques employed will prove more effective than the testimonials of someone fooled by the deceptions.

And so Edward's Syracuse audience regarded their belief in otherworldly communication as fully vindicated. There appeared to be only about four skeptics in the audience. Ironically, Edward seemed not to know they were there—even though one has been a particular thorn in his side. Couldn't he feel all those bad vibes coming from an area of the orchestra?

Chapter 31

THE REAL "GHOST WHISPERER"

The character Melinda Gordon in CBS's fantasy TV series *Ghost Whisperer*, played by Jennifer Love Hewitt, is based on a real-life resident of North Royalton, Ohio. Her name is Mary Ann Winkowski, and she sports a silver Cadillac with a license plate reading "SPIRIT" (Kachuba 2007, 202). But can she really talk to ghosts?

INTRODUCTION

Winkowski does not claim to communicate with spirits who have "crossed over" to the Other Side, the purview of "mediums"; rather, she says she "can only see and talk to earthbound spirits," claiming, "I talk to the spirits and find out who they are and why they didn't cross over."

Her belief in a dimension where ghosts hang out is nothing new. It is basically a version of purgatory, which in Catholic dogma is a place (or state) "where souls are purged of sin before going to heaven" (Severy 1971, 381). Not surprisingly, Winkowski was raised Catholic. And just as the faithful are urged to assist those in purgatory by prayer and penance (Stravinskas 2002, 626–27), Winkowski believes she and others can guide spirits who lag behind for whatever reason—such as being attached to a thing or place, seeking revenge, fearing judgment (for suicide or other wrongdoing), and so on (Winkowski 2007, 81–104).

She claims to have been freeing earthbound spirits since the age of four, when her Italian grandmother began taking her to neighborhood funerals. She would "see" the dead—who are "always there, right by the casket," she says—then envision "the White Light" and direct spirits to it. Eventually, after becoming a wife and a mother, she was so sought after that she "had to start asking for a little bit of money" and was "basically forced into making it a business" (Winkowski 2000, 11–13, 19–20, 35). In her work, she mixes Catholic and New Age practices—for example, using holy water (water blessed by a priest) to dispel malignant entities and scattering quince seeds around a house "as protection" (2000, 162–67; 2007, 228–34). By means of the power of suggestion, such actions can have a beneficial effect, at the expense of encouraging superstition.

A QUESTION OF EVIDENCE

In her books—*As Alive, So Dead* (2000) and *When Ghosts Speak* (2007)—Winkowski provides no acceptable proof of her alleged ability. Some of her evidence is laughable. One published photo, sent by a client, purportedly depicts spirit energy but is actually the result of the flash rebounding from the camera's wrist strap, a common phenomenon (Nickell 2001, 128–31). Other "spirit" photos showing orbs, mists, and shapes (Winkowski 2007, illustration following page 82) have similar mundane explanations (see chapter 38, "Photoghosts: Images of the Spirit Realm?" and Nickell 2008b).

The same is true of other phenomena reported by—or to—Winkowski, including the sounds of footsteps and other noises, the effects of drafts and warm spots, and indeed almost anything: Headaches may be "a sign of a curse or negative energy," she says, and insomnia can be a sign of "an earthbound spirit in your home" (Winkowski 2007, 198–210). Missing pieces of a board game, drained batteries, a broken toy—all may be caused by "child ghosts," asserts Winkowski (2007, 208). She experiences a ghostly visitation (Kachuba 2007, 206) that is obviously only a common "waking dream" (one that occurs in the twilight between being fully awake and asleep—see Nickell 1995, 55). She even naively relates versions of the "vanishing hitchhiker" folktale (Winkowski 2000, 189–91).

Contradictorily, she describes ghosts as "pure energy," a life force that survives death (Winkowski 2007, 41), yet she maintains that earthbound spirits "smoke, comb their hair, change their clothes—all those things we always do, too. Only I've never been able to figure out where they get the stuff from" (2000, 150). Indeed, the supposed spirit-world existence of *inanimate* objects is revealing: apparitions of people appear fully clothed and are often accompanied by objects, just as they are in dreams, because the clothes and objects are required by the apparitional drama (Tyrrell 1973). That is to say, the source of "the stuff" that puzzles Winkowski is the imagination.

As to her ability to talk with ghosts, Winkowski offers only anecdotal evidence, nothing constituting scientific proof. In fact, we know that death brings a cessation of brain function and consequently an end to the ability to think, walk, or talk. So why do Winkowski and others believe they can converse with spirits?

FANTASY PRONENESS

Although Winkowski distinguishes herself from both mediums and psychics (she claims no future-telling ability), she nevertheless shares much in common with them and other paranormal claimants, including alien abductees. Such persons tend to exhibit an array of traits that indicate a fantasy-prone personality. In their pioneering study, psychologists Cheryl C. Wilson and Theodore X. Barber (1983) listed several identifying characteristics of people who fantasize profoundly. Called "fantasizers," such individuals fall within the normal range and represent an estimated 4 percent of the population.

For the past several years, I have been applying Wilson and Barber's findings to the biographies and autobiographies of a number of contemporary and historical individuals, ranging from psychics, like Sylvia Browne and Dorothy Allison, to prophets, like Jeane Dixon and Edgar Cayce, as well as others, including many alien abductees, like Whitley Strieber. I have considered the possession of six or more of the identified characteristics to indicate fantasy proneness. As shown by her own statements, Winkowski—like the others mentioned here—clearly fits the profile of a fantasizer.

For example, (1) as a child she had apparent imaginary playmates (Winkowski 2000, 10–14), although she insists they were not imaginary; (2) she claims to receive special messages from paranormal entities (2000; 2007); (3) she is a good hypnotic subject and (4) through past-life regression she has had fantasy identities in the form of "several lives" (2000, 28); (5) she has had hypnagogic/hypnopomic experiences, or waking dreams, with (6) classic strange imagery (Kachuba 2007, 206–207); (7) she frequently encounters apparitions (Winkowski 2000; 2007), and (8) while she insists she is "not psychic—at least not in the traditional sense"—she believes she channels energy, creates "White Light" and directs spirits to it, lifts curses, and so on (2000, 92, 176; 2007, 222).

Taken together, the evidence strongly indicates that Mary Ann Winkowski, "the Real Ghost Whisperer," is only participating in elaborate encounters of her own imagination. Like "visionaries" who receive messages from the Virgin Mary or "contactees" or "abductees" who are in touch with space aliens, mediums and ghost whisperers are merely communicating with an adult version of a child's imaginary playmate. Such fantasizers have rich imaginative lives and, often, a receptive audience, since they tap into shared hopes and fears. But they simply deceive first themselves, then others.

Chapter 32

SYLVIA BROWNE: DOES SHE TALK TO THE DEAD?

Self-claimed "psychic, medium, clairvoyant, channel" Sylvia Browne has gained notoriety by appearing on *The Montel Williams Show* and *Larry King Live*, as well as by writing books that bill her as a "*New York Times* bestselling author." However, there is another side to the spiritualist—a revealing and often-troubling side—as shown by some events others and I have investigated.

UNFORESEEN CRIMINAL CONVICTION

Long before adding an *e* to her surname, Sylvia Celeste Brown was involved in selling securities to a gold-mining venture while failing to foresee the true consequences: the venture failed, and she and her estranged husband were subsequently indicted on several counts of investment fraud and grand theft.

The criminal complaint, filed in the Superior Court of Santa Clara County, California, on May 26, 1992, alleged that the Browns sold securities in the venture under false pretenses. Although telling a couple their $20,000 investment was to be used for immediate operating costs, the complaint stated, the Browns transferred the money to an account for their Nirvana Foundation for Psychic Research. Just one month later, in April 1988, the complaint stated, they declared bankruptcy in the venture.

Reporting on the pair's arraignment, the June 6, 1992, *San Francisco Chronicle* noted that "Sylvia Brown claimed to have strong psychic 'feelings' that the mine would pay off." (The *Chronicle* clipping resurfaced in a review of some old files, and at my request investigator Vaughn Rees undertook the job of obtaining certified copies of the papers for criminal case #16303.)

The documents show that Sylvia and her estranged husband Kenzil Dalzell Brown pleaded no contest to a felony charge of "sale of security without permit," made restitution in the case, and received one year probation each. Dalzell's disposition included "County Jail *4 mos*[.] with credit for time served of *21 days*," while Sylvia's included two hundred hours of community service.

In her book *Adventures of a Psychic* (written with Antoinette May, 1998 ed.), Browne blames her 1988 bankruptcy declaration on her ex-husband's "attempt to hide his illegal doings," without mentioning her felony conviction in the gold-mine case. She laments that while "ignorant people" say, "Well, if you're so psychic, why didn't you . . . ," the answer, she says, is that "I am not psychic about myself." Frankly, one might not wish to buy that excuse, or much of anything else involving claimed psychic powers, from Sylvia Browne—with or without the *e*.

VISION? OR ADVANCED KNOWLEDGE

A little over two years later, Sylvia was ghost hunting at "haunted" Brookdale Lodge (figure 32.1), near Santa Cruz, California (which I subsequently investigated for a Discovery Channel documentary that aired May 24, 1998). Sylvia appeared on an episode of the television show *Sightings*, which aired on November 27, 1994. On camera, she told lodge employees about the alleged spirit of a little girl named Sarah. Browne claimed to have had a vision in which the child reenacted her death by drowning. Astonishingly, seeming to confirm Browne's vision, the employees said that, yes, decades ago, a girl so named had in fact drowned on the property!

Now, Brookdale indeed has an actual brook—a landscaped mountain stream named Clear Creek—that flows charmingly through the middle of its dining room (aptly named the Brookroom). Some claim that the girl— variously said to be six or nine years old (Stollznow 2007, 22)—drowned here. But could Sylvia have known the story of the alleged drowning before arriving at the lodge?

In her book *Visits from the Afterlife*, she insisted she had visited Brookdale "with no clue what to expect." Sounding defensive, she stated, "I'd give up my career in a heartbeat if the only way I could keep going would be to fool people" (Browne 2003, 46, 47).

Figure 32.1. Brookdale Lodge was visited by "psychic" and "medium" Sylvia Browne—with questionable results. (Photo by Joe Nickell.)

As it happens, nearly four years before, the *San Jose Mercury News* had reported on the very incident Browne claimed to see in her vision. The article told of a reported apparition of a little girl at Brookdale: "According to Brookdale legend, the little girl is named Sarah. The niece of the lodge owner 50 years ago, she drowned in the creek that runs through the dining room, the story continues, and her spirit remains to this day in the building" (Rogers 1991). So Sylvia could have received the information when, prior to the *Sightings* taping, she was "filled in on the lodge's fairly chaotic history" (Browne 2003, 46). There is even evidence that she not only *could* have previously heard the story of the girl's death but that she *probably did*.

As the *Mercury News* related, "two Gnostic ministers who work with Campbell [California] psychic Sylvia Browne conducted a 'house blessing'" at Brookdale "to try to communicate with and rid the lodge of ghosts" (Rogers 1991). They returned the next day to appear in a television news story on the "haunting" (Lancaster 2007a). According to Browne critic Robert S. Lancaster (2007a), "members of Browne's church in Campbell at the time" stated that "the lodge's 'ghostly history'—including that of 'Sarah'—was common knowledge at the church." He concluded, "It strains credulity to think that Browne would not have read the newspaper article or watched the TV news story, both of which prominently featured her assistants."

PLAGIARISM BY SPIRIT GUIDES

In 2005, Browne published yet another tome, titled *Secrets & Mysteries of the World*. It is an exception to Browne's usual practice of collaborating on a book "with" so-and-so. This time the cover simply reads, "Sylvia Browne." In producing this book, she says, she augmented her "intense search" with her "psychic abilities," including assistance from "Francine," the imaginary playmate of her childhood who became Browne's "spirit guide" (2005, 11).

In the various chapters, Browne says she used psychometry (psychic object reading) at Stonehenge, saw and talked with a tall extraterrestrial from planet "PX41," determined that spontaneous human combustion is a real phenomenon,[1] and so on.

However, if readers will stop laughing, it is Browne's ideas on the Shroud of Turin (the reputed burial cloth of Jesus) that interest me most. Some believe the images on the cloth, of a seemingly crucified man, were produced by Jesus at the moment when, lying in his tomb, he rose from the dead. Browne shows some admirable skepticism, concluding: "I believe that the Shroud is a representation and not a true relic—but I don't think that should put a dent in our Christian belief" (2005, 199). Citing a fourteenth-century bishop's report that the image was painted, Browne (196) writes:

> If the Shroud were in fact painted, it would explain some image flaws that have always raised questions. For example, the hair hangs as for a standing rather than a reclining figure; the physique is unnaturally elongated (like figures in Gothic art); and the "blood" flows are unrealistically neat (instead of matting the hair, for instance, they run in rivulets on the outside of the locks). You see, real blood soaks into cloth and spreads in all directions rather than leaving picturelike images.

I found that passage intriguing, since I had written (in the July/August 1998 *Skeptical Inquirer*, p. 21):

That the Shroud is indeed the work of a medieval artist would explain numerous image flaws. For example, the physique is unnaturally elongated (like figures in Gothic art!). Also, the hair hangs as for a standing rather than recumbent figure.

. . . Everywhere the "blood" flows are unrealistically neat. Instead of matting the hair, for instance, they run in rivulets on the outside of the locks. . . . In addition, real blood soaks into cloth and spreads in all directions, rather than leaving picturelike images.

Now, the shared phrasing between Browne's passage and mine may give new meaning to the term *ghostwritten*. Considering the book's lack of any reference to my article, one may wonder: Has Francine stooped to plagiarism? What does Browne know about this? Was she in a trance when she wrote it? Are there other *Secrets & Mysteries of the World* yet to be revealed?

THE MISSING DEAD

Then there is Browne's track record in supposedly helping police find dead people. In that pursuit, her "spirit guides" should be especially useful, contacting for her the ghosts of persons missing and presumed dead to learn where their remains are. Actually, most such "psychic sleuths" merely use a technique called retrofitting (or after-the-fact matching). They throw out a few vague "clues" (like "water" or "the number seven") then wait and attempt to match them with the actual facts once they become known, so as to maintain the pretence of accuracy (Nickell 1994).

Yet in the case of Chandra Levy, who disappeared in Washington, DC, in 2001, Browne did not do well. Although she visualized that the missing intern's remains were in the area police were concentrating on, Rock Creek Park, Browne said they were "down in a marshy area." Instead, when they were discovered by a man walking his dog, they were scattered on a steep wooded slope (Lancaster 2009; Nickell 2009).

Worse, in one case, Browne erroneously told the parents of a missing eleven-year-old boy, Shawn Hornbeck, that he was dead. He had gone missing from his Richwood, Missouri, home on October 6, 2002, and four months later (February 26, 2003) his parents, Pam and Craig Akers, appeared with Sylvia Browne on *The Montel Williams Show*. There, Browne told the parents that Shawn "is no longer with us" and stated her impression that his body was near two jagged boulders in a wooded area some twenty miles from Richwood in a southwesterly direction (Lancaster 2007b).

Actually, Browne was describing a general area that had already been searched several times. In fact, all the while, Shawn was alive, being held along with another boy, by a kidnapper in St. Louis. The youths were found by law enforcement on January 12, 2007. Subsequently, CNN's *Anderson Cooper 360* show devoted a segment to Browne's many psychic failures titled *Dead Wrong*, which aired January 19, 2007. For the show, Sylvia Browne provided a list of her supposed successes, but Cooper and his staff subjected the cases to scrutiny and found them seriously wanting, including claims that were unverifiable and some that were documented only after the fact (Lancaster 2009).

FANTASY PRONE

None of the foregoing means, of course, that Sylvia Browne is an out-and-out charlatan. In fact, she could very well believe she has special powers—whether or not she engages in trickery to boost her appearance of success.

Those who fancy themselves psychics often exhibit traits associated with a "fantasy-prone" personality—a designation for an otherwise normal person with an unusual ability to fantasize, as we have seen. As a child, he or she may have an imaginary playmate and live much of the time in make-believe worlds. As an adult, the person continues to spend much time fantasizing, and may report apparitional, out-of-body, or near-death experiences; claim psychic or healing powers; receive special messages from higher beings; be easily hypnotized; and/or exhibit other traits (Wilson and Barber 1983). Anyone may have some of these traits, but fantasizers have them in profusion.

Sylvia Browne, for example, as a child had what her parents called "made-up friends," particularly her "spirit guide" named "Francine." Browne undergoes "trances" in which "Francine" provides alleged information from "Akashic records, individual spirit guides, and messages from the Godhead." Browne also claims to see apparitions, talk to ghosts, have clairvoyant visions, make psychic medical diagnoses, divine past lives, and so forth. She has even started her own religion, Novus Spiritus ("New Spirit"). (Browne and May 1998; Browne 1999)

MILLION-DOLLAR CHALLENGE

Putting aside the question of Sylvia Browne's sincerity, the question remains: does she have psychic powers and the ability to speak with the dead?

On *Larry King Live* (aired September 3, 2001), Browne appeared with famed magician and psychic investigator James Randi, who offers, as he told Larry, one million dollars "to any person or persons who can provide evidence of any paranormal or supernatural event or ability of any kind under proper observing conditions." Randi challenged Browne to take the test.

She was defensive, saying, "I don't care about his million dollars," and switching the subject to whether or not Randi believes in God. However, pressed by Randi, she did agree to be tested, and Larry King volunteered to use his website for the purpose. When the show finally ended, Larry said: "And we're going to see that the two get together and go through this test. And we'll let you know about it." Yet, at this writing, well over a decade later, Browne still has not submitted herself to being tested by Randi. Maybe she guesses what the results will be.

PART 4:
GHOST HUNTING

Chapter 33

GHOST HUNTING

As shown in chapter 1, on the history of ghosts, visits made to check out a "haunted" site date as far back as 1 CE. More intentional ghost hunting is known from at least the second half of the sixteenth century. According to Harry Price (1936, 37):

> Ghost-hunting (even professional ghost-hunting) is of ancient origin and was fully discussed as long ago as 1572 when [Ludwig] Lavater's famous book, *Of Ghostes and Spirites Walking by Nyght*, was published. In many respects, the book might have been written yesterday, instead of in the sixteenth century, and it is a fact that Shakespeare drew largely from the work when he wrote *Hamlet*. The first chapter "Concerning certaine wordes which are often used in this Treatise of Spirits" deals with the terms *spectrum*, defined as "a substance without a body, which beeing hearde or seene, maketh men afrayde," visions, and apparitions. The author then warns his readers to be critical of the evidence for spirits: "Melancholike persons, and madde men, imagin many things which in verie deede are not. Men which are dull of seing and hearing imagine many things which in very deed are not so." Lavater's words should be emblazoned in neon lights over the portals of every *séance*-room. Lavater then proceeds to describe various fraudulent phenomena and again warns us "That many naturall things are taken to be ghosts, as for example, when they heare the crying of rats, cats, weasles, martins, or any other beast, or when they heare a horse beate his feete on the plankes in the stable at midnight, by and by they sweate for feare, supposing some buggs [hobgoblins] to walke in the dead of the night. . . . If a worme whiche fretteth wood, or that breadeth in trees chaunce to gnawe a wall or waynescot, or other tymber, many will judge they heare one softly knocking uppon an andvill with a sledge."

The rest of Lavater's treatise deals with supposedly genuine phenomena.

Today's emphasis on physical phenomena that are thought to prove the reality of ghosts is interesting. If ghosts are nonmaterial (as evidenced by reports of their walking through walls), how is it that they produce heavy, thudding footsteps on stairs (as also reported)—or that they use stairs at all? And if ghosts represent a dead person's "spiritual energy" (as is often claimed), how is it that they are invariably clothed, that clothing and other inanimate objects pass into an afterlife? The answer (as we discussed in chapter 2) seems to be that all are really only figments of the mind; they appear because they are required by the imagined ghostly drama (Nickell 2001a, 216–17). People, even ghosts, are appropriately clothed both in our memory and in our imagination.

Nevertheless, the notion that ghosts are at least somewhat physical is the basis for spiritualism's *physical mediumship* (slate writing, materializations, etc.) as well as much of so-called *ghost hunting*. Of the physical evidence supposedly supporting both, none is more prevalent than photographs. Interestingly, the first experimental photographs (in the 1820s) as well as the first types of commercial photos—daguerreotypes (invented in 1839), ambrotypes (from 1855), and tintypes (from 1856)—failed to record ghosts. Not until glass-plate negatives came on the scene (about 1859), and made double exposures possible, did "ghosts" begin to appear in photographs (first in 1862). Photography became a ghost-hunting tool that has seen increasing use as photography became accessible to amateurs. (See chapter 38, "Photoghosts: Images of the Spirit Realm?")

After photography, other technological developments began to be enlisted in the search for ghosts. In 1920, for example, the prolific American inventor Thomas A. Edison was reported to be working on a device for communicating with the dead. However, while Edison was fascinated with the occult—conducting experiments in mind reading, mind control, and spirit communication (Gardner 1996)—he spoke rather skeptically of the latter:

> I have been thinking for some time of a machine or apparatus which could be operated by personalities which have passed on to another existence or sphere. Now follow me carefully; I don't claim that our personalities pass on to another existence, or sphere. I don't claim anything because I don't know anything about the subject. For that matter, no human being knows. But I do claim that it is possible to construct an apparatus which will be so delicate that if there are personalities in another existence or sphere who

wish to get in touch with us in this existence or sphere, this apparatus will
at least give them a better opportunity to express themselves than the tilting
tables and raps and ouija boards and mediums and the other crude methods
now purported to be the only means of communication. (Edison 1948, 239)

Edison went on to describe his concept as being "in the nature of a valve, so
to speak" that would tremendously magnify any exerted force. A collaborator of his having recently died, Edison went on to say, "In that he knew
exactly what I am after in this work, I believe he ought to be the first to use
it if he is able to do so." He added, "Of course, don't forget that I am making
no claims for the survival of personality; I am not promising communication
with those who have passed out of this life. I merely state that I am giving
the psychic investigators an apparatus which may help them in their work"
(Edison 1948, 240). The important point to note is that Edison did not
report any further progress in spirit communication, certainly not any message from his deceased collaborator.

Undaunted, those attempting to prove the reality of ghosts continued
their efforts. In 1936, another researcher, one Atilla von Szalay, attempted to
capture spirit voices on phonograph records. Others followed with tape
recorders, culminating in Konstantin Raudive's book *Breakthrough* (1971). It
sparked the craze known as "electronic voice phenomena" (EVP), which
began to spread in the 1980s (Guiley 2000, 120–21). The reputed ghost
voices are unheard during taping but are supposedly manifested on playback.

Such voices actually have natural explanations (discussed in chapter 34),
but one celebrated invention, called Spiricom—which could allegedly
permit two-way communications with people who have died—was ultimately revealed to be "no more than a fairly transparent hoax" (Peterson
1987, 97).

The father of today's ghost hunting, England's Harry Price (1881–
1948), became one of the first to use "modern technology" to supposedly
detect spirits of the dead (Nickell 2006a, 25). Having married an heiress,
Price was able to indulge his interests in psychical research. Although he was
a member of the SPR (Society for Psychical Research), he felt the society
was too skeptical of physical phenomena and he therefore established his
own research lab.

Seeking evidence of "haunting" activity, Price famously had a "ghost-
hunting" kit (see Price 1936, photo facing p. 32). He employed a variety of

devices, including a reflex camera (with film packs and flash bulbs), a camera with infrared filter and film (for photographing in the dark), a remote-control motion-picture camera, and "a sensitive transmitting thermograph, with charts, to measure the slightest variation in temperature in supposed haunted rooms."[1] He also utilized "an electronic signaling instrument" to reveal the "movement of any object in any part of the house" (Price 1940, 5–6). Less technological equipment included a tape measure, electric torch (flashlight), string, chalk, notebook and pencils, tape (for sealing windows), a bowl of mercury (used for detecting building tremors), and other items, including "bandages, iodine and a flask of brandy in case member of investigating staff or resident is injured or faints" (Price 1940, 5–6). He rejected "cranks and inventors with machines to sell—pieces of apparatus guaranteed to detect a ghost a mile off" (Price 1940, 107).

Price combined the use of gadgetry with a psychic approach. As early as the 1920s he had a séance with a "famous physical medium" in a reputedly haunted dressing room of the Adelphi Theatre (Price 1940, 46–47). In his famous investigation of Borley Rectory, he noted "the phantasms seen by various people," statements produced as automatic writing "through the Planchette," and a séance he held at midnight in the rectory's "Blue Room" (1940, 33, 34, 41–43). Price (1940, 93, 95) also reported that at Borley he suggested reciting the Rosary, "asking our Lord and the Blessed Virgin to assist us," and he "had several Masses offered in connection with this house." He even rented Borley Rectory for a year, enlisted some forty volunteer "observers" to monitor it in shifts, and created protocols and report-writing instructions (Price 1940, 193–97, 248).

Despite all his efforts, however, Price was still unable to prove the reality of ghosts. Worse, he remains "suspected of fraud in connection with several of his investigations, including the most famous one, the Borley Rectory haunting" (Guiley 2000, 299), the subject of his *The Most Haunted House in England* (1940). (For a discussion, see Dingwall, Goldney, and Hall 1956.) Among Price's many other works is his seminal *Confessions of a Ghost-Hunter* (1936).

His most recent biographer (Morris 2006, xv) said of him—in words that might describe some of today's so-called ghost hunters:

> He claimed that his findings were bolstered through his training as a scientist and engineer but in reality the man who had left school at 15 was an academic failure. His scientific methods were nothing more than an act,

using scientific apparatus and the trappings of a chemical laboratory merely to convince people he was a scientist. He thought instinctively and impulsively and, instead of trying to disprove his theories, he sought only to prove them.

(This is called *confirmation bias*.) Harry Price's style of ghost hunting was slow to catch on in America. Instead, there were many armchair collectors of popular haunting stories. Often riddled with errors or omissions and characterized by a mystery-mongering attitude, the collections include Susy Smith's *Ghosts around the House* (1970) and Scott and Norman's *Haunted Heartland* (1985). There have also been many collections of fictional ghost stories, including Marvin Kaye's *Haunted America* (1990), which presents tales by Nathaniel Hawthorne, Washington Irving, Mark Twain, Ambrose Bierce, Isaac Asimov, and many others.

Among Americans who really did go on-site to "investigate" reputedly haunted places was Hans Holzer (1920–2009). One of his 138 books on the occult and supernatural billed him as "the world's leading expert on haunted houses" (1991). However, despite labeling himself in the title of another book as *Ghost Hunter* (1963), which thus links his pursuits to those of Harry Price, he largely avoided gadgetry and instead favored a "psychic" approach. That is, he visited spooky places with an alleged clairvoyant or medium, like the self-styled "witch" Sybil Leek (1922–1982). (See Holzer 1991, 192; Nickell 2001b, 298–99.)

Such reputed sensitives have claimed to shed light on historical matters of all kinds, including solving old crimes, revealing hidden treasures (or at least their supposed existence), locating archaeological sites, authenticating artifacts, and explaining historical enigmas—although the offered "information" is notoriously undependable (Holzer 1991, 40, 68, 94, 112; Nickell 2007, 48–58; Christopher 1970, 127–29; Archer 1969, 11–23).

Holzer's work was once examined in the *Journal of the Society for Psychical Research* (December 1970). He had taken two mediums to a reputedly haunted house, and they had made certain pronouncements:

They identified the ghost as Nell Gwyn and gave the cause of the haunting as the murder of one of her lovers on orders from Charles II who had given the house to her. She was supposed to have acted at the adjacent Royalty Theatre. It was also stated that the house had formerly housed the Royal Stables.

Unfortunately, however,

> The JSPR article reveals that just about everything the mediums said was incorrect, the house not having been built until after Nell Gwyn's death, the theatre not having been built until about 150 years later, and the Royal Stables never having been located anywhere near the site. "Whatever may be the truth about the ESP investigations carried out by Mr. Holzer, his treatment of his historical sources is so unsatisfactory, on the evidence of this case, as to cast considerable doubt on the objectivity and reliability of his work as a whole." (quoted in Berger and Berger 1991, 183)

In 1950, Holzer even conceived of "a television series based on actual hauntings." However, it is unclear from his statement whether he had "started to work" on such a series, whether it materialized or not (Holzer 1963, 15). He was involved in other television ghost documentaries, including having "made a television film" about Governor Clinton's haunted carriage house in New York City (Holzer 1991, 63), and he participated in the Search for Haunted Hollywood, a 1989 "tour of Tinseltown's most terrifying sites" ("Search for Haunted Hollywood" 2007).

A markedly different approach to Holzer's was that of Ed and Lorraine Warren, who also styled themselves, in a book title, as *Ghost Hunters* (1989). Actually the Warrens' approach was to arrive at a "haunted" house, transform it into a case of alleged demonic attack, then produce a sensationalized book—usually written with a professional writer. They were called various things, from "passionate and religious people" to "scaremongers" and "charlatans." Reportedly, some of their coauthors have since admitted that the Warrens encouraged them to make up scary incidents and details (Nickell 2006b). (See chapter 36.)

Ghost-hunting organizations originated in England in the wake of spiritualism, first the Cambridge Ghost Club and then in 1862 the Ghost Club in London. In 1993 Peter Underwood left the latest embodiment of the latter club to form his own Ghost Club Society, of which he became president for life. Members have included science-fiction writer Colin Wilson, medium Rosemary Brown, and horror actor Peter Cushing (Guiley 2000, 153). By 1995, English writer Ian Wilson (1995, 205) was observing, in his *In Search of Ghosts*, that "several more localised ghost-hunting groups have mushroomed in recent years, among these the Grimsby-based Ghostbusters UK, who wear 'Ghostbuster' T-shirts, and travel to reputedly haunted sites in their 'Ghostmobile,' crammed with ghost-detecting equipment."

In the United States, usually only one or two ghost seekers visited a site, and their equipment could be quite limited. For instance, in 1959, according to his *Occult America*, paranormal writer John Godwin (1972, 184) went on his first haunting vigil with a photographer: "Our equipment consisted of a camera, two flashlights, a tape recorder and one (unlicensed) .32-caliber pistol." Fortunately no one was killed.

As ghosts rode the crest of a boom in paranormal interest in the 1970s, a few skeptics began to investigate alleged hauntings from a rational, scientific, and evidential perspective. They included noted magician Milbourne Christopher (1970), who followed in the Houdini tradition, and psychologist Robert A. Baker, who went to haunted houses to study puzzling phenomena. Baker explained ghostly activity in physical or psychological terms, and he was fond of saying that there were no haunted houses, "only haunted people" (see Baker and Nickell 1992, 124).

However, like their British counterparts, most American ghost hunters disagreed. Writing in his *The Haunted House Handbook*, D. Scott Rogo suggested:

> An ideal ghost-hunter should be equipped with all sorts of fancy gadgets as he makes his investigation. If you happen to be rich, that's no problem. You could bring cameras to continually film the house in hopes of photographing either the ghost or perhaps some object floating about. You could even set up T.V. monitors all through the building. Then you could sit in one room, and still watch what is going on every place else. You could also bring in delicate thermometers to check if any odd temperature changes are taking place. Unfortunately, few ghost-hunters are so nicely equipped. However, even an amateur can conduct a few simple experiments in a haunted house or at least carry out a thorough investigation.

Rogo (1978, 156) went on to state, "The simplest method of actively investigating a haunted house is to just sit and wait there until something happens!"

Ghost-hunting clubs gained in popularity in the United States in the late 1970s. At that time the Chicago-area Ghost Trackers Club was founded. In 1981, it became the Ghost Research Society (GRS), headed the following year by Dale Kaczmarek (a former army chaplain's assistant turned grocery-distribution employee). He advocated ghost hunting that involved a team effort (Miller 1990, 62). According to *The Encyclopedia of Ghosts and Spirits*, "his investigations, using increasingly sophisticated technology, have yielded promising, but still inconclusive, evidence" (Guiley 2000, 206).

Loyd Auerbach's 1986 *ESP, Hauntings, and Poltergeists: A Parapsychologist's Handbook* suggested that equipment "that might be used in an investigation" for ghosts might include photoelectric cells ("to see if a ghost walks through the beam"), microwave and ultrasonic detectors ("like those used in security work"), and strain-gauge plates ("to detect minute stresses and vibrations, such as footsteps as the apparition walks down a hallway"). Yet Auerbach (370) conceded that the American Society for Psychical Research's sophisticated equipment reportedly "has yet to yield up as much information as a human detector."

Parapsychologist Charles Tart was among those recommending that sensitive electronic devices for ghost detecting—for example, heat sensors, infrared imaging devices, biosensors, magnetic and radiation sensors (such as Geiger counters)—be connected to a computer in order for changes in the local environment to be displayed and correlated (Cochran 1988). However, Robert A. Baker noted that it hardly represented "anything new." He questioned the supposition "that the ghost is some sort of energy form that is part of the electromagnetic spectrum and is thus detectable" (Baker and Nickell 1992, 123). He quoted skeptical parapsychologist Susan Blackmore, who stated, "Much of the research is based on pseudophysical theories. The problem with this field is that we keep coming up with mad ideas that lead nowhere" (Cochran 1988).

Nevertheless, the notion that there was equipment to detect ghosts continued to spread. *The Encyclopedia of Ghosts and Spirits* notes, "Since the mid-1990s, sophisticated high-technology equipment has dramatically changed the nature of ghost investigation, especially in the United States. Most contemporary researchers prefer to use the terms 'ghost investigation' or 'ghost research' instead of 'ghost hunting,' which has become associated with sensationalism" (Guiley 2000, 153). Some ghost hunters call themselves "parapsychologists," a term that best applies to those within the field of psychology who use scientific methodology in the laboratory to conduct tests for ESP and other "psychical" phenomena (Berger and Berger 1991, 312). However, the National Research Council of the National Academy of Sciences concluded in 1987 that "the Committee finds no scientific justification from research over the last 130 years for the existence of parapsychological phenomena" (quoted in Berger and Berger 1991, 312).

Modern ghost-hunting manuals tout phenomena that supposedly indicate ghosts but typically have mundane causes (as explained in the following chapters). (See Hope and Townsend 1999, 22–32; Keene, Bradley-Stevenson, and Saunders 2006, 23–27; Nickell 2006a; Southall 2003, 41–82; Underwood 1998, 109–15.) Richard Southall's *How to Be a Ghost Hunter* (2003) recommends "scientific" equipment to detect ghosts. However, he is like most other ghost hunters who are nonscientists using equipment that was never designed to detect ghosts and has never been scientifically demonstrated to have detected a single ghost. Southall even shows his ignorance of science when he speaks of "electromagnetic energy as opposed to microwave radiation" (2003, 75): in fact, microwaves are part of the electromagnetic spectrum.

Paul Roland (2007), author of *The Complete Book of Ghosts*, is another who champions the pseudoscientific approach. He insists that among the "items of equipment which no self-respecting ghost hunter can afford to be without" is "the most essential item," namely "an EMF meter which measures fluctuations in the electromagnetic field." He adds, "Orthodox science considers these to be a natural phenomenon, but paranormal researchers believe these disturbances to be proof of the presence of ghosts" (Roland 2007, 188)—as if belief were more dependable than evidence.

Joshua Warren's *How to Hunt Ghosts* (2003) suggests the use of some quite-contrasting materials and methods. He offers, on the one hand, age-old superstitious practices of using dowsing rods and pendulums, Ouija boards, and the pronouncements of psychics and mediums, and, on the other, such modern gadgetry as the electromagnetic field meter, electrostatic generator, strobe light, and audio enhancer. Warren (2003, 183) looks forward to being able to combine various technologies into a single "ghost meter" designed specifically for spectral detection. Actually, as early as 1988 Tony Cornell (2002, 87) was reportedly using for that purpose a multi-instrument package he had developed called Spontaneous Psychophysical Incident Data Electronic Recorder (SPIDER). However, he concludes, "Considering the number of cases and the time involved, one must recognize that the use of such equipment has not produced any great weight of evidence to confirm the paranormal nature of those events it has been designed to record" (Cornell 2002, 381).

Yet Warren (2003, 116) is among those already looking to the future—as a means of looking to the past. "Imagine a day," he says, "when you can take a special pair of goggles and headphones to any location and, by turning through various 'frequencies,' watch any moment in that location's past." (*Imagine* is, of course, the operative word.)

Others, however, believe they can accomplish the same by mental means and hark back to Hans Holzer's mediums and the biblical Witch of Endor. One is a woman known as Michelle Whitedove, who as a child had invisible friends and now styles herself—in the title of a book—*Ghost Stalker* (2003). She clearly exhibits many of the traits associated with a fantasy-prone personality (see appendix).

Paralleling books on ghosts and ghost hunting are television shows on these topics. In addition to those already mentioned, there have been numerous documentaries—often with a "reality TV" style (involving real people "in unusual circumstances"). The documentaries include the series *In Search Of...*, which aired weekly from 1976 to 1982 and included episodes on "Ghosts," "Haunted Castles," "Ghostly Stakeout," "The Amityville Horror," and "Ghosts in Photography" (*"In Search Of..."* 2007). Another series, *Sightings*, also focused on the paranormal, with segments like "Ghost of Brookdale Lodge" in 1994, featuring "psychic" Sylvia Browne (Lancaster 2007). Others include *Hauntings across America* (the Learning Channel, October 25, 1998) and *America's Haunted Houses* (Discovery Channel, May 24, 1998). A video documentary also appeared, titled *Seeing Ghosts: A How-To Video for the Amateur Ghost Hunter* (Peter Kuehn Productions, 1996) (Edwards 2001). The *Ghost Hunters* "reality TV" show, which debuted October 6, 2004, on the Sci-Fi Channel (now known as Syfy), features a team headed by a pair of Roto-Rooter plumbers who investigate supposedly haunted places, Grant Wilson and Jason Hawes (see chapter 34) ("Ghost Hunters" 2007).

Ever looking for ways to capitalize on the interest in spirits, ghost hunters have enlisted celebrities—the dead as well as the living—in their productions. Holzer's book *Star Ghosts* (1979), for instance, presents encounters with the alleged spirits of Marilyn Monroe, Elvis Presley, and other film greats. And living celebrities have hosted TV ghost shows, for instance Linda Blair, *The Scariest Place on Earth* (2006); Leonard Nimoy and Stacy Keach, *Haunted Lives* (1995–1998); and William Shatner, *Hollywood Ghost Stories* (1998) (*"The Scariest Places"* 2007; "Haunted Lives" 2007; Edwards 2001).

Chapter 34

GHOST HUNTERS

Belief that spirits of the dead exist and can appear to the living is both ancient and widespread, yet the actual study of ghostly phenomena has largely been lacking. So-called investigation has ranged from mere collecting of ghost tales to the use of "psychic" impressions to a pseudoscientific reliance on technology applied in a questionable fashion. Real science has largely been ignored.

COLLECTING TALES

Even in a given era, ghosts seem to behave according to individual expectations, being as likely to walk through a wall as to knock on a door before entering (Finucane 1984, 223).

While collecting ghost stories can be helpful in showing just such trends, much that is claimed as the "investigation" of hauntings never rises above mere mystery mongering. Necessarily there is a reliance on anecdotal, eyewitness testimony. Moreover, accounts may be exaggerated and are frequently offered with the implication that the "unexplainable" phenomena are proof of the reality of spirits. Actually, such a view is an example of a logical fallacy called *arguing from ignorance* ("we don't know what caused the door to slam, therefore it was a ghost"). One cannot draw a conclusion from a lack of knowledge. Besides, an event may simply be unexplained rather than unexplainable. That is, the riddle of the mysterious phenomenon may later be solved (e.g., a slamming door might have been caused by a draft or an event may have been the result of a prank).

Uncritical collections of ghost tales—rife with weaselly phrases like "is said to be" and "some believe that" (e.g., Hauck 1996, 1, 12)—are ubiquitous. They include Dennis William Hauck's *Haunted Places: The National*

Directory (1996) and *The International Directory of Haunted Places* (2000), as well as a hundred or so books by "ghost hunter" Hans Holzer alone.

THE "PSYCHIC" METHOD

Hans Holzer was a leading figure in the use of "psychics" in ghost hunting, for which—as we discussed in the previous chapter—he was taken to task by serious psychical researchers as well as skeptics. I happened to be able to follow up on one of Holzer's "investigations" with my own on-site investigation. This was at Ringwood Manor in northern New Jersey.

Holzer arrived at Ringwood with "psychic" Ethel Meyers in tow, a dubious choice given her involvement in the "Amityville Horror" case, wherein she failed to realize it was a hoax. She supposedly made contact with former servants at Ringwood, saying that one, "Jeremiah," had "complained bitterly about his mistress," a Mrs. Erskine. However, the curator of Ringwood told me he doubted the house was haunted, and he disparaged the notion that Mrs. Erskine mistreated any servant—whether "Jeremiah" or not. He observed that the present house was never seen by her and "isn't even near the location of the original house!" (Prol 1993). Thus when Holzer writes, "The center of the hauntings seems to be what was once the area of Mrs. Erskine's bedroom" (Holzer 1991, 125), he betrays an utter lack of historical credibility.

As such evidence demonstrates—whether alleged psychics claim to enter a "trance" state, like Holzer's favorite mediums, Ethel Meyers and Sybil Leek (Holzer 1991, 24, 36), or whether they rely on "channeling tools" such as a Ouija board, dowsing rod, or psychic pendulum, as others prefer (Belanger 2005, 17)—psychics have a poor track record. They typically offer unsubstantiated, even unverifiable claims, or information that can be gleaned from research sources or from knowledgeable persons by "cold reading" (an artful method of fishing for information). Alternatively, the psychic may simply make a number of pronouncements, trusting that the credulous will count the apparent hits and ignore, or interpret appropriately, the misses.

Still, not all such offerings are insincere. As we have seen, those who fancy themselves psychics may exhibit traits associated with a "fantasy-prone" personality—a designation for an otherwise normal person's heightened propensity to fantasize. Some field research I have done shows a correlation between the number and intensity of ghostly experiences on the one hand and the number of exhibited traits associated with fantasy proneness on the other (Nickell 2000).

GHOSTBUSTERS

With the resurgence of spiritualism in the mid-nineteenth century, mediums sought to prove the existence of spirits through certain physical phenomena. In dark-room séances, spirits allegedly materialized, spoke, wrote messages on slates, posed for photographs, and produced apports (teleported objects)—or so it appeared. Magician Harry Houdini (1874–1926) spent his last years crusading against such phony spirit tricks (Nickell 1995, 17–38).

One of the first to use "modern technology" for ghost hunting was England's Harry Price (1881–1948), as we discussed in chapter 33. Despite his gadgets, Price still was unable to prove the reality of ghosts. Worse, he "is suspected of fraud in connection with several of his investigations, including the most famous one, the Borley Rectory haunting" (Guiley 2000, 299), which he wrote about in his *The Most Haunted House in England* (1940). (For a discussion, see Dingwall, Goldney, and Hall 1956.)

Ghost hunting began to be popular in the late 1970s with the founding of the Chicago-area Ghost Tracker's Club. It became the Ghost Research Society (GRS) in 1981. The popularity of the *Ghostbusters* movie of 1984 may have boosted the proliferation of ghost clubs. Some include psychics and dowsers, but virtually all utilize high-tech equipment for the supposed detection of ghostly "energy" or ghosts' supposed impact on the environment (e.g., changes in temperature). Unfortunately, that is unknown to science, and the approach of the typical ghost hunter—a nonscientist using equipment for a purpose for which it was not made and has not been shown to be effective—is sheer pseudoscience.

Here is a brief overview of their alleged findings and the equipment involved.

Ghost photos. The earliest photographs—daguerreotype (from 1839), ambrotypes (1855) and tintypes (1856)—did not show ghosts. However, following the advent of glass-plate negatives (about 1859), which permitted double exposures, various means of faking ghost photos followed. As well, unintended ghostly effects have been caused by imperfections in film or camera or by conditions under which the photo was made (Nickell 1994, 146–59). Some "ghosts" are only simulacra—faces or other shapes perceived due to the mind's tendency to "recognize" images in random patterns (Nickell 2004). (Chapter 38 discusses ghost photos in more depth.)

Orbs. Typically unwitnessed but showing up in photographs—especially flash photos—orbs are bright spheres touted as "spirit energy" (Belanger 2005, 342). In fact, however, orbs are easily made anywhere (as I have done in experimental photographs). When they are not mere reflections from shiny surfaces, they most often result from the flash rebounding from particles of dust or droplets of water close to the lens (Nickell 2002). The characteristics of orbs can vary, depending on how they are photographed. Orbs are more likely to be caused by cameras having the flash located close to the lens, according to Fujifilm (2006). Also, digital cameras, having a greater depth of field, may be a more frequent offender ("Orbs" 2006). Responding to the evidence, some ghost hunters now claim to be able to differentiate "genuine" ghost orbs from "false orbs" (Guiley 2000, 270), while still being unable to prove the existence of the former.

Ectoplasm. Ghost hunters often tout the existence of "ectoplasm"— originally a substance supposedly extruded from the body of a medium. It was shown in photographs, extending umbilical-like from the medium's mouth, nose, or ears, but again and again it was revealed to have been faked with strips of gauze, chewed-up paper, concoctions of soap and gelatin, and so forth (Guiley 2000, 116–17). Ghost hunters have seized on ectoplasm as a pseudo explanation for various strand and mist effects in photos. Such effects can be caused by the flash rebounding from the camera's wrist strap, jewelry, hair, insects, a wandering fingertip, and so on (Nickell 1996; 2002). Or they may be due to other glitches.

Spirit energy. In addition to photography, ghost hunters search for their elusive quarry with a panoply of devices, notably electromagnetic field (EMF) meters. These are highly sensitive and—depending on the model— can be influenced by a number of very real energy sources, including faulty electric wiring, inadvertently magnetized objects (such as a metal bed frame), radio waves, microwave emissions, solar activity, electrical thunderstorms, and many other influences—even the human body! Watching hapless ghost hunters on TV crockumentaries, one often sees them operating EMF meters while holding them in the hand and moving about—a sure recipe for "unexplained" (to them) fluctuations. See figure 34.1.

Figure 34.1. Paranormal investigator Vaughn Rees mimics ghost hunters, demonstrating how *not* to find a ghost. (Photo courtesy of Vaughn Rees.)

Electronic Voice Phenomena (EVP). Following the nineteenth-century attempts to amplify spirit voices with tin trumpets, Thomas A. Edison suggested it might be possible to make an electronic device that permitted spirit communication (Gardner 1996). That never materialized, but today's ghost hunters make audiotape recordings of what they believe are "voices of the dead." These are unheard during taping but are manifested on playback. Skeptics contend they are either voices from radio, television, or two-way radio transmissions, or they are imagined. Like visual simulacra, syllablelike effects may be perceived in the randomness of static and background noise (Guiley 2000, 120–21; Flynn 2006).

Cold spots. Ghost buffs tout temperature fluctuations and "cold spots" as evidence that a house is haunted. Supposedly, they indicate areas where ghosts reside, and in the past they were picked by alleged psychics. To counter the inherent subjectivity of such an approach (a spooky place may give one "cold chills"), modern ghost hunters employ heat sensors, such as digital thermal scanners that measure instant temperature changes. The practice persists despite a lack of scientific evidence or a theory to support equating the temperature with ghosts. Furthermore, temperatures routinely vary throughout a building due to normal causes (Warren 2003, 171–72; Guiley 2000, 155; Baker and Nickell 1992, 123).

The pseudoscientific approach is presented—one might almost say caricatured—by a ghostly reality show that airs weekly on Syfy (formerly the Sci-Fi Channel). Called *Ghost Hunters*, it features two hapless paranormalists—Jason Hawes and Grant Wilson—who, by day, are Roto-Rooter plumbers in New Jersey, and, by night, are leaders of the Atlantic Paranormal Society (TAPS). With some skepticism to enhance overall credibility (a token nonbeliever on each show), the duo present "evidence" for alleged hauntings. This we take a look at in the next chapter.

SCIENTIFIC INVESTIGATION

The scientific approach to hauntings does not begin with the unproven, seemingly contradictory notion that entities are at once nonmaterial and quasi physical. Rather, in scientific inquiry one seeks to gather, study, and follow the evidence, only positing a supernatural or paranormal cause when all natural explanations have been decisively eliminated. Investigation seeks neither to foster nor debunk mysteries but instead to solve them.

This approach can involve scholarly methods (such as historical research and folkloristic analysis) as well as scientific techniques like those used in crime-scene investigation. (See chapter 37, "Ghost Forensics").

As shown by examples throughout this book, it is the scientific approach that solves mysteries. Indeed, we could see the advance of science as a progression of solved mysteries.

Chapter 35

SCIENTIFIC INVESTIGATIONS vs. *GHOST HUNTERS*

I have often crossed paths with the Atlantic Paranormal Society (TAPS), headed by Jason Hawes and Grant Wilson, stars of the popular *Ghost Hunters* series on Syfy (formerly the Sci-Fi Channel). On Saturday, July 26, 2008, my wife, Diana Harris, and I attended their presentation at Lily Dale, the spiritualist village in Western New York. Jason and Grant were kind enough to single me out—favorably—during their talk, and I accepted their invitation for a beer afterward. They graciously bestowed on me an autographed copy of their book *Ghost Hunting: True Stories of Unexplained Phenomena from the Atlantic Paranormal Society*, produced with, well, ghostwriter Michael Jan Friedman (Hawes and Wilson 2007). Interestingly, Friedman authors "science fiction and fantasy novels." (See figure 35.1.)

Figure 35.1. The author (*right*) meets with Grant Wilson (*left*) and Jason Hawes after their presentation at Lily Dale spiritualist village. (Author's photograph by Diana Harris.)

The book gave me a chance to compare notes with Hawes and Wilson. Because I had preceded them in examining several of the "haunted" places featured on the show, I was able to contrast my findings with theirs. Our mutual cases include the Myrtles Plantation (in St. Francisville, Louisiana), the Winchester Mystery House (San Jose, California), and the St. Augustine Lighthouse (on Florida's east coast).

THE MYRTLES

Located in the Louisiana bayou, the Myrtles Plantation (figure 35.2) is actively promoted by its owners as a haunted place. Indeed, says Jason, "Grant and I could barely contain ourselves. The Myrtles was known as one of the most haunted places in America. It was every paranormal investigator's dream to check the place out" (Hawes and Wilson 2007, 137). Well, I had been there, done that—courtesy of the Discovery Channel—for a documentary.

Figure 35.2. The Myrtles Plantation, picturesquely nestled among trees hung with Spanish moss, is reputedly a very haunted place. (Photo by Joe Nickell.)

In February 2005, the TAPS team members got off to a good start at the Myrtles. They were shown a "ghost" photo, but it had been so enhanced by a "paranormal guy" that they promptly labeled it "tampered." But then came the incident with the lamp: in the plantation's "slave shack" (a structure of recent vintage that never held a slave), a lamp glided eerily across a table behind the pair while they were on camera. Although they conceded that "Grant might have snagged the lamp cord with his foot and dragged it without knowing it," the pair later decided to attribute this incident to "a supernatural force" (Hawes and Wilson 2007, 146). Unfortunately, as reported by *TelevisionWeek*, "Upon close inspection, fans concluded the lamp was being pulled by its own cord. Even worse: a night-vision shot appears to show the cord extending from behind the table to Mr. Wilson's hand" (Hibbard 2005, 19). Yet Grant maintained, "If we were looking for a sign that we were doing something worthwhile, we couldn't have asked for a better one than the lamp." The pair concluded, "The place was haunted" (Hawes and Wilson 2007, 146, 147).

In my own investigation at the Myrtles (including staying alone overnight there August 14–15, 2001), I had reached a very different conclusion about the place. Although its owners and staff hype the tale of a murderous slave named Chloe—a "legend" that Hawes and Wilson repeat in some detail—my research revealed Chloe to be fictitious and the tale to be fakelore rather than folklore. Ghostly phenomena reported at the site can be explained without invoking the supernatural. For instance, a mysteriously swinging door was simply hung off center, and banging noises heard at night were attributable to a loose shutter (Nickell 2003).

RETURN TO WINCHESTER

As discussed in chapter 6, San Jose's Winchester Mystery House is remarkable indeed. Even after the gothic Victorian mansion was greatly reduced in size by the 1906 San Francisco earthquake, eccentric widow Sarah Winchester continued to add to the architectural wonder until her death in 1922. At that time it contained 160 rooms and included bizarre architectural details such as stairways that led nowhere. As we have seen, legend holds that a Boston spirit medium had directed Mrs. Winchester to go west and build, without ceasing, a home for spirits. This was to halt an alleged curse on the Winchesters resulting from the "terrible weapon" (the repeating firearm) they had produced.

Jason and Grant retell the legend without skepticism, although the tale is unproved, exists in many contradictory versions, and lacks proof that Mrs. Winchester was herself a spiritualist.

Visiting the mansion in July 2005, Hawes and Wilson (2007, 225–29) "didn't find anything of a supernatural origin"—and even concluded that "odd banging sounds" were probably "the result of a plumbing problem." Nevertheless, they and their TAPS team continued their pseudoscientific approach to ghost hunting (Hawes and Wilson 2007, 225–29). That is, they relied heavily on alleged ghost-detecting equipment that does not, in fact, detect ghosts. A reading on an electromagnetic field (EMF) meter, for instance, can be caused by faulty wiring, microwaves, solar activity, or any of a number of other nonghostly sources. There is no credible scientific evidence that ghosts exist, let alone that they are electromagnetic—or radioactive: the TAPS team also on occasion uses a "portable Geiger counter" ("St. Augustine Lighthouse" 2006). Other ghost-hunting equipment is similarly useless, especially in the hands of nonscientists (Nickell 2006).

I investigated the Winchester mansion in 2001 (with colleague Vaughn Rees) and found that temperature variations, the settling of an old structure, and other similar characteristics accounted for cold spots, odd noises, and ghostly phenomena (Nickell 2002). I have learned that people's level of ghost experiences is approximately proportional to their psychological tendency to fantasize (Nickell 2000).

ST. AUGUSTINE LIGHTHOUSE

Among the tallest such structures in the United States, the St. Augustine Lighthouse (figure 35.3) is claimed to feature, in the keeper's dwelling, a girl in a red dress who suddenly vanishes and the lingering smell of cigar smoke. In the tower, various unexplained noises are often perceived (Elizabeth and Roberts 1999, 40–49).

Once again, the TAPS team lugged in the fancy equipment on which their pseudoscientific approach to ghost hunting depends. They placed a wireless audio unit up in the tower; at the bottom, a thermal camera was positioned to shoot upward "just to see what we could pick up" (Hawes and Wilson 2007, 234–35). The team claims to have seen a shadowy figure and heard a woman's cry as they went up the stairs. Jason ran toward it but "couldn't catch more than a glimpse of the dark figure" as he gained the stairs (2007, 236). Afterward, their "video footage clearly showed a shadow at the top of the stairs. A moment later, we heard a female voice crying for help, and saw the shadow dart to the right" (2007, 238). They concluded that the St. Augustine Lighthouse was indeed haunted.

Figure 35.3. At the St. Augustine Lighthouse ghost hunters may have been detecting—themselves! (Photo by Joe Nickell.)

That lighthouse was one of many I have investigated (Nickell 2008). (My wife and I even stayed as "assistant keepers" at a couple of remote sites. See chapter 13.) On March 23, 2004, I climbed the 219 steps to check out the St. Augustine Lighthouse's tower and also explored the keeper's house. The occasional perception of cigar smoke in the latter may have a ready explanation, as discussed in chapter 13. There is often confusion as to the true nature of the smoke (attributed alternately to cigars, cigarettes, burning wiring, etc.), and real smoke can drift inside or its smell be carried in on people's clothing. The power of suggestion may be at work as well. Similarly, apparitions at "haunted" sites are also explainable. For example, private citizens who rented the St. Augustine keeper's dwelling (after the light was automated in 1955) sometimes woke to see a young girl at their bedside (Elizabeth and Roberts 1999, 44). Such sightings are easily explained scientifically as "waking dreams," which occur in the state between sleep and wakefulness (see appendix).

As to noises in the tower, there are a number of plausible explanations, beginning with the wind. Indeed, Hawes and Wilson (2007, 238) themselves found one culprit in the form of a window "free to swing with the wind." Temperature changes can also cause old steel to make noises as it expands and contracts (Thompson 1998, 73). One such screeching sound was interpreted as "a female voice crying for help." (Another possibility is seagulls; the birds may "shriek" and "sound almost like humans screaming" [Vercillo 2008, 50].)

Glimpsed shadows might have an equally simple explanation. I studied the video of the TAPS team's St. Augustine Lighthouse episode ("St. Augustine Lighthouse" 2006) with two colleagues, Timothy Binga and Tom Flynn, and all of us were underwhelmed. Flynn, the Center for Inquiry's video expert, summed up the evidence by stating: "These visual effects are so ambiguous that they may signify nothing at all." He added, "The observed effect might even be the shadows of the ghost hunters themselves as they moved about, several landings below" (Flynn 2009).

As this comparison of cases shows, the approach of so-called ghost hunters is simply one of mystery mongering. Like claims for the paranormal in general, their assertions that certain places are haunted are based on the logical fallacy of arguing from ignorance: "We don't know what caused such-and-such (a noise, say), so it must have been a ghost." In fact, one cannot draw a conclusion from a lack of knowledge. The problem is exacerbated by the pseudoscientific use of scientific equipment and by the distinct possibility that ghost hunters are actually causing—even if unintentionally—some of the very phenomena they are experiencing!

In contrast is the scientific investigator's approach: begin with the phenomenon in question, try to ascertain whether it in fact happened, develop hypotheses to explain it, and seek to find the most likely explanation—keeping in mind that one cannot explain one mystery by attributing it to another.

Chapter 36

GHOST HUSTLING
IN CONNECTICUT

Shades of *The Amityville Horror*! Take a house reeking of death, bring in a "demonologist," commission a professional writer to enhance the alleged events, Hollywoodize the resulting book into a horror/thriller flick, and shamelessly bandy about the word *true* in promotional copy. This formula lured moviegoers to *The Amityville Horror* (1979); now—current hucksters hope—*The Haunting in Connecticut*, "based on true events," will entice a new generation of credulous screamers. But here is some of the real truth I encountered in my investigation of the case in 1992 and 1993.

Figure 36.1. An image from the Lions Gate
feature film *The Haunting in Connecticut*.

BACKGROUND

It's an old story—in more ways than one. In 1986 the family of Allen and Carmen Snedeker (respectively a stone-quarry foreman and former bowling-alley cocktail waitress) moved into an old residence, known as the Hallahan House, in Southington, Connecticut (figure 36.2). The family included three sons, ages thirteen, eleven, and three (the two oldest being Carmen's by a previous marriage), and a six-year-old daughter; two nieces would later follow.

Figure 36.2. The "haunted" former funeral home known as the Hallahan House. (Watercolor by Joe Nickell.)

It is disputed whether the Snedekers knew when they moved in on June 30 that the house had been a funeral home. They maintained they did not; however, some neighbors insisted otherwise, and the previous owners emphatically stated that the Snedekers were informed of the house's former use prior to their moving in. In any case, the family soon discovered in the basement a box of coffin handles, a chain-and-pulley casket lift, and a blood drainage pit—unmistakable relics of the previous business, the Hallahan Funeral Home.

The creepy setting may well have had a powerful suggestive effect. Spooky phenomena began with the oldest son, Philip, whose basement bedroom was adjacent to the gruesome area. Soon he reported seeing ghosts, although his parents say they first attributed this to cobalt treatments he was receiving for Hodgkin's disease. Philip's personality changed drastically: he began wearing leather, developed an interest in demonology, and even reportedly broke into a neighbor's home, telling his mother he wanted a gun so he could kill his stepfather (Corica and Smith 1988a; Rivard 1988; Carpenter 1988).

The phenomena allegedly continued for two years. A seventeen-year-old niece claimed an unseen hand fondled her on occasion as she lay in bed, and there were many other reported occurrences, including more apparitions, noises, and physical attacks—especially alleged demonic sexual attacks on Carmen Snedeker (Carpenter 1988; Corica and Smith 1988a).

Then the Snedekers brought in notorious "demonologist" Ed Warren and his "clairvoyant" wife Lorraine. The couple made a business—some would say a racket—of spirits. They came to be called many things, ranging from "passionate and religious people" to "scaremongers" and "charlatans" (Duckett 1991). Already having helped promote the Amityville "horror" and a similar West Pittston, Pennsylvania, "nightmare" (Curran 1988), they continued their modus operandi of arriving at a "haunted" house and transforming the case into a "demonic" one, in keeping with their own medieval-style Catholic beliefs. (Like the Lutzes at Amityville and the Smurls at West Pittston, the Snedekers were self-described devout Catholics.)

Bringing with them two "psychic researchers" (the Warrens' grandson and nephew), Ed and Lorraine Warren moved into the house for nine weeks. While denying there was any book deal in progress, the researchers had in fact made just such an arrangement. Mrs. Snedeker had already told her upstairs neighbor about the deal, saying she and her husband were to receive one-third of the profits (Carpenter 1988; Corica and Smith 1988a, 1988b).

Soon both Al and Carmen Snedeker were publicly claiming to have been raped and sodomized by demons—the same claim made in a previous case involving the Warrens (Nickell 1995, 131). They would repeat these claims on national television shows—notably on *Sally Jessy Raphael*—to promote their book with the Warrens, *In a Dark Place: The Story of a True Haunting*

(Warren et al. 1992). It was written with professional horror-tale writer Ray Garton and timed—like the *Sally* show—for Halloween promotion, 1992.

INVESTIGATION

Although I had earlier appeared with Carmen Snedeker on *The Maury Povich Show* (taped March 2, 1992), my investigation intensified when *Sally Jessy Raphael* producers sent me an advance copy of the Warrens and Snedekers' book and invited me on the show. I later visited Southington as a guest of one of the Snedekers' neighbors.

On the *Sally* show (taped October 19, aired October 30), I appeared with the Warrens and Snedekers as well as several of the latter's skeptical Southington neighbors. Ed made veiled threatening asides to me (not aired) and, offstage, swore like a sailor. During the taping, the Snedekers sat on a brass bed while telling their story of demonic sexual attack.

Among their most effective critics was Mrs. Kathy Altemus, who lived across the street from the Snedekers during their entire residence in the Hallahan House. Beginning in mid-July 1988, Mrs. Altemus kept a journal of events relating to 208 Meriden Avenue. As she told Sally, "I discovered that there were usually things going on in the neighborhood that explained the things they put in the newspaper." The journal—which she generously shared with me to help "expose the truth" (Altemus 1993)—juxtaposes her written records with news clippings arranged chronologically. The result is revealing. For instance, the television program *A Current Affair* mentioned the sound of clanking chains in the house, presumably from the coffin lift in the basement. But Mrs. Altemus's journal shows that the noise most likely was from a truck that passed by, making a sound like it was "dragging a chain." Other events also had credible explanations, some attributable to various passersby mentioned in the journal as "pulling pranks on the 'haunted house'" (Nickell 1995, 137, 147n98).

The journal also sheds light on another event. As sensationalized in the *New Britain Herald*, either a "bizarre coincience or ghost" was indicated by a power outage—caused by a tree limb that fell onto an electrical line outside the Hallahan House just after *A Current Affair* broadcast "a segment on the Snedeker family of that address." According to the paper, a utility spokesman "was at a loss to explain just why the limb chose that particular time to knock out the power." In fact, however, the incident did not occur at the time of the television program but approximately two hours later. Besides, as the journal makes clear, such outages have occurred several times on tree-lined Meriden Avenue, when limbs have fallen on the uninsulated line. Such an event, in fact, actually occurred when I was in Southington at the Altemus home in June 1993. It seems unlikely that demonic forces were heralding my arrival or had no better means of attempting to scare me away.

Long before the *Sally* show, in response to the Warrens' shameless media exploitation, the Snedekers' landlady—who had served them with an eviction notice for failing to pay their rent—had responded to the supernatural claims. She and her husband, she said, had owned the property for two and a half years and had experienced no problems with it.

"Personally, my husband and I do not believe in ghosts and to us, the whole issue seems ridiculous. I find it ironic that after more than two years as tenants, suddenly we are told about these alleged ghosts and then read in the paper that the Warrens will be conducting a seminar and will be charging the public for it.

"If the ghosts really are there, then why did the Snedekers stay there over two years and why are they staying there now? Are they looking for publicity or profit, or what?" the landlady said (quoted in DiMauro and Starmack 1989).

The Snedekers' upstairs neighbor had similar views. Calling the Warrens "con artists," she said: "I haven't experienced anything. I definitely know that no one has been raped up here." She told reporters that the Warrens, who she was convinced were exploiting the situation for personal gain, "have caused a lot of problems here and they are not ghost problems" (Corica and Smith 1988b).

Other revealing information came to light in Southington—about Philip Snedeker's drug use, vandalism, and other misbehavior. There was even an explanation for the sexual touching that Carmen's niece had felt "from an unseen hand." The boy was actually caught fondling his nieces while they slept. "Steven" (as he is called in the book) "was taken away by the police that afternoon. He was questioned, at which time he confessed that he'd been fondling the girls while they slept at night, and that he'd attempted unsuccessfully to have sex with his twelve-year-old cousin." He was later taken to the juvenile detention center, where a psychiatrist diagnosed him as schizophrenic (Warren et al. 1992, 145–47).

CONCLUSIONS

Many people branded the Warren-Snedeker-Garton book fiction. Said the husband of the Snedekers' landlady: "It's a fraud. It's a joke. It's a hoax. It's Halloween." He added, "It's a scheme to make money." Those comments appeared in a brilliantly titled newspaper article (Schmidt 1992), "Couple Sees Ghost; Skeptics See through It." As indicated by the evidence—the publicity-seeking actions in the case and the timing of the book for Halloween promotion—there is reason to doubt the motives of those involved. If the case did not originate as a hoax, I concluded from my original investigation (Nickell 1995, 139), people could scarcely be blamed for thinking it has been transformed into one.

Subsequent developments have only supported that conclusion. Some of the coauthors of the Warrens' books have reportedly since admitted that Ed Warren (who died in 2006) told them to make up incidents and details to create "scary" stories (Nickell 2006). Ray Garton, the award-winning horror writer who wrote the book about the Southington case—on which the movie *The Haunting in Connecticut* is based—has now effectively repudiated that book. He says he is glad that it went out of print, adding: "The family involved, which was going through some serious problems like alcoholism and drug addiction, could not keep their story straight, and I became very frustrated; it's hard writing a non-fiction book when all the people involved are telling you different stories" ("Ray Garton" 2009). So much for the movie being "based on true events."

Chapter 37

GHOST FORENSICS

We have come a long way since the time of the first real-life "scientific detective," an Austrian attorney named Hans Gross (1847–1915). Gross seemed to embody, in real life, Sherlock Holmes's fictional ability to glean much information from a bit of evidence others had overlooked. His "manual for examining magistrates," published in 1893 (and eventually republished in English as *Criminal Investigation*) advocated the use of forensic medicine, ballistics, toxicology, and other sciences. He coined the term *criminalistics* (Nickell and Fischer 1999, 8–10).

Since the early 1970s I have endeavored to apply forensic techniques to the paranormal—including spirit phenomena and hauntings. Incidentally, today's popular acronym "CSI" stands not only for crime-scene investigation (or investigator) but also for Committee for Skeptical Inquiry—my employer and the publisher of *Skeptical Inquirer* science magazine. I am, indeed, a CSI for CSI.

The following are abstracts of several of my important early cases, illustrating how particular applications of forensic science have helped solve purportedly otherworldly mysteries.

LASER-LIGHT EXAMINATION

A case I investigated in 1985 began when some forty persons each paid twenty dollars to attend a séance in Lexington, Kentucky. There, alleged spirit productions called "precipitations on silk" were manifested (figure 37.1). The "medium" placed an open bottle of ink on a table and, as the attendees sat in the darkened room, each had a small square cloth placed in his or her lap. After suitably invoking the spirits, who then purportedly spoke through the entranced channeler, he went about the room carrying a lamp with a dim red bulb. This created an eerie effect. As each person turned over his or her square cloth, three or four thumbprint-sized "spirit" faces were seen to have apparently materialized onto the fabric.

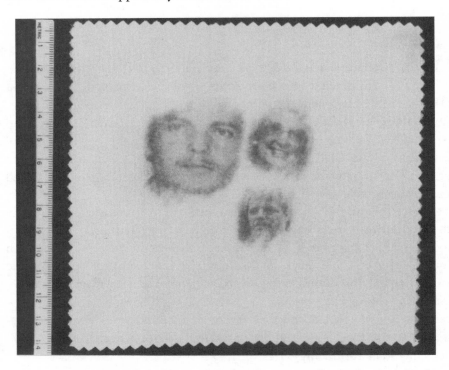

Figure 37.1. Alleged "spirit precipitations" supposedly depict the sitter's "spirit guides." (Photographed by John F. Fischer for Joe Nickell.)

I was made aware of the case of a young woman who had attended the séance. She felt she had been scammed. I submitted her cloth swatch to examination by forensic analyst John F. Fischer. While infrared and ultraviolet light showed nothing, argon laser light revealed a circular stain around each face: this was evidence of a different type of spirits—a solvent such as ammonia or alcohol—used to a transfer a newspaper or magazine photograph onto fabric, using a hot iron (figures 37.2–37.3).

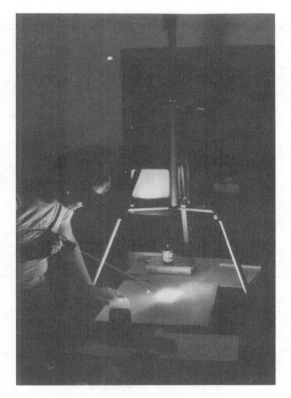

Figure 37.2. Forensic analyst John F. Fischer examines evidence with the argon laser. (Photographed by John F. Fischer for Joe Nickell.)

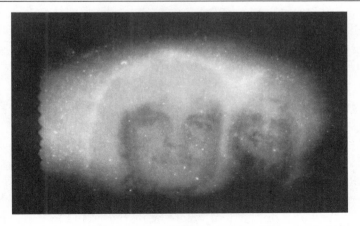

Figure 37.3. Laser light reveals telltale solvent-produced areas around "spirit images." (Photographed by John F. Fischer for Joe Nickell.)

Figure 37.4. Images experimentally produced by author replicate "spirit" pictures. (Photographed by John F. Fischer for Joe Nickell.)

Obviously the swatches shown the sitters were blank, but after the lights were extinguished, those were switched for prepared ones. The book *The Psychic Mafia* (Keene and Spraggett 1976, 64–66) tells how such fakes were made at the spiritualist Camp Chesterfield in Indiana—the very place the medium in question resided (see figure 37.4). Although I obtained police warrants against him, the small fee he had charged each victim kept the offense within the misdemeanor range, and so he could not be extradited. However, until his death he did not again ply his fraud in Kentucky. (See Nickell 1988, 47–60.)

FORENSIC SEROLOGY

My first direct encounter with a claimed paranormal origin of blood occurred in 1978. It involved an eastern Kentucky farmhouse located, curiously, on "Deadening Branch." The deserted house had a front door that reportedly bled—indeed bore mysterious streaks that supposedly correlated with a century-old tragedy: a boy crushed to death in a cane-mill mishap was reportedly "laid out" on the door before being buried in the cemetery overlooking the site. Here was a popular folklore motif, the "ineradicable bloodstain after bloody tragedy."

Actually, the grayish streaks visible on the door were consistent with water-borne substances such as dirt, tar, decaying leaves, and so forth, that had washed down from the roof. I lightly scraped off some of the deposit, carefully wrapping it in paper for future testing. This was carried out by forensic analyst John F. Fischer, who conducted several preliminary tests for various hemoglobin-related compounds, using reagents that yield color reactions in the presence of those compounds. The various tests were negative, indicating no blood was present, even in trace amounts. When mysterious noises and other phenomena that made up the "haunting" were explained, the case gave up the ghost. (See Nickell 1988, 119–28.)

BLOOD-PATTERN ANALYSIS

Atlanta's "House of Blood" mystery began on September 8, 1987, at the home of an elderly African American couple. Blood began to flow from the walls and spring up from the floor "like a sprinkler." Police were called and, although they took color crime-scene photos (figure 37.5), they abandoned the case after concluding no crime had occurred. Soon, however, exaggerated accounts of the "unexplained" case began to be circulated, and the bizarre phenomenon was attributed to poltergeist activity.

Figure 37.5. Blood-pattern analysis from police photographs revealed the "House of Blood" mystery was a hoax. (Photograph courtesy of the Atlanta Police Department.)

I began an investigation of the occurrence in 1991. I obtained special access to the police file and discussed the case—both on and off the record—with the homicide commander. From the photographs it did not appear to me that the blood had manifested in the manner described, so I submitted copies of the photos to forensic blood-pattern analyst Judith Bunker. Her subsequent report detailed how the blood had been applied in "spurt" patterns *onto* the floor and walls, discrediting the witnesses' statements and supporting additional evidence that suggested a hoax. As one police investigator said somewhat cryptically, "Some adults will act like children just to get attention." (See the section titled "House of Blood" in chapter 3 of Nickell 1995, 92–97.)

ACOUSTICS

Among my early paranormal investigations—and my first "haunting"—was that of Canada's famous ghost residence, Mackenzie House in downtown Toronto. Prior to my visits in 1972–1973, strange occurrences there were attributed to the spirit of William Lyon Mackenzie. Among the most interesting of the varied phenomena were sounds of heavy footsteps on the old stairs. These occurred when caretakers were lying abed in a rear bedroom on the other side of the house. During these occasions the couple were alone in the locked house. On occasion they heard other sounds, such as piano music, even though the piano sat unused in the parlor.

The sounds were puzzling until, on a tip from one earwitness, I visited the adjacent building. There, against the proximate wall, separated by just forty inches, was a parallel iron staircase. On those stairs the noisy footfalls of real people—members of the building superintendent's family or the nighttime cleanup crew—created the illusion that someone was treading the staircase in Mackenzie House, especially to those lying quietly and thinking of ghosts. As to the piano music, the super's apartment jutted above the flat expanse of the rest of the Macmillan building. He explained how his son's piano music wafted across the flat roof, struck the taller brick house, and was consequently amplified by a sort of echo-chamber effect caused by the hollow space between the two buildings. Privately, the custodian had determined that the sounds actually seemed louder inside the house due to the effect of the amplification. Over time, unexplained sounds and other occurrences had developed into a full-blown case of what psychologists call *contagion* (see appendix)—a sort of bandwagon effect in which people's ghostly experiences prompt others to have experiences of their own (Nickell 1988, 17–27).

MACROSCOPY

Macroscopy (distinguished from microscopy) is the scrutiny of things that are visible to the naked eye or with a simple magnifying glass. Sometimes even a lay person may be able to make a close inspection and see the obvious. Take the case of America's most infamous haunted house. As told in Jay Anson's *The Amityville Horror*—falsely subtitled *A True Story* (1977)—in 1975 the Lutz family moved into a six-bedroom Dutch colonial home on Long Island, New York, in the community of Amityville, where, the previous year, young Ronald DeFeo had murdered his parents and siblings in cold blood. Just weeks after moving in, the Lutzes were telling a fantastic tale of being driven out by demonic spirits. They said a door was ripped off its hinges, among other damage, and that one entity had left clover-hoofed tracks in the snow outside! Now there are actually forensic techniques for recording footprints in snow (Nickell and Fischer 1999, 151), but in this case there was a bigger problem: The whole story began to fall apart.

I contacted the later owners, talking with Barbara Cromarty on three occasions, including when I visited Amityville as a consultant to the *In Search Of . . .* television series. She told me the damage to doors and windows never occurred. Not only was the old hardware obviously still in place but, upon close inspection, one could see that there were no disturbances to the original paint and varnish. When the TV show *That's Incredible* featured the case in its premier episode, the producers took my advice and had Mrs. Cromarty guide them through the house, the camera taking a close look at the features she pointed out. As to the cloven footprints in the snow, researchers discovered that, on the date given, there had been no snowfall on the ground. Other claims were similarly disproved, and eventually William Weber, attorney for Ronald DeFeo, admitted colluding with the Lutzes on a book deal: "We created this horror story over many bottles of wine that George Lutz was drinking" (Nickell 1995, 122–29).

OBLIQUE-LIGHT EXAMINATION

Among the "physical phenomena" commonly manifested during the heyday of spiritualism were paintings produced in various media and under a variety of conditions but attributed to spirit entities. Frequently the pictures were ordinary pastels like those produced by the notorious Bangs Sisters (whose methods I have discussed elsewhere at length [Nickell 2001, 267–75]). However, a rather unusual spirit painting—exhibited at the spiritualist village Lily Dale, in Western New York—is of particular interest. It was produced by the Campbell "Brothers" (actually a gay couple, Allan B. Campbell [1853–1919], and Charles "Campbell" Shrouds [d. 1926]). Supposedly portraying Allan Campbell's spirit guide, Azur, the picture is a striking forty-by-sixty-inch oil painting that reportedly materialized—from a blank canvas, through several stages of development—over an hour and a half's time. The "spirits," accompanied by an allegedly entranced Campbell, worked behind a curtain; each time it was drawn back, séance attendees saw a new stage of the painting.

I examined the artwork at Lily Dale in 1999 using oblique light. In this technique, light is aimed at a low angle, which helps to reveal surface irregularities such as erasures, indentations, and the like (Nickell and Fischer 1999, 177). In the case of "Azur," I discovered surface damage in each of the four corners, consistent with a known technique for producing such fake pictures. This involves lightly gluing, say, two canvases over the finished one: the first partially painted and the second one a blank that hides the others. Additional work was probably done on the partially finished canvas using brushes and paints that were probably kept in the drawer of the "small table" on which the painting seems to have been stood (Nickell 2001, 259–66).

HANDWRITING

A case in Kentucky that Dr. Robert Baker and I were involved in concerned an apparently haunted houseboat. As related in our book *Missing Pieces: How to Investigate Ghosts, UFOs, Psychics, and Other Mysteries* (1992), the boat was moored at a marina, where a widow had put it up for sale. One evening, the twenty-five-year-old caretaker reported having seen lights on in the houseboat. Although the boat was locked, he found signs that it had been recently occupied. Setting everything right, he returned to the office, but soon he saw the lights come on again. In fact there were several more occurrences, and, even when he cut off the only source of electricity to the boat, the lights continued to mysteriously come on. Finally, the young caretaker left a note for the ghost, asking what he wanted. The ghost replied!

Not only did the ghost write a note to the caretaker, insisting he only wished to be left in peace, but he also penned a cordial missive to the Kentucky State Police river patrolman who was stationed at the marina and who was investigating the poltergeistlike disturbances. This was the "ghost's" error in judgment. The patrolman obtained a specimen of the caretaker's handwriting, and it was a simple matter (the "ghost" handwriting not being disguised) to compare the two. They matched. Confronted, the young man confessed that he had been perpetrating a hoax. He believed the publicity it engendered would help sell the houseboat as well as increase business at the marina (Baker and Nickell 1992, 128–29).

FINGERPRINTS

The following case is a historical one I studied during my tenure as resident magician at the Houdini Magical Hall of Fame (Niagara Falls, Ontario) from 1970 to 1972. It concerned "Margery," the medium (real name Mina Crandon) whose séance effects were branded deceptions by Houdini, the famed magician, escape artist, and exposer of phony spiritualists. One of her later effects, shown after Houdini's death (on Halloween 1926), was the production of a "spirit" thumbprint. She claimed it was that of her dead brother, Walter, and indeed it was authenticated as such by a police expert.

However, spiritualist researcher E. E. Dudley had begun to catalog each fingerprint "Walter" had produced, and he then decided to collect the prints of those who had attended the various séances. He was startled to discover that the prints that were supposedly Walter's actually matched those of Mrs. Crandon's dentist, Dr. Frederick Caldwell. Caldwell's involvement in the deception was unintentional. He had, at her request, supplied Mrs. Crandon with dental wax for her séance and had showed her how well it recorded thumbprints when softened in hot water, even pressing his own thumbs into it to demonstrate its preservation of detail! With those thumbprints, Mrs. Crandon could make casts and so produce additional impressions as desired. As to the police fingerprint expert, he was a phony, a Margery plant. Houdini's accusations against her were vindicated (Polidoro 2001, 229–30).

FORENSIC LINGUISTICS

Like "spirit paintings," bogus mediums also produced so-called spirit writings, often chalked on slates. One such slate, with a signed message purportedly from Abraham Lincoln, is displayed in the Lily Dale Museum. The late curator there, my friend Joyce LeJudice, graciously permitted me to examine and photograph it. Not only was I able to demonstrate that the handwriting and signature were positively not those of Lincoln, but—as a member of the International Association of Forensic Linguists, I determined to scrutinize the text as well.

I found several elements of the language suspicious, including the use of *thy*, which is both uncharacteristic of Lincoln and a common ploy used by pretentious writers trying to adopt a lofty tone. Most significant was the slate writer's use of *should of* for *should have*—a grammatical error that is unimaginable for such a skilled writer as Abraham Lincoln. Putting that evidence with the bogus handwriting, I had no hesitation in pronouncing the entire production fraudulent (Nickell 2001, 39–47).

RE-CREATION EXPERIMENTS

Quite often in forensic cases, it becomes desirable to attempt to re-create some effect as a means of demonstrating how it most likely occurred. Experts conduct experiments in every forensic field. (For example, in one homicide case colleague John F. Fischer and I fired bullets in an experimental manner into the thin bone of deer skulls' eye sockets to re-create an unusual wound defect in the eye socket of the deceased, with successful results [Nickell and Fischer 1999, 91].) Re-creations are also useful in paranormal investigation. For instance, at Austria's Salzburg Castle, I took experimental photographs in an attempt to learn whether an anomaly in a photo made there might have a different cause than a "ghost."

My re-creation (shown earlier in figure 16.1) demonstrates that what appears in some photos taken at "haunted" sites and attributed to a "spiraling mist" of "paranormal energy" is probably nothing more than the flash bouncing off the carelessly placed wrist strap! (See also chapter 38, "Photoghosts: Images of the Spirit Realm?") Such effects need not occur only at "haunted" sites, but can be made at will anywhere.

Chapter 38

PHOTOGHOSTS: IMAGES OF THE SPIRIT REALM?

S ince it was founded in London in 1882, the Society for Psychical Research (SPR) has conducted research into paranormal claims. Its founders' hope was to validate spiritualist phenomena and so unite science and religion (Guiley 2000, 353). Over the subsequent century and a quarter, the society's archives have amassed an important collection of anomalous photographs that (with other collections, such as the Fortean Picture Library) have been tapped for the book *Ghosts Caught on Film: Photographs of the Paranormal?* The compilation is by Dr. Melvyn Willin, the SPR's honorable archive officer. It is at once an invaluable compendium—a selection of curious paranormal photos, many of which are treated with appropriate skepticism—and an annoying presentation with outright fakes sometimes obfuscated by excessive credulity.

Figure 38.1. *Ghosts Caught on Film: Photographs of the Paranormal?* by Dr. Melvyn Willin.

PARANORMALITIES

Willin appropriately debunks such notorious images as the 1917 Cottingley Glen fairy photographs produced by two schoolgirls using obvious cutouts (but fooling the likes of Sir Arthur Conan Doyle) (2007, 16–17), and a supposed séance materialization of spirit "Katie King" that is in fact a depiction of the medium Florence Cook posing "in her underwear" (Willin 2007, 18–19). He also correctly explains some images—a "Madonna and Child" seen in a fountain's splashing water, the face of a "cherub" gazing from a wedding posy, and the "Virgin Mary" outlined in tree branches (Willin 2007, 52–57)—as simulacra resulting from our ability to interpret random patterns, like inkblots or clouds, as recognizable pictures. Indeed, a "sacred elephant in the sky" (Willin 2007, 62–63) is merely a pachyderm-shaped cloud.

Still, Willin is unwilling, it seems, to avoid mystery mongering altogether. For example, he is too uncritical of "aura" photographs, including Kirlian photos (Willin 2007, 36–37, 12–43; cf. Nickell 2001, 142–49) and the allegedly psychically projected "thoughtographs" of Ted Serios (Nickell 1994, 197–98; Randi 1982, 222–27). Willin's main focus (so to speak), as his book's title makes clear, is on ghosts, and the majority of his questioned pictures are of that genre: here a spook, there a specter, elsewhere an apparition or a phantom—a ghost (or a spirit of the dead) by any other name.

However, it is important to realize that the earliest photographic processes recorded not a single ghost: not the early, impermanent experimental images of J. Nicephore Niepce in the first quarter of the nineteenth century nor the later experiments (1834–1839) by Fox Talbot, who produced "fixed" prints on paper. The first practical photographic process, the daguerreotype (after L. J. M. Daguerre), which was announced in 1839, likewise recorded no ghosts. And the same is true of ambrotypes (from 1855) and tintypes (patented in 1856) (Coe 1989, 8–37; Nickell 1994, 4–29, 147–49).

DEBUT OF SPIRITS

Not until glass-plate negatives came on the scene (about 1859), facilitating double imaging, did "ghosts" begin to appear in photographs. The first such fakes were produced by Boston photographer William H. Mumler (figure 38.2). He discovered that when he recycled glass photographic plates, a faint image could remain and so appear as a dim image in subsequent pictures if the glass was not thoroughly cleaned. Spiritualism then being all the rage, Mumler went into business in 1862 as a "spirit photographer," eventually attracting such clients as Mary Todd Lincoln, whose portrait included a "spirit" image of her assassinated husband (Willin 2007, 22–23). However, Mumler was exposed as a fraud when people recognized that some of the supposed spirits were still among the living (Nickell 1994, 146–59, 192–96).

W. H. MUMLER.   MRS. W. H. MUMLER.—BY MUMLER.

SPIRIT PHOTOGRAPH BY MUMLER.   SPIRIT PHOTOGRAPH BY MUMLER.

Figure 38.2. Engravings show the "spirit" photographer, Mumler, and some of his bogus productions. (*Harper's Weekly*, May 8, 1869.)

Nevertheless, "spirit" photography was off and running (figure 38.3), later followed—if we make a distinction that Willin does not—by "ghost" photography. The difference? The former began in the studio and moved to include the séance room, the idea being that spirits of the departed were usually conjured up, summoned to appear in order to communicate with the living. In contrast, ghost photographs were typically made at supposedly haunted sites. And whereas spirit photos were invariably charlatans' productions, ghost photos could either be faked or appear inadvertently—as by reflection, accidental double exposure, or the like.

Figure 38.3. Mumler's fake spirit photos were widely imitated, like this *carte de visite* example. Note that the sitter is posed low in the picture to allow room for the "spirits." (Author's collection.)

Willin would do well to note that ghost photos began to proliferate after portable cameras became available to amateurs during the 1880s—especially at the end of the decade, when George Eastman introduced celluloid roll film for his Kodak® camera (Nickell 1994 22–28, 158). Like the earliest spirit photos, those supposedly depicting ghosts showed them to look just like people, only more ethereal. In modern times, that would change when a variety of ghostly forms—such as strands of "ectoplasm" (an imagined spirit substance) or "orbs" (bright balls of "energy")—began to appear in snapshots. The main culprit was the pocket camera with a built-in flash. The burst of light could rebound from the wrist strap to produce the ectoplasmic strands, or from dust particles or water droplets to yield orbs, or from a wandering fingertip, strand of hair, or piece of jewelry to produce various other shapes or blurs (Nickell 1994, 159).

PHOTO ANALYSIS

To show how additional facts and analysis can help illuminate many alleged ghost photographs, here are a few from Willin's compendium that are especially deserving of such treatment.

Posing Spirits. A circa 1875 image by the notorious English spirit photographer Frederick Hudson depicts a seated man surrounded by shrouded figures. "Although known to dress up and pose as his own 'ghosts' and to use double exposure for cheating," concedes Willin, "Hudson was ultimately believed to have leavened his frauds with much genuine spirit photography" (Willin 2007). Reputedly, in this instance the sitter and two friends were permitted to operate the camera without Hudson's interference.

Never mind that Hudson allegedly used a specially gimmicked Howell camera; it supposedly held a framed, pre-exposed image that moved into position while the sitter was being photographed (Willin 2007, 25). There are other inherent indicators that the photograph is bogus. If the extra figures are subtracted from the picture, the composition is unaccountably bad: the sitter is positioned not only off-center (being both too far to the right and too low), but also too far away, so as to leave an unusual amount of surrounding space. One can rationalize that the additional space was left to make room for the spirits, but how would they have known just where to place themselves to make a pleasing arrangement? Most likely the chair and camera had been prepositioned by Hudson, who had already photographed the "spirits." Still another indicator of faking comes from the figures' wearing shrouds. This seems less a convincing attire for ghosts than a suspiciously dramatic convention (as Willin himself notes in the following case).

Haunted Doorway. A figure, shrouded head-to-toe and appearing semitransparently before the doorway of a thatched-roof building, was supposedly photographed in the 1920s. However, the image did not surface until 1993, and its place of origin is only assumed to be "probably England." Willin admits that "most people are suspicious of the dramatic drapery," since the majority of ghost sightings look like "real people in real clothes" (Willin 2007, 146–47). Yet he adds: "One day, technology could well tell us this apparition is exactly what it seems to be: a genuine paranormal presence."

What it *really* seems to be is a staged ghost photo. There is a well-known technique for producing such fakes that does not require any tampering with the negative or other darkroom deception. It was used by some spirit photographers: while the sitter remained motionless for the lengthy exposure, a confederate—suitably attired—simply appeared briefly behind the unwitting person, the result being a photo with a semitransparent "spirit" (Nickell 1994, 152). The same effect can be produced accidentally when someone steps briefly into or out of a scene that is photographed with a long exposure (Nickell 1994, 158–59). Several other photos published by Willin may be of this type, as he himself somewhat grudgingly admits (e.g., Willin 2007, 76–77, 86–87, 116–17, 132–33, 144–45).

Specter on the Stairs. A famous 1936 photograph of a too-good-to-be-true ghostly figure on a staircase was made at Raynham Hall in Norfolk, England, by a pair of reporters who claimed first to see the apparition and then to quickly take a picture of it. Willin sits on the fence—or is it the banister?—on this one, acknowledging that "there appear to be inconsistencies in the photo on the stair rail," while insisting that the negative appeared to be "genuine" and there was "a tradition of haunting" at the house (Willin 2007, 128–29). He adds, "Let the viewer decide."

And so expert viewers have. A careful examination of the photograph (in much greater enlargement than given in Willin's book) shows evidence of double exposure. "For example," note John Fairley and Simon Welfare (1987, 140) in *Arthur C. Clarke's Chronicles of the Strange and Mysterious*, "there is a pale line above each stair-tread, indicating that one picture has been superimposed over the other; a patch of reflected light at the top of the right-hand banister appears twice." What likely happened is that the camera was shifted slightly during a long, two-stage exposure, one with a real figure briefly standing on the stairs. Hence, the negative would be unaltered. Photo expert Tom Flynn (2008) agrees with this assessment and cites clear evidence that the photo was not flash illuminated but rather was shot with available light, thus requiring a long exposure. This gives away the lie of the reporters' claim of having made a quick snapshot.

Spirit of "Old Nanna." A 1991 photo depicts a little boy who seems to be gazing up at a bright vortex of mist that intrudes into the photo. But is he really looking at the spirit of Old Nanna, his late great grandmother, as family members have suggested? Unfortunately, no one in the room at the time the picture was snapped perceived anything out of the ordinary. Although acknowledging that "there is not enough verifiable fact to support the appearance and photographing of a spirit," Willin cautions: "If the picture is fraudulent then the misty cloud should be explainable but it's far too big and dense to be, say, cigarette smoke. Neither is there anything to suggest a human form but, of course, what the boy saw and what we are permitted to see could be quite different" (Willin 2007, 20–21).

Ironically, the effect is clearly due to something that Willin is well aware of—acknowledging elsewhere (2007, 72) how frequently the "camera-strap syndrome" can cause just such an anomaly. He fails to recognize it in this instance even though it has the classic appearance produced by an unsecured strap getting in front of the lens. The braiding of the strap is even evident, an effect I have captured in experimental photographs (Nickell 1996, 13–14).

Palatial Apparition. At Middlesex, England's famed Hampton Court Palace, on October 7, 2003, surveillance-camera footage captured a spooky, robed figure emerging from open fire doors. (This is the photo that graces the cover of Willin's book.) Alarms sounded on three occasions, but each time the doors were found closed. Although Willin cites the opinion of skeptic Richard Wiseman that the figure is likely a person in a costume, he ends by wondering, "Could this be the genuine image of an apparition on film, one of the most rare things in the world?" (2007, 142–43).

I studied the photograph for *Skeptical Inquirer* magazine (Nickell 2004) and similarly determined that the image probably depicted an actual person. Examining a high-resolution electronic copy of the photo, I found a clearly solid figure accompanied by shadow patterns that are consistent with a real, human figure appearing in ambient light. The picture thus contrasts with most traditional "ghost" photos that depict transparent, ethereal figures. I suggested that although the footage might be unaltered, the actual event could well have been staged—as suggested by the repeated opening and closing of the doors and the fact that the incidents occurred during the pre-Halloween season.

These are only a few examples from Willin's compendium. Many others could be noted. Time and again, a spooky picture can best be explained by invoking Occam's razor—the rule that the simplest tenable explanation (the one requiring the fewest assumptions) is preferred. And so, other anomalous photos are likewise attributable to such factors as deliberate hoaxing (figures 38.4 and 38.5), reflections, rebounding flash, defects of camera or film, simulacra, and other factors—factors not of another world, but of this one. (See also figure 38.6.)

Figure 38.4. The phantom figure of the "Gray Lady" of Liberty Hall in Frankfort, Kentucky, is of a type that is easily faked—see figure 38.5. (Photographic copy courtesy of Bill Rodgers.)

Figure 38.5. Experimental photograph made by having someone move quickly downstairs while the shutter is locked open. (Photograph made for the author by Clint Robertson.)

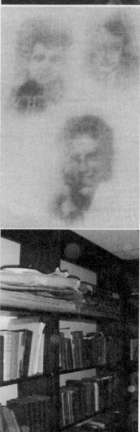

Figure 38.6. Some common "ghost"-photo effects. *Top left:* "Spirit" photo (ca. 1880) made with a double exposure. (Note the sitter is posed off-center to make room for the "extra.") (Author's collection.). *Top right:* Late nineteenth- or early twentieth-century multiple-exposure photograph incorporating cutouts. (Author's collection, gift of Vaughn Rees.) *Middle left:* Photo of author as "ghost" was created by stepping away during a long exposure. (Author's photo by Clint Robertson.) Middle right: "Spirit precipitations" were made by using a solvent and burnisher to transfer newspaper or magazine photos onto cloth. (Produced by Joe Nickell from a spiritualist recipe.) *Bottom left:* This "ectoplasmic strand" actually resulted from the flash rebounding from the camera strap. (Experimental photo by Joe Nickell.) *Bottom right:* "Orbs" caused by scattering dust in the air and taking a flash photo. (Produced by Joe Nickell.)

Chapter 39

GHOSTLY EXPERIENCES: MAGNETIC FIELDS OR SUGGESTIBILITY?

Some skeptics have embraced Michael A. Persinger's studies, which supposedly demonstrate that electromagnetic stimulation of the brain can produce religious or paranormal experiences. Persinger's findings received extensive media attention, including television coverage by the BBC, CNN, and the Discovery Channel, in addition to numerous citations in print, especially in popular-science magazines. Recent experimental results, however, cast doubt on Persinger's claims.

Persinger—a professor of psychology and biology at Laurentian University in Sudbury, Ontario, Canada—has claimed that a majority of test subjects (up to 80 percent) sense an unexplained presence when their temporal lobes are targeted by weak magnetic fields. Skeptics have been tempted to argue from Persinger's work that certain paranormal experiences may merely be due to brain stimulation. Supposedly, sightings of ghosts, angels, and aliens, as well as out-of-body experiences, might all be caused by exposure to electromagnetic fields (as from electronic equipment or power lines) or Earth's geomagnetic fields (Roll and Persinger 2001; Shermer 1999; Granqvist et al. 2004).

Others (myself included) were troubled by some of Persinger's writings, such as "Investigations of Poltergeists and Haunts: A Review and Interpretation," coauthored with parapsychologist William G. Roll (Roll and Persinger 2001). This work suggests, for instance, that some poltergeist ("noisy spirit") disturbances that skeptical investigators have attributed to human tricks or other mundane causes (Christopher 1970, 142–63; Randi

1985; Randi 1995, 52–53, 186; Baker and Nickell 1992, 135–39; Nickell 2001) may instead be due to "a psychoenergetic force." The two collaborators opine that, possibly, "electromagnetic components of mental states can interact with electromagnetic energy in the environment to produce the events" (Roll and Persinger 2001, 152).

In late 2004, however, a joint study by scientists from two Swedish universities called into question much of Persinger's research. The scientists attempted to replicate Persinger's findings using the identical magnetic-field apparatus. Their experiments involved eighty-nine students in psychology and theology.

The researchers found no evidence that paranormal or religious experiences were caused by the electromagnetic stimulation. However, there were such reported experiences in both the test and control group subjects who were highly suggestible (as determined by use of a special questionnaire). The researchers concluded that "suggestibility might well account for the previously reported effects" (Granqvist et al. 2004). To explain the discrepancies between their results and those of Persinger and his coworkers, the Swedish scientists noted that the previous studies were not clearly double blinded. (To avoid influencing the results, neither the test subjects nor experimenters should know who was exposed to the weak magnetic fields and who was not.)

Persinger countered that some of his studies were effectively double blinded and that the Swedish researchers did not expose their test subjects to magnetic fields for a sufficiently long time (Khamsi 2004). That seems an odd claim, since the scientists sought specific instruction from Persinger and his coworker, Stanley Koren, with regard to optimal replication (Granqvist et al. 2004, 5).

Clearly, the claim that application of magnetic fields can prompt certain mystical experiences has been seriously challenged. On the other hand, the Swedish results further demonstrate the powerful role suggestibility plays in such experiences. As the researchers commented, regarding commercially available devices that produce weak complex fields (devices that, while having a different design, function on the same principles as the one used in the various studies), "Insofar as prospective purchasers of such equipment are high on suggestibility, placing the helmet or their heads in a sensory deprivation context might have the anticipated effects, whether or not the cord is plugged in" (Granqvist et al. 2004).

Chapter 40

GHOST HUNTING'S
OTHER SIDE

Ghost hunting—as shown by such popular TV shows as *Ghost Hunters* and *Paranormal State*—may seem an engaging activity. But it often has another side—sometimes comic, frequently controversial, on rare occasions even tragic. Here are examples from my investigative files.

THERMAL-IMAGE "GHOSTS"

During the weekend of January 7–9, 2011, amateur "ghost hunters" were invited to "investigate" so-called paranormal activity in Eureka Springs, Arkansas, at the Crescent Hotel and Spa (built in 1886). The property has become a sensation since the stars of SyFy's *Ghost Hunters*, Jason Hawes and Grant Wilson, using a thermal-imaging camera at the Crescent, photographed a shadowy "apparition" in front of a locker door.

At first the ghost hunters believed the image was merely a thermal reflection of Grant—that is, the result of his body heat reflecting off the locker door. However, when the duo were supposedly unable to re-create the effect, they gushed about having obtained "the holy grail of ghost hunting." But not so fast.

A technical analysis makes a convincing case that the image was indeed "a thermal reflection of Grant." The figure's "hat," which Jason imagines he sees, is apparently only an effect of Grant's shock of hair. The analyst concluded that the duo's two re-creation attempts involved—among other problems—Grant putting his hand into the shot each time, which altered the temperature scale. (See "Crescent Hotel Analysis" 2011.) Thus, the ghost hunters' effort to reproduce the effect was apparently as inept as their creation of it in the first place.

There is, of course, no scientific proof that ghosts exist, despite the pseudoscientific efforts of ghost-hunting amateurs (Grant and Jason actually work as Roto-Rooter plumbers). Their glitch-prone equipment was not manufactured for, nor is it effective for, ghost detection—neither their electromagnetic field meters nor their portable Geiger counters nor their thermal-imaging cameras. (See my "Scientific Investigations vs. *Ghost Hunters*," chapter 35.)

In fact, in 2010 a TV crew and I filmed a series of ghost-hunting techniques, showing how "unexplained" phenomena are often caused—not necessarily intentionally—by ghost hunters themselves. Shown here is our thermal photo of a wall where—just before—a crewmember had stood (figure 40.1).

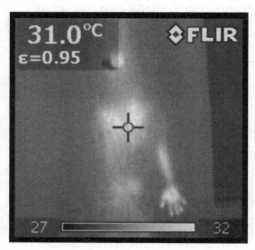

Figure 40.1. Detailed thermal-image photograph of a "ghost"—note the clarity of the hand. (Author's photograph.)

CHIP COFFEY AND *PARANORMAL STATE*

In 2011 the *Miami Herald* contacted me for a feature on Chip Coffey, who claims to communicate with the dead. I shared with reporter Serena Dai (2011) my insights as to how such alleged psychic mediums give the impression they know the unknown, which she included in her article, "Chip Coffey: Sixth Sense, Showbiz, or Both?" As it happens, Coffey—who appeared regularly in A&E's *Psychic Kids* (a program I regard as shamefully exploitive) and *Paranormal State*—has been accused of outright deception involving the latter show.

In an online posting, "Paranormal State—Caught Faking Entire Show,"

Chip Coffey, host Ryan Buell, and other staffers are accused of hoaxing an episode of the popular ghost-hunting show (Ryan 2008). At issue is season two's eighth episode, "The Messenger," which allegedly featured a headless apparition. The accuser—Kelli Ryan (2008), whose home in Gold Beach, Oregon, was the "investigated" site—claims that Coffey had been in town for "48 hours prior to his 'first arrival' on the scene." She says, "Chip Coffey only playacted at being psychic. He was given every bit of information regarding our case and the identity of the ghost of the past-previous owner of our home. . . ." Ryan (herself an alleged psychic medium) also asserts that glimpses of ghostly figures were staged by crew members, that a "cold spot" showing on a monitor was simulated with a chilled beer, and that instances of alleged electronic voice phenomena (EVPs) were actually picked up from local ham radio transmissions (Ryan 2008; "Paranormal State" 2011).

As an outcome, Chip Coffey (2008) branded Kelli Ryan's assertions as "*Fraught* with total outright lies," while *Paranormal State*'s producers issued a revised DVD of *Paranormal State*'s second season, minus "The Messenger" ("Paranormal State" 2011).

"GHOST TRAIN" DEATH

In the early hours of Friday, August 27, 2010, about a dozen amateur ghost hunters were standing on a railway trestle in Iredell County, North Carolina, waiting for a legendary "ghost train" to manifest itself. Suddenly a real train, from the Norfolk Southern Railroad, rounded a bend and surprised the group. Everyone fled to the trestle's eastern end, but twenty-nine-year-old Christopher Kaiser didn't make it. His body was later found in a steep ravine below the trestle (Lytle 2010). A woman in the group was also seriously injured. Reportedly, Kaiser's last act was pushing her to safety.

The tragic irony is that the so-called ghost train appears to be nothing more than the interplay of imagination and folklore. Like many other phantom-train tales, this one originated after a disaster. The disaster occurred at the site, Bostian Bridge, on August 27, 1891, when a passenger train derailed and fell some nine stories into the ravine, killing almost thirty people and injuring some two dozen more. Ever since, at 3:00 a.m. (though different times are given) on the anniversary of the tragedy, one "is said to be" able to hear the sounds of metal twisting and breaking, steam pipes bursting, and passengers screaming at the site. The apparition of a killed baggage master is also reported.

The Bostian Bridge narrative contains a number of common folk motifs, or story elements (indicated below by their standard folk-motif numbers):

- Ghost haunts place of great accident or misfortune (E275);
- Phantom railway train (E535.4);
- Sounds of accident reenact tragedy (E337.1.2); and
- Persons who die violent or accidental deaths cannot rest in grave (E411.10).

(See Thompson 1955, vol. 2)

As I learned while doing graduate studies in folklore, such stock motifs suggest that the story was influenced by the general climate in which ghost stories are told with spine-tingling relish. In this environment, story elements have been known to migrate from tale to tale and place to place.

Most ghost-train tales date back to a time before the advent of modern safety practices and devices. The stories are told and retold (hence the designation *folktales*), often becoming embellished in the process. For example, an unverified incident attributed to an anonymous group of curiosity seekers that walked near the bridge on the wreck's first anniversary, allegedly involved the baggage master, Hugh K. Linster, who had been killed in the train wreck. He was said to have asked for the time and then to have vanished. Now this action is reported as having happened repeatedly: "Sometimes the ghost of baggage master H. K. Linster appears and asks for the correct time, so he can set his gold watch" (Hauck 1996, 319).

A ghost train, of course, contradicts the common definition of a ghost as the spirit of a dead person. Modern ghost hunters postulate that the entity exists as a form of life "energy" (which, however, science cannot find; indeed, once the brain is dead, there would be a cessation of mental activity and motor function). Be that as it may, how is it that *inanimate* things—like clothing, walking sticks, or other objects that accompany people in their alleged apparitional forms, and even means of conveyance like trains and stagecoaches—can become ghostly? The answer is that all such forms appear in apparitional encounters just as they do in dreams, memories, and imaginings, because all are purely mental images. Indeed, sightings of ghosts are linked to dreams, reveries, and other altered states of consciousness. (See appendix for "apparitional experience.")

Chapter 41

GHOSTLY ENDEAVOR: ETHICAL ISSUES HAUNT KENTUCKY PRESS

This is the story of how a respectable university press—the University Press of Kentucky (UPKY), "scholarly publisher for the Commonwealth"—came to contradict its legacy of science and scholarship. It is also the story of how I, one of its most-published authors—attempting to raise a question of ethics in the interest of the press, the state's universities, science, and the public—was treated in the process.

"FOLK"-LURE

At issue is a ridiculous book on ghosts—another mystery-mongering, proparanormal collection that is based on a logical fallacy known as *argumentum ad ignorantiam* ("argument from ignorance," i.e., a lack of knowledge). The notion is that if you "can't explain" something (say a noise in an old house), it must therefore be paranormal (surely a ghost). Although that illogic permeates *Spookiest Stories Ever: Four Seasons of Kentucky Ghosts*, beginning with the very first sentence of the very first story, there are other problems with the book.

Take the title: Please! I've read spooky stories, and these don't compare. For my money, Ruth Ann Musick's *Coffin Hollow and Other Ghost Tales* (1977), published by the same press, is much spookier. Besides, Musick's book offers a bibliography and source notes, whereas Roberta Simpson Brown and Lonnie E. Brown—the authors of *Spookiest Stories Ever*—rather embarrassingly confess, "We were not collectors when we heard many of these stories, so we did not record the storyteller's name or the time and place of the stories" (Simpson Brown and Brown 2010, xvi).

They add, "Some of these stories are based on our own experiences." This is interesting, because the book's jacket copy suggests a work of traditional folklore, stating that *Spookiest Stories Ever* "transports readers into the past with chilling tales that have been passed down from generation to generation." So not only do the authors not know many of their stories' antecedents, but by relating their "own experiences"—and those of family, friends, and acquaintances, which actually make up over half of the book—they reveal that theirs is not, substantially, a work of classic folklore. (In contrast, Musick's book is a collection of folktales with folk motifs, keyed to standard motif-indexes of folklore that are helpfully identified.)

In fact, as a press release for the book observes, "the authors explore paranormal phenomena and investigate some of the most haunted places in the world" (University Press of Kentucky 2010). So this is basically a ghost hunter's book—one promoting belief in spirits of the dead through allegedly empirical means: personal experiences, presumably by psychically sensitive persons, and/or the use of cameras and other equipment that supposedly record spirit "energy."

GHOST HUNTING

The authors of *Spookiest Stories Ever* are in fact self-styled conductors of "paranormal investigations with the Louisville Ghost Hunters and the American Ghost Society" (Simpson Brown 2009)—groups whose approach is widely viewed as fundamentally pseudoscientific. Here and there throughout the book, ghost hunters make forays into "haunted" places where alleged spirit pictures (Simpson Brown and Brown 2010, 146), camera malfunctions (133), and the like are reported, along with various alleged psychical encounters (e.g., 146, 149, 153, 156). (For a discussion of ghost hunters, see Nickell 2006.)

Coauthor Roberta Simpson Brown repeatedly reports her own psychic experiences. Since the age of seven (Simpson Brown and Brown 2010, 5), she has witnessed apparitions (150, 157–58, 215–16), had prophetic dreams (127), experienced "visitations" (32, 33), communicated with spirits (32, 33, 60, 244), encountered "signs" (239–45), sensed a presence (38, 61, 75, 143), felt paranormal cold spots (62, 147), and so on. Some of these paranormal experiences have come from her "ghost-hunting activities" (149). In fact, Simpson Brown—who has an "interest in the supernatural" (29)—exhibits several traits associated with a fantasy-prone personality (see Wilson and Barber 1983): she is highly imaginative, has vivid dreams, receives messages from otherworldly entities, and has "psychic" experiences, among other traits. Some of Roberta Simpson Brown's experiences seem consistent with common "waking dreams" that occur in the interface between being fully asleep and awake (Nickell 2004, 228–40). If she is aware of this phenomenon, she never says so.

When I first heard about the Browns' proposed book and raised the alarm, I was assured by a University Press of Kentucky editor that the collection was just "ghost stories" such as would be told around a campfire and that the press was not presenting them "as true"—certainly not as actual evidence for the supernatural. But they ended up doing just that. The book's jacket copy promises "a wealth of real-life experiences with the supernatural." The foreword refers to "moments when extraordinary events have suggested the presence of the supernatural," and it also touts a book by another press that "introduces the reader to forty-four ghost-hunting groups that have generated interesting stories" (Tucker 2010, xi).

"TRUE" VS. THE TRUTH

When Simpson Brown and Brown (2010) gush that a story "is incredible, but true" (28), we are apparently supposed to understand this statement as, "Well, not *true* true." The authors disclaim: "If you are looking for scientific proof that ghosts exist, or even an exact definition of what they are, you will not find the answers in this book. This is a collection of true personal experiences and stories we heard as true. We will not attempt to convert you to our way of thinking" (4–5). Oh, really? Much of the book is just such an attempt, a litany of alleged firsthand testimonials that invite the very kind of reaction that one credulous reader had: noting that the book's narratives "are offered as 'true stories,'" he added, "While it's easy to raise a jaundiced eyebrow at this notion, the cumulative effect of these plain-spoken tales inspires belief rather than skepticism" (Patterson 2010).

So the disingenuity in the book—and in its publishing campaign—is immense, with "true" being treated the way "real" is used on a carnival side-show banner (meaning a real fake, as opposed to an imaginary one). Yes, the stories in *Spookiest Stories Ever* are "true"—in that they are not presented as fiction.

The real truth is that the stories are convincing only to those who are unaware of just how little validity such anecdotal accounts have and of the fallacy of arguing from ignorance. Actually, many of the book's reported incidents are unexplained merely because the evidence they offer is some-where between nonexistent and doubtful. They are not at all unexplainable. Such phenomena are quite easily explained as waking dreams, mispercep-tions, alternative natural phenomena, electronic glitches, pranks by others, and so on (Nickell 2001; 2004; 2006; 2007). One suspects many of the Browns' reports are confabulated at best and partially or completely fiction-alized at worst. Not a single ghost has ever been validated by mainstream science, and pseudoscientific ghost hunters are on a fool's errand, unaware that when the brain is dead, brain function ceases—and with it, thought, speech, and motor function.

Realizing they have no "scientific proof that ghosts exist," the authors still try to have it both ways, insisting, "You must decide for yourself what you believe about ghosts" (4–5). But how can someone possibly decide when given only a phony choice? For one, we are presented "true" experiences of the supernatural, and for the other, the authors' assurance that there is no other tenable position because the experiences simply "can't be explained." This takes disingenuity to a new level. That it would bear the imprimatur of the University Press of Kentucky, which represents the state's scholarly insti-tutions, is appalling. Will there be further such books, perhaps "true" expe-riences with angels or encounters with extraterrestrials?

MESSENGER SHOT

Because of my concerns, I talked by phone with the head of the press, Stephen Wrinn, who was defensive (to say the least) and decried what he suggested was my attempt at censorship. Of course it is not censorship to hold works to standards of science and scholarship as befits a university press. He did not like my use of the word *ethics*, and he stated that he did not intend to have, financially, another year like the previous one. He insisted I look at the book's manuscript, which he thought I would find acceptable after all, and I agreed to take a look.

I subsequently received from an editor a copy of the manuscript (although it was missing several pages). After reading it and seeing that it was as bad as I had feared, I wrote a seven-page critique, concluding, "Surely the Press can find a more suitable collection of ghost tales to publish—perhaps a statewide anthology of folktales, ballads, etc.—rather than try to patch and prop up the Browns' unacceptable manuscript" (Nickell 2009).

But patch and prop they did—deleting a ghost hunter's term ("orbs"), for example, and making other cosmetic changes, as well as adding a foreword by a folklorist. (She mentions other collections of ghost tales, some published by UPKY, but acknowledges that "an important difference between the present volume and the books just mentioned is that the Browns tell stories from their own family and friends.")

Meanwhile, I waited for the publisher to reply to my report. An editor said Wrinn was "very interested in reading it, but he's on vacation until after the fourth" (of July 2009). That is the last I heard (a long vacation indeed!). I've heard nothing about the book, nothing about one of mine I was discussing with the press at the time (it would have been my thirteenth with them, but it has now been published by Prometheus Books). And, although UPKY had just published my *Real or Fake: Studies in Authentication*, for the first such time they did not ask me to appear at the annual Kentucky Book Fair. Having provided other reader reports to UPKY in the past that were acknowledged and acted upon, the board's silence was perplexing. Given my past experiences, I have no reason to believe that my report was ever shown to the UPKY board, which must approve all books based on readers' reports and the advice of staff. Did the board have access to all available and relevant information?

No doubt *Spookiest Stories Ever* will sell more than most of my books. Wrinn is correct in noting that popular books often make possible the publishing of scholarly ones (Nardini 2004), although when both are at their best (thorough, honest, and well documented on the one hand and interesting and readable on the other), there may not be so much difference after all. But if it takes a book cynically promoting ignorance and superstition to support one advocating science and reason, I will take a pass. My integrity is not for sale.

Chapter 42

CATCHING GHOSTS

D espite the popular antics of inept "ghost hunters," ghosts continue to remain elusive—as if they are only productions of the imagination rather than purportedly still-living entities of a supernatural realm. Nevertheless, actively ghost hunting since 1969, I have actually "caught" a few "ghosts."

BACKGROUND

True, in most cases I have found plausible explanations for haunting phenomena. At Mackenzie House in Toronto (as related in chapter 37), mysterious footfalls had been heard on the stairs for much of a decade until, during 1972–1973, I investigated and discovered that the iron stairway in the adjacent building was regularly traversed by a late-night cleanup crew (Nickell 2001, 217). At various haunted inns, many apparitions have turned out to be due to the percipient experiencing a common "waking dream" (Nickell 2001, 290–92). And aboard a haunted ship, the mysterious blurring of a dead sailor's picture whenever it was photographed was caused by its nonglare glass softly reflecting the camera's flash (Nickell 2001, 187).

Such physical illusions are common, but they also tend to have a psychological component. Belief in ghosts caused the superstitious folk who lived at Mackenzie House to assume they heard ghostly activity. They did not stop to consider how nonphysical entities could produce manifestly physical effects. I, on the other hand, thought there might indeed have been a source for the sounds—reported by multiple earwitnesses—and I investigated by looking for the most obvious potential sources.

The effects of memory can also play a role in enhancing a reported occurrence. The fallibility of memory is demonstrated in several studies. For example, Wiseman and Morris (1995) compared paranormal believers with

319

disbelievers by showing them videotapes featuring pseudopsychic trickery. The believers tended to recall less contradictory information than the skeptics.

The power of suggestion is a potent force in reported hauntings. One person may excitedly influence another (or the latter may acquiesce to preserve domestic tranquility), resulting in what the French term *folie à deux*— the folly of two! Important also is what psychologists term *contagion*: the spreading of an idea, action, or the like from person to person. Thus, as a house, inn, or other place becomes thought of as "haunted," more and more ghostly encounters are reported. At Kentucky's Liberty Hall mansion, for example, spooky phenomena flourished during the tenure of a manager who found the "ghost" good for business but waned under the more professional direction of a subsequent curator (Nickell 1995, 49). Research by Lange et al. (1996) shows that when people are "alert" to the paranormal (i.e., given to expect paranormal events), they tend to notice those conditions that would confirm their expectations. Also, suggestion effects were more frequently associated with groups of paranormal percipients than with individual ones, indicating that groups are more susceptible to the effects of contagion. "Seeing is believing," goes the old saying, but it may also be said that sometimes "believing is seeing."

FLICKERING LIGHTS

And then there are hoaxes. At a reputedly haunted restaurant in Georgia, various strange phenomena were reported, including lights that flickered on and off in the barroom. The bartender, whom I interviewed, was initially convinced it was the work of a spirit entity. Parapsychologists who had earlier "investigated" the site using electromagnetic field meters failed to uncover the young worker who admitted that she would sneak up to the doorway, reach for the light switch, then dart away, giggling silently. Similar pranks, minor accidents and glitches, as well as misperceptions coupled with contagion, could easily account for the phenomena reported at the restaurant.

Perception—actually misperception—can transform a hoaxed occurrence into a seemingly supernatural one. A young lady told me of an incident at her apartment in which a light was turned on and off. When I suggested she might be the victim of a prankster and related the case of the Georgia barroom lights, she at first told me she had actually seen the light switch move.

On further thought, however, she withdrew that "memory" and concluded that her boyfriend was responsible. He had wanted to spend the night, she said, her tone warming as she recalled the situation, and probably faked the phenomenon so she would be frightened—just as young men used to take their sweethearts to horror features at drive-in movies to induce "snuggling."

As related in "Haunted Inns," chapter 45 of *Real-Life X-Files* (Nickell 2001, 296), I once caught such a "ghost" in action, namely a hotel desk clerk who was unaware I was looking in his direction as chandelier lights flickered mysteriously. There, as at many other places, ghosts were apparently thought to be good for business (see figure 42.1).

Figure 42.2. Rustic Hand Hotel in the old mining town of Fairplay, Colorado, is reputedly home to prankish ghosts. (Photo by Joe Nickell.)

POLTERGEIST ANTICS

As we saw in the previous chapter, such antics are the explanation for almost an entire class of physical hauntings, known as *poltergeist* cases. Typically, small objects are hurled through the air by unseen forces, furniture is overturned, or other disturbances occur—usually by a juvenile trickster determined to plague credulous adults (e.g., Randi, 1985). However, where such cases are properly investigated by magicians and detectives, using such tactics as installing hidden cameras, using or threatening the use of lie detectors, or dusting objects with tracer powders, they usually turn out to be the pranks of children, teenagers, or immature adults.

For instance, consider a case that occurred in the summer of 1957 in Hartsville, Missouri. A nine-year-old girl was the focus of poltergeist attacks that included a flying comb, spilled water buckets, shaking laundry baskets, and other odd events. The girl told reporters she was terrified by the happenings, but a magician who visited the house to investigate concluded otherwise: he actually observed a can opener fall from its place of concealment under the girl's arm (Christopher 1970, 145). In another case, events centered around a thirteen-year-old girl whose fingerprints were discovered on a dish she claimed the poltergeist had tossed out of a window. On *Arthur C. Clarke's Mysterious World* program, a revealing bit of footage showed a little girl slipping from bed to break an object, then scampering back under the covers. And a Tulsa, Oklahoma, poltergeist case was solved when tracer powder dusted on certain objects in the house were subsequently discovered on the hands of the plagued couple's twelve-year-old adopted daughter (Nickell 1995, 85–88). Simply having a talk with the mischief maker proved successful in ending many poltergeist outbreaks, whether it took the form of a police grilling or sympathetic counseling.

Such was a case I investigated with Robert A. Baker (1921–2005), a professor of psychology at the University of Kentucky and author of numerous books. While I was completing doctoral work at the university, he and I teamed up to examine a number of paranormal cases, and in 1992 we published our investigative manual *Missing Pieces: How to Investigate Ghosts, UFOs, Psychics, and Other Mysteries*.

Dr. Baker and I were called to an Indiana farmhouse that was experiencing a spate of haunting activity. The yard contained religious statues that may have been placed for their presumable protective value. The main percipient was the young wife and mother. Due to the various noises and prankish antics that she perceived, mostly upstairs where her children slept, she seemed at her wit's end. Afraid for her children, she made them sleep downstairs on sofas and day beds.

We listened to her story, went through the house, and talked to each family member separately. One little boy, being rather pointedly quizzed by the sage Dr. Baker, suddenly blurted out, "You aren't going to tell on me, are you?" No, the understanding psychologist replied, while insisting that we must nevertheless have an end to the "haunting" activity. We kept in touch with the family for a while, and apparently the little ghost had heeded Hamlet's imploring, "Rest, rest, perturbed spirit" (*Hamlet*, act 1, scene 5).

THE SHIFTING PICTURES

Another supposedly haunted place is the Golden Lamb Inn in Lebanon, Ohio, whose sign proclaims it is "the oldest Inn still operating as a hotel in Ohio." Serving travelers since 1803, it has hosted ten presidents, including John Quincy Adams, as well as notables Henry Clay, Harriet Beecher Stowe, and Mark Twain. In 1842, Charles Dickens refused to stay there when he learned it was "a temperance hotel," one that did not serve alcohol (Woodyard 2000, 22, 24).

The inn is allegedly haunted by the ghost of Sarah Stubbs, a little girl whose family once managed the hotel. "Sarah" is blamed for most of the ghostly hijinks that are reported at the Golden Lamb. There is even a museum room containing a couple of pieces of children's furniture once owned by her, along with additional period furniture, pictures, and other artifacts. The first such "Sarah's Room" was located on the fourth floor next to the stairs. Unfortunately, guests either blocked the stair traffic as they viewed the display or else missed their footing when they glanced at it on their way downstairs. As a consequence, the exhibits were moved to a room across the hall. Reportedly, that was when the "haunting" began (Woodyard 2000).

According to a display card at the room, "Housekeepers mentioned that pictures on the wall in Sarah's Room were sometimes crooked after being straightened the day before" (figure 42.2). Not surprisingly, the claim is elaborated in the *Ghost Hunter's Guide to Haunted Ohio* (Woodyard 2000, 25). I wondered about the phenomenon as I prepared to check into the hotel on February 7, 2002.

I had just given a lecture on the paranormal at the University of Cincinnati, sponsored by UC Skeptics, and had just had dinner, so it was rather late. Local skeptics Robert Sexton and Liz Upchurch were helping me check into the original Sarah's Room (room number 2, renamed the Harriet Beecher Stowe Room).

As I brought up the subject of haunting, the night clerk told us a secret: sometimes, she confided, because she found the housekeeping staff so superstitious and credulous, she would slip upstairs at night and "turn the pictures" in Sarah's Room just to "mess with" their minds.

Once again, I had confirmed the value of on-site investigating over armchair debunking. I had caught another ghost, this time at the very beginning of a stay. I have to admit, I slept especially well that night.

Figure 42.2. In "Sarah's Room," in Ohio's historic Golden Lamb Inn, pictures on the wall were repeatedly found askew—to the consternation of the housekeeping staff. (Photo by Joe Nickell.)

Chapter 43

POLTERGEIST ATTACKS!

The *poltergeist*—German for a noisy (*poltern*) spirit (*geist*)—is said to be responsible for certain types of ghostly disturbances, usually of a mischievous nature, for which there is no apparent cause. Once attributed to the devil, today's paranormal believers often link the phenomenon to repressed hostilities of the pubescent child that somehow manifest themselves as psychokinetic energy (Roll 1972)—hardly a scientific theory. Skeptics have a simpler explanation.

OUTBREAKS

In the typical poltergeist outbreak, small objects are hurled through the air by unseen forces, furniture is overturned, or other disturbances occur—usually just what could be accomplished by a juvenile trickster determined to plague credulous adults. Unfortunately, in many instances the adults prohibit knowledgeable investigators from becoming involved (e.g., Randi 1985; Kurtz 1986–1987). This can help make the case seem "unexplainable."

The "poltergeists'" motives are varied. One young Alabama boy, who was responsible for several mysterious fires, wished to cause his parents to return to their previous home because he missed his former playmates. In one schoolhouse outbreak, the children involved admitted that the gullibility of their teacher as well as townsfolk had been tempting, and they delighted in all the excitement their pranks had produced. Still another poltergeist, perpetrated by an eleven-year-old girl, was merely looking for attention. However, her comment is revealing of eyewitness misperception. "I didn't throw all those things," she stated. "People just imagined some of them" (Christopher, 1970, 142–63).

Not all ghostly mischief is caused by children, however. For example, it was a young maid in the employ of an elderly widow who played poltergeist in Stockton, Surrey, in 1772. She later confessed to a clergyman that she was the "unseen agency" that had tossed objects, dislodged rows of plates (by using a fine wire), and instigated other disturbances. Nor was it children who produced the Atlanta House of Blood hoax in 1987. When the sub-urban home was reported to spurt blood "like a sprinkler," police took samples and made photographs. The photos reveal (by blood-pattern analysis) that the blood had not sprung from the floors and walls as claimed by the residents (a neglected elderly black couple) but rather that it had been *squirted onto* surfaces, giving the lie to the claims (see Nickell 1995, 92–97).

THE NEWBURY DEMON

An instructive historical poltergeist case I investigated is found in the writings of the American Puritan Increase Mather (1663–1728).

In his *An Essay for the Recording of Illustrious Providences* (1684), Mather gives an account of a house in Newbury, Massachusetts, "lately troubled with a Daemon" (quoted in Quinn et al. 1938).[1] The events, which began on December 3, 1679, and continued until at least early February of the following year, are catalogued in considerable detail over several pages. For example, Mather says that at the home of William Morse,

> people were sometimes Barricado'd out of doors, when as yet there was nobody to do it: and a Chest was removed from place to place, no hand touching it. Their keys being tied together, one was taken from the rest, & the remaining two would fly about making a loud noise by knocking against each other. But the greatest part of this *Devils* feats were his mischievous ones, wherein indeed he was sometimes Antick enough too, and therein the chief sufferers were, the Man and his Wife, and his Grand-Son. The Man especially had his share in these *Diabolical* Molestations. For one while they could not eat their Suppers quietly, but had the Ashes on the Hearth before their eyes thrown into their Victuals; yea, and upon their heads and Clothes, insomuch that they were forced up into their Chamber, and yet they had no rest there; for one of the Man's Shoes being left below, 'twas filled with Ashes and Coals, and thrown up after them. (Quinn et al. 1938)

The boy, Abel Powell, slept with his grandparents in their bed. Frequently one or all would be pricked as they lay in the dark. On searching, on one occasion they found an awl and on another "found in the Bed a Bodkin, a knitting Needle, and two sticks picked at both ends" (Quinn et al. 1938, 40, 41).

At other times sticks, stones, and bricks were thrown through an open window; the grandfather's inkhorn was "taken away" while he was writing; and objects were frequently thrown at him or his wife.

As to the boy, Mather writes,

> There remains much to be said concerning him, and a principal sufferer in these afflictions: For on the 18. of *December*, he sitting by his Grandfather, was hurried into great motions and the Man thereupon took him, and made him stand between his Legs, but the Chair [in which the grandfather sat] danced up and down, and had like to have cast both Man and Boy into the fire. (Quinn et al. 1938, 41)

On another occasion, Mather says of the lad:

> He barked like a Dog, and clock't like a Hen, and after long distraining to speak, said, there's *Powel*,[2] I am pinched; his Tongue likewise hung out of his mouth, so as that it could by no means be forced in till his Fit was over, and then he said 'twas forced out by *Powel*. (Quinn et al. 1938, 42)

When the boy was taken to the home of a doctor, the disturbances ceased, only to resume when he returned home that evening. He was found to be "best at a Neighbors house" (Quinn et al. 1938).

Like other poltergeist disturbances, that of the Morse family eventually came to an end. Mather states that a seaman who often visited at Morse's home told him that his wife was not guilty of witchcraft, as some suspected, and that, if he could have the child for a single day, he would put an end to the troubles. Morse agreed and the seaman fulfilled his promise. Mather considers the possibility that a witch or "Conjurer" had been responsible for the disturbances, but he adds: "Or it may be some other thing as yet kept hid in the secrets of providence might be the true original of all this Trouble." (Quinn et al. 1938; see also Lowance 1974, 96.)

Clearly it is indeed some other thing, what we today would classify as an example of so-called poltergeist phenomena. The particulars in this account are extremely similar to those in cases we have examined thus far. In Mather's account there is little that is not readily explained by the hypothesis that the grandson contrived the mischief. In fact, on one occasion when he was taken to an aunt's home, he boldly "threw a great stone at a Maid in the house" (Quinn et al. 1938). He was also seen, by his brother, throwing a shoe at their grandfather (*Salem* 1860, 30). The day spent with the seaman that ended the affair rings true. No doubt the wise seafarer lent the boy a sympathetic ear, counseled him about his problems, and urged him to end his hijinks. His troubles likely stemmed from what seems to have been a broken home, since the boy lived with his grandparents.

LINDLEY STREET INFESTATION

The so-called Lindley Street Infestation is named after the site of similar developments in Bridgeport, Connecticut, that came to light in 1977. At the home of "devout Catholic" Gerald Goodin and his wife, the disturbing events had actually begun two years earlier, with noises occurring each night like the house was being pelted with stones. The disturbances, which seemingly centered around the Goodin's newly adopted Native American daughter, Marcia, began to escalate in November 1974. Dishes began rattling, furniture moved and toppled, and a chair in which ten-year-old Marcia was seated was propelled against a wall. Soon, police and firemen were at the scene. So was Ed Warren, the notorious "demonologist" discussed in chapter 36.

Before long, however, police closed the case. Police superintendent Joseph A. Walsh, who had earlier told reporters, "There are no ghosts in Bridgeport," made an announcement. The whole affair was a hoax, admitted to by Marcia. She confessed it was she who had banged on the walls, threw items, and created other effects that credulous adults had attributed to demonic activity. Not surprisingly, Ed Warren accused the police of calling the affair a hoax only "to get things quieted down." He huffed, "If the whole thing is a hoax, it's one of the biggest hoaxes I've ever seen." Eventually—after the girl was taken for psychiatric evaluation, and after psychical researchers, priests, and demonologists had left—the outbreak ceased (Nickell 1995, 89–92).

In 1993, researching the case for my book *Entities* (1995), I visited Bridgeport, but turned up little additional information. Police public relations officer, Sgt. W. Chapman laughingly told me that, although one policeman had been genuinely frightened by the Lindley Street events, he would have had to himself witness paranormal events in order to become a believer (Nickell 1995, 92).

ENFIELD DISTURBANCES

This case, taking its name from that of a northern London suburb, began in August 1977. The disturbances included overturned and even supposedly "levitated" furniture, as well as a rock the size of a softball that "manifested out of thin air in the middle of the living room and slammed to the floor with a thud!" This case was also "investigated" by Ed and Lorraine Warren, who (again recall chapter 36) invariably arrived at the scene of a "haunting" or "poltergeist" outbreak and soon transformed the case into one of "demonic possession." Enfield was no exception, and it is included in a chapter in *The Demonologist: The True Story of Ed and Lorraine Warren, the World-Famous Exorcism Team* by Gerald Brittle (1980).

As it happens, however, British parapsychologist Anita Gregory examined the case and found it overrated. Reporting in the *Journal of the Society for Psychical Research*, she characterized several episodes of behavior concerning the family's two girls, aged eleven and thirteen, as clearly suspicious. Gregory concluded that the children had *nonpsychically* effected many of the occurrences. Her view was that the case quickly became a farcical performance staged for overly credulous investigators and reporters eager for a sensational story. As well, skeptical investigator Melvin Harris cast doubt on some of the photos that allegedly depict the Enfield poltergeist phenomena, demonstrating the ease with which they could have been faked (Clark 1981).

Revealingly, magician Milbourne Christopher—a psychical investigator whose work was an important early influence on my own—had a chance to become involved in the case. He regarded the Enfield poltergeist as one of the most intriguing occurrences of reputed paranormal phenomena he was ever involved in. Christopher (1970, 184–85) stated: "I was there when the 'strange' things started happening in this little suburban section of London. It was one of the few alleged poltergeist cases in which I was involved where the strange things happened when I was in the house. Normally when I go to a poltergeist house the 'haunting' influences disappear immediately. But there I had a chance to observe the techniques." Christopher concluded they were the hijinks of "a little girl who wanted to cause trouble and who was very, very clever."

COLUMBUS POLTERGEIST

Again, in 1984, a supposed poltergeist overturned furniture, sent telephones flying, smashed picture frames, set lamps swinging, and caused much other mischief in the household of John and Joan Resch of Columbus, Ohio. Once again, the disturbances centered around a family member, in this case the Resches' fourteen-year-old adopted daughter Tina (Nickell 1995, 88).

Fortuitously, some photographs and even television news tapes captured the girl in the act of producing certain phenomena—for example, toppling a lamp. Also, a television technician saw Tina secretly move a table using her foot. Noted magician and psychical investigator James Randi (1985, 234) extensively followed the case and concluded that "she was admittedly under stress and had good reason to want to attract media exposure: she wanted to trace her true parents, against the wishes of the Resches." Randi (1995, 69–70) observes that "descriptions given by parapsychologist William Roll, who specializes in poltergeist investigations and had examined the situation in person, turned out to be quite impossible sequences."

Although the Columbus poltergeist case ran its course, as typically happens in such cases, and faded into relative obscurity, there is a tragic sequel. In 1994 Tina Resch Boyer was sentenced to life imprisonment in Georgia for the murder of her three-year-old daughter. The child, whose body had been badly bruised, had died of injuries to the head (Nickell 1995, 88; Randi 1995, 70).

THE POLTERGEIST THAT WASN'T

Of course, not all poltergeist outbreaks are hoaxes, as my friend and fellow ghostbuster, the late Robert A. Baker, found when he investigated one case. While there was a variety of reported events—such as a bedroom door slamming and a telephone flying off its table—Dr. Baker noted that the events were atypical of the usual hoax pattern, in which events often suggest outright vandalism and tend to center around a particular suspect. Instead, the disturbances seemed more like random events.

Visiting the home, he discovered simple explanations for each occurrence. For example, air pressure from the quickly opened kitchen door caused the bedroom door to shut; when a chair leg was placed inside the phone cord on the floor and the chair scooted forward, the telephone was yanked off the table; and so on. Concluded Dr. Baker: "The most fascinating aspect of this case is just how clearly it demonstrates the power of expectation and how our attitudes and mental sets can influence our perceptions and beliefs" (Baker and Nickell 1992, 135–39). Likewise, Houran and Lange (1996) have shown that ambiguities in normal—unhaunted—houses tend to go unnoticed unless subjects are predisposed (as by suggestion) to notice them.

THE POLTERGEIST-FAKING SYNDROME

As countless historical examples demonstrate, cases of so-called poltergeist phenomena typically have a number of shared features. Although each is different, these common features are often so characteristic as to define what I term the *poltergeist-faking syndrome.*

This describes both the cause and the effect of episodes of disturbance by a hidden agency, which the superstitious attribute to a "poltergeist" and some psychical theorists suggest are psychokinetic (mind-over-matter) phenomena. However, proper investigation and the principle of Occam's razor repeatedly demonstrate that the occurrences are centered around an individual (rarely individuals)—who is motivated to cause the mischief. In numerous instances an obvious suspect is actually observed perpetrating a surreptitious act, and many confessions of such misbehavior have been recorded—with motives ranging from a simple desire for attention to more serious psychological causes. On the other hand, never has a poltergeist or a psychokinetic force been confirmed by mainstream science.

The term *poltergeist-faking syndrome* may be used to describe an investigated case of poltergeistlike phenomena having the previously mentioned characteristics as well as to diagnose such misbehavior in a subject when the evidence warrants. It should not be used in an *a priori* manner (that is, antecedent to inquiry), although one could certainly refer to a *suspected* case of the syndrome when evidence warrants.

Chapter 44

RAMPAGING MIND: THE SEAFORD POLTERGEIST CASE

C alled "the first modern investigation by parapsychologists of poltergeist disturbances," the 1958 case of the Seaford poltergeist, asserts Guiley (2000, 339), "remains unsolved." Actually, the solution—suspected from the onset—was convincingly argued by a distinguished skeptic, magician Milbourne Christopher (1970, 149–60). Here I add to the evidence and make a complete new study and assessment, having been fortunate to obtain a copy of the sixty-page police file on the case.

OUTBREAK

At a ranch-style house at 1648 Redwood Path, the home of James M. Herrmann (age 43), his wife, Lucille (38), and their children, Lucille (13) and James Jr. (12), peculiar disturbances began on Monday, February 3. Mr. Herrmann was away when Mrs. Herrmann, according to the police report,

> heard noises of bottles popping their caps and on checking found that a small Holy Water bottle on her dresser in the master bedroom had its cap unscrewed and was laying on its side with the contents all spilled. In her son's bedroom, which is right next to the master bedroom, a small ceramic doll had its neck broken and a few small pieces had broken off a plastic ship model. In the bathroom cabinet there were two bottles with the caps unscrewed and the contents spilled. In the kitchen there was a bottle of starch under the sink with the cap off and the contents spilled. In the cellar directly under the kitchen a gallon bottle of bleach was also spilled. (Tozzi 1958)

Three days later, more bottles were found open and spilled, or even broken, when the two children were the only ones present, and there were additional incidents on February 7 and 9. Subsequently, Mrs. Herrmann contacted the police and became the "complainant" in what was prosaically labeled "Local Investigation (Broken Bottles)." On February 11, Detective Joseph Tozzi was assigned to the case full-time, as "the disturbances appeared to be increasing in both number and magnitude" (Pratt 1964, 81).

Early on, Detective Tozzi (1958, 2) interviewed the children, and "both were informed that if they were in any way connected with this case in that they were causing this disturbance in some way that it was a serious matter." Mr. Herrmann was also interviewed and stated that his own prior talk with the children had convinced him they were not causing the disturbances. However, after more incidents occurred, Tozzi (1958, 8) again questioned the children, indicating that his suspicions were continuing. Indeed, on February 20, the detective and young James had just gone to the basement when "a small metal horse that was on the cellar stair shelf struck the floor at the writer's [Tozzi's] feet. . . . The writer accused James of having thrown this figure and interrogated him for quite some time. James again denied having done any of these disturbances and also denied knowing anything about this latter occurrence."

COMPETING EXPLANATIONS

As the movement of objects continued and drew the attention of the Long Island newspaper *Newsday* and other media sources, famed Duke University ESP pioneer J. B. Rhine dispatched two parapsychologists, first J. Gaither Pratt and later William Roll, who investigated both separately and together but were ultimately unable to explain the phenomenon. Pratt and Roll (1958) did suggest that such cases might be due to what they termed "recurrent spontaneous psychokinesis" (RSPK). This proposes that the person around whom the disturbances center may be *unconsciously* causing them by psychic force ("mind over matter"). However, the existence of psychokinesis has never been proved, and the Pratt/Roll "theory" has not been accepted by mainstream science.

For their part, the police considered a bewildering variety of possible explanations, including earth tremors, high-frequency radio waves, a magnetic field caused by the electrical wiring, the oil burner going on, a downdraft from the chimney, vibrations from the TV antenna, and so on. But as experts came and went—setting up an oscillograph, checking the wiring, searching maps for underground streams, and the like—nothing proved fruitful, not even the efforts of a dowser wielding a willow rod. Members of the public sent numerous letters suggesting other possibilities, ranging from "publicity stunt" to "poltergeist," "black magic spell," and "Satan." Proposed solutions included burning sulfur, praying, sprinkling holy water, performing an exorcism, and so on. A few suggested the incidents were children's pranks (Tozzi 1958).

The obvious possibility that the incidents were the pranks of one or both children could be all but ruled out, however, the parapsychologists concluded. Pratt conceded that "the mysterious events centered around James rather than Lucille (or any other member of the family)," and he admitted that in numerous instances—perhaps fifty out of some sixty-seven recorded events—James could have been responsible, such as when a bread plate was dumped on the floor while "James was sitting at the dining-room table alone" (Pratt 1964, 85, 99, 103–104). However, he and Roll believed there were seventeen events that "cannot, if correctly reported, be explained as easily performed, single pranks" (Pratt 1964, 104).

POSSIBLE TRICKERY?

Let us consider one of the incidents, described in the police report. On February 19, Detective Tozzi was in the basement with Mrs. Herrmann and Lucille, at which time young James was reportedly doing homework at the dining-room table. Suddenly there was a loud noise, and the detective, Mrs. Herrmann, and Lucille rushed upstairs. Tozzi reported that in the living room a "porcelain figurine had left the end table at the south end of the sofa and flown through the air approximately 10 feet" where it struck a desk, breaking off an arm. "No one was in the living room at this time," wrote Tozzi, "and it would have been impossible for James to have left the dining room, thrown the figurine and returned to the dining room" without being heard by those downstairs, since the floors were wooden and "every sound can be heard through them" (Tozzi 1958, 11–12).

However, Tozzi could easily have been mistaken. Moreover, young James might have produced the effect by a method Tozzi had not imagined. Suppose the boy had obtained the small object earlier and had hidden it, say under a book, where he was doing his homework. He could then have thrown the object through the open doorway into the living room. The distinguished magician Milbourne Christopher analyzed the reported disturbances in conjunction with a floor plan of the Herrmann house and stated (1970, 157–58):

> It should be stressed that Mr. Herrmann refused to allow lie-detector tests to be made on his family and that the police and the investigators from Duke accepted Jimmy's statements. Let us suppose that what the boy said was not true, that he was in one room when he said he was in another in some instances. Also let us suppose that what people thought they saw and what actually happened were not precisely the same. It has been shown that the police notes record that the boy and his mother "actually saw" the bleach bottle leave a box and crash on the floor. Yet Dr. Pratt discovered during his interviews that neither witnessed the out-of-the-carton action. Any trial lawyer will testify that witnesses often believe that they have seen things that did not occur. For example, a woman hears a loud noise, then sees a pistol. She may be confident she heard the pistol fire, though the noise came from another source—the backfire of an automobile or an exploded firecracker.

Christopher adds:

> Take the single instance where an outsider, Miss Murtha, saw a statuette take off and land. A television set was on at the time. It is logical to suppose her attention was there. A quick movement by the occupant of the sofa could have jarred the small end table with enough impact to send the upright figurine falling to the floor the mere two feet away.

The parapsychologists understood little of the possibility of magic tricks. Pratt was completely baffled by Christopher who was able to duplicate the Seaford "poltergeist" effects when the parapsychologist visited him. Pratt had no idea of the simplicity with which the effects were accomplished, and Roll imagined James's tricks would have had to be produced by special "devices" which would then have to be "installed, operated, and removed" in "the presence of adult witnesses" (Roll and Persinger 2001, 127). In explaining the tricks involved, the biggest problem is in determining what really happened, since there are often multiple versions of a given incident (for example, see Pratt 1964, 93–95). As usual, the devil—or rather the non-devil in this case—is in the details.

SEARCHING FOR PSYCHOKINESIS

In my reopening of the Seaford matter I was faced with a very cold case, yet I had the full police report to work with and, of course, my professional background as a magician and mentalist, a private detective, and—since 1969—a ghostbuster.

My starting point was the realization that natural causes were effectively ruled out, leaving two competing hypotheses: first, a paranormal claim involving supposed psychokinesis, and, second, a nonparanormal possibility (what I have called the *poltergeist-faking syndrome*). Both hypotheses accept Roll's assertion, "There is little doubt that [James] was instrumental in bringing about the incidents in his home." The disagreement is over Roll's further assertion, "It also seems clear that he was unaware of this" (Roll and Persinger 2001, 130). In other words, we must ask, did James cause the "poltergeist" events by inadvertent psychic force or by deliberate deception? In examining the evidence I used a number of strategies, as follows.

1. *Track the central figure.* As we have seen, the events in question centered around young James. He was not only in the house during each of the events (while other family members were often absent), but, as Pratt acknowledges (1964, 113), "the disturbances took place nearer to James, on the average, than to any other member of the family." For example, "a globe of the world came bouncing into the living room from the boy's room" when he was in his room (though found in bed) (Tozzi 1958, 21). On occasion, James was the first to arrive on the scene of some disturbance (e.g., Tozzi 1958, 17), or, in fact was frequently the only one present when an event did occur.

2. *Focus on the disturbances.* Whenever James was at school or elsewhere (the family stayed with relatives for several nights), there were not only no disturbances in the house, but the supposed "poltergeist" or unconscious psychokinetic force did not follow the boy (Tozzi 1958, 15; Pratt 1964, 109). In other words, the mysterious events would

occur only at James's home and then only when he was present. Was this because he was on familiar territory, where he could best carry out his secret actions, and possibly because he had some family issue that provoked his rebellion? In fact, psychological tests administered to the children revealed, in James's case, "passive demandingness, hostility to father figures, impersonal violence, and isolation of affect [emotion]." One psychologist "thought the boy felt on the one hand protected and tenderly cared for, but on the other hand oppressed and held down." When he was asked to make up stories, one "concerned a boy who is 'living with a guardian whom he hates,'" while "in another a father accuses his son of being 'a liar or a cheater'; the son fights him and is killed" (Roll and Persinger 2001, 128–29).

3. *Consider the "clandestine effect"*—the way the secret agency that caused the disturbances seemed not to want to be caught in the act. They invariably happened when no one was nearby, or when James was behind a possible observer, or the person had looked away from him, or the like. When police specially placed some previously disturbed objects (secretly dusted with a fluorescent powder) and asked family members not to touch them (in hopes of subsequently detecting the powder on a prankster's hands using an ultraviolet lamp), those particular bottles were never disturbed again (Tozzi 1958, 9, 10), suggesting the prankster suspected a trap. Moreover, when publicity brought numerous strangers into the house (parapsychologists, reporters, etc.), "the poltergeist activities ceased," according to Pratt (1964, 85), who thought it was because that "completely changed the psychological atmosphere"; was it instead because the increased presence made it more difficult to act unobserved?

4. *Examine the nature of the disturbances.* Pratt (1964, 113) observed: "The occurrences were not randomly scattered throughout the house," but, once again, were associated with James and his activities. More objects were disturbed in James' room than anywhere else (Roll and Persinger 2001, 129). Also, Pratt suggested that "some pattern can be discerned in the kinds of objects that were disturbed" (1964, 113). He divided these into two types (1964, 105), of which I make three: (1) "bottle poppings" and (2–3) "displacements of furniture and household objects." In each case the movement of the objects suggested simple trickery such as a boy could effect.

First, the bottles had screw tops that could not (experiments showed) pop open; they required unscrewing (Pratt 1964, 105–106), which I suggest could be achieved more easily by a human hand than by psychic force. Christopher (1970, 158–59) demonstrated that the bottle openings that apparently occurred remotely could be accomplished by opening a bottle somewhere unobserved, then later surreptitiously making a noise (such as a knock with the knuckles) while directing attention toward another room—what magicians call *misdirection*. As bad as eyewitnesses are, earwitnesses may be even worse. On occasions, people in the Herrmann home thought sounds came from one place, say the basement, when an object was subsequently found disturbed elsewhere, such as in James's room (e.g., Tozzi 1958, 17–18). Pratt (1964, 101) says of one incident that "the noise itself was not sufficiently well localized to establish definitely that it had come from the unfinished cellar rather than from the bathroom where James was at that time."

Second, the displacement of furniture was very closely related to young James and generally went unwitnessed by anyone else. The first such large item was the dresser in James's room, which fell on February 23, while the boy claimed he had his back to it (Tozzi 1958, 18). It fell again the next day, reportedly when "James Junior was coming up the cellar stairs" (Tozzi 1958, 20). However, *Newsday* reporter David Kahn was at the home, and parapsychologist Roll asked if Kahn could verify that James was indeed in the cellar at the time: "Mr. Kahn replied that he could not so state; by the time he reached the hallway, James was standing in the hall looking through the open doorway into his bedroom" (Pratt 1964, 96–97). Additional disturbances involved a picture over James's bed that twice fell while he was in his room alone, a portable phonograph in the basement that crashed while James was the only one there, a lamp on James's night table that fell, whereupon, as his father ran to the room, the table itself twisted and fell, while James was lying in bed and "appeared very frightened," and so on (Tozzi 1958, 22, 24, 35). Roll blithely noted that the "energy" causing the disturbances "was less strong at a distance" (Roll and Persinger 2001, 128), whereas I would postulate that heavier objects required James to be nearby so he could physically move them.

As to small objects sent flying—an ink bottle, figurines, a bread plate, and so forth—these were as easily dispatched as they were available. The cap of the ink bottle was unscrewed and the bottle sailed from the dining room into the living room, splashing its contents around. Mrs. Herrmann was on the phone at the time, with James "right next to her" (Tozzi 1958, 13). I suspect that, as she was distracted by the call, James was just out of her sight and easily managed to toss the bottle. Small objects would have permitted James to use a simple trick I alluded to earlier: secretly removing an object from its usual location, then later throwing it from a secure vantage point. For example, the small metal horse (mentioned earlier) that was tossed from behind Tozzi had probably been picked up by James from "the cellar stair shelf" as he followed the detective down the steps.

There were also some minor incidents that can be classed as miscellaneous. On an early occasion (February 16), James "complained twice that it felt like someone had stuck him in the back with a pin" (Tozzi 1958, 5). Also, there were a few noises that occurred without objects being disturbed. For instance, on March 9, when James was in bed, a dull thump was heard from the direction of his room, although nothing was found displaced. About five minutes later, there was a louder thump, which caused all the adults present to make a search. States Pratt (1964, 100), "Lucille, still in bed, said it came from James's wall just as if he had hit it with his fist or elbow. I asked James to do this and he was able to nearly get the same sound." Yet Pratt does not pursue the implications of these incidents, which he regarded as "trivial."

CASE CLOSED

Taken as a whole, the evidence strongly points to twelve-year-old James Herrmann Jr. as having been the deliberate cause of the Seaford "poltergeist" outbreak. The motive, means, and opportunity were his, and the case was unwittingly prolonged by the credulousness of adults. His father, an ex-marine and law-school graduate, first harshly accused James, but he later came to believe his son's tearful denials, abetted by James's mother, who disapproved of her husband's accusations (Pratt 1964, 103). Throughout, she seemed quick to defend and alibi the boy. Police were at a disadvantage, since they were usually called to the house *after* a disturbance, and they were discouraged from using tactics that might have exposed the trickster. Not only did Mr. Herrmann reject polygraph tests, but when Detective Tozzi passed on to Mr. Herrmann Milbourne Christopher's offer to explain what was probably going on, the magician learned that "Mr. Herrmann had said in no uncertain terms that he did not want a magician in the house"

(Christopher 1970, 155). However, the Herrmanns did make a request "to the Catholic Church for the Rites of Exorcism to be performed." Instead, a parish priest came on February 17 and blessed the house ("Poltergeist Phenomenon" n.d.), although the disturbances continued for at least three more weeks. The last recorded incident was on March 10, and the police file ended on March 25, without any indication the case had been closed (Tozzi 1958, 49, 60).

Had the prolonged tantrum simply run its course? Or had something dramatic occurred—such as the "poltergeist" having been caught *in flagrante delicto*, but the fact kept hidden within the household? Either way—and there is no justification for proposing unconscious psychokinesis as a cause—the case clearly demonstrates yet another example of the poltergeist-faking syndrome.

AFTERWORD

As my more than four decades of investigations illustrate, not a single ghost has ever been validated by science.

Despite the understandable impulse to believe in survival of consciousness, the fact remains that once the brain is dead, brain function ceases, and the phenomena on which worldwide belief in spirits rests has other, simpler explanations. This is notwithstanding the enthusiastic but misguided approach of would-be ghost hunters and "sensitives."

As the late psychologist Robert A. Baker observed (1995, 275), ghosts only exist "within the human head, where they are produced by the ever-active, image-creating human mind." As with other alleged paranormalities, belief in ghosts is sparked by our deepest hopes and fears, and so is worthy of our serious attention. That is why I decry alike the mystery-mongering approach of those who hype belief in ghosts and the dismissive, debunking attitude of others. As R. C. Finucane (1984, 1) sagely observed in his *Appearances of the Dead*, "Even though ghosts or apparitions may exist only in the minds of their percipients, the fact of that existence is a social and historical reality: the phenomena represent man's inner universe just as his art and poetry do.

Thus we can be sympathetic to the impulse to believe in spirits of the dead while nevertheless recognizing such belief as a superstition that we can overcome. I hope others will share with me the desire to investigate claims of ghosts and hauntings—for what they can tell us about ourselves—and embrace the continuing evidence that we live in a real, natural world. "No ghosts," as Sherlock Holmes insisted (in "The Adventure of the Sussex Vampire"), "need apply."

APPENDIX:
THE HAUNTED MIND —
A GLOSSARY OF MENTAL STATES, ATTITUDES, AND PERCEPTIONS ASSOCIATED WITH GHOSTLY ENCOUNTERS

Altered state of consciousness. As defined in B. Wortman and Elizabeth F. Loftus's *Psychology* (1981, 613), an altered state of consciousness is "any qualitative alteration in mental functioning, such that a person feels that his or her consciousness is distinctly different from the way it functions." A dissociative state is an example.

Apparitional experience. Many "ghosts" are perceived as apparitions, that is, ghost sightings. Often they are merely a waking dream that occurs in the interface between wakefulness and sleep. Other dissociative states, like daydreaming, can also produce ghost sightings, whereby the spectral image wells up from the subconscious and is superimposed onto the visual scene. The evidence that many ghostly perceptions are so derived is well established. For instance, Haraldsson (1988) specifically found that sightings of apparitions were linked to periods of reverie. And Andrew Mackenzie (1982) showed that in one-third of hallucinatory cases he examined, the incidents occurred to percipients just prior to or following sleep, or while they were in a relaxed state or performing routine work or concentrating on some activity like reading. The relationship between apparitional states and a dreamlike state was also observed by G. N. M. Tyrrell (1973). He noted that apparitions of people appear fully clothed and are often accompanied by objects, just as they are in dreams, because the clothes and objects are required by the apparitional drama.

Channeling. The supposed communication with such "higher beings" as angels, spirits, extraterrestrials, or the like—allegedly in an altered state of consciousness, such as a dissociative state—is called channeling. When it is not done as a deliberate deception, it is usually found to be an expression of fantasy proneness.

Clairvoyance. The supposed "seeing" of objects, people, or events through extrasensory perception (ESP). (With telepathy it constitutes one of the two main categories of ESP.) The term is French for "clear seeing." "Psychics" reportedly using clairvoyance (or *clairaudience* ["clear hearing"] when voices or other sounds are perceived, or *clairsentience* ["clear sensing"] when involving smell, taste, or other sensations) often claim to experience ghostly phenomena (Guiley 1991, 109–13). However, clairvoyants typically exhibit fantasy proneness, and all forms of ESP remain scientifically unproved. (For a specific case, see Nickell 1995, 61–63.)

Confabulation. A distortion of memory, in which gaps in one's recollection are unintentionally filled in with fictional experiences (Goldenson 1970, 1:249). Thus, someone's relating of a paranormal experience, especially one of long ago, may be partially confabulated. (See also "memory distortions.")

Contagion. Such simple phenomena as waking dreams, sleep paralysis, and out-of-body experiences can be transformed into ghostly encounters. The mechanism is what psychologists call *contagion*—the spreading of an idea, behavior, or belief from person to person by means of suggestion (Baker and Nickell 1992, 101). Historical examples of widespread contagion (often incorrectly termed "mass hysteria") are the Salem witch craze of 1692–1693, the spiritualist excitement of the nineteenth century, and the modern ghost-hunting fad. Today contagion is hugely aided by the mass media.

Déjà vu. Among the most common of anomalistic experiences is the phenomenon known as *déjà vu* (French for "already seen"). It is a strange feeling of familiarity, such as arriving at a never-before-visited site but experiencing the sensation of "having been here before." Often, it is accompanied by the feeling that one knows what is to happen next. The brief experience then passes. Although often claimed as proof of reincarnation (see "past-life recall"), psychic phenomena, or spiritualistic information transfer, psychologists usually attribute the phenomenon to partial recall and faulty recognition—that is, one has seen similar places, perhaps in photos or on television (Baker and Nickell 1992, 103–107; Alcock 1996).

Dissociative state. Dissociation is the unconscious process in which a group of mental activities is separated from the main stream of consciousness, and so functions as a separate unit. (A simple example of dissociation is illustrated by the common experience of driving an automobile for miles while lost in thought, yet scarcely remembering the drive.) Such a divided mind is the explanation for the medium's automatic writing and drawing and the like (Goldenson 1970, 1:137, 339–40; Baker 1990a, 182–91; Wortman and Loftus 1981, 385–86).

Expectancy. Expectation plays a major role in reports of ghostly phenomena. Rupert T. Gould (1976, 112–13) applied the term "expectant attention" to the tendency of people who are expecting to see a certain thing to be misled by something having a resemblance to it. The result is an illusory experience. Expectancy can be prompted by suggestion (see "suggestibility") as well as by wishful thinking. Research by Lange et al. (1996) shows that when people are "alert" to the paranormal (i.e., given to expect paranormal events) they tend to notice those conditions that would confirm their expectations. Also, suggestion effects were more frequently associated with groups of paranormal percipients than with individual ones, indicating that groups are more susceptible to the effects of contagion.

Extrasensory perception (ESP). Supposedly beyond the normal senses and therefore popularly referred to as a "sixth sense," the questionable phenomenon of extrasensory perception—consisting of clairvoyance and telepathy—is said to be the source of psychic ability. Mainstream science has not established the validity of either ESP or psychokinesis (PK, also known as "mind-over-matter"), which together make up what is known as "psi." (For a brief discussion, see "psychic phenomena.")

Fantasy proneness. Certain individuals, perhaps 4 percent of the public, have what is termed a *fantasy-prone personality*. Such a person possesses an exceptional ability to fantasize. In their classic study of fantasy proneness, Wilson and Barber (1983) found a number of identifying characteristics: (1) susceptibility to hypnosis, (2) having imaginary playmates in childhood, (3) frequently fantasizing as a child, (4) adopting a fantasy identity, (5) experiencing imagined sensations as real, (6) having vivid sensory experiences, (7) reliving past experiences (not merely recalling them), (8) believing they have psychic powers, (9) having out-of-body experiences, (10) receiving messages from higher beings, spirits, and so on, and (11) experiencing a "waking dream." Of course, many of us will have some of these traits, but exhibiting several (say six or more) suggests a notable tendency to fantasize.

Folie à deux. The power of suggestibility is a potent force in reported hauntings. One person may excitedly influence another (or the latter may acquiesce to preserve domestic tranquility!), resulting in the phenomenon the French term *folie à deux*—the folly of two! Typically, as psychologist Robert A. Baker has explained, the more "dominant personality—highly imaginative and convinced of the existence of ghosts—persuades the less imaginative member of the duo that specters exist" (Baker and Nickell 1992, 129).

Hallucination. Under certain conditions a person may perceive something that is unrelated to an external stimulus. That is, "the person hears, or more rarely sees, something that is not there" (Wortman and Loftus 1981, 491–92). Called a *hallucination*, this is not to be confused with the misperception of something actually seen (see "illusory experience"; "pareidolia"). Hallucinations may be caused by such factors as exhaustion, starvation, stress, or periods of sustained emotion, as well as by certain drugs. The common waking dream is a form of hallucination (Baker and Nickell 1992, 41, 130).

Hypnosis. The induced "trance" state in which people experience such alleged phenomena as past-life recall, channeling, or the like is called *hypnosis*. In fact, the condition is one of a dissociative state, in which, due to suggestibility and imagination, compliant people are prompted to play roles. Susceptibility to hypnosis is one of the traits associated with fantasy proneness, and fantasizing individuals often practice self-hypnosis (Baker 1990a, 161–98; Baker and Nickell 1992, 52).

Ideomotor effect. This is the psychological phenomenon in which, unconsciously, a subject moves his or her hand sufficiently to affect such "spirit phenomena" as Ouija-board messages, automatic writing and drawing, and table tipping, as well as operate dowsing rods and pendulums (which are sometimes used to "detect" ghosts). That such movement is indeed due to the ideomotor effect has been demonstrated by proper testing (such as by blindfolding the Ouija-board subject, whereupon only gibberish is produced [Randi 1995, 169–70, 223]).

Illusory experience. Simple illusions (deceptive appearances) are often responsible for paranormal perceptions. For example, when one woman was in her bedroom sewing, she would sometimes see a ghostly flash of white pass by her door. Investigation revealed that "when lights were on in the bath or the headlights from a passing car shown in the bathroom window, they were reflected off the mirror in the door, and when the door moved it was as if someone had flashed a searchlight across the bedroom door" (Baker and Nickell 1992, 127). Similarly, Milbourne Christopher (1970, 172) explains how "a billowing curtain becomes a shrouded woman" and "a shadow becomes a menacing intruder to those with vivid imaginations." (See "imagination.")

Imaginary companionship. Having an imaginary companion as a child or as an adult, or having a guardian angel, a spirit guide, or another entity with which one supposedly communicates, is a trait strongly indicative of fantasy proneness, the tendency of certain normal individuals to perceive as real things from their imagination.

Imagination. The imagination—the mental ability by which we create images and ideas—enables us to perceive supposedly otherworldly phenomena (see "expectancy"). As psychologist Robert A. Baker observed, "We tend to see and hear those things we believe in" (Baker and Nickell 1992, 129).

Intuition. Sometimes referred to as a hunch or a "gut feeling," intuition is the sense of knowing something without understanding why. It is sometimes attributed to psychic phenomena or to "inner voices," such as from one's imagined spirit guide (Guiley 1991, 285–88). One problem is that people make guesses, then count the hits and disregard (rationalize away) the misses. However, we humans are constantly responding to subtle cues, unconsciously collecting and assembling bits of information, rather like jigsaw-puzzle pieces, thus often arriving at the realization of some greater concept (Nickell 2007, 166–71)

Memory distortions. The effects of memory can play a critical role in enhancing a reported paranormal occurrence. According to Elizabeth Loftus (1980, 37):

> Memory is imperfect. This is because we often do not see things accurately in the first place. But even if we take in a reasonably accurate picture of some experience, it does not necessarily stay perfectly intact in memory. Another force is at work. The memory traces can actually undergo distortion. With the passage of time, with proper motivation, with the introduction of special kinds of interfering facts, the memory traces seem sometimes to change or become transformed. These distortions can be quite frightening, for they can cause us to have memories of things that never happened. Even in the most intelligent among us is memory thus malleable.

Among common distortions is the tendency for people to confuse what occurred on one occasion with what happened on another. Also, when memories become vague, people tend to "fill in the gaps with what they *believe* to be true," that is, to engage in confabulation (Wortman and Loftus 1981, 189–91). As a result, the stories that people tell of their alleged ghost encounters and experiences of haunting phenomena cannot be relied upon no matter how sincerely they are related. Such anecdotal evidence, therefore, is disparaged by scientific investigators.

Near-death experience (NDE). People having close encounters with death, as from heart failure, sometimes report having near-death experiences (NDEs), which are offered as proof for survival of death. Some describe out-of-body experiences (OBEs), others a sense of passing through a tunnel; still others see their life flash before them, or they visit otherworldly realms. Actually, British parapsychologist Susan Blackmore (1991) has shown that these phenomena are quite explicable: effects of the brain. The OBE is a hallucination, as is the tunnel experience (the effect of oxygen depletion on the visual cortex), while the life review results from stimulation of memory-associate areas of the brain, and the otherworldly visits are a product of the imagination. (See also Nickell 1995, 172–76.)

Out-of-body experience (OBE). The sensation that one floats out of one's body is a type of hallucination that can occur during an altered state of consciousness, as by the ingestion of certain drugs or, commonly, during the experience of a waking dream (Baker and Nickell 1992, 41, 130).

Pareidolia. Ghostly faces and figures are often perceived in photographs, in the random forms of shadow patterns, and in foliage or other shapes, like inkblots or pictures in clouds, that are interpreted as recognizable figures. Such images are called simulacra, and the tendency to see them is known as pareidolia, a neurological-psychological phenomenon by which the brain interprets vague images as specific ones. In other words, it is the mind's tendency to "recognize" common shapes in random patterns (DeAngelis 1999; Novella 2001). Similarly, one may perceive seemingly spoken spirit words or phases in random sounds—as from a tape recorder's internal noise.

Past-life recall. The alleged remembering of previous lives—supposed evidence for reincarnation—is typically done by so-called hypnotic regression. Hypnosis is essentially an invitation to fantasize, and being easily hypnotized is a trait linked to fantasy proneness. Déjà vu is sometimes held to be another indicator of "remembering" a past life.

Possession. Belief in possession by spirits—especially demonic spirits—flourishes in times and places where there is ignorance about mental states. Some early notions of possession may have been based on the symptoms of such brain disorders as epilepsy, migraine, and Tourette's syndrome (Beyerstein 1988). Psychiatric historians have long attributed demonic manifestations to such aberrant mental conditions as schizophrenia and hysteria, noting that as mental illness began to be recognized as such after the seventeenth century, there was a consequent decline in demonic superstitions and reports of possession. In many cases, however, supposed possession can be a learned role that fulfills certain important functions for those claiming it—such as acting out sexual frustrations, protesting restrictions, escaping unpleasant duties, attracting attention and sympathy, and fulfilling other psychologically useful or necessary functions (Baker and Nickell 1992, 192–217; Nickell 2004, 14–27).

Psychic phenomena ("psi"). Certain people known as "psychics" are held to be sensitive to psychic phenomena, of which there are two main types: extrasensory perception (ESP), which itself consists of clairvoyance and telepathy, and psychokinesis (PK), or mind-over-matter, such as by mentally moving objects. Mainstream science has not validated the existence of psi. Moreover, Ray Hyman (1996) has observed that forms of psi are invariably defined *negatively*—that is, as an effect remaining after other normal explanations have supposedly been eliminated. He noted that a mere glitch in the experimental data could thus be counted as evidence for psi. "What is needed, of course," he stated, "is a positive theory of psychic functioning that enables us to tell *when psi is present and when it is absent*." He added, "As far as I can tell, every other discipline that claims to be a science deals with phenomena whose presence or absence can clearly be decided" (23).

Psychokinesis (PK). The alleged ability to influence matter (say by moving objects) using sheer mental power is called *psychokinesis* (PK). It is popularly referred to as "mind-over-matter." With extrasensory perception (ESP), PK composes "psi." (For a brief discussion, see "psychic phenomena.") Some people believe that subconscious PK from an individual is the cause of some "haunting" phenomena (such as mischievous or malevolent moving of objects, noisy disturbances, fiery outbreaks, or the like) that are otherwise usually attributed to a *poltergeist* (German for "noisy spirit"). In fact, most poltergeist attacks turn out to be the work of disturbed children or adolescents, or immature adults seeking attention. (For a discussion of poltergeists see Nickell 1995, 79–103.)

Sleep paralysis. With a "waking dream," especially in the case of a hypnopompic (waking-up) hallucination, one may also experience sleep paralysis—an inability to move because the body is still in the sleep mode. In the middle ages this led to reports of demons (incubi in the case of sleeping women, and succubi with men) that were perceived as sitting or lying on the person's body, rendering him or her immobile. In the Victorian era, sleep paralysis could cause one to report being transfixed by the sight of a "Grey Lady" specter, and today the phenomenon is commonly interpreted as the experience of being tied down by aliens aboard their flying saucer (Nickell 2001, 216; Baker and Nickell 1992, 130–31).

Suggestibility. Many people are quite suggestible; that is, they uncritically accept an idea or adopt a course of action. Some—especially those with fantasy proneness—are more suggestible than others, making them good candidates for hypnosis. Suggestibility has profound consequences to the paranormal. For example, someone who is led to believe a place is haunted is more likely to attribute some experience—real or imagined—to a ghost (Baker and Nickell 1992, 142–43; Nickell 2001, 218–19).

Synchronicity. To describe coincidences that are "meaningful"—for example, hearing a dead loved one's favorite song come on the radio after just thinking of that person—psychologist Carl Jung (1960) coined the dubious term *synchronicity*, which he defined as an "acausal connecting principle." In fact, however, there may sometimes be cause-and-effect relationships of which we are simply unaware. Moreover, the extraordinariness of the coincidence may be misjudged due to the "selection fallacy": Ruma Falk (1981–1982) explains, "Instead of starting by drawing a random sample and then testing for the occurrence of a rare event, we select rare events that happened and find ourselves marveling at their nonrandomness. This is like the archer who first shoots an arrow and then draws the target around it." (See also Nickell 1988, 75–88.)

Telepathy. One of the two main categories of extrasensory perception (clairvoyance is the other), telepathy is supposedly mind-to-mind communication. Deriving from the Greek *tele* ("distant") and *pathe* ("occurrence"), the word was coined by British psychical researcher F. W. H. Meyers in 1882 to replace such terms as "thought-reading" and "thought-transference." That telepathy's success or failure is not affected by distance or barriers—an observation made by ESP pioneer J. B. Rhine (Guiley 1991, 607–608)—is one of many arguments against its being a physical phenomenon rather than a product of the imagination. (For a skeptical discussion, see Baker and Nickell 1992, 169–75.)

Trance. See "dissociative state."

Waking dream. Many people on occasion have an apparitional experience that occurs in a state between sleeping and waking. If one is falling asleep, the experience is called *hypnagogic*; if it occurs when one is waking, it is termed *hypnopompic*. Either hallucination is known popularly as a "waking dream," which has features of both wakefulness and sleep: imaginary elements that are perceived as real. Consider, for example, this ghostly occurrence described by a caretaker's wife at Toronto's "haunted" Mackenzie House (the historic home of William Lyon Mackenzie [1795–1861]):

> One night I woke up at midnight to see a lady standing over my bed. She wasn't at the side, but at the head of the bed, leaning over me. There is no room for anyone to stand where she was. The bed is pushed against the wall. She was hanging down like a shadow but I could see her clearly. Something seemed to touch me on the shoulder to wake me up. She had long hair hanging down in front of her shoulder. . . . She had a long narrow face. Then she was gone. [Nickell 1995, 41]

Such experiences are exceedingly common—not only in sightings of alleged ghosts, but in visitations of extraterrestrials, demons, vampires, and other bedside visitors. Sometimes, the experience is coupled with so-called sleep paralysis (Nickell 2001, 215–16).

Wishful thinking. Being influenced, often unconsciously, by one's desires is a form of bias commonly known as "wishful thinking," and it can influence nearly every aspect of the perceptions and reporting of alleged hauntings. Cautioning about the pitfalls of bias caused by wishful thinking, W. I. B. Beveridge (n.d. 67–68), in his *The Art of Scientific Investigation*, advised, "The best protection against these tendencies is to cultivate an intellectual habit of subordinating one's opinions and wishes to objective evidence and a reverence for things as they really are."

NOTES

CHAPTER 2. NAKED GHOSTS!

1. Tyrrell's "theory of apparitions" (1953, 83–115) accounts for much, but it is flawed by his belief in telepathy, the existence of which is unproved and doubtful.

CHAPTER 3. HEADLESS GHOSTS I HAVE KNOWN

1. This is according to the genealogical chart of my mother, the late Ella T. Nickell (n.d.), which records Rev. Haute Wyatt as her eighth great-grandfather. He was a great-grandson of Sir Thomas Wyatt (Perkins 2004).

2. December 30, 1970.

CHAPTER 8. ELVIS LIVES!

1. Interviews by Joe Nickell (with Vaughn Rees), March 7, 2004. The information agent wrote her first name, "Roseanne," on a hotel business card but did not otherwise want to be identified.

2. The "Elvis impersonators" phenomenon actually started years prior to the star's death ("Elvis Presley Phenomenon" 2008).

CHAPTER 10. CONJURING GHOSTS

1. A sign at the garden site mentions the dowsing and the discovery of bones in the vicinity. Actually it was a single bone ("Van Horn Mansion" 2011), and since there was no expert determination that it was human, the evidence is worthless. Also, the use of "cadaver dogs" ("Van Horn Mansion" 2011) was applied in what strikes me as a particularly pseudoscientific manner, even apart from the fact that the dogs followed the dowsers and were obviously encouraged to support their finding.

2. To test the word choice, I used my close-up photo of the inscription, enlarged it 250 percent on a photocopier, then cut letters from one copy, arranging them on strips of clear tape to form the respective words, and compared them to the available space. Although both have the same number of letters, the word *calmly*, with the very broad letter *m*, failed the experiment, whereas *softly*, having a series of narrow letters, fit perfectly.

CHAPTER 12. GHOST OF AN
ALASKA MURDERER?

1. Adams (2006) has also given the conflicting stories as two different incidents, attributing one to room 315, the other to 318.

2. See for example, "Ghost Haunts Place of Great Accident or Misfortune" (motif E275), in Thompson 1955, 2:428.

CHAPTER 14. THE STORIED
LIGHTHOUSE GHOST

1. Some online sources reprint the article under an incorrect title, "The Haunted Lighthouse," and wrongly attribute it to "Vol. 11" of "Pacific Monthly" [*sic*]. The correct citation appears in the references (Miller 1899).

CHAPTER 16. AN AUSTRIAN CASTLE
HAUNTED BY PARACELSUS?

1. Actually, his father's name was Wilhelm Bombast von Hohenheim; *bombast* is an old word for cotton stuffing ("Paracelsus" 2008).

CHAPTER 18. CONVICT SPECTERS
AT ALCATRAZ

1. I turned twelve on December 1, 1956, just before the events of January 6, 1957, that I now relate.

2. After Alcatraz closed the following year, he was transferred back to Atlanta, where he was eventually paroled. He remained, took college courses, and worked as a lab technician yet again. In 1976, however, he was again robbing banks. He returned to prison (though he briefly escaped once from a prison bus), and finally ended up at the federal prison in Tallahassee, Florida, where he died on February 22, 1987 (Esslinger 2003, 397–412).

3. See the video *Joe Nickell Investigates: Alcatraz* on YouTube®, produced by Adam Isaac for the Committee for Skeptical Inquiry, 2010.

CHAPTER 21. STAGE FRIGHT

1. See darkhaunts.com (Dark Haunts, http://darkhaunts.com/ArizonaGhost Stories/BirdCageTheatre.htm); sgha.net (Southwest Ghost Hunters Association, http://www.sgha.net/az/birdcage/birdcage.html); hauntedarizona.freeiz.com (Haunted Places of Arizona, http://hauntedarizona.freeiz.com/tourism/ birdcage.html); legends ofamerica.com (Legends of America, http://www.legendsofamerica.com/az -tombstoneghosts2.html); what-when-how.com (page titled "Birdcage Theater, Tombstone, Arizona [Haunted Place]") http://what-when-how.com/haunted-places/ birdcage-theater-tombstone-arizona-haunted-place/; and strangeusa.com (Strange USA, http://www.strangeusa.com/Viewlocation.aspx?id=12236&desc=BirdCage Theater/OperaHouseTombstone az) (all accessed June 21, 2011).

CHAPTER 24. SPIRIT SEARCH

1. In addition to Blum's discussion of Paladino's trickery, see Hansel 1966, 209–17.

CHAPTER 25. GHOSTWRITTEN TEXTS?

1. For these statistical analyses, I chose two passages from "Ingersoll" (*Message from Robert G. Ingersoll* 1904), the third paragraph on page 7 and the first full paragraph on page 20. From Ingersoll (1887), I selected a paragraph beginning at the bottom of page 421 and ending on page 422 and another beginning at the bottom of page 423 and ending on page 424.

CHAPTER 28. "MESSAGES" FROM THE 9/11 DEAD

1. There are two types of waking dreams: the hypnagogic experience, in which one is going to sleep, and the hypnopompic experience, in which one is waking up. Sometimes the person is unable to move—experiencing what is called sleep paralysis—because the body is still in the sleep mode. (See Baker and Nickell 1992, 130–31.)

CHAPTER 29. SYNCHRONICITIES

1. For a discussion of forensic pathology, see my *Crime Science* (Nickell and Fischer 1999, 246–68).

CHAPTER 30. JOHN EDWARD

1. The transcript was of the June 19, 1998, *Larry King Live* show on CNN.

CHAPTER 32. SYLVIA BROWNE

1. For a contrary, scientific view, see my *Real-Life X-Files* (Nickell 2001, 28–36, 240–44).

CHAPTER 33. GHOST HUNTING

1. According to physicists who debunk the idea (Efthimiou and Gandhi 2007, 28), "It has become a Hollywood cliché that the entrance of a ghostly presence is foreshadowed by a sudden and overwhelming chill (see, for example, *The Sixth Sense*)."

CHAPTER 43. POLTERGEIST ATTACKS!

1. All quotes from Mather are from Quinn 1938.
2. *Powel* seems to refer to the boy, Abel Powell, as if he's being mentioned by a demon speaking through him. (See also *Salem* 1860, 30–31.)

REFERENCES

INTRODUCTION

Guiley, Rosemary Ellen. 2000. *The Encyclopedia of Ghosts and Spirits*. New York: Checkmark Books.

Nickell, Joe. 2011. *Tracking the Man-Beasts: Sasquatch, Vampires, Zombies, and More*. Amherst, NY: Prometheus Books.

Stravinskas, Peter M. 2002. *Catholic Dictionary*. Huntington, IN: Our Sunday Visitor.

CHAPTER 1. GHOSTS

Baker, Robert A. 1990. *They Call It Hypnosis*. Amherst, NY: Prometheus Books.

Baker, Robert A., and Joe Nickell. 1992. *Missing Pieces: How to Investigate Ghosts, UFOs, Psychics, and Other Mysteries*. Amherst, NY: Prometheus Books.

Benet's Reader's Encyclopedia. 1987. 3rd ed. New York: Harper & Row.

Blum, Deborah. 2006. *Ghost Hunters: William James and the Search for Scientific Proof of Life after Death*. New York: Penguin.

Brandon, Ruth. 1983. *The Spiritualists: The Passion for the Occult in the Nineteenth and Twentieth Centuries*. New York: Alfred A. Knopf.

Brunvand, Jan Harold. 1996. *American Folklore: An Encyclopedia*. New York: Garland.

Christopher, Milbourne. 1970. *ESP, Seers, and Psychics: What the Occult Really Is*. New York: Thomas Y. Crowell.

Cohen, Daniel. 1984. *The Encyclopedia of Ghosts*. New York: Dorset.

Crowe, Catherine. 1848. *The Night-Side of Nature; or Ghosts and Ghost-Seers*. Reprint, Wellingborough, England: Aquarian, 1986.

Edwards, Emily. 2001. "A Filmography." In *Hauntings and Poltergeists: Multidisciplinary Perspectives*, by James Houran and Rense Lange. Jefferson, NC: McFarland, pp. 100–19.

Finucane, R. C. 1984. *Appearances of the Dead: A Cultural History of Ghosts*. Amherst, NY: Prometheus Books.

———. 2001. Historical introduction in Houran and Lange 2001, pp. 9–17 (below).

The Ghost Breakers (plot summary). 2007. IMDb. http://www.imdb.com/title/tt003 2520/ (accessed October 19, 2007). See this site for other movie plot summaries.

Guiley, Rosemary Ellen. 2000. *The Encyclopedia of Ghosts and Spirits*. 2nd ed. New York: Checkmark Books.

Haining, Peter. 1982. *A Dictionary of Ghosts*. Reprint, New York: Dorset, 1993.

Hansel, C. E. M. 1966. *ESP: A Scientific Evaluation*. New York: Charles Scribner's Sons.

Haunted Lives (show summary). 2007. tv.com. http://www.tv.com/haunted lives/show/13147/summary.html (accessed October 20, 2007).

Houdini, Harry. 1924. *Houdini: A Magician among the Spirits*. New York: Ayer.

Houran, James, and Rense Lange. 2001. *Hauntings and Poltergeists: Multidisciplinary Perspectives*. Jefferson, NC: McFarland.

Internet Movie Database. 2007. IMDb. http://www.imdb.com/title/tt0280312/full credits (accessed October 30, 2007).

Keene, M. Lamar, and Allen Spraggett. (1976.) 1997. *The Psychic Mafia*. Reprint, Amherst, NY: Prometheus Books.

Moore, David W. 2005. "Three in Four Americans Believe in Paranormal." Gallup, June 16, 2005. http://www.gallup.com/poll/16915/Three-Four-Americans -Believe-Paranormal.aspx (accessed July 1, 2005).

Moorman, F. W. 1905. "Shakespeare's Ghosts." *Modern Language Review* 1, no. 196. Quoted in Finucane 1984, p. 112 (above).

Nickell, Joe. 1995. *Entities: Angels, Spirits, Demons, and Other Alien Beings*. Amherst, NY: Prometheus Books.

———. 1999. "The Davenport Brothers." *Skeptical Inquirer* 23, no. 4 (July/August): 14–17.

———. 2001. "Phantoms, Frauds, or Fantasies?" In *Hauntings and Poltergeists: Multidisciplinary Perspectives*, edited by James Houran and Rense Lange. Jefferson, NC: McFarland, pp. 214–23.

Scot, Reginald. 1584. *The Discoverie of Witchcraft*. Reprint, New York: Dover, 1972 (from 1930 edition).

Summers, Montague. 1930. Introduction to Scot 1584, pp. xvii–xxxii (above).

Warren, Joshua. 2003. *How to Hunt Ghosts: A Practical Guide*. New York: Simon & Schuster.

CHAPTER 2. NAKED GHOSTS!

Answer Fella. 2005. "Pickled Eggs, Naked Ghosts & Getting Stood up Gracefully." *Esquire*, September, p. 118.

Belanger, Jeff. 2007. *The Ghost Files*. Franklin Lakes, NJ: New Page Books.

Cawthorne, Nigel. 2006. *Witches: History of a Persecution*. Edison, NJ: Chartwell Books.

Evans, Hilary, and Patrick Huyghe. 2000. *The Field Guide to Ghosts and Other Apparitions*. New York: HarperCollins.

Finucane, R. C. 1984. *Appearances of the Dead: A Cultural History of Ghosts*. Amherst, NY: Prometheus Books.

"Ghosts Gone Wild." 2009. Carnivalia, http://www.carnivalia.com/ghosts_gone _wild.htm (accessed April 22, 2009).

Houran, James, and Rense Lange. 2001. *Hauntings and Poltergeists: Multidisciplinary Perspectives*. Jefferson, NC: McFarland.

Maxwell-Stuart, P. G. 2006. *Ghosts: A History of Phantoms, Ghouls & Other Spirits of the Dead*. Stroud, Gloucester, England: Tempus.

Nickell, Joe. 1988. *Secrets of the Supernatural*. Amherst, NY: Prometheus Books.

———. 1995. *Entities: Angels, Spirits, Demons, and Other Alien Beings*. Amherst, NY: Prometheus Books.

———. 2001a. *Real-Life X-Files*. Lexington: University Press of Kentucky.

———. 2001b. "Phantoms, Frauds, or Fantasies?" In *Hauntings and Poltergeists: Multidisciplinary Perspectives*, edited by James Houran and Rense Lange. Jefferson, NC: McFarland, pp. 214–23.

———. 2006. "Ghost Hunters." *Skeptical Inquirer* 30, no. 5 (September/October): 23–26.

Permutt, Cyril. 1988. *Photographing the Spirit World*. Wellingborough, England: Aquarian.

Podmore, Frank. 1909. *Telepathic Hallucinations: The New View of Ghosts*. New York: Frederick A. Stokes.

Roffe, Alfred. 1851. *Essay upon the Ghost-Beliefs of Shakespeare*. Cited in Finucane 1984, p. 209 (above).

Stenger, Victor J. 1990. *Physics and Psychics: In Search of a World beyond the Senses*. Amherst, NY: Prometheus Books.

Tyrrell, G. N. M. 1953. *Apparitions*. Rev. ed. London: Gerald Duckworth.

Waters, Colin. 1993. *Familiar Spirits: Sexual Hauntings through the Ages*. London: Robert Hale.

White, John, and Stanley Krippner. 1977. *Future Science: Life Energies and the Physics of Paranormal Phenomena*. Garden City, NY: Anchor Books.

CHAPTER 3. HEADLESS GHOSTS I HAVE KNOWN

Creason, Joe. 1972. *Joe Creason's Kentucky*. Louisville, KY: Courier-Journal.

De Vaux, Samuel. 1839. *The Falls of Niagara*. Cited in Dunnigan 1989, p. 100 (below).

Diachun, Elizabeth (former assistant director of Old Fort Niagara). 2003. Interview by Joe Nickell, September 24.

Dunnigan, Brian Leigh. 1985. *A History and Guide to Old Fort Niagara*. Youngstown, NY: Old Fort Niagara Association.

———. 1989. "The Ghost of Old Fort Niagara." *New York Folklore* 15 (1–2): 99–104.

Gutjahr, Mirko. 2002. Interview by Joe Nickell and Martin Mahner, October 8.

Hauck, Dennis William. 2000. *The International Directory of Haunted Places*. New York: Penguin.

Hibbert, Christopher, et al. 1971. *Tower of London*. New York: Newsweek.

Johnson, Arthur. 1974. *Early Morgan County*. West Liberty, KY: Privately printed.

Jones, Richard. 2004. *Haunted London*. New York: Barnes & Noble.

Kasprzyk, Elaine. 2002. Interview by Joe Nickell, April 27.

Nickell, Ella T. N.d. Personal genealogical papers.

Nickell, Joe. 1991. *Raids & Skirmishes: The Civil War in Morgan*. West Liberty, KY: Nickell Genealogical Books, pp. 11, 17.

———. 2001. "Phantoms, Frauds, or Fantasies?" In *Hauntings and Poltergeists: Multidisciplinary Perspectives*, edited by James Houran and Rense Lange. Jefferson, NC: McFarland, pp. 214–23.

———. 2003. "Germany: Monsters, Myths, and Mysteries." *Skeptical Inquirer* 27, no. 2 (March/April): 24–28.

———. 2004. "Rorschach Icons." *Skeptical Inquirer* 28, no. 6 (November/December): 15–17.

Perkins, Steven C. 2004. "Ancestry of Rev. Haute/Hawte Wyatt." Ancestry.com. http://www.freepages.genealogy.rootsweb.com/~scperkins/hwyatt.html (accessed July 17, 2006).

"Pirate Biographies: Klaus Störtebeker." 2002. http://www.extraweb.com/bpirates/bios/bio58.htm (accessed December 10, 2002).

Tour Guide of Burg Reichenstein. N.d. Pamphlet published by Reichenstein, "the castle of the family Schmitz." Rhineland-Palatinate, Germany.

Webster's New Universal Encyclopedia. 1997. New York: Barnes & Noble.

CHAPTER 4. EXPERIENCING THE OTHER SIDE

Baker, Robert A., and Joe Nickell. 1992. *Hidden Memories: Voices and Visions from Within*. Amherst, NY: Prometheus Books.

Blackmore, Susan. 1991. "Near-Death Experiences: In or Out of the Body?" *Skeptical Inquirer* 16, no. 1 (Autumn): 34–35.

Cockell, Jenny. 1993. *Across Time and Death: A Mother's Search for Her Past Life*. New York: Simon & Schuster.

Guiley, Rosemary Ellen. 1991. *Harper's Encyclopedia of Mystical and Paranormal Experience*. New York: HarperCollins.

———. 2000. *The Encyclopedia of Ghosts and Spirits*. 2nd ed. New York: Checkmark Books.

Nickell, Joe. 1988. *Secrets of the Supernatural*. Amherst, NY: Prometheus Books.

———. 2001. *Real-Life X-Files: Investigating the Paranormal*. Lexington: University Press of Kentucky.

———. 2007. *Adventures in Paranormal Investigation*. Lexington: University Press of Kentucky.

Smith, Susy. 1970. *Ghosts around the House*. New York: World Publishing.

Wilson, Sheryl C., and Theodore X. Barber. 1983. "The Fantasy-Prone Personality: Implications for Understanding Imagery, Hypnosis, and Parapsychological Phenomena." In *Imagery, Current Theory, Research and Application*, edited by Anees A. Sheikh. New York: Wiley, pp. 340–90.

Woerlee, G. M. 2004. "Darkness, Tunnels, and Light." *Skeptical Inquirer* 28, no. 3 (May/June): 28–32.

CHAPTER 5. ENTOMBED ALIVE!

Bell, Betty. 2003. Interview by Joe Nickell, August 29.

Broeke, Robbert van den. 2005. *Robbert—Van zorgenkind tot medium (Robbert—From Problem Child to Medium)*. Utrecht: Kosmos.

Bunson, Matthew. 1993. *The Vampire Encyclopedia*. New York: Gramercy Books.

Catholic Apologetics. 2006. http://www.catholicapologetics.net/qb130 (accessed October 26, 2006).

Citro, Joseph A., and Diane E. Foulds. 2003. *Curious New England: The Unconventional Traveler's Guide to Eccentric Destinations*. Hanover: University Press of England.

Hauck, Dennis William. 1996. *Haunted Places: The National Directory*. New York: Penguin.

Marquard, B. K. 1982. "Beating the Grim Reaper." *Rutland Daily Herald* (Rutland, VT), May 27.

Meder, Theo. 2005. "Het spook van het Singraven." October 18. http://www .meerten.sknaw.nl/volksverhalenbank/detail_volksverhalen.php?id=thm00267 (accessed October 22, 2007).

Mulder-Bakker, Anneke. 2005. *Lives of the Anchoresses: The Rise of the Urban Recluse in Medieval Europe.* Philadelphia: University of Pennsylvania Press.

Nanninga, Rob. 2005. "Van zorgenkind tot wonderman: De avonturen van Robbert van den Broeke." *Skepter* (Netherlands) 18, no. 4 (Winter): 24–29.

Nickell, Joe. 1995. *Entities: Angels, Spirits, Demons, and Other Alien Beings.* Amherst, NY: Prometheus Books.

———. 2001. "Phantoms, Frauds, or Fantasies?" In *Hauntings and Poltergeists: Multidisciplinary Perspectives,* edited by James Houran and Rense Lange. Jefferson, NC: McFarland, pp. 214–23

———. 2005. "Legends of Castles and Keeps." *Skeptical Inquirer* 29, no. 6 (November/December): 24–26.

———. 2007. "The Netherlands: Visions and Revisions." *Skeptical Inquirer* 31, no. 6 (November/December): 16–19.

Palmer, John. 2003. Interview by Joe Nickell, August 29.

Robinson, Duane L. 1950. *General Catalogue of Middlebury College.* Middlebury, VT: Publications Department of Middlebury College.

Roth, Hans Peter, and Niklaus Maurer. 2006. *Orte des Grauens in der Schweiz: Von Spukhausern, Geister-plätzen und unheimlichen Begebenheiten (Sites of Horror in Switzerland: Of Haunted Houses, Ghost Sites, and Spooky Occurrences).* Baden, Switzerland: AT Verlaq.

Schloss Neu-Bechburg. 2007. File of miscellaneous articles from city hall. Oensingen, Switzerland, copy obtained May 25.

Scott, Sir Walter. 1808. *Marmion: A Tale of Flodden Field.* Edinburgh: Archibald Constable.

Wynia, Sjouke, René Notenboom, Ans Zekhuis-Stroot, and Leen van Rooden (tour guides at Singraven). 2006. Interviews by Joe Nickell, October 26; supplemented by typescript history of Singraven (in English), n.d.

CHAPTER 6. GHOSTLY LORE AND LURE

Belote, David. 2006. Quoted in "Ghost of Clement Hall" 2006 (below).

Bender, William N. 2008. *Haunted Atlanta and Beyond.* Toccoa, GA: Currahee Books.

Christian, Reese. 2008. *Ghosts of Atlanta: Phantoms of the Phoenix City*. Charleston, SC: Haunted America.

"The Ghost of Clement Hall: Is She Real or Just a Myth?" 2006. *Pacer*. http://www.utmpacer.com/sports/the-ghost-of-clement-hall-is-she-real-or-just-a-myth-1.2202396 (accessed March 24, 2010).

Guiley, Rosemary Ellen. 2000. *The Encyclopedia of Ghosts and Spirits*. 2nd ed. New York: Checkmark Books.

Hauck, Dennis William. 1996. *The International Directory of Haunted Places*. New York: Penguin.

"Haunted Tour." 2010. http://www.wwtntoday.com (accessed April 14, 2010).

Minervini, Peter. 2010. Interview by Joe Nickell, September 4.

Mueller, Stephanie. 2010. Interview by Joe Nickell, March 24.

Nickell, Joe. 2004. *The Mystery Chronicles: More Real-Life X-Files*. Lexington: University Press of Kentucky. (Additional sources are given in this source.)

The Winchester Mystery House. 1997. San Jose, CA: Winchester Mystery House.

Winer, Richard, and Nancy Osborne. 1979. *Haunted Houses*. New York: Bantam Books.

Wright, Earl. 2006. Quoted in "Ghost of Clement Hall" 2006 (above).

CHAPTER 7. THE DOCTOR'S GHOSTLY VISITOR

Brunvand, Jan Harold. 1978. *The Study of American Folklore*. New York: W. W. Norton.

———. 1981. *The Vanishing Hitchhiker: American Urban Legends and Their Meanings*. New York: W. W. Norton.

———. 2000. *The Truth Never Stands in the Way of a Good Story!* Chicago: University of Illinois Press.

Colby, C. B. 1959. *Strangely Enough* (abridged). New York: Scholastic Book Services.

Edwards, Frank. 1961. *Strange People*. New York: Signet.

Graham, Billy. 1975. *Angels: God's Secret Agents*. Garden City, NY: Doubleday.

Hurwood, Bernhardt J. 1967. *Strange Talents*. New York: Ace Books.

Mitchell, S. Weir. (1891.) 1909. *Characteristics*. New York: Century.

Musick, Ruth Ann. 1965. *The Telltale Lilac Bush and Other West Virginia Ghost Tales*. Lexington: University of Kentucky Press.

Nickell, Joe. 1995. *Entities: Angels, Spirits, Demons, and Other Alien Beings*. Amherst, New York: Prometheus Books.

———. 2007. *Adventures in Paranormal Investigation*. Lexington: University Press of Kentucky.

Ronan, Margaret. 1974. *Strange Unsolved Mysteries*. New York: Scholastic Book Services.

Strange Stories, Amazing Facts. 1976. Pleasantville, NY: Reader's Digest Association.

Tyler, Steven. 1970. *ESP and Psychic Power*. New York: Tower.

CHAPTER 8. ELVIS LIVES!

Banks, Amanda Carson. 1996. In Brunvand 1996, pp. 221–22 (below).

Berger, Arthur S., and Joyce Berger. 1991. *The Encyclopedia of Parapsychology and Psychical Research*. New York: Paragon House.

"Best Epiphany." 1994. *Hamilton This Month* (now *Hamilton Magazine*), summer.

Brewer-Giorgio, Gail. 1988. *Is Elvis Alive?* New York: Tudor.

Brunvand, Jan Harold. 1996. *American Folklore: An Encyclopedia*. New York: Garland.

Christopher, Milbourne. 1975. *Mediums, Mystics and the Occult*. New York: Thomas Y. Crowell.

Collier's Encyclopedia. 1993. New York: P. F. Collier.

"Elvis Is Alive Museum again for Sale on eBay." 2008. *Buffalo News*, September 23.

"Elvis Presley Phenomenon." 2008. *Wikipedia*. http://www.en.wikipedia.org/wiki/Elvis_sightings (accessed August 4, 2008).

Elvis Sighting Bulletin Board. 2008. http://www.elvissightingbulletinboard.com (accessed August 4, 2008).

Hauck, Dennis William. 1996. *Haunted Places: The National Directory*. New York: Penguin.

"Haunted Places: Las Vegas Hilton." 2008. Haunted Honeymoon. http://www.hauntedhoneymoon.com/hauntedplaces/lvhilton.html (accessed August 6, 2008).

Holzer, Hans. 1979. *Star Ghosts*. New York: Leisure Books.

"Is 'Weeping' Elvis Statue a Hose Job?" 1997. *Buffalo News*, August 10.

McElroy, Rob. 2001. Report of February 18, together with interview notes and the like in author's extensive case file.

Nickell, Joe. 1993. "Outlaw Impostors." In Stein 1993, pp. 112–13 (below).

———. 1995. *Entities: Angels, Spirits, Demons, and Other Alien Beings*. Amherst, NY: Prometheus Books.

———. 2001. "Phantoms, Frauds, or Fantasies?" In *Hauntings and Poltergeists: Multidisciplinary Perspectives*, edited by James Houran and Rense Lange. Jefferson, NC: McFarland, pp. 214–23

———. 2004. *The Mystery Chronicles*. Lexington: University Press of Kentucky.

Southwell, David, and Sean Twist. 2004. *Conspiracy Files*. New York: Gramercy Books.

Stein, Gordon. 1993. *Encyclopedia of Hoaxes*. Detroit: Gale Research.

West, Red, Sonny West, and Dave Hebler. 1977. *Elvis: What Happened?* As told to Steve Dunleavy. New York: Ballantine.

Wilson, Sheryl C., and Theodore X. Barber. 1983. "The Fantasy-Prone Personality: Implications for Understanding Imagery, Hypnosis, and Parapsychological Phenomena." In *Imagery, Current Theory, Research and Application*, edited by Anees A. Sheikh. New York: Wiley, pp. 340–90.

CHAPTER 9. ENCOUNTERING PHANTOM SOLDIERS

Belanger, Jeff. 2006."Civil War Re-enactors and the Ghost Experience." http://www.ghostvillage.com/legends/2006/legends44_09152006.shtml (accessed September 7, 2011).

Evans, Hilary, and Patrick Huyghe. 2000. *The Field Guide to Ghosts and Other Apparitions*. New York: Quill.

"Ghosts." 2006. The Civil War Reenactors. http://www.cwreenactors.com/ (accessed September 7, 2011).

Haining, Peter. 1993. *A Dictionary of Ghosts*. New York: Dorset.

Hauck, Dennis William. 1996. *Haunted Places: The National Directory*. New York: Penguin.

Hawkins, Jonathan M. 2011. Interview by Joe Nickell at Kennesaw Mountain Battlefield, September 4.

"Mistaken for a Ghost?" 2011. Posting for Facebook group Civil War Reenactors. http://www.facebook.com (accessed September 7, 2011). This posting is no longer available online.

Nesbitt, Mark. 1991. *Ghosts of Gettysburg: Spirits, Apparitions, and Haunted Places of the Battlefield*. Gettysburg, PA: Thomas.

Nickell, Joe. 1995. *Entities: Angels, Spirits, Demons, and Other Alien Beings*. Amherst, NY: Prometheus Books.

———. 2011. *Tracking the Man-Beasts: Sasquatch, Vampires, Zombies, and More*. Amherst: NY: Prometheus Books.

O'Day, Patty. 1993. Interview by Joe Nickell, June 8.

Winfield, Mason. 2009. *Ghosts of 1812: History, Folklore, Tradition, and the Niagara War*. Buffalo, NY: Western New York Wares.

CHAPTER 10. CONJURING GHOSTS

Crocitto, John. "The Van Horn Mansion." Examiner, May 7, 2010. www.examiner
.com/paranormal-travel-in-buffalo/the-van-horn-mansion (accessed September
13, 2011).

Ganz, Kathleen. 1989. "'Ghosts' Haunt Van Horn Mansion." *Union-Sun Journal*
(Lockport, NY), June 3.

"The Ghost of the Van Horn Mansion." 2011. http://www.angelfire.com/ny4/
bigT/adventure.html (accessed September 14, 2011).

"Ghosts, Dollhouses at Home at Landmark Bertie Hall." N.d. Unidentified newspaper clipping (datelined Fort Erie, ON) displayed at Van Horn Mansion.

Hauck, Dennis William. 1996. *Haunted Places: The National Directory*. New York:
Penguin.

Heck, Judson H. N.d. [ca. 1979.] Malinda Van Horn tombstone. Typescript report
of town of Newfane historian. Copy in Nickell 2011 (below).

———. 1988. "Van Horn Mansion Has Colorful History." *Union-Sun Journal*
(Lockport, NY), October 8.

———. 1989. "Van Horn Mansion Has a Lot of Spirit." *Union-Sun Journal* (Lockport, NY), January 2.

Lee, Helene R. 2008. "The Van Horns." *Western New York Heritage* 10, no. 4
(Winter): 58–65.

Nelson, Bill. 1970. "Do Spirits Hover inside Van Horn? These People Think So!"
Union Sun and Journal (Lockport, NY), October 31.

Nickell, Joe. 2001. *Real-Life X-Files*. Lexington: University Press of Kentucky.

———. 2004. *The Mystery Chronicles: More Real-Life X-Files*. Lexington: University
Press of Kentucky.

———. 2011. Van Horn Mansion file (begun 2003) in author's case files, accessed
and updated during September 2011.

Sherwood, Anne. 1986. "Newfane Historical Society Plans to Restore Fabled Bit of
the Past." *Buffalo News*, June 9.

Smitten, Susan. 2004. *Ghost Stories of New York State*. Auburn, WA: Lone Pine.

Townsend, Avis A. 2005. *Newfane and Olcott*. Charleston, SC: Arcadia.

"The Van Horn Mansion." 2011. http://www.angelfire.com/ny4/miaja38/van
horn.html (accessed September 14, 2011).

Winfield, Mason. 1997. *Shadows of the Western Door: Haunted Sites and Ancient Mysteries of Upstate New York*. Buffalo, NY: Western New York Wares.

———. 2003. *Haunted Places of Western New York*. Buffalo, NY: Western New York
Wares.

Wiseman, Sharon. 2000. "Re: Melinda [*sic*] Van Horn & Van Horn Mansion." July 27. http://genforum.genealogy.com/vanhorn/messages/657.html (accessed September 14, 2011).

CHAPTER 11. ANIMAL SPIRITS

Baker, Robert A. 1990. *They Call It Hypnosis*. Amherst, NY: Prometheus Books.

Cohen, Daniel. 1989. *The Encyclopedia of Ghosts*. New York: Dorset.

Cooper, Paulette, and Paul Noble. 1996. *100 Top Psychics in America*. New York: Pocket Books.

Guiley, Rosemary Ellen. 2000. *The Encyclopedia of Ghosts and Spirits*. New York: Checkmark Books.

Psychic Pets and Spirit Animals. 1996. New York: Gramercy Books.

Schäuble, Rosemarie. 2002. Interview by Joe Nickell, October 10.

CHAPTER 12. GHOST OF AN ALASKAN MURDERER

Adams, Joshua. N.d. *The Life and Times of the Alaskan Hotel*. 2nd ed. Privately printed.

———. 2006. "A Brief Walking Tour of the Alaskan Hotel." Computer printout supplied by Joshua Adams to Joe Nickell.

Murdoch, John. 1885. "Ethnological Results of the Point Barrow Expedition (1881–1883)." In *Ninth Annual Report of the Bureau of Ethnology*, edited by J. W. Powell. Washington, DC: Smithsonian Institution, 1892 [1893]. Cited in Wendt 2002 (below).

Nickell, Joe. 1995. *Entities: Angels, Spirits, Demons, and Other Alien Beings*. Amherst, NY: Prometheus Books.

———. 2000. "Haunted Inns." *Skeptical Inquirer* 24, no. 5 (September/October): 17–21.

———. 2006. "Ghost Hunters." *Skeptical Inquirer* 30, no. 5 (September/October): 23–26.

Thompson, Stith. 1955. *Motif-Index of Folk-Literature*. Rev. ed. 6 vols. Bloomington: Indiana University Press.

Wendt, Ron. 2002. *Haunted Alaska: Ghost Stories from the Far North*. Kenmore, WA: Epicenter.

CHAPTER 13. LIGHTHOUSE SPECTERS

Brunvand, Jan Harold. 1978. *The Study of American Folklore: An Introduction*. 2nd ed. New York: W. W. Norton.

Christopher, Milbourne. 1970. *ESP, Seers, and Psychics*. New York: Thomas Y. Crowell.

Elizabeth, Norma, and Bruce Roberts. 1999. *Lighthouse Ghosts: 13 Bona Fide Apparitions Standing Watch over America's Shores*. Birmingham, AL: Crane Hill.

———. 2004. *Lighthouse Ghosts and Carolina Coastal Legends*. Morehead City, NC: Lighthouse Publications.

Grant, John, and Ray Jones. 2002. *Legendary Lighthouses*. Vol. 2. Guilford, CT: Globe Pequot.

Guiley, Rosemary Ellen. 2000. *The Encyclopedia of Ghosts and Spirits*. New York: Checkmark Books.

Hermanson, Don. N.d. *True Lighthouse Hauntings*. VHS. Houghton, MI: Keweenaw Video Productions.

Nickell, Joe. 1995. *Entities: Angels, Spirits, Demons, and Other Alien Beings*. Amherst, NY: Prometheus Books.

———. 2001. "Phantoms, Frauds, or Fantasies?" In *Hauntings and Poltergeists: Multidisciplinary Perspectives*, edited by James Houran and Rense Lange. Jefferson, NC: McFarland, pp. 214–23.

———. 2008. "Catching Ghosts." *Skeptical Briefs* 18, no. 2 (June): 4–6.

"Peggy's Cove, Lady in Blue." 2008a. *Creepy Canada*. http://www.creepy.tv/season 2_e3.html (accessed February 18, 2008).

"Peggy's Cove, Nova Scotia, Lady in Blue." 2008b. Ghost Study Message Board. http://www.paranormalsoup.com/forums/index.php?showtopic=21962&mode=thread (accessed February 18, 2008).

"Seul Choix Point Lighthouse on Lake Michigan." 2005. http://www.exploringthe north.com/seulchoix/seul.html (accessed October 4, 2005).

Shanklin, Bob. 1999. Quoted in Elizabeth and Roberts 1999, pp. 15–21 (above).

Smith, Barbara. 2003. *Ghost Stories of the Sea*. Edmonton, AB: Lone Pine.

Stonehouse, Frederick. 1997. *Haunted Lakes: Great Lakes Ghost Stories, Superstitions, and Sea Serpents*. Duluth, MN: Lake Superior Port Cities.

———. 2000. *Haunted Lakes II: More Great Ghost Stories*. Duluth MN: Lake Superior Port Cities.

"Thirty Mile Point Light: 2001–2007." Guest books 1–3, various entries; copies in author's files.

Thompson, William O. 1998. *Lighthouse Legends and Hauntings*. Kennebunk, ME: 'Scapes Me.

————. 2001. *Coastal Ghosts and Lighthouse Lore*. Kennebunk, ME: 'Scapes Me.

Tyrrell, G. N. M. 1973. *Apparitions*. London: Society for Psychical Research.

Zepke, Terrance. 1999. *Ghosts of the Carolina Coasts: Haunted Lighthouses, Plantations, and Other Historic Sites*. Sarasota, FL: Pineapple.

CHAPTER 14. THE STORIED LIGHTHOUSE GHOST

Castle, Darlene, et al. 1979. *Yaquina Bay 1778–1978*. Newport, OR: Lincoln County Historical Society.

Davis, Jefferson. 1999. *Ghosts, Critters & Sacred Places of Washington and Oregon*. Vancouver, WA: Norseman Ventures.

————. 2001. *A Haunted Tour Guide to the Pacific Northwest*. Vancouver, WA: Norseman Ventures.

Garner, Sue. 2011. Personal communication, July 22.

Gibson, Scott. 2007. *Oregon Lights*. DVD. http://www.OregonLightsDVD.com (accessed February 27, 2012).

Hauck, Dennis William. 1996. *Haunted Places: The National Directory*. New York: Penguin.

Miller, Lischen M. 1899. "The Haunted Light. At Newport by the Sea." *Pacific Monthly* 2, no. 4 (August): 172–75.

Norman, Michael, and Beth Scott. 1995. *Historic Haunted America*. New York: Tom Doherty Associates.

"Yaquina Bay Lighthouse History." 2011. http://www.splintercat.org/YaquinaBay Lighthouse/YaquinaBayHistory.html (accessed July 2, 2011).

CHAPTER 15. PIRATE'S GHOSTS

Beck, Horace. 1973. *Folklore and the Seas*. Edison, NJ: Castle Books.

Belanger, Jeff. 2005. *Encyclopedia of Haunted Places: Ghostly Locales from around the World*. Franklin Lakes, NJ: New Page Books.

Benet's Reader's Encyclopedia. 1987. 3rd ed. New York: Harper & Row.

Bultman, Bethany Ewald. 1998. *New Orleans*. Oakland, CA: Compass American Guides.

"Captain Flint." 2009. *Wikipedia*, http://www.en.wikipedia.org/wiki/Captain_Flint (accessed March 16, 2009).

Cawthorne, Nigel. 2005. *A History of Pirates: Blood and Thunder on the High Seas*. Edison, NJ: Chartwell Books.

Cook, Samantha. 1999. *New Orleans: The Mini Rough Guide*. New York: Rough Guides.

Crooker, William S. 1993. *Oak Island Gold*. Halifax, NS: Nimbus.

D'Agostino, Thomas. 2008. *Pirate Ghosts and Phantom Ships*. Atglen, PA: Schiffer.

Dickinson, Joy. 1997. *Haunted City: An Unauthorized Guide to the Magical, Magnificent New Orleans of Anne Rice*. Secaucus, NJ: Citadel.

Downs, Tom, and John T. Edge. 2000. *New Orleans*. 2nd ed. Hawthorn, Victoria, Australia: Lonely Planet.

Elizabeth, Norma, and Bruce Roberts. 2004. *Lighthouse Ghosts and Carolina Coastal Legends*. Morehead City, NC: Lighthouse Publications.

Groom, Winston. 2006. *Patriot Fire*. New York: Knopf.

Hauck, Dennis William. 1996. *Haunted Places: The National Directory*. New York: Penguin.

Herczog, Mary. 2000. *Frommer's 2001 New Orleans*. Foster City, CA: IDG Books Worldwide.

"History." 2009. The Pirates' House. http://www.thepirateshouse.com/history.html (accessed March 13, 2009).

Howard, Julia. 2006. Interview by Joe Nickell, April 11.

Klein, Shelley. 2006. *The Most Evil Pirates in History*. New York: Barnes & Noble.

Klein, Victor C. 1999. *New Orleans Ghosts II*. Metairie, LA: Lycanthrope.

"The Legend of the Pirates' House." 2009. http://www.bestreadguide.excursia.com/destinations/USA/GA/savannah/stories/20000712/att_pirates.shtml/ (accessed March 13, 2009).

Nickell, Joe. 1994. *Camera Clues: A Handbook for Photographic Investigation*. Lexington: University Press of Kentucky.

———. 1995. *Entities: Angels, Spirits, Demons, and Other Alien Beings*. Amherst, NY: Prometheus Books.

———. 2001. *Real-Life X-Files: Investigating the Paranormal*. Lexington: University Press of Kentucky.

———. 2006. "Headless Ghosts I Have Known." *Skeptical Briefs* 16, no. 4 (December): 2–4.

———. 2008. "Photoghosts: Images of the Spirit Realm?" *Skeptical Inquirer* 32, no. 4 (July/August): 54–56.

Nott, G. William. 1928. *A Tour of the Vieux Carré*. New Orleans: Tropical Printing.

O'Connor, D'Arcy. 1988. *The Big Dig: The $10 Million Search for Oak Island's Legendary Treasure*. New York: Ballantine.

Pickering, David. 2006. *Pirates*. London: HarperCollins.

"Pirate's Alley Café Reviews." 2009. http://www.tripadvisor.com/Search?returnTo=__2F__&q=Pirates+Alley+Caf%C3%A9&sub-search.x=0&subsearch.y=0&subsearch=Go&geo=1 (accessed March 13, 2009).

Rondthaler, Alice K. N.d. *The Story of Ocracoke* (pamphlet). Ocracoke, NC: Channel.

Shute, Nancy. 2002. "Kidding about the Captain." *U.S. News and World Report*, August 26–September 2, p. 52.

Sillery, Barbara. 2001. *The Haunting of Louisiana*. Gretna, LA: Pelican.

Thompson, Stith. 1955. *Motif-Index of Folk-Literature*. Rev. ed. 6 vols. Bloomington: Indiana University Press, 1989.

Walser, Richard. 1980. *North Carolina Legends*. Raleigh: North Carolina Department of Cultural Resources.

Wilson, Sheryl C., and Theodore X. Barber. 1983. "The Fantasy-Prone Personality: Implications for Understanding Imagery, Hypnosis, and Parapsychological Phenomena." In *Imagery, Current Theory, Research and Application*, edited by Anees A. Sheikh. New York: Wiley, pp. 340–90.

CHAPTER 16. AN AUSTRIAN CASTLE HAUNTED BY PARACELSUS?

Chevallier, Andrew. 1996. *The Encyclopedia of Medicinal Plants*. New York: DK.

Collier's Encyclopedia. 1993. New York: P. F. Collier.

Cridlan, Avril, ed. 1997. *Webster's New Universal Encyclopedia*. New York: Barnes & Noble.

D'Emilio, Frances. 2008. "Pope Visits Grotto in Lourdes, Calls Attention to Faith." *Buffalo News*, September 14.

Hauck, Dennis William. 2000. *The International Directory of Haunted Places*. New York: Penguin.

Nickell, Joe. 1995. *Entities: Angels, Spirits, Demons, and Other Alien Beings*. Amherst, NY: Prometheus Books.

———. 1996. "Ghostly Photos." *Skeptical Inquirer* 20, no. 4 (July/August): 13–14.

———. 2007. *Adventures in Paranormal Investigation*. Lexington: University Press of Kentucky.

"Paracelsus." 2008. *Wikipedia*. http://www.en.wikipedia.org/wiki/Paracelsus (accessed September 30, 2008).

"Salzburg Sightseeing Tours." N.d. (current 2007). Tourism booklet. Salzburg, Austria: Salzburg Sightseeing.

Steves, Rick. 2007. *Rick Steves' Germany and Austria 2007*. Emeryville, CA: Avalon Travel Publishing.

"Mirabell Palace and Gardens." 2007. Salzburg.info. http://www.salzburg.info/en/service/infos/mirabell-palace-and-gardens_az-259662 (accessed May 21, 2007).

CHAPTER 17. INCARCERATED GHOSTS

Brownstone, David M., and Irene M. Franck. 1989. *Historic Places of Early America*. New York: Atheneum.

Cain, Suzy. 1997. *A Ghostly Experience: Tales of St. Augustine*. St. Augustine, FL: Tour Saint Augustine.

Cipriani, John. 2004. Interview by Joe Nickell, March 23.

Davis, Richard. 1998. *The Ghost Guide to Australia*. Sydney, Australia: Bantam Books.

Dickens, Charles. 1842. "Philadelphia and Its Solitary Prison." Chap. 7 of *American Notes for General Circulation*. London: Chapman and Hall. Available online at Project Gutenberg. http://www.gutenberg.org/ebooks/675 (accessed February 27, 2012).

Greco, Gail. 1994. *The Romance of Country Inns*. Nashville, TN: Rutledge Hill.

Hauck, Dennis William. 1996. *Haunted Places: The National Directory*. New York: Penguin.

"Haunted Jail." 1909. Unidentified newspaper clipping (courtesy of Jailer's Inn) dated May 21, reprinting a story signed *Bardstown Record*.

Hawes, Jason, and Grant Wilson (with Michael Jan Friedman). 2007. *Ghost Hunting: True Stories of Unexplained Phenomena from the Atlantic Paranormal Society*. New York: Pocket Books.

Hurst, Ann. 1993. Interview by Joe Nickell, November 12.

Lapham, Dave. 1997. *Ghosts of St. Augustine*. Sarasota, FL: Pineapple.

Lawrence, Cathy. 1993. Interview by Joe Nickell, November 12.

McCoy, Fran. 1993. Interview by Joe Nickell, November 12.

Moore, Joyce Elson. 1998. *Haunt Hunter's Guide to Florida*. Sarasota, FL: Pineapple.

Nickell, Joe. 2001. "Mysterious Australia." *Skeptical Inquirer* 25, no. 2 (March/April): 15–18.

———. 2008. "Entombed Alive!" *Skeptical Inquirer* 32, no. 2 (March/April): 17–20.

Sarro, Katharine. 2008. *Philadelphia Haunts*. Atglen, PA: Schiffer.

Smith, Terry L., and Mark Jean. 2003. *Haunted Inns of America: National Directory of Haunted Hotels and Bed & Breakfast Inns*. Birmingham, AL: Crane Hill.

CHAPTER 18. CONVICT SPECTERS AT ALCATRAZ

"Alcatraz Hauntings." 2007. Cited in Vercillo 2008, p. 118 (below).

Blackwell, O. G. (Alcatraz warden). 1962. "Reports to Bureau of Prisons." Cited in Esslinger 2003, pp. 403–10 (below).

Collier's Encyclopedia. 1993. New York: P. F. Collier.

Esslinger, Michael. 2003. *Alcatraz: A Definitive History of the Penitentiary Years*. Carwell, CA: Ocean View.

Ginsberg, Paul (president of Professional Audio Laboratories). 2009. Appearing on "Devil's Island," an episode of *Mystery Quest* (first aired November 4, 2009).

Guiley, Rosemary Ellen. 2000. *The Encyclopedia of Ghosts and Spirits*. 2nd ed. New York: Checkmark Books.

Heaney, Frank. 1987. *Inside the Walls of Alcatraz by Frank Heaney, Alcatraz's Youngest Guard*. Cited in Vercillo 2008, pp. 81–82 (below).

Nickell, Joe. 1991. "Historical Sketches: Bank Robber." *Licking Valley Courier* (West Liberty, KY), November 14, 1991.

———. 2001. *Real-Life X-Files: Investigating the Paranormal*. Lexington: University Press of Kentucky.

———. 2008. "Catching Ghosts." *Skeptical Briefs*, June 4–6.

Senate, Richard. 1998. *Ghost Stalker's Guide to Haunted California*. Ventura, CA: Charon.

Smith, Barbara. 2004. *Haunted San Francisco*. San Francisco, CA: Heritage House. Cited in Vercillo 2008, p. 85 (below).

Vercillo, Kathryn. 2008. *Ghosts of Alcatraz*. Atglen, PA: Shiffer.

CHAPTER 19. GHOSTS IN THE MIRROR

Finley, Rush. 2011. Interview by Joe Nickell, March 19.

Finley, Ruth. 2002. Interview by Joe Nickell, April 12.

"Ghostly Encounters." 2007. *Charleston* [WV] *Gazette Mail*, February 18.

Guiley, Rosemary Ellen. 1991. *Encyclopedia of the Strange, Mystical, and Unexplained*. New York: Gramercy Books.

———. 2007. "The Lowe Hotel: Haunted Rooms in Mothman Territory." *Fate*, August, pp. 24–27.

Hauck, Dennis William. 1996. *Haunted Places: The National Directory*. New York: Penguin.

King, Francis X. 1991. *Mind & Magic*. New York: Crescent.

"The Lowe Hotel." 2010. *Pennsylvania Haunts & History*. http://www.hauntsand history.blogspot.com/2010/12/lowe-hotel.html (accessed April 13, 2011).

"Marilyn Monroe's Ghost in Mirror." 2000. http://www.hollywoodroosevelt.com/ tt.htm (accessed April 22, 2000).

Moody, Raymond. 1993. *Reunions*. New York: Villard Books.

Nickell, Joe. 2001. *Real-Life X-Files*. Lexington: University Press of Kentucky.

———. 2007. *Adventures in Paranormal Investigation*. Lexington: University Press of Kentucky.

———. 2011. *Tracking the Man-Beasts: Sasquatch, Vampires, Zombies, and More.* Amherst, NY: Prometheus Books.

Rule, Leslie. 2008. *Ghost in the Mirror: Real Cases of Spirit Encounters.* Kansas City, MO: Andrews McMeel.

Senate, Richard. 1998. *Ghost Stalker's Guide to Haunted California.* Ventura, CA: Charon.

"Sid Hatfield." 2011. *Wikipedia.* http://www.en.wikipedia.org/wiki/Sid_Hatfield (accessed April 13, 2011).

Wicker, Christine. 2003. *Lily Dale: The True Story of the Town That Talks to the Dead.* New York: HarperSanFrancisco.

CHAPTER 20. HAUNTED DUTCH MINES

Dieteren, Frans. 1984. *Koale en eike (Coals and Oaks).* Beijnsberger: Heythuysen. Translated excerpt provided by J. W. Nienhuys.

Harmans, Gerard M. L. 2005. *Holland.* Eyewitness Travel Guides. New York: DK.

Lemmens, Gerard. 1936. *Mijnwerkersfolklore in Limburg.* Maastricht, Limburg, Netherlands: Veldeke Advertising Bureau.

Meder, Theo. 2005. "Details Volksverhall." Posted October 18. http://www.beleven .org/verhalen/data/verhaal.php?id=6646 (accessed July 2, 2007).

———. 2006. Personal communication, October 24.

Nienhuys, Jan Willem. 2006. Personal communication (citing Lemmens 1936, above), December 10.

CHAPTER 21. STAGE FRIGHT

"Area Landmarks: Lancaster Opera House." 1998. *Buffalo News,* December 20.

"Arthur J. Lamb." 2011. Virginia Tech Multimedia Music Dictionary Composer Biographies. http://www.music.vt.edu/musicdictionary/appendix/composers/L/ArthurJLamb (accessed June 24, 2011).

Belanger, Jeff, ed. 2005. *Encyclopedia of Haunted Places: Ghostly Locales from around the World.* Franklin Lakes, NJ: New Page Books.

"Bird Cage Theatre." 2011a. Dark Haunts. http://darkhaunts.com/ArizonaGhost Stories/BirdCageTheatre.htm (accessed June 21, 2011).

"Bird Cage Theatre." 2011b. StrangeUSA. http://www.strangeusa.com/View location.aspx?id=12236 (accessed June 21, 2011).

Bondrow, David. 2008. Interview by Joe Nickell, January 22.

Claud, Dwayne, and Cassidy O'Connor. 2009. *Haunted Buffalo: Ghosts of the Queen City*. Charleston, SC: History Press.

Cottrill, Janice. 2005. In Belanger 2005, pp. 170–71.

Dabkowski, Colin. 2006. "Lots of Treats." *Buffalo News*, October 27.

"Ghost Light." 1995. Shaksper: The Global Electronic Shakespeare Conference. http://shaksper.net/archive/1995/103-february/3014 (accessed January 24, 2008).

Guiley, Rosemary Ellen. 2000. *The Encyclopedia of Ghosts and Spirits*. 2nd ed. New York: Checkmark Books.

"Harry Von Tilzer." 2011. Parlor Songs. http://www.parlorsongs.com/issues/2004-2/thismonth/feature.php (accessed June 24, 2011).

Hauck, Dennis William. 1996. *Haunted Places: The National Directory*. New York: Penguin.

Houran, James, and Rense Lange, eds. 2001. *Hauntings and Poltergeists: Multidisciplinary Perspectives*. Jefferson, NC: McFarland.

Kachuba, John. 2007. *Ghosthunters: On the Trail of Mediums, Dowsers, Spirit Seekers, and Other Investigators of America's Paranormal World*. Franklin Lakes, NJ: New Page Books.

Kazmierczak, Thomas, III. 1998. Interview by author, October 13. (Kazmierczak was executive director of the Lancaster Opera House.)

LaChiusa, Matthew, Thomas LaChiusa, and Robert Kupezyk. 2008. *Ghostlights: Folklore, Skepticism & Belief*. DVD. Buffalo, NY: Morphine Hearts Productions.

The Legend of Sleepy Hollow (program booklet). 2009. Ghostlight Theatre, October (various dates).

"Myths & Legends of the Bird Cage Theater." 2011. Sonoran Paranormal Investigations. http://www.sonoranparanormal.com/joomla/index.php?option=com_content&view=article&id=86:myths-a-legends-of-the-bird-cage-theater&catid=29:haunted-places&Itemid=116 (accessed June 22, 2011).

Nelson, Burt Erickson. 1992. "Phantoms of the Opera House." *Buffalo Magazine*, April 5.

Nickell, Joe. 2001. "Phantoms, Frauds, or Fantasies?" In Houran and Lange 2001, pp. 214–23 (above).

———. 2005. *Unsolved History: Investigating Mysteries of the Past*. Lexington: University Press of Kentucky.

———. 2008. "Catching Ghosts." *Skeptical Briefs*, June, pp. 4–6.

———. 2010. "Ghost of Clement Hall." Center for Inquiry. May 4, 2010. http://www.centerforinquiry.net/blogs/entry/ghost_of_clement_hall (accessed February 27, 2012).

Ogden, Tom. 2009. *Haunted Theaters: Playhouse Phantoms, Opera House Horrors, and Backstage Banshees*. Guilford, CT: Globe Pequot.

Rubinsky, Yuri. 1976. "Museum Reopens June 21 Officially." *Whitehorse Star* (Whitehorse, YT), June 9.

Smith, Barbara. 2002. *Haunted Theaters*. Edmonton, AB: Lone Pine.

"What's a Ghost Light?" 2008. Theatrecrafts. http://www.theatrecrafts.com/glossary/pages/moreghostlight.html (accessed January 24, 2008).

Wilson, Sheryl C., and Theodore X. Barber. 1983. "The Fantasy-Prone Personality: Implications for Understanding Imagery, Hypnosis, and Parapsychological Phenomena." In *Imagery, Current Theory, Research and Application*, edited by Anees A. Sheikh. New York: Wiley, pp. 340–90.

Winfield, Mason. 2006. *Village Ghosts of Western New York, Book I: Actors in the Half-Light*. Buffalo, NY: Western New York Wares.

CHAPTER 22. WORLDWIDE HAUNTINGS

Barosio, Guido. 2001. *Morocco: Past and Present*. New York: Metro Books.

Bernhardson, Wayne. 2004. *Moon Handbooks Argentina*. Emeryville, CA: Avalon Travel Publishing.

Blackman, W. Haden. 1998. *The Field Guide to North American Hauntings*. New York: Three Rivers.

Brunvand, Jan Harold. 1981. *The Vanishing Hitchhiker: American Urban Legends and Their Meanings*. New York: W. W. Norton.

Cheng, Phoebe. 2010. "Bidding Fashionable Farewell to the Dead." *China Daily*, October 21.

Colombo, John Robert. 1988. *Mysterious Canada*. Toronto: Doubleday Canada.

Corliss, William R. 1995. *Handbook of Unusual Natural Phenomena*. New York: Grammercy.

Creighton, Helen. 1957. *Bluenose Ghosts*. Reprint, Halifax, NS: Nimbus, 1994, pp. 118–20.

Davis, Richard. 1998. *The Ghost Guide to Australia*. Sydney, Australia: Bantam Books.

Eliade, Mircea. 1995. *The Encyclopedia of Religion*. Vol. 5. New York: Macmillan.

Finucane, R. C. 1984. *Appearances of the Dead: A Cultural History of Ghosts*. Amherst, NY: Prometheus Books.

Fodors.com. 2004. Cited in Nickell 2006 (below).

Fowler, Verlie. 1991. *Colonial Days in Campbelltown: The Legend of Fisher's Ghost*. Rev. ed. Campbelltown, NSW, Australia: Campbelltown & Airds Historical Society.

Hauck, Dennis William. 2000. *The International Directory of Haunted Places*. New York: Penguin.

Leach, Maria. 1984. *Funk & Wagnalls Standard Dictionary of Folklore, Mythology, and Legend*. San Francisco: Harper & Row.

Luski, Paola. 2005. Interview by Joe Nickell, September 16.

Mooney, Paul. 2008. *National Geographic Traveler: Beijing*. Washington, DC: National Geographic.

Morocco. 2011. http://www.aulia-e-hind.com/dargah/Intl/Morocco.htm (accessed July 29, 2011).

Nickell, Joe. 2001. *Real-Life X-Files: Investigating the Paranormal*. Lexington: University Press of Kentucky. (Additional sources are given in this source.)

———. 2004. *The Mystery Chronicles: More Real-Life X-Files*. Lexington: University Press of Kentucky. (Additional sources are given in this source.)

———. 2006. "Argentina Mysteries." *Skeptical Inquirer* 30, no. 2 (March/April): 19–22. (Additional sources are given in this source.)

———. 2007. *Adventures in Paranormal Investigation*. Lexington: University Press of Kentucky. (Additional sources are given in this source.)

Supreme Criminal Court. 1827. Proceedings published in *Gazette* (Sydney), February 5.

Wachler, Martin. (1931.) 1984. *Die Weisse Frau*. Reprjnt, Kulmbach, Germany: Freunde der Plassenburg.

Winter, Brian. 2001. "Ghosts of the Present Haunt Argentine Cemetery." http://www.funeralwire.com (accessed September 26, 2005).

CHAPTER 23. A SKELETON'S TALE

"Bones in 'Old Spook House.'" 1904. *New York Times*, November 23.

Cadwallader, M. E. 1922. *Hydesville in History*. Chicago: Progressive Thinker.

Christopher, Milbourne. 1970. *ESP, Seers, and Psychics*. New York: Thomas Y. Crowell.

Doyle, Arthur Conan. (1926.) 1975. *The History of Spiritualism*. 2 vols. Reprint, New York: Arno.

"Editorial." 1909. *Journal of the American Society for Psychical Research*. March, p. 191.

"The Fox House Figures Again in a Sensation." 1904. *Arcadian Weekly Gazette*, November 23.

Guiley, Rosemary Ellen. 2000. *The Encyclopedia of Ghosts and Spirits*. New York: Checkmark Books.

"Headless Skeleton in Fox Sisters' Home." 1904. *New York Times*, November 24.

Keeler, P. L. O. A. 1922. "The Skeleton in the Fox Cottage." In Cadwallader 1922, pp. 59–60 (above).

Lewis, E. E. 1848. *A Report of the Mysterious Noises Heard in the House of Mr. John D. Fox, in Hydesville, Arcadia, Wayne County.* Canandaigua, NY: E. E. Lewis.

Muldoon, Sylvan. 1942. *Famous Psychic Stories, Psychic Series Volume II.* Darlington, WI: New Horizon.

Mulholland, John. 1938. *Beware Familiar Spirits.* Reprint, New York: Charles Scribner's Sons, 1979.

Nagy, Ron. 2006. Interview by Joe Nickell and Diana Harris, September 1.

Nickell, Joe. 2004. "Joseph Smith: A Matter of Visions." Chap. 35 of *The Mystery Chronicles: More Real-Life X-Files.* Lexington: University Press of Kentucky, pp. 296–303.

———. 2007. *Adventures in Paranormal Investigation.* Lexington: University Press of Kentucky.

Pressing, R. G. N.d. *Rappings That Startled the World.* Lily Dale, NY: Dale News.

"Topics of the Times." 1904. *New York Times*, November 25.

Weisberg, Barbara. 2004. *Talking to the Dead.* New York: HarperSanFrancisco.

CHAPTER 24. SPIRIT SEARCH

Blum, Deborah. 2006. *Ghost Hunters: William James and the Search for Scientific Proof of Life after Death.* New York: Penguin.

Gardner, Martin. 1992. "Communicating with the Dead: William James and Mrs. Piper." *Free Inquiry*, part 1 (Spring): 20–27; part 2 (Summer): 34–48.

Gottlieb, Anthony. 2006. "Raising Spirits" (review of Blum 2006, above). *New York Times*, August 20.

Gurney, Edmund. 1886. *Phantasms of the Living.* London: Trubner.

Gurney, E., and F. W. H. Myers. 1884. "Visible Apparitions," *Nineteenth Century* 16 (July): 89–91. Cited in Hansel 1966, pp. 185–89 (below).

Hansel, C. E. M. 1966. *ESP: A Scientific Evaluation.* New York: Charles Scribner's Sons.

"The Proceedings of the American Society for Psychical Research." 1907. *Journal of Society for Psychical Research* (London) 13 (1907–1908) (October): 124–26.

CHAPTER 25. GHOSTWRITTEN TEXTS?

Christopher, Milbourne. 1970. *ESP, Seers, and Psychics.* New York: Thomas Y. Crowell.

Flournoy, Theodore. (1901.) 1963. *From India to the Planet Mars.* Reprint, New Hyde Park, NY: University Books.

Gaines, Helen Fouché. 1956. *Cryptanalysis.* New York: Dover.

Gardner, Martin. 1957. *Fads & Fallacies in the Name of Science.* New York: Dover.

Guiley, Rosemary Ellen. 1991. *Encyclopedia of the Strange, Mystical, and Unexplained.* New York: Gramercy Books.

Ingersoll, Robert. (1887.) 1929. "A Tribute to Henry Ward Beecher (June 26)." In *Tributes and Miscellany.* Vol. 12 of *The Works of Robert G. Ingersoll.* Reprint, New York: Ingersoll League, pp. 419–24.

Kalush, William, and Larry Sloman. 2006. *The Secret Life of Houdini: The Making of America's First Superhero.* New York: Atria Books.

A Message from Robert G. Ingersoll Transmitted by Automatic Writing through a Philadelphia Psychic. 1904. N.p. Twenty-three-page pamphlet.

Nickell, Joe. 1987. *Literary Investigation: Texts, Sources, and "Factual" Substructs of Literature and Interpretation.* PhD diss., University of Kentucky.

———. 1991. *Wonder-Workers! How They Perform the Impossible.* Amherst, NY: Prometheus Books.

———. 1999. "Ingersoll among the Spirits." *Ingersoll Report* 6, nos. 1–3.

———. 2004. "Abraham Lincoln: An Instance of Alleged 'Spirit Writing.'" *Skeptical Briefs* 14, no. 3 (September): 5–7, 11.

Smith, Frank. 1990. *Robert G. Ingersoll: A Life.* Amherst, NY: Prometheus Books.

Wilson, Sheryl C., and Theodore X. Barber. 1983. "The Fantasy-Prone Personality: Implications for Understanding Imagery, Hypnosis, and Parapsychological Phenomena." In *Imagery, Current Theory, Research and Application,* edited by Anees A. Sheikh. New York: Wiley, pp. 340–90.

CHAPTER 26. THE SÉANCES OF "HELLISH NELL"

Churchill, Winston. 1944. "Letter to Home Secretary, April 3." Quoted in Shandler 2006, p. 3 (below).

Gibson, Walter B. 1930. *Houdini's Escapes and Magic.* New York: Blue Ribbon Books.

Gibson, Walter B., and Morris N. Young, eds. 1953. *Houdini on Magic.* New York: Dover.

Houdini, Harry. 1921. *Magical Rope Ties and Escapes*. London: Will Goldston, pp. 71–77.

Keene, M. Lamar, and Allen Spraggett. (1976.) 1997. *The Psychic Mafia*. Reprint, Amherst, NY: Prometheus Books.

Nickell, Joe. 2001. *Real-Life X-Files: Investigating the Paranormal*. Lexington: University Press of Kentucky.

———. 2004a. *The Mystery Chronicles: More Real-Life X-Files*. Lexington: University Press of Kentucky.

———. 2004b. Investigative notes, Cassadaga file, March 22.

Official Helen Duncan Website. 2009. http://www.helenduncan.org.uk (accessed June 23, 2009).

Price, Harry. 1931. *Regurgitation and the Duncan Mediumship*. London: National Laboratory of Psychical Research.

———. 1933. *Leaves from a Psychic's Case-Book*. London: Victor Gollancz.

Rauscher, William V. 2006. *Religion, Magic, and the Supernatural: The Autobiography, Reflections, and Essays of an Episcopal Priest*. Woodbury, NJ: Mystic Light.

Shandler, Nina. 2006. *The Strange Case of Hellish Nell: The Story of Helen Duncan and the Witch Trial of World War II*. Cambridge, MA: Da Capo.

Wilson, Sheryl C., and Theodore X. Barber. 1983. "The Fantasy-Prone Personality: Implications for Understanding Imagery, Hypnosis, and Parapsychological Phenomena." In *Imagery, Current Theory, Research and Application*, edited by Anees A. Sheikh. New York: Wiley, pp. 340–90.

Woolley, V. J. 1932. "Review of Harry Price's *Regurgitation and the Duncan Mediumship*." *Journal of the Society for Psychical Research* 27 (January): 187–90.

CHAPTER 27. SÉANCE UNDERCOVER

Keene, M. Lamar, and Allen Spraggett. (1976.) 1997. *The Psychic Mafia*. Amherst, NY: Prometheus Books.

Nickell, Joe. 2004. *The Mystery Chronicles: More Real-Life X-Files*. Lexington: University Press of Kentucky.

———. 2007. *Adventures in Paranormal Investigation*. Lexington: University Press of Kentucky.

"Phil Jordan the Psychic Venue." 2003. *Insights* (Official Newspaper-Menu of the Grand Hotel), no. 4 (Summer): 1.

CHAPTER 28. "MESSAGES" FROM THE 9/11 DEAD

Baker, Robert A., and Joe Nickell. 1992. *Missing Pieces: How to Investigate Ghosts, UFOs, Psychics, and Other Mysteries*. Amherst, NY: Prometheus Books.

Dunbar, David, and Brad Reagan, eds. 2006. *Debunking 9/11 Myths: Why Conspiracy Theories Can't Stand Up to the Facts*. New York: Hearst Books.

Frazier, Kendrick, and James Randi. 1981. "Prediction after the Fact: Lessons of the Tamara Rand Hoax." *Skeptical Inquirer* 6, no. 1 (Autumn): 4–7.

Gardner, Martin, ed. 1986. *The Wreck of the Titanic Foretold?* Amherst, NY: Prometheus Books.

Griffin, David Ray. 2007. *Debunking 9/11 Debunking*. Northampton, MA: Olive Branch.

Houran, James, and Rense Lange, eds. 2001. *Hauntings and Poltergeists: Multidisciplinary Perspectives*. Jefferson, NC: McFarland.

Lamon, Ward Hill. 1895. *Recollections of Abraham Lincoln 1847–1865*. Chicago: A. C. McClurgy.

McEneaney, Bonnie. 2010. *Messages: Signs, Visits, and Premonitions from Loved Ones Lost on 9/11*. New York: William Morrow.

Nickell, Joe. 1999. "Paranormal Lincoln." *Skeptical Inquirer* 23, no. 3 (May/June): 16–19.

———. 2001. "Phantoms, Frauds, or Fantasies?" In *Hauntings and Poltergeists: Multidisciplinary Perspectives*, edited by James Houran and Rense Lange. Jefferson, NC: McFarland, pp. 214–23.

———. 2010. "John Edward: Spirit Huckster." *Skeptical Inquirer* 34, no. 2 (March/April): 17–18.

Nickell, Joe, and John F. Fischer. 1999. *Crime Science: Methods of Forensic Detection*. Lexington: University Press of Kentucky.

Wilson, Sheryl C., and Theodore X. Barber. 1983. "The Fantasy-Prone Personality: Implications for Understanding Imagery, Hypnosis, and Parapsychological Phenomena." In *Imagery, Current Theory, Research and Application*, edited by Anees A. Sheikh. New York: Wiley, pp. 340–90.

CHAPTER 29. SYNCHRONICITIES

Amatuzio, Janis. 2002. *Forever Ours: A Forensic Pathologist's Perspective on Immortality and Living, a Collection of Real-Life Stories*. Minneapolis: Midwest Forensic Pathology.

———. 2006. *Beyond Knowing: Mysteries and Messages of Death and Life from a Forensic Pathologist*. Novato, CA: New World Library.

Falk, Ruma. 1981. "On Coincidences." *Skeptical Inquirer* 6, no. 2 (Winter): 24–25.

Hansel, C. E. M. 1966. *ESP: A Scientific Evaluation*. New York: Scribner.

Hill, Myron G., Howard M. Rossen, and Wilton S. Sogg. 1978. *Evidence*. St. Paul, MN: West.

Jung, C. G. 1960. "Synchronicity: An Acausal Connecting Principle." In *The Collected Works of C. G. Jung*, edited by Sir Herbert Read et al. Bollingen Series, no. 20. New York: Pantheon, pp. 418–519.

Nickell, Joe. 2004. *The Mystery Chronicles: More Real-Life X-Files*. Lexington: University Press of Kentucky.

———. 2006. "Headless Ghosts I Have Known," *Skeptical Briefs* 16, no. 4 (December): 2–4.

Nickell, Joe, and John F. Fischer. 1999. *Crime Science: Methods of Forensic Detection*. Lexington: University Press of Kentucky.

Orloff, Judith. 2000. *Dr. Judith Orloff's Guide to Intuitive Healing*. New York: Times Books.

Wilson, Sheryl C., and Theodore X. Barber. 1983. "The Fantasy-Prone Personality: Implications for Understanding Imagery, Hypnosis, and Parapsychological Phenomena." In *Imagery, Current Theory, Research and Application*, edited by Anees A. Sheikh. New York: Wiley, pp. 340–90.

CHAPTER 30. JOHN EDWARD

Ballard, Chris. 2001. "Oprah of the Other Side." *New York Times Magazine*, July 29, pp. 38–41.

Edward, John. 1999. *One Last Time*. New York: Berkeley Books.

———. 2001. *Crossing Over: The Stories behind the Stories*. San Diego, CA: Jodere Group.

Gibson, Walter B. 1977. *The Original Houdini Scrapbook*. New York: Corwin/Sterling.

Jaroff, Leon. 2001. "Talking to the Dead." *Time*, March 5, p. 52.

Nickell, Joe. 1998. "Investigating Spirit Communications." *Skeptical Briefs* 8, no. 3 (September): 5–6.

———. 2001. "John Edward: Hustling the Bereaved." *Skeptical Inquirer* 25, no. 6 (November/December): 19–22.

CHAPTER 31. THE REAL "GHOST WHISPERER"

Kachuba, John. 2007. *Ghosthunters: On the Trail of Mediums, Dowsers, Spirit Seekers, and Other Investigators of America's Paranormal World*. Franklin Lakes, NJ: New Page Books.

Nickell, Joe. 1995. *Entities: Angels, Spirits, Demons, and Other Alien Beings*. Amherst, NY: Prometheus Books.

———. 2001. *Real-Life X-Files: Investigating the Paranormal*. Lexington: University Press of Kentucky.

———. 2008a. "Catching Ghosts." *Skeptical Briefs* 18, no. 2 (June): 4–6.

———. 2008b. "Photoghosts: Images of the Spirit Realm?" *Skeptical Inquirer* 32, no. 4 (July/August): 54–56.

Severy, Merle, ed. 1971. *Great Religions of the World*. Washington, DC: National Geographic Society.

Stravinskas, Peter M. J. 2002. *Catholic Dictionary*. Huntington, IN: Our Sunday Visitor.

Tyrrell, G. N. M. 1973. *Apparitions*. London: Society for Psychical Research.

Wilson, Sheryl C., and Theodore X. Barber. 1983. "The Fantasy-Prone Personality: Implications for Understanding Imagery, Hypnosis, and Parapsychological Phenomena." In *Imagery, Current Theory, Research and Application*, edited by Anees A. Sheikh. New York: Wiley, pp. 340–90.

Winkowski, Mary Ann. 2000. *As Alive, So Dead: Investigating the Paranormal*. Avon Lake, OH: Graveworm.

———. 2007. *When Ghosts Speak: Understanding the World of Earthbound Spirits*. New York: Grand Central.

CHAPTER 32. SYLVIA BROWNE

Browne, Sylvia. 2003. *Visits from the Afterlife*. New York: New American Library.

———. 2005. *Secrets & Mysteries of the World*. Carlsbad, CA: Hay House.

Browne, Sylvia, and Antoinette May. 1998. *Adventures of a Psychic*. Carlsbad, CA: Hay House.

Browne, Sylvia, with Lindsay Harrison. 1999. *The Other Side and Back*. New York: Dutton.

Lancaster, Robert S. 2007a. "Sightings: Ghost of Brookdale Lodge." Stop Sylvia Browne. http://www.stopsylvia.com/articles/sightings_ghostofbrookdalelodge.shtml (accessed November 27, 2007).

———. 2007b. "Montel: Shawn Hornbeck Reading." Stop Sylvia Browne. http://

www.stopsylvia.com/articles/montel_shawnhornbeck.shtml (accessed February 1, 2007).

———.2009. "AC360: Sylvia Browne's Best Evidence." Stop Sylvia Browne. http://www.stopsylvia.com/articles/ac360_brownesbestevidence.shtml (accessed March 5, 2009).

Nickell, Joe, ed. 1994. *Psychic Sleuths*. Amherst, NY: Prometheus Books.

———. 2001. *Real-Life X-Files*. Lexington: University Press of Kentucky.

———. 2009. "Levy Case a Psychic Failure." *Investigative Briefs with Joe Nickell*. Center for Inquiry. March 10. http://www.centerforinquiry.net/blogs/show/levy_case_a_psychic_failure/ (accessed February 28, 2012).

Rogers, Paul. 1991. "Dislodging the Ghosts? Eerie Events at Hotel Rattle Owners, Lead to 'Exorcism.'" *San Jose Mercury News*, January 4.

Stollznow, Karen. 2007. "The Paranormal Conference." *Skeptic* (Winter): 19–23.

Wilson, Sheryl C., and Theodore X. Barber. 1983. "The Fantasy-Prone Personality: Implications for Understanding Imagery, Hypnosis, and Parapsychological Phenomena." In *Imagery, Current Theory, Research and Application*, edited by Anees A. Sheikh. New York: Wiley, pp. 340–90.

CHAPTER 33. GHOST HUNTING

Archer, Fred. 1969. *Crime and the Psychic World*. New York: William Morrow.

Auerbach, Loyd. 1986. *ESP, Hauntings, and Poltergeists: A Parapsychologist's Handbook*. New York: Warner Books.

Baker, Robert A., and Joe Nickell. 1992. *Missing Pieces: How to Investigate Ghosts, UFOs, Psychics, and Other Mysteries*. Amherst, NY: Prometheus Books.

Berger, Arthur S., and Joyce Berger. 1991. *The Encyclopedia of Parapsychology and Psychical Research*. New York: Paragon House.

Christopher, Milbourne. 1970. *ESP, Seers, and Psychics: What the Occult Really Is*. New York: Thomas Y. Crowell.

Cochran, Tracy. 1988. "The Real Ghostbusters." *OMNI* 10, no. 11 (August): 35, 78–83. Cited in Baker and Nickell 1992, 123–24 (above).

Cornell, Tony. 2002. *Investigating the Paranormal*. New York: Helix.

Dingwall, Eric J., Kathleen M. Goldney, and Trevor H. Hall. 1956. *The Haunting of Borley Rectory*. London: Gerald Duckworth.

Edison, Thomas. 1948. *The Diary and Sundry Observations of Thomas Alva Edison*, edited by Dagobert D. Runes. New York: Philosophical Library.

Edwards, Emily. 2001. "A Filmography." In *Hauntings and Poltergeists: Multidiscipli-*

nary Perspectives, edited by James Houran and Rense Lange. Jefferson, NC: McFarland, pp. 100–19.

Efthimiou, Costas J., and Sohan Gandhi. 2007. "Cinema Fiction vs. Physics Reality." *Skeptical Inquirer* 31, no. 4 (July/August): 27–34.

Gardner, Martin. 1996. "Thomas Edison, Paranormalist." *Skeptical Inquirer* 20, no. 4 (July/August): 9–12.

"Ghost Hunters." 2007. *Wikipedia*. http://en.wikipedia.org/wiki/Ghost_hunters (accessed October 1, 2007).

Godwin, John. 1972. *Occult America*. New York: Doubleday.

Guiley, Rosemary Ellen. 2000. *The Encyclopedia of Ghosts and Spirits*. 2nd ed. New York: Checkmark Books.

"Haunted Lives." 2007. http://www.tv.com/shows/haunted-lives/ (accessed October 20, 2007).

Holzer, Hans. 1963. *Ghost Hunter*. New York: Bobbs-Merrill.

———. 1979. *Star Ghosts*. New York: Leisure Books.

———. 1991. *America's Haunted Houses*. Stamford, CT: Longmeadow.

Hope, Valerie, and Maurice Townsend. 1999. *The Paranormal Investigator's Handbook*. London: Collins & Brown. "*In Search Of . . .*" 2007. *Wikipedia*. http://en.wikipedia.org/wiki/In_Search_of..._(TV_series) (accessed November 27, 2007).

Kaye, Marvin. 1990. *Haunted America*. New York: Doubleday.

Keene, Paul, Gemma Bradley-Stevenson, and Bryan Saunders. 2006. *The Ghost Chaser Chronicles*. New York: Barnes & Noble.

Lancaster, Robert S. 2007. "Sightings: Ghost of Brookdale Lodge." Stop Sylvia Browne. http://www.stopsylvia.com/articles/sightings_ghostofbrookdalelodge.shtml (accessed November 27, 2007).

Miller, Paul Richard. 1990. "Chicago: The World's Biggest Ghost Town. *Fate*, November, pp. 53–68.

Morris, Richard. 2006. *Harry Price: The Psychic Detective*. Stroud, Gloucestershire, UK: Sutton.

Nickell, Joe. 1994. *Camera Clues: A Handbook for Photographic Investigation*. Lexington: University Press of Kentucky.

———. 2001a. "Phantoms, Frauds, or Fantasies?" In *Hauntings and Poltergeists: Multidisciplinary Perspectives*, edited by James Houran and Rense Lange. Jefferson, NC: McFarland, pp. 214–23.

———. 2001b. *Real-Life X-Files*. Lexington: University Press of Kentucky.

———. 2006a. "Ghost Hunters." *Skeptical Inquirer* 30, no. 5 (September/October): 23–26.

———. 2006b. "Death of a Demonologist: Ed Warren Dead at 79." *Skeptical Inquirer* 30, no. 6 (November/December): 23–26.

———. 2007. *Adventures in Paranormal Investigation*. Lexington: University Press of Kentucky.

Peterson, Terrence. 1987. "Spiricom or Spiricon?" *Fate*, January.

Price, Harry. 1936. *Confessions of a Ghost-Hunter*. London: Putnam.

———. 1940. *The Most Haunted House in England: Ten Years' Investigation of Borley Rectory*. London: Longmans Green.

Raudive, Konstantin. 1971. *Breakthrough: An Amazing Experiment in Electronic Communication with the Dead*. New York: Taplinger.

Rogo, D. Scott. 1978. *The Haunted House Handbook*. New York: Grossett & Dunlap.

Roland, Paul. 2007. *The Complete Book of Ghosts*. London: Chartwell Books.

"*The Scariest Places on Earth*." 2007. IMDb. http://www.imdb.com/title/tt0280312/fullcredits (accessed October 30, 2007).

Scott, Beth, and Michael Norman. 1985. *Haunted Heartland: True Ghost Stories from the American Midwest*. New York: Dorset.

"The Search for Haunted Hollywood." 2007. Turner Classic Movies. http://www.tcm.com/tcmdb/title/476861/Search-For-Haunted-Hollywood-The/ (accessed November 27, 2007).

Smith, Susy. 1970. *Ghosts around the House*. New York: World.

Southall, Richard. 2003. *How to Be a Ghost Hunter*. St. Paul, MN: Llewellyn.

Underwood, Peter. 1998. *Ghosts and How to See Them*. London: Brockhampton.

Warren, Ed, and Lorraine Warren, with Robert David Chase. 1989. *Ghost Hunters: True Stories from the World's Most Famous Demonologists*. New York: St. Martin's.

Warren, Joshua. 2003. *How to Hunt Ghosts: A Practical Guide*. New York: Simon & Schuster.

Whitedove, Michelle. 2003. *Ghost Stalker: A Psychic Medium Visits America's Most Haunted Sites*. Ft. Lauderdale, FL: Whitedove.

Wilson, Ian. 1995. *In Search of Ghosts*. London: Headline.

CHAPTER 34. GHOST HUNTERS

Baker, Robert A. 1992. "Investigating Ghosts, Haunted Places and Things, Poltergeists, and Other Nonentities." Chap. 4 in Baker and Nickell 1992, pp. 113–51 (below).

Baker, Robert A., and Joe Nickell. 1992. *Missing Pieces: How to Investigate Ghosts, UFOs, Psychics, and Other Mysteries*. Amherst, NY: Prometheus Books.

Belanger, Jeff. 2005. *Encyclopedia of Haunted Places: Ghostly Locales from around the World*. Franklin Lakes, NJ: New Page Books.

Dingwall, Eric J., Kathleen M. Goldney, and Trevor H. Hall. 1956. *The Haunting of Borley Rectory*. London: Gerald Duckworth.

Finucane, R. C. 1984. *Appearances of the Dead: A Cultural History of Ghosts*. Amherst, NY: Prometheus Books.

———. 2001. "Historical Introduction." In *Hauntings and Poltergeists: Multidisciplinary Perspectives*, edited by James Houran and Rense Lange. Jefferson, NC: McFarland.

Flynn, Thomas. 2006. Personal communication, January 12.

Fujifilm. 2006. "What's Gone Wrong?" http://www.home.fujifilm.com/products/digital/shooting/flash.html (accessed January 17, 2006).

Gardner, Martin. 1996. "Thomas Edison, Paranormalist." *Skeptical Inquirer* 20, no. 4 (July/August): 9–12.

Guiley, Rosemary Ellen. 2000. *The Encyclopedia of Ghosts and Spirits*. 2nd ed. New York: Checkmark Books.

Hauck, Dennis William. 1996. *Haunted Places: The National Directory*. New York: Penguin.

———. 2000. *The International Directory of Haunted Places*. New York: Penguin.

Holzer, Hans. 1991. *America's Haunted Houses*. Stamford, CN: Longmeadow.

Nickell, Joe. 1994. *Camera Clues: A Handbook for Photographic Investigation*. Lexington: University Press of Kentucky.

———. 1995. *Entities: Angels, Spirits, Demons, and Other Alien Beings*. Amherst, NY: Prometheus Books.

———. 1996. "Ghost Photos." *Skeptical Inquirer* 20, no. 4 (July/August): 13–14.

———. 2000. "Haunted Inns." *Skeptical Inquirer* 24, no. 5 (September/October): 17–21.

———. 2002. "Circular Reasoning: The 'Mystery' of Crop Circles and Their 'Orbs' of Light." *Skeptical Inquirer* 26, no. 5 (September/October): 17–19.

———. 2004. "Rorschach Icons." *Skeptical Inquirer* 28, no. 6 (November/December): 15–17.

"Orbs—The Skeptical Approach." 2006. http://www.btinternet.com/~dr_paul_lee/orbs.htm (accessed January 17, 2006).

Price, Harry. 1940. *The Most Haunted House in England: Ten Years' Investigation of Borley Rectory*. London: Longmans Green.

Prol, Elbertus. 1993. Interview by Joe Nickell, June 12.

Warren, Joshua P. 2003. *How to Hunt Ghosts*. New York: Simon & Schuster.

CHAPTER 35. SCIENTIFIC INVESTIGATIONS vs. *GHOST HUNTERS*

Elizabeth, Norma, and Bruce Roberts. 1999. *Lighthouse Ghosts: 13 Bona Fide Apparitions Standing Watch over America's Shores*. Birmingham, AL: Crane Hill.

Flynn, Thomas. 2009. Video analysis and interview by Joe Nickell, September 1.

Hawes, Jason, and Grant Wilson, with Michael Jan Friedman. 2007. *Ghost Hunting: True Stories of Unexplained Phenomena from the Atlantic Paranormal Society*. New York: Pocket Books.

Hibbard, James. 2005. "In Search of Ghost Stories." *TelevisionWeek*, August 22, pp. 1, 19.

Nickell, Joe. 2000. "Haunted Inns." *Skeptical Inquirer* 24, no. 5 (September/October): 17–21.

———. 2002. "Winchester Mystery House." *Skeptical Inquirer* 26, no. 5 (September/October): 20–23.

———. 2003. "Haunted Plantation." *Skeptical Inquirer* 27, no. 5 (September/October): 12–15.

———. 2006. "Ghost Hunters." *Skeptical Inquirer* 30, no. 5 (September/October): 23–26.

———. 2008. "Lighthouse Specters." *Skeptical Inquirer* 32, no. 5 (September/October): 22–25.

"St. Augustine Lighthouse." 2006. Ghost Hunters *Season Two: Part 2*. DVD.

Thompson, William O. 1998. *Lighthouse Legends and Hauntings*. Kennebunk, ME: 'Scapes Me.

Vercillo, Kathryn. 2008. *Ghosts of Alcatraz*. Atglen, PA: Schiffer.

CHAPTER 36. GHOST HUSTLING IN CONNECTICUT

Altemus, Kathy. 1988–1992. Personal journal, copy provided to Joe Nickell, with cover letter of January 16, 1993.

Carpenter, Bryant. 1988. "Southington Haunting Is Daunting." *Record-Journal* (Meriden, CT), August 13.

Corica, Susan, and Glenn Smith. 1988a. "An Unworldly Being." *Herald Extra* (New Britain, CT), August 15.

———. 1988b. "Haunted House Claim Clouded by Tenant, Landlord Dispute." *Herald Extra* (New Britain, CT), August 29.

Curran, Robert, with Jack Smurl, Janet Smurl, Ed Warren, and Lorraine Warren. 1988. *The Haunted: One Family's Nightmare*. New York: St. Martin's.

DiMauro, Ken, and Jeanne Starmack. 1989. "Demonic Presence Said to Plague Family." *Observer*, August 18.

Duckett, Jodi. 1991. *Morning Call* (Allentown, PA), November 5, 1991.

"I Was Raped by a Ghost." 1992. *Sally Jessy Raphael* show transcript (no. 1084), Multimedia Entertainment, October 30.

Nickell, Joe. 1995. *Entities: Angels, Spirits, Demons, and Other Alien Beings*. Amherst, New York: Prometheus Books.

———. 2006. "Death of a Demonologist: Ed Warren Dead at 79." *Skeptical Inquirer* 30, no. 6 (November/December): 8.

"Ray Garton." 2009. *Wikipedia*. http://www.en.wikipedia.org/wiki/Ray_Garton (accessed February 27, 2009).

Rivard, Kathy. 1988. "Southington Family Spooked by House." *Bristol Press* (Bristol, CT), August 11.

Schmidt, Karen. 1992. "Couple Sees Ghost; Skeptics See through It." *Hartford Courant*, October 30.

Warren, Ed, Lorraine Warren, Al Snedeker, and Carmen Snedeker, with Ray Garton. 1992. *In a Dark Place: The Story of a True Haunting*. New York: Villard Books.

CHAPTER 37. GHOST FORENSICS

Baker, Robert A. and Joe Nickell. 1992. *Missing Pieces: How to Investigate Ghosts, UFOs, Psychics, and Other Mysteries*. Amherst, NY: Prometheus Books.

Keene, M. Lamar, and Allen Spraggett. (1976.) 1997. *The Psychic Mafia*. Reprint, Amherst, NY: Prometheus Books.

Nickell, Joe. 1988. *Secrets of the Supernatural*. Amherst, NY: Prometheus Books.

———. 1995. *Entities: Angels, Spirits, Demons, and Other Alien Beings*. Amherst, NY: Prometheus Books.

———. 2001. *Real-Life X-Files: Investigating the Paranormal*. Amherst, NY: Prometheus Books.

Nickell, Joe, and John F. Fischer. 1999. *Crime Science: Methods of Forensic Detection*. Lexington: University Press of Kentucky.

Polidoro, Massimo. 2001. *Final Séance: The Strange Friendship between Houdini and Conan Doyle*. Amherst, NY: Prometheus Books.

CHAPTER 38. PHOTOGHOSTS

Coe, Brian. 1989. *The Birth of Photography: The Story of the Formative Years, 1800–1900*. London: Spring Books.

Fairley, John, and Simon Welfare. 1987. *Arthur C. Clarke's Chronicles of the Strange and Mysterious*. London: Collins.

Flynn, Thomas. 2008. Interview by author, February 29.

Guiley, Rosemary Ellen. 2000. *The Encyclopedia of Ghosts and Spirits*. 2nd ed. New York: Checkmark Books.

Nickell, Joe. 1994. *Camera Clues: A Handbook for Photographic Investigation*. Lexington: University Press of Kentucky.

———. 1996. "Ghostly Photos." *Skeptical Inquirer* 20, no. 4 (July/August): 13–14.

———. 2001. *Real-Life X-Files: Investigating the Paranormal*. Lexington: University Press of Kentucky.

———. 2004. "Hampton Court Photo: Ghost or Guest?" *Skeptical Inquirer* 28, no. 2 (March/April): 13.

Randi, James. 1982. *Flim Flam: Psychics, ESP, Unicorns, and Other Delusions*. Amherst, NY: Prometheus Books.

Willin, Melvyn. 2007. *Ghosts Caught on Film: Photographs of the Paranormal*. Cincinnati, OH: F & W.

CHAPTER 39. GHOSTLY EXPERIENCES

Baker, Robert A., and Joe Nickell. 1992. *Missing Pieces: How to Investigate Ghosts, UFOs, Psychics, and Other Mysteries*. Amherst, NY: Prometheus Books.

Christopher, Milbourne. 1970. *ESP, Seers, Psychics: What the Occult Really Is*. New York: Thomas Y. Crowell.

Granqvist, Pehr, et al. 2004. "Sensed Presence and Mystical Experiences Are Predicted by Suggestibility, Not by the Application of Transcranial Weak Complex Magnetic Fields." *Neuroscience Letters* 379, no. 1 (April 29): 1–6.

Houran, James, and Rense Lange, eds. 2001. *Hauntings and Poltergeists: Multidisciplinary Perspectives*. Jefferson, NC: McFarland.

Khamsi, Roxanne. 2004. "Electrical Brainstorms Busted as Source of Ghosts." *Nature*. http://www.nature.com/news/2004/041206/full/news041206-10.html (accessed February 28, 2012).

Nickell, Joe. 2001. "Phantoms, Frauds, or Fantasies?" In *Hauntings and Poltergeists: Multidisciplinary Perspectives*, edited by James Houran and Rense Lange. Jefferson, NC: McFarland, pp. 214–23.

Randi, James. 1985. "The Columbus Poltergeist Case." *Skeptical Inquirer* 9, no. 3 (Spring): 221–35.

———. 1995. *An Encyclopedia of Claims, Frauds, and Hoaxes of the Occult and Supernatural.* New York: St. Martin's Griffin.

Roll, William G., and Michael A. Persinger. 2001. "Investigations of Poltergeists and Haunts: A Review and Interpretation." In Houran and Lange 2001, pp. 123–63 (above).

Shermer, Michael. 1999. "A Skeptic in the Trenches." *Skeptic* 7, no. 3 (September): 11–12.

CHAPTER 40. GHOST HUNTING'S OTHER SIDE

Coffey, Chip. 2008. "Smears, Lies & Videotape." *Psychic/Medium Chip Coffey's Blog.* http://www.myspace.com/chipcoffey/blog (accessed July 21, 2011).

"Crescent Hotel Analysis." 2011. Ultimate TechLinks. http://www.ultimatetech links.com/CrescentHotelAnalysis.html (accessed January 4, 2011).

Dai, Serena. 2011. "Chip Coffey: Sixth Sense, Showbiz, or Both?" *Miami Herald,* April 23, 2011. http://www.miamiherald.com/2011/04/23/2182489/chip -coffey-sixth-sense-showbiz.html (accessed April 26, 2011).

Hauck, Dennis William. 1996. *Haunted Places: The National Directory.* New York: Penguin.

Lytle, Steve. 2010. "Man Killed while Waiting for 'Ghost Train.'" *Charlotte Observer,* August 27.

"Paranormal State." 2011. *Wikipedia.* http://www.en.wikipedia.org/wiki/ Paranormal_State (accessed July 21, 2011).

Robinson, Kirby. 2008. Letter in posting, "Paranormal State" 2011 (above).

Ryan, Kelli. 2008. Quoted in Robinson 2008 (above).

Ryan, Kelly. 2008. "Paranormal State—Caught Faking Entire Show." Ghost Theory. http://www.ghosttheory.com/2008/11/04/paranormal-state-caught -faking-entire-show (accessed July 18, 2011).

Thompson, Stith. 1955. *Motif-Index of Folk Literature.* Rev. ed. 6 vols. Bloomington: Indiana University Press.

CHAPTER 41. GHOSTLY ENDEAVOR

Musick, Ruth Ann. 1977. *Coffin Hollow and Other Ghost Tales*. Lexington: University Press of Kentucky.

Nardini, Bob. 2004. "Two Days in Knoxville in the Year of the University Press." Baker & Taylor YBP Library Services. http://www.ybp.com/acad/features/1204 _up.html (accessed December 17, 2010).

Nickell, Joe. 2001. *Real-Life X-Files: Investigating the Paranormal*. Lexington: University Press of Kentucky.

———. 2004. *The Mystery Chronicles: More Real-Life X-Files*. Lexington: University Press of Kentucky.

———. 2006. "Ghost Hunters." *Skeptical Inquirer* 30, no. 5 (September/October): 23–26.

———. 2007. *Adventures in Paranormal Investigation*. Lexington: University Press of Kentucky.

———. 2009. "Response to 'Kentucky Ghosts for All Seasons'" [manuscript title of Simpson Brown and Brown 2010, below]. Report to University Press of Kentucky, June 24.

Patterson, D. H. 2010. "Review of *Spookiest Stories Ever: Four Seasons of Kentucky Ghosts*." Amazon.com. http://www.amazon.com/Spookiest-Stories-Ever-Seasons -Kentucky/product-reviews/0813125952/ref=dp_top_cm_cr_acr_txt?ie=UTF8 &showViewpoints=1 (accessed December 20, 2010).

Simpson Brown, Roberta. 2009. "Roberta's Bio." Roberta Simpson Brown. http://www.robertasimpsonbrown.com/node/10 (accessed June 15, 2009).

Simpson Brown, Roberta, and Lonnie E. Brown. 2010. *Spookiest Stories Ever: Four Seasons of Kentucky Ghosts*. Lexington: University Press of Kentucky.

Tucker, Elizabeth. 2010. Foreword in Brown and Brown 2010, pp. ix–xiii (above).

University Press of Kentucky. 2010. "Ghosts Aren't Just for Halloween" (press release), August 20.

Wilson, Sheryl C., and Theodore X. Barber. 1983. "The Fantasy-Prone Personality: Implications for Understanding Imagery, Hypnosis, and Parapsychological Phenomena." In *Imagery, Current Theory, Research and Application*, edited by Anees A. Sheikh. New York: Wiley, pp. 340–90.

CHAPTER 42. CATCHING GHOSTS

Baker, Robert A., and Joe Nickell. 1992. *Missing Pieces: How to Investigate Ghosts, UFOs, Psychics, and Other Mysteries.* Amherst, NY: Prometheus Books.

Christopher, Milbourne. 1970. *ESP, Seers, and Psychics.* New York: Thomas Y. Crowell.

Lange, Rense, et al. 1996. "Contextual Mediation of Perceptions in Hauntings and Poltergeist-Like Experiences." *Perceptual and Motor Skills* 82, no. 3 (June): 755–62.

Nickell, Joe. 1995. *Entities: Angels, Spirits, Demons, and Other Alien Beings.* Amherst, NY: Prometheus Books.

———. 2001. *Real-Life X-Files: Investigating the Paranormal.* Lexington: University Press of Kentucky.

Randi, James. 1985. "The Columbus Poltergeist Case." *Skeptical Inquirer* 9, no. 3 (Spring): 221–35.

Wiseman, Richard, and R. L. Morris. 1995. "Recalling Pseudo-psychic Demonstrations." *British Journal of Psychology* 86, no. 1 (February): 113–25.

Woodyard, Chris. 2000. *Ghost Hunter's Guide to Haunted Ohio.* Dayton, OH: Kestrel, pp. 22–30.

CHAPTER 43. POLTERGEIST ATTACKS!

Baker, Robert A., and Joe Nickell. 1992. *Missing Pieces: How to Investigate Ghosts, UFOs, Psychics, and Other Mysteries.* Amherst, NY: Prometheus Books.

Brittle, Gerald. (1980.) 1991. *The Demonologist: The True Story of Ed and Lorraine Warren, the World-Famous Exorcism Team.* Reprint, New York: St. Martin's, pp. 219–37.

Christopher, Milbourne. 1970. *ESP, Seers, and Psychics.* New York: Thomas Y. Crowell.

———. 1984–1985. Interview by Michael Dennett. *Skeptical Inquirer* 9, no. 2 (Winter): 159–65.

Clark, Jerome. 1981. "Update . . ." *Fate,* July, p. 94.

Houran, James, and Rense Lange. 1996. "Hauntings and Poltergeist-Like Episodes as a Confluence of Conventional Phenomena: A General Hypothesis." *Perceptual and Motor Skills* 83, no. 3 (December): 1307–16.

Kurtz, Paul. 1986–1987. "A Case Study of the West Pittston 'Haunted' House." *Skeptical Inquirer* 11, no. 2 (Winter): 137–38, 146.

Lowance, Mason I. 1974. *Increase Mather*. New York: Twayne.

Nickell, Joe. 1995. *Entities: Angels, Spirits, Demons, and Other Alien Beings*. Amherst, NY: Prometheus Books.

Quinn, Arthur Hobson et al., eds. 1938. *The Literature of America*. Vol. 1. New York: Scribner, 38–43.

Randi, James. 1985. "The Columbus Poltergeist Case." *Skeptical Inquirer* 9, no. 3 (Spring): 221–35.

———. 1995. *The Supernatural A–Z: The Truth and the Lies*. London: Brockhampton.

Roll, William. 1972. *The Poltergeist*. Garden City, NY: Nelson Doubleday.

Salem. 1860. In *Historical Collections of the Essex Institute*. Vol. 2. Salem: Henry Whipple & Son.

CHAPTER 44. RAMPAGING MIND

Christopher, Milbourne. 1970. *ESP, Seers, and Psychics: What the Occult Really Is*. New York: Thomas Y. Crowell.

Guiley, Rosemary Ellen. 2000. *The Encyclopedia of Ghosts and Spirits*. 2nd ed. New York: Checkmark Books.

Houran, James, and Rense Lange. 2001. *Hauntings and Poltergeists: Multidisciplinary Perspectives*. Jefferson, NC: McFarland.

"Poltergeist Phenomenon." N.d. Unidentified, undated short article from a publication reporting on Nassau County police cases, accompanying police file (see Tozzi 1958, below).

Pratt, J. Gaither. 1964. *Parapsychology: An Insider's View of ESP*. London: W. H. Allen.

Pratt, J. G., and W. G. Roll. 1958. "The Seaford Disturbances." *Journal of Parapsychology* 22:79–124.

Roll, William G., and Michael A. Persinger. 2001. "Investigations of Poltergeists and Haunts: A Review and Interpretation." In Houran and Lange 2001, pp. 123–63 (above).

Tozzi, Joseph. 1958. Detective Division Report No. 242-7-1958 (and supplements), Nassau County, NY, Police Department, February 11 and February 14–March 26, with some accompanying clippings and letters. (In the quotations from this source, misspellings and grammatical errors have been corrected.)

AFTERWORD

Baker, Robert A. 1995. Afterword in Nickell 1995, pp. 275–85 (below).

Finucane, R. C. 1984. *Appearances of the Dead: A Cultural History of Ghosts*. Amherst, NY: Prometheus Books.

Nickell, Joe. 1995. *Entities: Angels, Spirits, Demons, and Other Alien Beings*. Amherst, NY: Prometheus Books.

APPENDIX: THE HAUNTED MIND

Alcock, James E. 1996. *Déjà vu*. In Stein 1996, pp. 215–22 (below).

Baker, Robert A. 1990a. *They Call It Hypnosis*. Amherst, NY: Prometheus Books.

———. 1990b. *Hidden Memories: Voices and Visions from Within*. Amherst, NY: Prometheus Books.

Baker, Robert A., and Joe Nickell. 1992. *Missing Pieces: How to Investigate Ghosts, UFOs, Psychics, and Other Mysteries*. Amherst, NY: Prometheus Books.

Beveridge, W. I. B. N.d. *The Art of Scientific Investigation*. New York: Vintage.

Beyerstein, Barry. 1988. "Neuropathology and the Legacy of Spiritual Possession." *Skeptical Inquirer* 12, no. 3 (Spring): 248–62.

Blackmore, Susan. 1991. "Near-Death Experiences: In or Out of the Body?" *Skeptical Inquirer* 16, no. 1 (Autumn): 34–45.

Christopher, Milbourne. 1970. *ESP, Seers, and Psychics*. New York: Thomas Y. Crowell.

DeAngelis, Perry. 1999. "Mother Mary Come to Me." *New England Journal of Skepticism* 2, no. 4 (Autumn): 1, 13–15.

Falk, Ruma. 1981–1982. "On Coincidences." *Skeptical Inquirer* 6, no. 2 (Winter): 24–25.

Goldenson, Robert M. 1970. *The Encyclopedia of Human Behavior*. 2 vols. Garden City, NY: Doubleday.

Gould, Rupert T. 1976. *The Loch Ness Monster and Others*. Secaucus, NJ: Citadel.

Guiley, Rosemary Ellen. 1991. *Encyclopedia of the Strange, Mystical, and Unexplained*. New York: Gramercy Books.

Haraldsson, E. 1988. "Survey of Claimed Encounters with the Dead." *Omega: Journal of Death and Dying* 19, no. 2: 103–13.

Houran, James, and Rense Lange, eds. 2001. *Hauntings and Poltergeists: Multidisciplinary Perspectives*. Jefferson, NC: McFarland.

Hyman, Ray. 1996. "Evaluation of the Military's Twenty-Year Program on Psychic Spying." *Skeptical Inquirer* 20, no. 2 (March/April): 21–26.

Jung, C. G. 1960. "Synchronicity: An Acausal Connecting Principle." In *The Collected Works of C. G. Jung*, edited by Sir Herbert Read et al. Bollingen Series, no. 20. New York: Pantheon, pp. 418–519.

Lange, Rense, et al. 1996. "Contextual Mediation of Perceptions in Hauntings and Poltergeist-Like Experiences." *Perceptual and Motor Skills* 82, no. 3 (June): 755–62.

Loftus, Elizabeth. 1980. *Memories Are Made of This: New Insights into the Workings of Human Memory*. Reading MA: Addison-Wesley.

Mackenzie, A. 1982. *Hauntings and Apparitions*. London: Heinemann.

Nickell, Joe. 1998. *Secrets of the Supernatural*. Amherst, NY: Prometheus Books.

———. 1995. *Entities: Angels, Spirits, Demons, and Other Alien Beings*. Amherst, NY: Prometheus Books.

———. 2001. "Phantoms, Frauds, or Fantasies?" In Houran and Lange 2001, pp. 214–23 (above).

———. 2004. *The Mystery Chronicles: More Real-Life X-Files*. Lexington: University Press of Kentucky.

———. 2007. *Adventures in Paranormal Investigation*. Lexington: University Press of Kentucky.

Novella, Robert. 2001. "Believing Is Seeing." *New England Journal of Skepticism* 4, no. 1 (Winter): 1, 16–17.

Randi, James. 1995. *The Supernatural A–Z: The Truth and the Lies*. London: Brockhampton.

Stein, Gordon, ed. 1996. *The Encyclopedia of the Paranormal*. Amherst, NY: Prometheus Books.

Tyrrell, G. N. M. 1973. *Apparitions*. London: Society for Psychical Research.

Wilson, Sheryl C., and Theodore X. Barber. 1983. "The Fantasy-Prone Personality: Implications for Understanding Imagery, Hypnosis, and Parapsychological Phenomena." In *Imagery, Current Theory, Research and Application*, edited by Anees A. Sheikh. New York: Wiley, pp. 340–90.

Wortman, Camille B., and Elizabeth F. Loftus. 1981. *Psychology*. New York: Alfred A. Knopf.

INDEX

Note: Italicized page numbers indicate images.